Phillippo Buonarroti

BUONARROTI'S HISTORY

OF

BABEUF'S CONSPIRACY

FOR

EQUALITY;

WITH

THE AUTHOR'S REFLECTIONS

ON THE

Causes & Character of the French Revolution,

AND HIS ESTIMATE OF THE

LEADING MEN AND EVENTS OF THAT EPOCH.

ALSO, HIS VIEWS OF

DEMOCRATIC GOVERNMENT,

COMMUNITY OF PROPERTY,

AND

POLITICAL AND SOCIAL EQUALITY.

TRANSLATED FROM THE FRENCH LANGUAGE, AND ILLUSTRATED BY
ORIGINAL NOTES, ETC.

By BRONTERRE,

EDITOR OF THE POOR MAN'S GUARDIAN, HETHERINGTON'S TWOPENNY
DISPATCH, ETC. ECT.

LONDON:
PRINTED AND PUBLISHED BY H. HETHERINGTON, 126, STRAND;
AND SOLD BY ALL BOOKSELLERS.

1836.

BIOGRAPHICAL SKETCH

OF

BUONARROTI.

THE author of this work, Phillippo Buonarroti, was born in Florence in 1760. He was of noble extraction, and descended, it is said, in a right line from the celebrated Michael Angelo; but, as Michael Angelo was never married, it is more probable that he belonged to a collateral branch of that family. Certain it is, at all events, that his immediate connexions were amongst the highest Order at Florence; a fact not only attested by the high favour in which he was held in early life at the court of the Grand Duke Leopold, but also by the powerful influences he was enabled to interest in his behalf, at several critical periods of his subsequent life.

He received his education at the University of Pisa, where he discovered great energy of mind, and an indefatigable zeal for study. He addicted himself in particular to the cultivation of philosophy, politics, and history. He also exhibited favourable specimens of his talents by several dissertations and essays on a variety of subjects.

These promising dispositions, united with the great name he bore, won him the esteem of the Grand Duke Leopold, who made it a point to favour all the descendants of the illustrious men of Florence, and especially the families of Buonarroti, Vespucci, and Galilei, whose ancestors had shed so much honour upon that nursery of Italian genius.

As soon as Buonarroti quitted the University, the Grand Duke created him a Knight of the Order of St. Stephen, and offered him a distinguished place in his Court, with a large pension. The Order of Knighthood he accepted; but, whether from a desire to be more free to prosecute his studies, or, what is more probable, from a hatred of the servilities and hypocrisy necessary to make a good courtier, he declined the latter offer. " The desire of enriching himself," observes one of his Tory biographers, " seems never to have possessed him ; his *errors* were of a very different character." Unfortunately for Buonarroti's own prospects, they were indeed of a very different character ; for if to unite, to a thorough knowledge of the causes of human misery, an ardent love of his fellow-creatures, and a burning desire to rescue them from tyranny and slavery, at the risk of every personal sacrifice and danger—be an *error*, no man was ever more deeply involved in error than Buonarroti. His life was a continued error of this kind. Hence the many difficulties and perils of his revolutionary career; hence his participation in Babeuf's " Conspiracy for Equality ;" and hence is now devolved on the writer of this the task of aiding to transmit this last monument of his patriotism and glory to the admiration, we trust, of the good and the oppressed of all nations.

When the French Revolution broke out, it was natural that a mind constituted like Buonarroti's should catch the electric spark that thrilled all generous hearts with the hope of a new era. He accordingly entered into it with all the ardour of an Italian, and with an energy of character which showed that the soul of Michael Angelo was inherited by his illustrious descendant. Making no secret of his feelings, he boldly announced, and became a propagator of, the new principles. The Grand Duke was soon alarmed ; his predilections for Buonarroti as a man were lost in the terrors he inspired as a politician. To the Duke's own fears were added those of his courtiers and ministers. Buonarroti was, of course, calumniated and defamed. He was accused of ingratitude, as though the Grand Duke had a right to his conscience, in return for the Order of Knighthood conferred on him ; and, by way of marking the Court's abhorrence of revolutionary principles, Buonarroti was exiled from Tuscany. From this period commenced at once his career of misfortune and glory.

He first took refuge in Corsica with his wife and children, and soon after his arrival began to publish a patriotic journal, entitled, " *L'Amico della Libertà Italica.*" (*The Friend of Italian Liberty.*) This journal, which breathed the true spirit of a patriot, besides attaching to him a host of admirers of the new principles, attracted the notice of Salicetti the Deputy, to whom Buonarroti had been formerly known ; and the Constituent Assembly having finished its functions, and the Corsican Deputies being returned from Paris, Salicetti was rejoiced to find an old friend in his native country— a friend rendered doubly dear to him by his recent writings and services in the popular cause.

Not long after (in 1792) the second legislature was dissolved, and a National Convention summoned, to which Salicetti was elected by the Corsicans. Reluctant to leave so valuable a coadjutor behind, Salicetti prevailed on Buonarroti to accompany him to Paris, where he would have a wider field for the exercise of his talents and labours in support of the Revolution. He accordingly repaired thither, was received by the Republicans with the highest marks of esteem, and adopted into the famous popular society of the *Friends of Liberty*, better known under the name of the " Jacobin Club." In this situation he became acquainted with all the great leaders of the Mountain party, and it was probably from what he observed there, that he was subsequently enabled to distinguish so shrewdly between the generous and comprehensive policy of Robespierre's party, and the selfish and hollow character of those sham-Radical Mountainists, who then co-operated with Robespierre for their own ends, but who afterwards immolated him on the 9th Thermidor, after those ends had been attained.

Some few months after the Convocation of the National Convention (in the winter of 1792), an aristocratic insurrection broke out in Corsica, and it being necessary to send a Commissioner there with full powers, the choice fell on Buonarroti, who possessed all the personal and local requisites for the mission. Having repaired to that island he made every possible exertion to restore order, but being badly supported by the people, who had been seduced by the Royalists, he not only proved unsuccessful, but well nigh lost his life as well. The Corsican Aristocrats resolved to throw off their allegiance to France, and, like all Aristocrats, unscrupulous as to means, formed a conspiracy to assassinate Buonarroti. His house was surrounded in the dead of night, and it was only by throwing himself out of a window, amidst a discharge of pistols, that he escaped the hands of the assassins.

Having with some difficulty effected his escape from Corsica, he returned to Paris, and from his known zeal and energy was immediately entrusted with a new and more dangerous mission. It was to suppress a counter-revolutionary movement in Lyons, which the rich manufacturers and shopocrats of that town were industriously organising against the authorities of the Convention, and which threatened every moment to assume the character of a rebellion. These vampires, whose colossal wealth was derived from the luxurious spendings of the old aristocracy on the one hand, and from the brutalization of the workpeople on the other, were alarmed at the progress of Robespierre's doctrines of equality. To emancipate France was to strip them of the means of robbing their neighbours; and seeing no security for the old system of monopoly and plunder, except in the re-establishment of Monarchy, they were all but in a state of insurrection before Buonarroti quitted Paris. The latter and Maillot, another active patriot, were armed with full powers to quell the insurrectionary spirit. This they hoped to effect tranquilly, and by the aid of the municipal body of Lyons, which had been revolutionarily organised; but they had scarcely made half their journey when the dread tidings reached them that the town was in actual rebellion against the Convention; that the municipal authorities had been deposed, and many of them massacred, by the insurgent shopocrats; and that Challièr, the famous Radical mayor (called a "*fanatic*" on account of his zeal and sincerity), had been judicially assassinated. The same fate was designed for Buonarroti and Maillot, but this did not deter those brave patriots from proceeding on their mission. As soon as they reached the insurgent city, they were arrested, and carried before the president of the rebellious sections, whence they were sent to a dungeon, preparatory to their undergoing the fate of Challièr.

But on the eve of the day appointed for their execution, Collot d'Herbois arrived, and the Republican army entering the place under his instructions, Buonarroti and his colleague were saved.

It is said that having thus for a second time escaped assassination, Buonarroti expressed a wish for an appointment to some more peaceable situation; but (as is justly observed by one of his commentators) "such a wish is not likely to have been formed by Buonarroti, than whom no man was ever less disposed to seek peace, and ensue it," to the neglect of his country's claims on his services. Be that as it may, Collot recommended him to his colleagues, Ricord and Robespierre's brother, who were then on a mission at Nice, and by them he was appointed a member of the military tribunal of the army of Italy; and after the conquest of Piedmont in the following year, agent of the Republic in all the conquered countries.

It was in this last capacity that Buonarroti's real generosity of character became a theme of admiration for all who knew him. " He exhibited," says his biographer, " a degree of justice and disinterestedness, " which acquired him great celebrity in the eyes both of " French and Italians. Although at the head of an im- " mense administration, he not only proved himself " inaccessible to bribery and peculation, but actually " expended the produce of all his appointments in " relieving and succouring patriots and soldiers, who " hazarded their lives for their country. Being asked " why he preferred poverty to affluence; he replied, that " his only motive in coming to France was to be " serviceable to the cause of liberty, and that if he had " preferred riches he would not have left his prosperous " situation in Florence." *

Happy would it have been for France had all her revolutionary agents acted with the like disinterestedness; but, unfortunately, the majority of them considered the Revolution as a game of hazard, in which each had a right to grasp for himself whatever fortune offered. The pro-consuls and commissioners of the then Government

* Phillips's Biographical Anecdotes of the Founders of the French Revolution, &c. &c.

were, with few exceptions, of this class. The system of
terror which Robespierre and his friends had adopted
and supported only as a safeguard against aristocrats
and traitors, was converted by these monsters into a
means of omnigenous robbery and self-aggrandisement.
Hence the horrid butcheries in the provinces organised
and perpetrated by Fouché, Tallien, Bourdon, Freron,
Barras, and other brigand deputies and commissioners
of the Convention.   Sprung from the lowest dregs
of society, a Revolution was necessary to push these
adventurers into affluence; but that once attained, a
counter-revolution was required to secure them in the
safe enjoyment of their blood-stained acquisitions.
Hence, and from other causes not necessary here to par-
ticularize, arose the catastrophe of the 9th Thermidor;
or, in other words, the immolation of Robespierre and
the sincere Republicans, by the brigand-Mountainists of
the Convention, acting in concert with the other aristocratic factions of that assembly.

This event, which changed the whole face of the Republic, occured whilst Buonarroti held the appointment
of agent-general of all the conquered countries. The
Revolution, which had hitherto progressed towards a
new social order, to be based on equality of rights and
general happiness, assumed a new character. The new
Aristocrats, forming a junction with the old, rapacity
and proscription of the patriots became the order of the
day. The friends of virtue and equality were everywhere devoted to destruction. Buonarroti was not forgotten. The Thermidorian assassins, aware of his
principles and inflexible character, immediately dispatched orders for arresting him and sending him to
Paris. Tureau, the representative at Nice, to whom
these orders were addressed, having the highest personal
esteem for Buonarroti, and wishing to give him an opportunity of escape, exclaimed publicly, " *Voila encore
une victime du Fréronisme*" (Behold another victim of
Freronism).* He even delayed executing the commands
of the Committee for ten days, so that Buonarroti was
not only apprised of the fate intended for him, but might

---

* Fréron was considered at the head of the then prevailing
party.

depart in safety if he wished. His secretary implored him to escape, and to provide against the future by carrying off the chest of the administration, which contained about 300,000 livres. Buonarroti, indignant at this advice, replied with firmness, "*Why should I leave so base a stain upon my character? Have I been guilty of any crime? No—I yield to my destiny, and consent to go to prison!!*"

Buonarroti was accordingly seized by the *gendarmerie*, and carried to Paris. In the prison Du Plessis, where he was immured, "he suffered," says his biographer, "the greatest distress, and endeavoured to earn a subsistence by teaching music." "*I find,*" said he, "*that Rousseau was altogether right when he recommended to his Emilius the attainment of some art which might prove useful to him in time of want. I had studied music for my recreation; I am now obliged to have recourse to it for my subsistence.*"

Two circumstances occurred during his imprisonment at Du Plessis, both strikingly illustrative of the true magnanimity of his character. The National Convention, by whose orders he was arrested, came, by a just retribution of Providence, to feel the effects of the counter-Revolution it had commenced. The middle classes of Paris, who desired a more complete re-action in their favour than the Convention was disposed to promote, rose in insurrection against it on the memorable 13th Vendemiaire. This movement, which was decidedly Royalist, filled the Convention, and the Thermidorians in particular, with alarm and dismay. Buonarroti being asked whether he did not rejoice to see the Convention menaced by the same Royalists whom the Thermidorian faction had so basely caressed, in order to secure their co-operation against Robespierre? He generously made answer—"*I sacrifice all personal resentment to the public welfare. If the Convention be sincere in defending the Republic against the Royalists, and if it want a soldier to fight for the public cause, I am ready again to take up arms in its support, though I have experienced the grossest injustice at its hands.*"

The other *trait* I alluded to is this: During Buonarroti's confinement, the Prince Corsini, ambassador from the Grand Duke of Tuscany, intimated to him that he would intercede with the Directory, and procure him his liberty, if he would engage to return to Florence, and resume there his rank and family honours. Buonarroti replied that he had relinquished his right for ever in Italy, that he was wedded to liberty, and that death or force alone should prevent him from remaining in France to enjoy the " *vestigia morientis libertatis* " (the last traces or remains of expiring liberty!) Such sublime devotedness was not without its reward even in Directorial France. A few days afterwards the Convention (feeling itself to be in more danger from the Royalists than from the Democrats, and desiring to use the latter as a sort of counterpoise to the growing ascendancy of the former), proclaimed a general amnesty to all the confined patriots, and Buonarroti regained his liberty once more. This, which was his third escape, was (considering the then state of parties) almost as marvellous as either of his two former ones. It was only the hope that his life would prove more useful than his death to the then dominant faction, that saved him on this occasion from adding one more to the numerous victims of the Thermidorian counter-Revolution.

From this period we hear no more of Buonarroti till he connected himself with the Pantheonists, and in conjunction with Babeuf and others, organised the famous conspiracy for equality which forms the subject of this work. But of these events he must be his own historian.

One circumstance, however, in this part of his eventful career I cannot forbear noticing here. It stamps the seal of conviction on all that is recorded in commendation of " this magnanimous and accomplished character— the gallant but unfortunate Buonarroti," as he is justly designated by one of his biographers. I allude to the dialogue which took place between him and the President of the Military Commission appointed to try him for the conspiracy :—

" Did you conspire ?" said the President.

" Yes," answered Buonarroti.

" What motive induced you to conspire ?"

" The love of mankind."

" What were the principles that directed you ?"

" The rights of man."

" But did you intend to overthrow the present Con-
" stitution ?"

" Yes ! and till I cease to live I will ever conspire
" against tyrants. Was it worth while to shed the blood
" of two millions of citizens, in order to restore slavery
" again ? Was it worth while to crush the *ci-devant*, in
" order to bow to the *ci-après* ?"

" But are you not a foreigner ?"

" No man is an alien to the cause of human nature."

It will be seen from the sequel that only two of the
conspirators were condemned to death—Darthé and
Babeuf; the former, most probably, because he was the
intimate friend of Robespierre ; and Babeuf, I should
suppose, in consequence of the inflexible perseverance
with which he preached and advocated in his journal a
" community of property." This doctrine was particularly
unpalatable to the then rulers of France, who were all upstart adventurers, enriched by public plunder, and reeking
with the blood and spoils of the Revolution. The rest
of the conspirators, including Buonarroti, were only sentenced to transportation ; but this apparent clemency to
parties equally culpable, as Babeuf and Darthé, is easily
accounted for. The *Quarterly Review* explains it well.
" They who were then in authority," observes that periodical, " had good reason for this. The appetite of
the Revolution for blood, which during a long and
dreadful time had ' grown by what it fed on,' had *gained
their ends in the Revolution*, and, therefore, wished it
to stop where it was ; and they were conscious, moreover,
that *against them Babeuf and his associates had but
too strong a case*."

Buonarroti's sentence, it appears, was never carried
into effect, owing, it is supposed, to the reiterated inter-
cession of the Court of Tuscany. Incarceration was substituted for transportation, and he was confined first at
Cherbourg, then at some place in the Maritime Alps,
where he was as late as 1806, and lastly in some other
remote extremity of France, the name of which is not
stated. The last account I heard of Buonarroti was
shortly after the Revolution of 1830, when it seems he
was arrested by some of Louis Philippe's agents. The

Times newspaper, which was then "on the Liberal side," noticed the matter in the way of indignant remonstrance. It upbraided Louis Philippe for cruelty in persecuting so venerable and (as the *Times* then *thought* him) so patriotic an old man. (Buonarroti must have been then upwards of 70.) Such an eulogium, upon such a man, it did certainly surprise me at the time to find in such a publication; nor was my surprise without good cause, as the honest *Times* itself soon proved; for, in a day or two after, out comes another leader in the *Times*, disclaiming all it said before, and pointing attention to some correspondent's letter, in which Buonarroti was abused as a leveller, and calumniated as a blood-thirsty follower of Robespierre. The *humane* and liberty-loving *Times* was, of course, shocked at this disclosure; and, though poor Buonarroti had done nothing in the mean time to excite our contemporary's wrath, all the praises and appeals to the French authorities in his behalf were retracted, and the " venerable and patriotic old man " was left to sink or swim, as he best could, under the tutelary protection of honest Louis Philippe. So much for Printing-house-square philanthropy.

What has since become of Buonarroti,—whether he is alive or dead, I have not heard. Should any of my readers be able to give me any information on the subject, I shall be most happy to publish it at the close of the work.

BRONTERRE.

TO THE READER.

My readers may desire to know my reasons for publishing Buonarroti's work. I will frankly explain. The motives that determined me are as follows:—

1st. Because Buonarroti's book contains one of the best expositions I have seen of those great political and social principles which I have so long advocated in the *"Poor Man's Guardian"* and other publications, and which I am still endeavouring to inculcate through the columns of *"Hetherington's Twopenny Dispatch."* The application of these principles I deem to be of paramount importance to the human race. Society has been hitherto constituted upon no fixed principles. The state in which we find it is the blind result of chance. Even its advocates do not claim for it any other origin. The right of the strongest—the only right acknowledged by savage man—appears to be still the fundamental charter of all "civilized" states. The wandering savage asks no other title to his neighbour's produce than his own superior strength or capacity to take it. The "civilized" man acts precisely, though disguisedly, on the same principle. Their means are different, but the objects and end are the same. What the savage or uncivilized man does *individually* and *directly*, by the exercise of mere personal prowess, the civilized man (so called) does *collectively* and *circuitously*, by cunningly-designed institutions. The effects of these institutions are well depicted by Buonarroti. He shows, with admirable ability, how, in trying to escape the evils of savage life, man has unconsciously plunged into another state far more calamitous—to wit, the present artificial state, which he terms that of "false civilization." He shows, that to correct the evils of this latter state, without at the same time retrograding to the former, was the grand problem sought to be resolved by the first French Revolution; and, in discussing the principles and institutions deemed necessary to that end by the leaders of the Revolution,

I was so forcibly struck by the coincidence of Buonarroti's ideas with my own, that I immediately resolved to translate the book, and thereby present to the English reader the doctrines of the " *Poor Man's Guardian* " under a new form and dress, which, if I mistake not, will add greatly to their popularity, in consequence of the superior abilities and practical experience of the author. Such, then, is my first and chief motive in sending forth this work.

2d. Because it contains what to me appears the most luminous and correct estimate, to be found in any language, of the leading men and events of the great French Revolution. In this respect I deem the republication of Buonarroti's work an imperative duty.

In no other book have I seen the frauds of history so effectually exposed. It is impossible to read it without being convinced that nearly all the books that have appeared on the French Revolution are masses of fabrication and misrepresentation, artfully designed to reconcile mankind to aristocratic tyranny. To believe these impostors, one would suppose that the Royalists and Girondists included all the public virtue in France at that epoch, and that Robespierre and his party were a band of illiterate and blood-thirsty monsters, who, under pretence of serving the public, sought only to aggrandize themselves, and who, to gain their selfish and criminal ends, would cover France with scaffolds and dead bodies. How different the reality! How utterly at variance with facts and reason are these representations! The then Royalists of France were exactly the same description of persons that now support Louis Philippe's despotism; that is to say, Aristocrats and rich usurers, who, caring only for themselves, would sacrifice half the human race to make slaves and brutes of the other half. The Girondists consisted of lawyers, bankers, and babbling literati, who, jealous of the nobility and privileged orders, sought to swindle the Government, and all the advantages derivable from it, into their own hands. Some good men there were, no doubt, amongst them; but, taken as a whole, the Girondists were the worst faction in France, except perhaps the sham-Radical portion of the Mountain party, that conspired with the committees of

Government to destroy Robespierre. The Royalists would concentre the whole national authority in the hands of the rich bourgeoisie, or make it absolute in the King and Council. The Girondists would extend the franchise to the small middlemen (just as our English Whigs did by the Reform Bill), in order the more effectually to keep down the working classes. The one would govern by the Church and a standing army; the other would govern by money, by lying journalism, and an armed shopocracy. Priestcraft and bayonets were the *materiel* of Royalist tyranny; Mammon and corrupt literature were the weapons of the other. The prevailing characteristics of the Royalists were sloth, monopoly, bigotry, hatred of change; those of the Girondists were restlessness, intrigue, falsehood, and cowardly ambition. The sham-Radical Mountainists differed from both in this—that wanting the riches of the former party, and the talents of the Girondists, they were obliged to make up for the double deficiency by brigand courage and enterprize. To this latter party belonged the Septembrizers—the chief terrorists of the Convention—and the ferocious pro-consuls and commissioners who shed so much blood in the provinces. Its leaders were Bourdon, Tallien, Fouché, Freron, Legendre; Barras and Rovère also belonged to it; but previously to Danton's death, that demagogue was considered the chief of the party. In the early stages of the Revolution, and, indeed, till a short period before his death, the necessity of opposing a strong force to the Royalists and Girondists, obliged Robespierre to act with these desperadoes, but there was no mutuality or congeniality of feeling between him and them. Robespierre and his friends desired to turn the Revolution to the account of humanity, by introducing a new social order into society, based on equality of rights and purity of morals. The Dantonists, on the other hand, cared nothing about rights or morals, provided they could acquire riches and power for themselves. The Revolution was in their eyes a game of hazard, in which every one had a right to seize all he could for himself, no matter at what cost or at whose expense. Such discordant elements could not long coalesce. Previously to the 31st of May, 1793, the necessity of combatting the Girondists, who had then a majority in the Convention, kept them united, but after that event the chasm became wider and wider every day. The Dantonists, who had combatted the Royalists and the Girondists, only with a view to succeed them in authority, formed the nucleus of a new Aristocracy; but having acquired their ascendancy solely by the people's favour, they found it convenient still to profess popular principles; conscious, however, that Robespierre knew their real designs, and dreading his extreme popularity, and still more his inflexible integrity, they naturally desired his downfall. Moreover, as Robespierre combatted against principles, not men, they felt that the same patriotic motives which had impelled him against the Royalists and the Girondists, would necessarily compel him at last to take a part against themselves, seeing that they had now usurped the places of the Aristocracy, to whose vices they added those also of brigandism and apostacy. These considerations necessarily hastened the shock of parties.

The result is well told by Buonarroti. Suffice it to observe here, that Robespierre was overwhelmed on the 9th Thermidor (27 July, 1794), by a conspiracy of all the factions in the Convention, headed by the Desperadoes or Dantonists just described. His accusation was decreed with acclamations, amid cries of " Down with the tyrant ;" and after his execution he was, of course, saddled with the chief share of all the crimes of the Revolution, and especially with those that had been committed by his assassins. This is the way in all Revolutions. The dominant party takes credit to itself for all that is good, and flings upon the vanquished the odium of all that is bad.

As a proof how little reliance can be placed in history, I shall just notice here some of the opinions promulgated respecting Robespierre. Mark their inconsistency with facts, and with one another.

M. DULAURE, in the course of a long article inserted in the *Censeur* of 1815, proves (as he thinks) that Robespierre was a secret Royalist traitor, who had sold himself first to Orleans, and afterwards to the foreign enemy, for gold. Dulaure asserts, that beyond doubt

Robespierre received bribes from foreign Courts; and that previously to his death he was meditating how to smooth the way for the return of royalty in the person of Louis XVIII. A strange character this, to give of a man whom France called the *Incorruptible*, from his well-known contempt of riches—a man of whom Napoleon said that if he had been offered 2,000,000f. to betray the Republic, he would have rejected it with disdain—of a man, in short, who, though the most influential in France during a period of eighteen months, and consequently with unbounded opportunities of enriching himself, nevertheless died so poor that the sale of all his effects after his death fetched only 240 livres, or less than 10*l.*!

Another character of Robespierre is, that he " was of a cold, sanguinary disposition, without conviction and without conscience—ready to exterminate three-fourths of the French people—devoid of all capacity, and aspiring to some inexplicable sort of bloody dictatorship," &c. Such is the sapient opinion of Fantin Desodoards, author of a history on the French Revolution. Dulaure and he would be not a little puzzled to reconcile these two characters. It would non-plus them to explain how a man, aspiring to a dictatorship for himself, could at the same time be plotting for the royalty of another. Both these writers, by the way, represent Robespierre as an unparalleled liar and hypocrite, &c. &c.

Now, what say Messrs. Thiers and Mignet? According to these worthies, Robespierre was "an honest fanatic (*un fanatique de bonne foi*), of mediocre capacity, devoured with envy and pride, incapable of courage; for the rest, a sincere and incorruptible Republican, but beneath the mission which he supposed himself called to fill," &c. &c. It would be a nice matter to reconcile this; with the two preceding characters. The honest fanatic does not harmonise well with the profound hypocrite " without conviction or conscience:" much less does the " incorruptible Republican " harmonise with Dulaure's mercenary conspirator receiving the wages of treason from the hands of royalty, &c.

Another writer, named Nodier, has improved on Thiers and Mignet. According to him, Robespierre was not only honest, but *horribly honest!* His expression is " *hor-*

rible bonne foi." " From these circumstances," observes Nodier, " I should consider Robespierre to be the
true personification of the Revolution—*his rare disinterestedness, his horrible honesty, and his appetite
for blood!"* What a jumble is here. Before I saw this
profound criticism I was not aware that there was any
thing horrible in honesty, much less did I imagine there
was any natural connexion between blood-spilling and
disinterestedness ; but historians are rare discoverers. If
we believe the Abbé de Montgaillard, or the *Conjuration
de Robespierre* (by Mountjoye), or Fantin Desodoard,
Robespierre was a compound of all the inferior qualities,
not only of human nature, but of brute and reptile natures also. He was " ignorant, ugly, grim, sombre, malignant, vulgar, lascivious, brutal, envious, a hater of
journalists, a second Omar against literature, a barbarous
proscriber of the arts and sciences, a murderer of his
enemies, an assassin of his friends, a bachelor only be-
canse the chastity of marriage did not suit his taste for
libertinism, a seducer of his host's daughter, and, to
complete the picture, a filthy beast that finished his daily
orgies of lust and the guillotine by a nocturnal debauch
amongst common prostitutes !!!" Such is the character
given by history of one of the noblest spirits that ever
adorned human nature.

History has been defined to be, " Philosophy teaching
by examples." A just definition, no doubt, if applied
to *true* history; but how melancholy to think that the
youth of a nation should have its opinions formed by
such " philosophy" as that just quoted—a " philosophy"
that has falsehood for its means, and slavery for its end !
But what, you may ask, is the secret of this ferocity—
of these unheard of calumnies against an individual ? Read
Buonarroti, my friends, and you will know. Buonarroti
will show you that Robespierre was a true friend of humanity; that he was the oppressed man's consolation and
the oppressor's scourge; that he devoted himself to the
emancipation of his fellow-citizens with a zeal and a
degree of success never witnessed before in the world ;
that he had a vast plan of regeneration in preparation
for France, by which the poor would be for ever delivered from the rich, and the reign of morals, of frater-

nity of relations, and real happiness established on earth. But the counter-revolutionary conspiracy of the 9th Thermidor destroyed all. Robespierre and his friends removed, the few honest Democrats in the Convention were left without weight or influence. The old Aristocrats uniting themselves to the new, that assembly soon became thoroughly anti-popular. Deprived of their party in the Convention, the friends of equality were soon driven from all their strongholds. The very day after Robespierre's death they lost the Commune, or Municipal Authority of Paris, which was broken up by order of the Convention, and never afterwards re-organised. They were next driven from the Committees of Government. The sectional meetings, which in Robespierre's time used to be held every day, were now reduced to one in every decade, or ten days; and the daily payment of forty sous to the sansculottes, to enable them to attend, was discontinued. As democracy declined in influence, the bourgeoisie and the Royalists raised their heads once more. The population of Paris, finding itself betrayed and disappointed, made a few insurrections to recover its lost power; but without chiefs, or a powerful Commune to lead, they proved feeble and abortive. To complete its humiliation, and to cut off all hope as well as chance of future success, the Convention, under pretence of preparing organic laws for the execution of the Constitution of 1793, abolished that Constitution altogether, and substituted for it the Constitution of the Year III. (1795), which made over the legislature to the middle classes, by annexing a money qualification to the franchise. This was the final blow at the democracy. The people now became universally sensible of the real character and motives of the Thermidorian Revolution. The destruction of Robespierre and his party was now viewed in its proper light—namely, as an essential preliminary to the new treason, which was to wrest the national sovereignty from the entire body of the citizens, in order that a single class might monopolize it. The Constitution of 1793 had been voted by 4,800,000 adult Frenchmen, exclusive of the armies, which were all devotedly attached to it. The Constitution of 1795, on the other hand, received but 900,000 votes, and the armies were all against it. Yet, because this latter established the Government of the middle class, the perfidious Convention was satisfied with the 900,000 votes, and took no account of the 4,800,000 in favour of the popular and legitimate Constitution. Perhaps the history of the world does not record a more hideous treason than this. Had such a measure been proposed only two years before in the Convention, the proposer would have been sent before the revolutionary tribunal as a traitor. But so great had been the reaction since Robespierre's death, that except in petitions and remonstrances, no resistance was offered by the people. The 900,000 shopocrats were quietly suffered to rob the 4,000,000 citizens of their rights and sovereignty; and there was no longer a power in the country to invade the Conventionalists in their hall, or to blow the swindling shopocracy to hell at the cannon's mouth. The people, deceived and disappointed, abandoned the struggle in despair. After all their sacrifices, they wondered to find themselves worse off than before the Revolution; they had not knowledge enough to know that, of all governments, a government of the middle class is the most grinding and remorseless; if they had, they would have felt less surprise at the dreadful distress at that time felt by the Parisian workmen. The Convention having suppressed the law of the *maximum* * in favour of the Shopocrats, as also those against monopoly and forestalling, the consequence was that usury and high profits became the order of the day. To add to the difficulty, assignats, the only money accessible to the labouring class, were in discredit. This arose in a great measure from the extravagance and wasteful system of finance adopted by the new Government, which had issued no less than 30,000 millions of assignats since the 9th Thermidor. The depreciation caused by these enormous issues rendered the assignats of no value. The Shopocrats would not receive them, and the people having no cash, and wanting provisions, were on the brink of destruction. Historians of all

---

* A Robespierrian law, by which the Shopocrats were prevented from charging an extortionate price on commodities, &c. This law was passed to prevent the middle classes from starving the sansculottes.

parties agree that this was a period of unexampled distress, although the harvest had been singularly abundant. The fact is acknowledged, but the cause is left to conjecture. The following, however, shows pretty clearly what the cause was :—" Such," observes Mignet, " was the distressing situation of the country after the fall of the Committee of Public Safety, which had during its reign provided against scarcity, both in the army and the interior, by requisitions and the *maximum*. No person could escape this financial regulation by which the mercantile and the wealthy classes were rendered tributary to the soldiers and the *mob*. During that period, therefore, the necessaries of life were not necessarily hoarded in warehouses. But since, when an end was put to violence and confiscation, the people, the Convention, and the armies had been at the mercy of proprietors and speculators; the consequence was, a frightful degree of poverty, the reaction of the *maximum*." &c. Mignet calls the requisitions and *maximum* violent, though they were absolutely necessary to support 1,400,000 soldiers fighting in defence of the country on the frontiers; but he does not call the hoarding by the vampire profit-hunters violent, although the effect of that was certain death, and torments the most excruciating, to hundreds of thousands. But so it is with aristocratic historians. The middleman's gains being of more consequence in his eyes than the poor man's life, whatever interferes with the one is " *violent*," while the other is very lightly dealt with. Thus Mignet sums up for the poor quietly—" *they attributed their distress to the merchants, to the contractors, to the landholders, to the Government* (all with good reason), *and they called to mind, not without regret, that not long ago they had both bread and power under the Committee of Public Safety.*"

Such was the condition of France two years after the death of Robespierre, when the famous conspiracy of Babeuf was formed,—and this brings me to my third reason for publishing this book.

3rd. Because " Babeuf's Conspiracy for Equality" appears to me the only event of the kind recorded in history that was sincerely and comprehensively designed

for the benefit of human kind. The only conspiracy to
match it in magnitude of means, was that of Cataline to
set fire to Rome during Cicero's consulship, but from
what history has transmitted relative to that event (a
good deal falsified no doubt) it does not appear that
Cataline and his accomplices had any other motives than
plunder and private revenge. Not that I believe what
Sallust and Cicero relate respecting him. The fact that
Cicero was obliged to put his accomplices to death *un-
condemned,* is enough for me. Had not the conspiracy
and its agents been more popular than it suited Sallust
or Cicero to state, the latter would not have feared to
send them for trial before the judges. Nevertheless,
putting the case most favourably for Cataline, there
is no evidence extant to show that that conspirator
was actuated by other than personal motives—motives
it may be justifiable and provoked—but still only personal and vindictive.

Of a very different character was the conspiracy of
Babeuf and his friends. Their's was a plot for the emancipation of France—for the regeneration and happiness
of mankind. It was a conspiracy to restore the democratic Constitution of 1793, and, through that Constitution, the reign of political and social equality. Nor was
the project a chimerical one. The conspirators had
abundant means and materials for success. Never,
perhaps, was a conspiracy conducted with better auspices, or more likely to succeed, up to the moment when
it was broken by the hand of perfidy. The then state of
France, and particularly Paris, was peculiarly favourable. The experience of two years had made the multitude regret the loss of Robespierre's Government. The
abundance enjoyed then, and the happy times that
promised to follow the accomplishment of his projects for
giving a milliard to the defenders of the country—for
dividing the lands of the emigrant traitors amongst the
poor—for extirpating mendicity—and, above all, for
putting the people in secure possession of the Constitution of 1793; these, and the like, contrasted strangely
with the misery and impotence experienced by the multitude under the new Government. Now, the object of
the conspirators (who were all devoted admirers of

Robespierre) being to resume the great work left off on the 9th Thermidor, it was pretty certain that the moment they declared themselves, the multitude would rise as one man for them. Besides, the doctrines of social equality had been recently rendered so universally popular by Robespierre's Government, that they no longer inspired feelings of incredulity (as they might now in France), but rather of enthusiasm and confidence. The principles to which the people were invited to rally were the same that had often led them to victory, and to the achievement of such prodigies. Upon the people, then, the conspirators had every reason to calculate. Moreover, they had 17,000 practised Revolutionists ready to act at a given signal. They had the Mountaineers* of the Convention with them, and the ex-officers of various kinds who had been in authority under Robespierre to the number of 1,500; they had the artillerymen of Paris, who were noted for their democratic spirit, the grenadiers of the legislative body, the whole corps of the Invalides, and almost the entire legion of police. They had also gained the guards, the magazines, and the artillery at the camp of Vincennes; and by Grisel, one of the conspirators (the same that afterwards betrayed them), they were assured of the good dispositions of the soldiers at the camp of Grenelle. With the aid of the two camps they promised themselves a speedy success; but should the troops hold out against the harangues of their orators, the blandishments of the women, who were to present them with garlands and refreshments, and the invitation of the Invalides to follow their example, preparations were made for barricading the streets against them, and showering upon them stones, slates, bricks, vitriol, and boiling water. But I anticipate the narrative—I have said so much only to show that the conspirators had no lack of means or materials, and considering the then aspect of affairs, their project appeared as feasible in execution as it was bold in conception and benevolent in design.

BRONTERRE.

* These devils, now sunk into contempt and impotence, by the return of the Girondists, and the general progress of the counter-revolutionary re-action, regretted bitterly the part they had taken against Robespierre on the 9th Thermidor.

P.S. I had intended to offer some remarks as to the credibility of Buonarroti as a historian, but the following extracts are, I think, considering the quarter from whence they come, sufficiently decisive on that point. A good word from the *Quarterly* is—in Buonarroti's case at least (to use his own words)—*omni exceptione major.*

(From the Quarterly Review.)

" The work of Buonarroti may be considered not only as the most curious one which has appeared concerning the French Revolution, but as the most important also."

Again—" Let us render justice both to Buonarroti and his work. That he was an accomplished person, and a man of great abilities, is beyond all doubt ; as little can it be doubted, that if his opinions had been compatible with the public welfare (Tory welfare he means), or if he had lived in peaceful times, he might in many respects have been an estimable and distinguished member of society. The estimation in which he was held at the Court of the Grand Duke, Leopold, is proof of this. To speak of him as intrepid, would be to use a word at once inadequate and inappropriate ; to use an expression of Marshal Soult, he was an *impassable* man ; he could have done whatever Sylla or Marius did ; whatever Timur or Nadir enjoined among barbarians, or Simon de Montford and Alva among persecuting Christians, he could have executed without hesitation and without remorse, &c. &c. * * * * He has rendered an important service to society by the publication of these Memoirs. There never was a book more trustworthy in all its statements," &c.

Again—" On the subject of the conspiracy his authority is *omni exceptione major ;* he is perfectly explicit both as to the object at which he aimed and the means by which it was to be brought about ; the object was to subvert the existing system, not of Government alone, but of society in France, and to introduce an absolute community of goods ; the means were, an insurrection first, the massacre of all who opposed them, the putting of the whole legislative body to death, and placing the operatives, the *malheureux*, as he sometimes calls them, in possession of the property and houses of the higher orders throughout the whole of France !" &c. &c. &c.

NEW PUBLICATIONS.

I take this opportunity to announce that I will shortly send forth to the public several new works, of which I have repeatedly given intimation in the *Poor Man's Guardian, Twopenny Dispatch,* &c. Amongst these will be—" *A True Life and Character of Maximilian Robespierre*"—" *A Real History of the French Revolution*" —" *A History of the English Commonwealth*"—and " *An Essay on the Existing State and Future Prospects of Society.*" I am now engaged in collecting materials for these works, and hope to have Robespierre's Life in stereotype before the last number of Buonarroti shall have appeared. The others shall follow with all the despatch compatible with the due execution of such important and, necessarily, laborious undertakings. Of their nature and principles I shall only observe here that I intend them to be instrumental in familiarising the public mind of England with those great principles of social and political reform, the application of which I consider essential to the regeneration and happiness of mankind.   BRONTERRE.

AUTHOR'S PREFACE.

———◆———

A MOMENT before our condemnation, Babeuf and Darthé* received from me, on the benches of the High Court of Vendôme, in presence of the aristocratic axe, which was ready to fall upon them, a promise to avenge their memory, by publishing an exact recital of our common intentions, which party spirit had so strangely misrepresented and disfigured. Now that I am near the close of life, it is time that I acquit myself of this obligation, which divers circumstances prevented me from discharging sooner.

Besides other duties, a long and rigorous detention, followed by a surveillance still longer, and oftentimes very embarrassing, on the three opposite extremities of France, precluded me for a long time from the possibility of discussing with ocular witnesses, the causes of the great events of the Revolution, and of procuring certain documents (*pieces*) that were necessary to elucidate particular facts, which I had proposed to my-

* The penalty of death had just been demanded against them, and that of deportation against Germain, Moroy, Cazin, Bouin, Méneissier, Blondeau, and myself.

B

self to make known. Nevertheless, I might possibly
have been able to publish this work much sooner, had I
not been withheld by the apprehension of furnishing
fresh pretexts for animosities and persecutions. Now,
however, that age presses me, I have decided to let it
appear; and I feel the greater confidence in so doing,
because, on the one hand, the men of that epoch have
almost all disappeared, and because, on the other, the
political doctrines of the present day being at an infinite
distance from those which were professed by the Democrats of the year IV of the French Republic, there
exists no longer any occasion to dread any dangerous
application. Besides, it is just that the democratic
party should be at length known in its true colours.

Having to render an account of a singularly bold enterprise, I have considered it my duty to make clearly
appear in what manner we conducted ourselves; and to
this end I have deemed it necessary to bring to recollection the situation in which the Revolution then stood,
the successive phases which had marked its progress,
and the virtues or vices which appeared to us to have
exercised any influence upon it. Accordingly, I have
commenced my narration with a rapid retrospect of this
Revolution, up to the period of those events which form
my subject-matter. I have not pretended to write a
history of them, I have only desired to sketch the impressions which we (the conspirators) received from
them.

To accomplish the task thus imposed upon me, it was
not sufficient to narrate what Babeuf and his friends
did, or wished to do, with the view of putting their

plan in execution; it was necessary also to explain the final end which they proposed to themselves, and the manner in which they demonstrated to their own satisfaction its justice and necessity. I have, therefore, followed up my recital of the facts of the conspiracy, by a development of their doctrines and of their projects.

The sources from which I derive all that I affirm relatively to this conspiracy, are my own recollections, the writings of my brother conspirators, the papers of the judicial proceedings instituted against them, and some few fragments that were, up to this moment, unknown.

All our papers were not seized by the police. Some of those which Babeuf had not about him, were destroyed by over-prudent friends; others I have been able to recover; these I publish in the imperfect state in which they have reached me.

I am not ignorant that the political and economical principles which I must avow, will meet with many disapprovers, but that is no reason for not publishing them; other opinions, pretended to be errors, have established themselves as incontestable truths. Are there not men whom the tinsel of civilized society has not dazzled, nor the systems which are preached up by those who arrogate to themselves the right of directing opinion? They, perhaps, will appreciate the importance of these opinions, and will give some regret to the memory of those courageous citizens who, being penetrated by their justice, and proud of exposing their lives in supporting them, sealed them at last with their blood.

Strongly knitted to them by the conformity of our sentiments, I partook in their conviction and efforts;

and if we deceived ourselves, our error was, at least, complete. They persevered in it to the grave; and for my own part, after subsequent long reflection, I remain convinced that that equality which they cherished, is the only institution proper for conciliating all real wants, for directing the useful passions, restraining the dangerous ones, and giving to society a free, happy, peaceful and durable form.

CONSPIRACY FOR EQUALITY

CALLED

BABEUF'S CONSPIRACY.

PARTIES AND THEIR CHARACTERS DURING THE REVOLUTION.

AMONGST the various parties which caused the French Revolution to assume so many different complexions, there was one which deserves to fix the attention of the philosopher, because of the constant devotion with which it consecrated its efforts to the real deliverance of humanity.

Whilst ambition, jealousy, cupidity, and the blind love of innovation, kept up a deplorable struggle among a people, of whom some combatted to reestablish the ancient monarchy—others to place upon the French throne a new dynasty—others, again, to transfer power from one caste of society to another; but all for the purpose of appropriating exclusively to themselves the national authority, and thereby those enjoyments of which authority is the source: amid all these parties there was slowly formed a certain class of citizens who, actuated by very different principles, desired also a great political change, but one altogether opposed to the passions of the former persons, who were only so many interested fomenters of civil discords. In fact, there was a variety of political sects that aspired, each to give to France a form of administration favourable to its own selfish views, but they were very few who sought a real radical reform of society in favour of the mass of the people.

Hence it happens that the bulk of those who figured on the stage of the Revolution, confined their efforts to the barren object of making one order of government prevail over another, without at all troubling themselves about the condition of those for whose advantage all legitimate government ought to exist; and owing to the same cause it was, that so many pretended legislators imagined themselves to have founded a Republic, when they had only condemned a king to death, and substituted the authority of several for that of an individual.

Our divisions during the Revolution were the results of opposing interests and principles. While one set of persons (the honest) supported a system because they believed it to be good, another set, far more numerous, united themselves to the party that appeared most favourable to their personal views of fortune or ambition. The former pursued with constant fidelity the path which they had originally traced out for themselves; the latter were always shifting their conduct, according to circumstances, or their own capricious passions.

It was only at successive stages of the Revolution, however, that one could discern the particular character of each political sect, for so long as they had a common enemy to combat, they were obliged (whatever their differences of opinion) to appear all to act in the same spirit; but at each succeeding step towards a new degree of amelioration, there was formed a fresh party of oppositionists, namely, of those interested in maintaining the vices against which the new movement was directed.

Thus, if certain nobles of the Constituent Assembly appeared popular at the dawn of the Revolution, they were not slow in revealing their true characters, by following an opposite course, the moment that the first aspirations were heard in favour of a real equality. If others, again, rose up against the reigning family, with the design of substituting another in its room, they were soon seen to range themselves under the banners of royalty, from the moment it became evident that the cause of all dynasties was hopeless. If, at first, the priests applauded the efforts of the reformers against the higher orders of the clergy, they became afterwards the bitterest propagators of fanaticism, when once the nation had refused its support to all forms of worship alike. If those who had wished to cashier the constitutional monarchy for their own profit, assumed the guise of Republicans to that end, they were to be found in open opposition to the more ardent defenders of the Republic, from the instant that the people seemed eager for the Republic as the most desirable of all things.

In the midst of the storms thus necessarily produced by the mixture of so many discordant elements, those individuals who, from the commencement of the Revolution, had conceived the hope of establishing in France the empire of true justice, seized with eagerness the frequent occasions which so great a fermentation presented, to habituate their fellow citizens to reflect on their rights, and to lead them gradually to desire the overthrow of all vicious institutions which interdicted the enjoyment of them.

The useful or dangerous passions that agitated Frenchmen in one sense or the other, were in some measure represented in the Assemblies, which during the Revolution exercised the supreme power. In these were developed the most abject vices and the most sublime virtues. In these was the signal given of so many combats. It was here that the members of the different political sects, laid hold on, and gave birth to those crises by which they sought to give prevalence to their respective systems and interests.

The party which remained firm to the cause of the people, saw itself, at distinct epochs, treacherously abandoned and threatened with destruction, by the very factions that had assisted in the triumph of its projects, up to the moment when those projects began to clash with their own selfish views. Whilst the Monarchy existed, the Republican party appeared very numerous; and although for a long time one might have perceived essential shades of difference amongst those that were then ranged under the banners of the Republic, the 10th of August, 1792, witnessed a multitude of men combating against the Court, who afterwards became divided, and amongst whom were many that have since espoused the cause of kings. Indeed, amongst these combatants, as well as amongst those that applauded their triumph, might be enumerated many who were animated only by personal jealousy and resentment, and a still greater number whom the probability of a Regency, or of a change of dynasty, flattered with the hope of a near and profitable influence. Be this as it may, however, there exists every reason to believe that the majority were at that time in favour of a Republican Government, although the different parties diverged widely from one another, both in respect of the ideas they had formed of Republicanism, and of the passions which impelled them to desire that form of Government.

All the various systems of politics and of public economy, served as motives or pretexts for the dissensions of the National Convention. Some preached the exclusive influence of the class favoured by fortune and by education; others regarded a participation by all in the sovereign power as an essential condition of the durable tranquillity and well-being of society. The former sighed after the riches, the superfluities, and the display of Athens; the latter desired the frugality, the simplicity, and the modesty of the fine days of Sparta. It is rendering, however, but a very imperfect view of the nature of these dissensions, to compare them with the political systems of the ancients. To understand it well, we must consider the state of manners, and our acquaintance with natural rights.

What passed in France immediately after the creation of the Republic, is, in my view, only the explosion of that discord, which ever exists between the partizans of opulence and distinctions on the one hand, and the friends of equality, or the numerous class of labourers, on the other.

System of Egoism, or Selfishness. By tracing the stream higher up, we shall find the source of the discussions which took place at that epoch, in the English doctrine of the economists,* on the one side, and in that of Jean Jacques Rousseau, Mably, and other modern philosophers on the other.

* I comprise under this denomination, as well those writers and statesmen who would subject industry and commerce to regulations, as those who would give the most extended freedom to their operations.

Let us call to mind, that very many writers have made the prosperity of nations to consist in the multiplicity of their wants—in the ever augmenting diversity of their material enjoyments—in an immense industry—in an unlimited commerce—in the rapid circulation of the monied metals—and (as the last step of the analysis) in the *restlessness and insatiable cupidity of the population.** At one time they prefer the heaping together of territorial property, at another, they declare for the multiplication of small proprietorships; and whilst some have believed that the misery and brutalization of the productive classes are essential to the opulence and tranquillity of the whole, others, by holding forth the unrestricted and unlimited freedom of industry and commercial transactions, as a means of remedying the established inequality, have only paved the way for a new system of corruption, and for new inequalities, more extensive and pernicious than what before existed. For, once the happiness and strength of society were placed in riches, it became a necessary consequence to debar from the exercise of political rights all the citizens who do not offer by their fortunes a guarantee or pledge of attachment to such an order of things—an order reputed, as it were, the perfection of the social state. In all social systems of this kind, the great majority of the citizens being incessantly subjected to painful drudgery are, in effect, condemned to languish all their days in misery, ignorance, and slavery.†

* It was always difficult for men to understand one another, with a view to the establishing of a rational social order. It was by a traffic in superfluities, and by the arts of luxury, that our forefathers, snatched without violence a part of their riches from the favoured sons of feudality. Slaves, by thus becoming necessary to their masters, enfeebled their power. An evil which served as a cure for another evil, was taken for the supreme good at the point, where, in the eyes of many, liberty is but another name for the unlimited faculty of acquiring and accumulating.

† From the vast disproportion between the numerically large class of labourers (*salariés*) and the comparatively small class of capitalists (*salarians*), must necessarily result the misery of the former. Overcharged as they are with labour, their ignorance becomes as much a matter of necessity to themselves, as it is a necessary safeguard to their taskmasters, who would have every thing to fear from their knowledge, in consequence of having thrown upon them their own proper share of the general burdens. From ignorance and misery arises the slavery of our country, which exists wherever men want the power or the knowledge to exercise their volition

B 5

Rousseau proclaimed the inalienable rights
System of Equality. of human nature. He pleaded for all mankind
without distinction. He placed the prosperity
of society in the happiness of each of its members, and
its strength in the attachment of all to the laws. In his
view, public riches consist in the industry and moderation
of the citizens, and liberty resides in the power of the
sovereign, which is the entire body of the people, and of
which each element preserves in itself the influence
necessary to the social body, by means of an impartial
distribution of enjoyments and of intelligence.

This social order subjects to the will of the sovereign
people the acts and properties of each individual, encourages the arts which are useful to all, proscribes those
which only flatter the vanities of the few, develops, without
predilection or partiality, the reason of each citizen,
substitutes for base cupidity the love of country and of
glory, and constitutes the whole of society into one vast,
peaceable family, in which each member is subject to the
will of the whole, but no member to that of another.
This social order of Rousseau is the same for which all
true philosophers have sighed from time immemorial, and
has had illustrious advocates in all ages, as, for example,
in ancient days, Minos, Plato, Lycurgus, and the law-
giver of the Christians (Jesus Christ); and in modern
times, Thomas Moore, Montesquieu,* and Mably.†

The system of the economists has been named the
ORDER OF EGOISM,‡ or the ARISTOCRATIC

---

* Montesquieu's Spirit of Laws (*Esprit des Lois*) book 4, cap. 6.

† Vide *Principes de Legislation*, and, promiscuously, his other
writings. Mably considers a community of property to be the
only social order, conformable to the true end or intent of society, which is the permanent happiness of all its members. According to him, all the evils which afflict human society, being the
effects of avarice and ambition, the science of politics reduces
itself to the art of effectually stifling these passions. Avarice
cannot be smothered unless by a community of goods. The principle of community does away with individual property, and thus,
at the same time, diminishing the attractions of power, it becomes
a rampart against ambition, which ought also to be restrained by
manners and by institutions.

‡ By this denomination is meant to be expressed, that in this
system, the only spring to sentiments and actions is the selfish
one of mere personal interest, without any regard whatever to the
general good.

SYSTEM. That of Rousseau—the ORDER OF EQUALITY. *

From the moment that the tendencies of the different political sects, which figured on the stage of the Revolu-

* Equality, the sentiment of which is the base of sociability, and the consolation of the wretched, is a chimera only in the eyes of men that are depraved by the love of riches and of power.

All systems and all passions apart, where is the human being that does not, in his heart, recognise an equal in an individual of his own species, whatever he may be? Where is the man, who, placed in the same situation, does not experience an equal pang of pity at beholding the sufferings of any of his fellow men? This sentiment, the effect of our earliest impressions, is justified by reason, which teaches us, that nature has made all men equal. But how, and in what respects? To comprehend this rightly is important.

The advocates of social inequalities pretend that they are inevitable, because, as they say, they are derived from those which nature herself has established between individuals of the human species. Mankind, they say, differing naturally in sex, size, colour, features, age, and vigour of limb and muscle, cannot possibly be equal either in power or riches; equality, whether natural or social, is, therefore, a mere creature of reason or of imagination.

But granting that the *natural* differences just mentioned do really exist, does it, therefore, follow that the inequalities of *institution* are necessary consequences of them? Why, according to this reasoning, opulence and authority would always go hand in hand with physical force, with majesty of size and beauty—a consequence utterly disclaimed by fact and experience. But, say the partizans of inequality, there is another natural difference which necessarily induces distinctions in intellect and social position; namely, that of mind or spirit (*esprit.*) Nay, they have gone so far as to pretend to recognise in the bumps of the brain, according to their various degrees of protuberance, infallible indices of our inclinations and passions. Notwithstanding this, however, our very instincts apprise us that things have not been so ordered by the author of Nature; and that if human beings, ordinarily well organized, do not all possess the same mental capacity, the existing differences in this respect is much less the effect of diversity in their conformation, than of the circumstances in which they have been trained and placed. Who can doubt that numbers of men now ignorant, would not be so if they had had opportunities of instruction? Does not the coarsest rustic apply, in the direction of his works, and in the discussion of his interests, as much intellectual acuteness as was required by Newton for discovering the laws of attraction? Everything depends on the object towards which our study is directed. Besides, were it even true that intellectual inequality exists by nature, to the degree pretended. it would nevertheless be impossible to discover in that circumstance the source of those distinctions in riches and power which exist in society, since it is by no means true that wealth and authority are generally the inheritance of knowledge and wisdom.

But, after all, are the qualities just spoken of necessary to the

tion, began to assume a marked character, it might be observed that all whose minds were perverted by corruption attached themselves to the promoters of the *Order of Egoism*, while, on the other hand, those only whose

question? Not at all. The natural equality we have in view, and for whose existence we contend, is only that uniformity of wants and desires which are born with us, or are developed by the first use that we make of our senses and organs. The want of food—the desire of procreation —self-love—pity—sympathetic affections —the disposition to feel, to think, to will, to communicate our ideas, and understand those of our companions, and to conform our actions to rules—hatred of constraint and love of freedom; these are what exist in pretty nearly the same degrees, in the bosoms of all sound and well-constituted human beings. Such is the natural law, from which emanate, for all men, the same natural rights.

In the eyes of him, who recognises in himself a being composed of two substances of distinct natures, a new argument, in favour of natural equality, may be derived from the spirituality of the *thinking principle*. This principle, which constitutes to him alone his entire human self (*tout le* moi *humain*), being indivisible and pure, and derived always from the same source, is necessarily equal in every individual of our species. As to the inequality of physical strength, it is certain that it can be no bar to the enjoyment of natural equality, at any rate no more than a momentary bar; and it was probably to obviate this evil that recourse has been had to conventions, and that civil society was instituted.

And here, for want of foresight, mankind have precipitated themselves into a greater calamity than the one they had wished to guard against. The equality established by nature, and avowed by reason, has been violated in society by a succession of these same Conventions which were designed to maintain it. For the transitory inconveniences produced by the inequalities of physical force have been substituted other inconveniences more fatal, more permanent, and more inevitable, by the conventional inequalities of riches and power. Thus, by a strange metamorphosis, the most foolish, the most vicious, the feeblest, and the least numerous, have been enabled to overburden with painful toils and duties, and to deprive of their natural liberty, the great majority of the strongest, most virtuous, and even best instructed.

From the unequal distribution of wealth and power arise all the disorders of which nine-tenths of the inhabitants of all civilized countries justly complain. From thence result to them privations, sufferings, humiliations, and slavery. From the same source results also that intellectual inequality which, through interested motives, is falsely ascribed to an exaggerated inequality of mental capacity. It is, therefore, to restrain within just limits the *riches* and *power* of individuals, that all true social institutions should tend—power, by subjecting all citizens equally to laws emanating from the whole—and riches, by providing such institutions for distribution, as would give to each enough, and to nobody more than enough. Behold in what consists the equality treated of in this work.

Indeed, at the point to which things have arrived now, this equality may be said to regard riches only; for wealth alone,

hearts were pure, and whose consciences were not perverted, became necessarily interested in the complete triumph of the *Order of Equality*. But amongst the partisans of the system based on *egoism*, there were, besides those whom old prejudices attached to it, many that aspired to preserve, and others that wished to conquer for themselves, exclusive enjoyments and pre-eminence. This latter party, devoid of all virtue, affected a love of equality, and even an affection towards its sincere friends, so long as they fancied they would be able to prevent its establishment, and to turn to their own profit the general fermentation they had themselves provoked.

False friends of Equality.

Since the commencement of the Revolution, the friends of equality, that is to say, of justice, exerted themselves to prepare a triumph for it, by opposing in the distance, the views of the parties that were its enemies.

Efforts and progress of the party of Equality.

Under the Constituent Assembly, they combatted against the unjust distinction of citizens into active and inactive —against the contribution of a mark of silver being required as a condition of eligibility to the national representation—against the royal veto, and against martial law. They thundered, at one and the same time, against the avowed Royalists, and against those who hypocritically covered themselves with the varnish of patriotism, they proposed the progressive impost—opposed the reinstatement of the King after his forced return from Varennes—sustained the courage of the patriots, when it was at the point of being extinguished after the massacre of the Champ de Mars—unmasked the aristocratic complots of those who prematurely demanded the Republic. These, and a variety of other services, they rendered under the Constituent. Under the first Legislative Assembly they denounced the dismissal of the military patriots, exposed to light the snare hidden under the declaration of war against Austria, caused crowns of honour to be decreed to the Swiss soldiers of the Château-Vieux, unmasked the dissimula-

nowadays, confers the passport to power. Wealth is become the sole title to power, as well in the eyes of the governors as of the governed. Money, money, is the sovereign power.

tion of the court, the crimes of the ministers, the treasons of Narbonne, and the tortuous proceedings of the Girondists; and preserved the sacred fire (of patriotism), which the rich and powerful had endeavoured to smother by calumny and persecution.

But it was especially after the 10th of August, 1792, that the men I have just described, conceived the most flattering hopes, and redoubled their noble efforts to secure the triumph of their sublime cause. To the merit of Rousseau's conceptions, they added the boldness of applying them to a society of five and twenty millions of men. At this same epoch, too, the struggle between the friends of equality and the partisans of the Order of Egoism became more characterized and more animated. The project of governing the state under a show of republican forms, while at the same time retaining all the institutions of the monarchy, was publicly supported. To this project, united themselves all those descriptions of persons who, in times of political trouble, fear to lose their consideration and enjoyments. And as the same fear had attached them to royalism, they furnished grounds of accusation against the leaders of their party, for conspiring to re-establish the throne.* So great was

Its triumph. at that time the number and credit of the sincere friends of equality, whom the poignards of the aristocracy had not as yet cut off—such was the activity excited in the multitude by the hope of a speedy deliverance from their sufferings, and such was the force of the sham-patriots, who had hypocritically become the apostles of an equality they abhorred, with a view to replace the old aristocracy—so great was the power of all these combined (for they were then united), that the avowed partisans of the Order of Egoism were attacked, vanquished, and reduced to silence. Behold what produced the divisions of the National Convention, before the 31st of May, 1793, and the civil war which followed upon that memorable day's proceedings.

* Some were effectually devoted to the royal cause. Others accommodated themselves with equal ease to every regime through which they hoped to preserve their consideration and power. The interest that both these parties took in the life of the king, during his trial before the Convention, gave great weight to the accusations of royalty urged against them.

From the victory of the 10th of August resulted immediately some progress of the popular cause. A few days after the fall of the throne, the exercise of political rights was extended to all citizens, without distinction. All were declared eligible to public functions, and it was solemnly recognized that no constitution could be imposed on the people without their consent. At the same time marriage was legally disembarrassed of that deplorable (*désespérinte*) indissolubility which often renders it as inimical to the happiness of individuals and families, as it is disastrous to morals and liberty. It is a fact deserving observation, that the energy of the nation in defence of the Revolution invariably expanded or diminished in proportion as the laws seemed to favour equality or to oppose it. It was the working class—that class so maltreated and so unjustly despised in society—which achieved all the prodigies of virtue and devotion to which the Revolution gave birth. The rest of the community (with very few exceptions) only threw obstructions in the way of the national regeneration.

It is an unquestionable fact that the Order of Egoism, or Aristocracy,* had very able and numerous advocates in the National Convention. For proofs of this [Aristocrats in the National Convention before 31st May.] we need only look to the crafty harangues and writings of Vergniaud, Guadet, Rabaud, Brissot, Gorsas, Condorcet, Lanjuinais, Louvet, Barbaroux, and so many others of the same stamp. We have further proofs in their transactions with the court—in their incessant invectives against the friends of equality—in their avowed hatred of the real directors of the insurrection of the 10th of August—in their connections with Narbonne, Dumouriez, Custine, and other faithless generals—in their persevering opposition to the establishment of the progressive impost †—in the prodigal interest they took in

* The aristocratic system, or exercise of sovereign power, by a part of the nation over the whole, is an inevitable consequence of the inequality consecrated by the Order of Egoism.

† The impost progressive differs from the proportional impost in this—that the relation of the latter to a man's income is always the same, the tax preserving a uniform ratio to his fortune—whereas in the impost progressive the ratio itself increases at the point where superfluity begins. In short, the progressive impost prevents large fortunes and spares small ones.

the King's fate, when he was brought before the tribunal
of the nation—in their hostile measures against the partisans of democracy—in the alarms with which they
sought to inspire the rich and corrupt classes—in the
firebrands of discord which, by such means, they scattered
throughout France—and last, not least, in their obstinate
perseverance to consecrate by the force of laws their
anti-popular principles. *   The question was, to give a

* The liberty of a nation is the result—1. Of the equality which
the laws produce in the condition and enjoyments of the citizens,
and 2. From the greatest possible extension being given to the
exercise of political rights. The *projet* of the first Constitutional
Committee of the National Convention, composed entirely of
Girondists, by absolutely neglecting the first of these conditions,
delivered over the people to the influence of the rich and intriguing, by the development which it seemed to give to the
second.

NAME OF THE GIRONDIST FACTION.—CAUSES OF DIVISION IN THE
CONSTITUENT ASSEMBLY.

This faction was called *Girondist*, because it recognised for its
chiefs almost all the deputies from the department of *La Gironde*,
to the Legislative Assembly, and to the Convention.

So soon as the first Declaration of Rights was proclaimed by
the Constituent Assembly, the frank and unqualified application
of the principles of natural justice with which some of them were
consecrated in it, proved revolting to men led astray by a false
science, or corrupted by the vices of civilization.   From that
moment they only meditated how they might best elude the principles, while they affected and appeared to applaud them.

This was the origin of the factions which, under the first three
National Assemblies, exerted themselves to arrest the impulse
(*élan*) of the French people towards complete emancipation, and
to confine the Revolution to those systems which they judged
most favourable to their passions, or most conformable to their
doctrines. These proved much more hurtful to the establishment
of liberty, than the open opposition of the privileged classes,
because they have deceived the people by borrowing from them
the language of patriotism.

Towards the close of the Constituent Assembly, the spirit of
these factions predominated in it, and the party which remained
faithful to the public cause would have been unnoticed, had it not
forced itself into attention by the energy of its remonstrances. It
is to this spirit we are to ascribe the retrograde movements and
contradictions of this Assembly.

In contempt of the equality of right which had been decreed by
the Constitution, millions of citizens were deprived of the right
of suffrage, and of eligibility. A law of blood was opposed to the
complaints excited by the misery of the people, and by the equivocal course of the legislature. The latter were obstinately bent,
in defiance of good sense and the national will, to replace the
safeguard of the constitution in the hands of a king who had just
openly avowed himself its enemy, and whose power, *instead of*
extinguishing, they had increased. They caused to flow in the

constitution to a rising republic.◦ The want of a regular authority had made itself generally felt, and it was pretty commonly believed that a good distribution of political

Champ de Mars the blood of those citizens who were preparing to solicit a contrary decision. They forced the people to have recourse to violence in order to obtain that justice which a simple decree might have peaceably operated. They struck a blow at the right to assemble and petition, and wished to chain the nation for ever to the chariot wheels of the aristocracy.

To the real contempt which the Constituent Assembly had for the mass of the people, we are to attribute the feebleness of their efforts against the royal power, which, while they pretended to shake, they really desired to convert into a rampart against democratic effervescence. Hence, also, its negligence to profit by the people's enthusiasm and the errors of the court, in order to annihilate the monarchy or tie it up within limits which would have made it, in effect, almost a republic.

Such are the causes of the suspicions which subsequently arose against the Lameths, against La Fayette, against the minority of the Noblesse, and against several distinguished members of the Third Estate. The same views were shared by the famous Mirabeau, the extreme corruption of whose morals, forced him through the allurements of gain, to become the champion of that monarchy against which he had just successfully combatted.

THE GIRONDIST FACTION.

But the love of luxury, the thirst of gold, and the desire to shine and govern, were not engrossed by the Noblesse alone ; there was between them and the immense class of working men, another numerous class of ignoble aristocrats, who shone by riches, by polished manners, by refined wit, by small talk, by laxity of morals, and by irreligion. This latter upstart class also despised the people—believed itself born to lord over them—pretended to be the *sound* part of the nation, and added suppleness and jealousy to the views of the nobles, whom they aspired to replace in authority.

This class was composed, for the greater part, of advocates, lawyers, physicians, bankers, rich merchants, opulent citizens, and men of letters, who trafficked in science, and made it the ladder of their ambition. Greedy, vain, and restless, it plunged into the first movements of the Revolution, and induced the multitude, whom poverty and want of instruction made dependent on them, to participate in their schemes of ambition. The members of this class being masters of most of the tribunes for haranguing the people (*tribunes aux harangues*), and of the administrations, pushed themselves, through the suffrages of their friends, into the Legislative Assembly and the Convention, where they formed the NUCLEUS of the Girondist faction.

Generally speaking, the Girondists did not desire the ancient *regime* in all its hideousness, but still less did they desire that the new regime should progress so far as to confound them with what they called the " low people" (*bas peuple*), and strip them of that superiority which was so profitable to them. As to whether France was governed in the manner of Monarchy or of a Republic, at bottom they cared not a rush, provided to *them* and their party should belong the possessors and dispensers of all favours emanating from power, and that the sovereignty of the people

power would in itself secure to the people the advantages of equality and liberty—the main object of their aspirations.

should be in reality but a *sound* invented the more effectually to ensure public submission and obedience to the laws—laws of which they (the Girondists) should have the sole enactment and execution.

Accordingly, we see them in the Legislative Assembly alternately combat or favour the particular interests of Louis XVI., just according as that monarch pretended to follow the plan of his ancient courtesans, or submit himself to the councils of this faction. The personal views of its chiefs in the secret negociations which they entered upon with the king—in the official councils they gave him to the effect of strengthening his power, were fully proved by living witnesses and documentary evidence. Indeed, some of the Girondists, most notable in their party, had not been ashamed to publish in their memoirs, their confession of attachment to the Monarchy, and their aspirations for its re-establishment after it had ceased to exist.

PROOFS OF THEIR HATRED OF REPUBLICANISM.

It is a gross error to suppose the Girondists were real friends of liberty, or frank Republicans. Had they been so, would they have so bitterly calumniated and persecuted the Parisian municipality of the 10th of August (the dethronement of the king), to whom was mainly due the triumph of that day? Would they have exerted themselves as they did, during the combat, to throw damp (under pretence of re-establishing order) upon the people's enthusiasm, which it was so important at the moment to cherish and increase? Would they have declaimed so much against those terrible but inevitable executions of the 2d and 3d of September, which were notoriously resolved upon as the only means of securing the Revolution, and which were but deplorable consequences of the avowed and concealed hostilities of the enemies of liberty, and of the grave and imminent dangers which just then threatened the French nation? Would they have converted the sanctuary of the laws into an arena of gladiators, by their virulent and calumnious accusations against the men who had contributed most to sustain the courage of the people? Would they have sought to terrify the rich, to sow division among the people, and speak of federalising France, at a time when the most perfect unity was necessary to repel the armed coalition of Europe's despots? Would they even, after their expulsion from the Convention, have erected altar against altar, kindled a civil war, and laboured to arm the departments against the heroic Commune of Paris, whose destruction the foreign tyrants most panted for? Could, they, in short, have been ignorant that the only means to consolidate the Revolution, and eternalize liberty, peace, and happiness, was to second the people's cause, to satisfy the secret wishes, and give effect to the aspirations of so many millions of oppressed men, and thus uniformly diffuse throughout society, for each and every one of its members, the benefit of the social state.

Unhappy Girondists! Neither was it without reason that you were inculpated of the design to re-establish the throne. Were there not some Royalists amongst those Girondists that fought at Lyons against the Republic under the orders of a king's officer, and received into their ranks the emigrants whom they had released

Nevertheless, the most clear-sighted of the friends of equality did not participate in this opinion. Whatever may have been said of the matter, the aristocrats of the Convention were more eager to set to work about this constitution than the friends of equality, who, being far less numerous, felt convinced that without an event calculated to terrify

The friends of equality opposed to the premature discussion of a constitution.

from prison, or who congregated in crowds into this revolted city? Were there not some Royalists amongst those other Girondists who delivered Toulon to the enemy, and re-established there the very same day the royal authority?

The servile spirit of the Girondists appeared palpable in the proposition, so obstinately supported by them, to submit the sentence against Louis to the ratification of the Primary Assemblies. Falsely did they pretend in that to render homage to the sovereignty of the people, since the question at issue was a mere judicial act, and not a law. Could they flatter themselves with engraving on the hearts of Frenchmen that hatred of royalty upon which the Republic should be based, by introducing in favour of the royal captive so new a privilege? How is it that they did not dread exposing France to weariness and distraction, which had well nigh dug a tomb for liberty? Was such an irresolution, cowardice, and servile respect for a demolished throne, the proper means to strengthen in the souls of the citizens that courage and virtue which they so much needed to escape the fury and perfidious snares of the enemies of the Revolution? Is it by tergiversation that characters elevate themselves? Is it by trembling, dastard-like, that we can break a nation's chains? But if, under all circumstances, people will have it that the Girondists were Republicans, then must it be confessed that their conduct was absurd, and that if they desired a Republic, it was one that would have crushed the people under such a weight of oppression as to give them abundant cause to regret their old servitude.

Unfortunate Girondists! the sport of your own vanity, you could neither be frankly Royalist nor positively Republican. You did us far more injury than our avowed enemies, inasmuch as you veiled your crimes under the appearances of patriotism and moderation, and rendered urgent and necessary that severity which at first saved the Republic, but which afterwards furnished so many auxiliaries to those by whom it was successively dismantled and destroyed.

Miserable Girondists! by combatting against the men sincerely devoted to the happiness of the people, you delivered them defenceless to the wicked and infatuated men that immolated them on the 9th Thermidor. Listening only to the counsels of vengeance, you provoked, after this epoch, the massacre of the Republicans; and your aristocratic spirit gave birth to the Constitution of the year III, to which we owe the tyranny of Buonaparte, which was, in great measure, your work. Let others vaunt the eloquence of the Girondists; to us they cannot be subjects for eulogy in any sense, because we are convinced that their influence has been one of the most active causes of the failure of the Revolution, of the fall of the Republic, and of the ruin of liberty.

their adversaries, not only could they not obtain a reform
in the civil elements of society, but that it was impossible
even to establish an organization founded on the equality
of political rights.   This eagerness of the aristocrats was
then a branch of the vast conspiracy against the natural
rights of man ; and it was necessary to divert from it its
chief instigators before one could reckon on the successful efforts of a handful of honest persons.

Conspiracy   A conspiracy was, in fact, formed against
of the 31st   the numerous conspirators that had intro-
May, 1793.   duced themselves into the chief offices of
authority in the republic—a conspiracy for the imprescriptible rights of humanity against the desolating
power of pride and avarice; and at the moment when
the aristocrats, concealed in the bosom of the Convention, were giving the signal for a general proscription
of the friends of equality, whom they called *anarchists*,
the people of Paris carried terror into the souls of their
perfidious representatives, and forced them to deliver up
(31 May, and the days following) to national justice the
chiefs of the counter-revolutionary plot.   The freedom
of the Convention was violated to save that of the
people; the power of the delegates was infringed to
make them respect the national sovereignty, which was
impudently made a jest of, by the majority of them.

In the absence of the writings, discourses, and facts,
which prove the reality of this plot, one may easily
recognize it in the almost universal coalition of the rich
against the revolution of the 31st May, and in the
rapidity with which democratic truths were subsequently
Democracy in   propagated. It must not be supposed that
France. Mean-   the revolutionists of France attached the
ing of the word. same idea to the democracy sought by
them that the ancients attached to that word.   Nobody
in France dreamt of convening the universal people to
deliberate on the acts of Government.   Democracy was
in their view, *that public order in which equality and
good morals place all the people in the same condition to exercise legislative power usefully.*

Small number   Later events have, methinks, sufficiently
of the sincere   proved that the true democrats were never
friends of equa- numerous in the National Convention.

The insurrection of the 31st of May was far from transmitting the supreme influence to the sincere friends of equality only. Its false and interested friends appeared to triumph with it; but the latter, who were active destroyers only for their own profit, immediately flung themselves into the old system they had combatted, when it became necessary to build up another for the people.

Amongst the individuals that shone in the revolutionary arena, there were a few who, from the outset, declared themselves for a complete emancipation of the French people. Marat, Maximilien Robespierre, and Saint Just, figured gloriously, with some others, in this honourable list of the champions of equality. Marat and Robespierre attacked in front the anti-popular system which prevailed in the Constituent Assembly. By these were the steps of the patriots directed before and after the 10th of August; elected to the Convention, they were there exposed to all the hatred and calumnies of the egoistical or aristocratic factions, whom they confounded and unmasked. In giving judgment on the king, they elevated themselves to the highest philosophy, and they had a principal share in the events of the 31st of May and days following,* the happy influence of which was afterwards destroyed by the false friends of equality.

Previously to the fall of the Girondists, Robespierre believed that it was impossible for the Convention, governed as it was by that faction, to originate good laws. He thought, moreover, that in the then critical state of the country, the first care of the people's mandatories ought to be to annihilate the hordes of enemies which, from within and without, menaced the existence of the Republic; but, seeing the eagerness of the Girondists to consecrate by

lity in the National Convention.

Declaration of Rights by Robespierre.

---

* France was indebted to the rational and vigorous policy which followed these events, for the generous and universal onset (*élan*) which made her crush in so short a time the factions of the interior, and the armies of the confederated despots, for which the aristocratic views and equivocal conduct of the Girondists prepared a safe and certain triumph. Such was the effect of the courage and firmness of the Mountainists, the adverse party to the Girondists in the Convention. At this epoch the Mountain was composed of the true friends of equality, and of those who from personal views affected and made use of its principles.

legislation their aristocratic principles, he opposed to their projects his *Declaration of Rights*, in which his popular designs are fully revealed. If the political doctrines comprised in this document, and in the discourses which Robespierre delivered in his last days, are viewed in juxta-position with the purity of his morals, his devotedness, his courage, his modesty, and his rare disinterestedness, we are forced to render a brilliant homage to so lofty a wisdom; and we cannot but detest the perversity, or deplore the incomprehensible blindness, of those that planned and consummated his assassination.*

* So much has this illustrious martyr of equality been calumniated, that it becomes a duty of every honest writer to consecrate his pen to avenge his memory. I know not that I can better effect this purpose than by transcribing here his project of the Declaration of Rights. This remarkable document lets in a full light on the real and ultimate designs of those men, so furiously proscribed since the death of this celebrated legislator. One cannot but admire in it the definition of the right of property, which ceases to rank in the number of principal rights, to give place to the power of preserving existence. One will also admire in it the limits placed to this same right of property—the institution of the progressive impost—the concurrence of all in the formation of the law—the extirpation of misery—the guaranteeing of instruction to all the citizens—and above all the right of resistance to oppression, determined in such a manner as to become an insurmountable barrier to the arbitrary will of public ministers, and against even the tyranny of the laws themselves.

DECLARATION
Of the Rights of Man, and of the Citizen,
BY MAXIMILIEN ROBESPIERRE.

The representatives of the French people, assembled as a National Convention, acknowledge that all human laws which do not emanate from the eternal laws of justice, are but criminal attempts of ignorance and despotism against humanity; and convinced that the forgetfulness and contempt of the natural rights of man are the sole causes of the crimes and calamities of the world, have resolved to lay open, in a solemn declaration, those sacred and inalienable rights, to the end, that all the citizens being always able to compare the acts of the Government with the design of all social institutions, may never suffer themselves to be oppressed and degraded by tyranny; and that the people may have perpetually before its eyes the bases of its liberty and happiness—the magistrate the rule of his duties—and the legislator the objects of his mission—in consequence, the National Convention proclaims, in presence of the universe and of the Supreme Legislator of the World, the following Declaration of the Rights of Man, and of the Citizen:—

Art. 1. The end of all political associations is the maintenance of the natural and imprescriptible rights of man, and the development of all his faculties.

The Constitution of 1793, however, which was drawn up in consequence of the insurrection of the 31st May, by the party then called the *Mountain*, did not com-

Art. 2. The principal rights of man are those of providing for the preservation of his existence and liberty.

Art. 3. These rights belong to all men equally, whatever difference may be in their physical and moral force. Equality of rights is established by Nature. Society, so far from invading it, constitutes its security against the abuse of force, which would render it illusory.

Art. 4. Liberty is the power which belongs to a man of exercising all his faculties at pleasure. It has justice for its rule, the rights of others for its boundaries, nature for its origin, and the law for its safeguard.

Art. 5. The right of peaceably assembling—of manifesting opinions, whether through the press, or by any other means—are so necessary consequences of the principles of man's liberty, that the necessity of declaring them supposes either the presence or the recent remembrance of despotism.

Art. 6. Property is the right which each citizen has to enjoy and to dispose of, at his pleasure, the portion of fortune or wealth that is guaranteed to him by the law.

Art. 7. The right of property is limited, like all other rights, by the obligation to respect the rights of others.

Art. 8. It can prejudice neither safety, nor liberty, nor existence, nor the property of our fellow-citizens.

Art. 9. All traffic that violates this principle is essentially illicit and immoral.

Art. 10. Society is under obligation to provide subsistence for all its members, either by procuring employment for them, or by ensuring the means of existence to those that are incapable of labour.

Art. 11. The relief indispensible to those that are in want of necessaries is a debt due from the possessors of superfluities. It belongs to the law to determine the manner in which the debt should be discharged.

Art. 12. Citizens, whose income does not exceed what is necessary to their subsistence, are dispensed from contributing to the public expenditure. The rest ought to contribute *progressively*, according to the extent of their fortunes.

Art. 13. Society ought to favour, with all its power, the progress of public reason, and place instruction within the reach of every citizen.

Art. 14. *The people is the sovereign*; Government is its work and its property; the public functionaries are its agents and officers; the people may, when it pleases, revoke its mandatories.

Art. 15. The law is the free and solemn expression of the people's will.

Art. 16. The law ought to be equal for all.

Art. 17. The law can forbid only what is hurtful to society; it can prescribe only what is useful.

Art. 18. Every law that violates the imprescriptible rights of man is essentially unjust and tyrannical; it is no law at all.

Art. 19. In every free state the law ought, above all, to defend public and individual liberty against the authority of those that govern. Every institution that does not suppose the people *good*, and the magistrate *corruptible*, is vicious.

pletely answer the wishes of the friends of humanity. One regrets to find in it the old deplorable ideas on the right of property.   For the rest, the political rights of

Art. 20. No *part* of the people can exercise the power of the *whole* people ; but the wish it expresses ought to be respected, as a wish of part of the people, which is to concur in forming the general will.   Each section of the sovereign assembly ought to enjoy the right of expressing its will with perfect liberty ; it is essentially independent of all constituted authorities, and competent to regulate its own policy and deliberations.

Art. 21. All the citizens are equally admissible to all public functions, without any other distinctions than those of virtue and talents—without any other title than the confidence of the people.

Art. 22. All the citizens have an equal right to concur in the nomination of the delegates of the people, and in the formation of the law.

Art. 23. In order that these rights be not illusory, and equality chimerical, society ought to pay the public functionaries, and to provide that the citizens who live by their labour may be able to assist at the public assemblies to which the law calls them, without compromising their means of existence, or that of their families.

Art. 24. Every citizen ought religiously to obey the magistrates and agents of the Government, whilst they are the organs and executors of the law.

Art. 25. But every act against the liberty, the safety, or against the property of a man, by whomsoever exercised, even in the name of the law itself, if not comprehended within the cases determined by the law, and within the forms it prescribes—every such act is arbitrary and null.   The very respect due to the law forbids submission to it, and if the attempt be made to execute such act by violence, it is permitted to repel force by force.

Art. 26. The right of presenting petitions to the depositaries of the public authority belongs to every individual.   Those to whom they are addressed ought to determine upon the points which constitute the object of them ; but they can never either interdict, or restrict, or condemn the exercise of the right.

Art. 27. Resistance to oppression is the consequence of the other rights of man and of the citizen.

Art. 28. There is oppression against the social body whenever one alone of its members is oppressed.   There is oppression against every member of it when the social body is oppressed.

Art. 29. When the Government violates the rights of the people, insurrection is for the people, and for every portion of the people the most sacred of rights, and the most indispensible of duties.

Art. 30. When the social guarantee or compact fails to protect a citizen, he resumes his natural right to defend *personally* all his rights.

Art. 31. In either of the two preceding cases, to subject to legal forms the resistance to oppression, is the last refinement of tyranny.

Art. 32. Public functions cannot be considered as distinctions, nor as recompenses, but as public duties.

Art. 33. The crimes of the delegates of the people ought to be severely and promptly punished.   No one has the right of pretending that he is more inviolable than other citizens.

the citizens are clearly enounced and strongly guaranteed. It places general education amongst the duties of society; it renders easy all changes favourable to the people; it opens the way to every improvement, and secures to the people the exercise of sovereign power, in a manner, and to a degree, unknown before. Is it to a prudent circumspection, commanded by the hostile attitude of the rich, who were set in motion by the Girondists? or is it to the prevailing influence of the Egoists, in the deliberations of the Convention, that we are to ascribe the wary reservations it had resort to, and the veil under which the honest members of that body were obliged to conceal their ulterior views of social equality? Whatever was the cause, certain it is, that the right, *attributed to the people, of deliberating on the laws—the submission of the people's mandatories to their orders, and the almost unanimous voice of the nation in accepting the Constitution of* 1793—caused that Constitution to be regarded (and never was title juster) as the *Palladium of French Liberty*.

But some of the parties that had laboured in digesting this Constitution (called afterwards the *democratic* Constitution by the patriots) felt that *it* alone was not enough to ensure to Frenchmen the happiness they demanded. They considered an antecedent reform of morals to be necessary to the enjoyment of liberty: they knew that before conferring on the people the exercise of sovereign power, it was necessary to render

Origin and motives of the Revolutionary Government.

Art. 34. The people has the right to know all the operations of its delegates. It is the duty of the latter to render to the people a faithful account of their behaviours, and to submit to its judgment with respect.

Art. 35. Men of all countries are brothers, and the people of each ought to yield one another mutual aid, according to their ability, like citizens of the same state.

Art. 36. He who oppresses one nation alone is the declared enemy of all.

Art. 37. Those who make war on a people, to arrest the progress of liberty, and to annihilate the rights of man, ought to be pursued everywhere, not as ordinary persons, but as assassins and brigand rebels.

Art. 38. Kings, aristocrats, tyrants of every description, are slaves in revolt against the sovereign of the earth, which is the human race, and against the legislator of the universe, which is Nature.

c

the love of virtue general—to substitute disinterestedness and modesty for avarice, vanity, and ambition,
which keep up a perpetual war amongst the citizens—
to extinguish the contradiction established by our institutions between want and the love of independance, and
to wrest from the natural enemies of equality the means
of deceiving, terrifying, and dividing. They knew that
the coercive and extraordinary measures, indispensable
to operate so happy and great a change, are irreconcilable with the forms of a regular organization. They
knew, in short—and subsequent experience has but too
well justified their views—that to establish, without
those preliminaries, the constitutional order of elections,
would be only to abandon their power to the friends of
all abuses, and thus lose for ever the opportunity of
establishing general happiness. Accordingly, at the
demand of 8,000 envoys from the people, they caused
the Constitution of 1793 to be replaced (until the peace)
by a form of authority, which preserved to those who
had commenced the great work the power of completing
it, and substituted at once, for the hazards of an open
war against the intestine foes of liberty, prompt and
legal means of reducing them to impotence. This form
was called the *revolutionary Government*, and had for
its directors the members of that Committee of Public
Safety, to which humanity might owe its complete redemption, had not subsequent events destroyed all.

Its prodigies.　　　It is impossible that honest minds should
not acknowledge the profound wisdom with
which the French nation was then directed towards a
state in which, equality established, it would have arrived at the full and tranquil enjoyment of a free constitution. One cannot too much admire the prudence
with which these illustrious legislators, turning reverses
and victories, to account, with equal skill, were able to
inspire the great majority of the nation with a self-denial
the most sublime, with contempt of riches, pleasures,
and even death, and to induce them to proclaim that
*all men have an equal right to the productions of the
earth and of industry.*

And who will be able to efface from the pages of history this astonishing metamorphosis, by which so vast a

population, hitherto, and but a season before, the sport of voluptuousness, cupidity, levity, and presumption, cheerfully renounced a thousand factitious enjoyments rivalled one another in zeal to offer up their superfluities on their country's altar, thundered in mass on the armies of the coalesced sovereigns, and contented themselves with demanding for their *all*, bread, steel, and equality? These facts, attested by an infinite number of addresses, reports, and decrees, by the public registers, by the annals of France, by the terror (not yet extinct) of the aristocratic classes, and by our own recollections, are alone a sufficient answer to the falsehoods, the calumnies, and the sophisms, by which it has been sought to blacken this brilliant portion of French history. To what high destinies might not a people attain, capable of being inspired with such generous devotion! What sage institutions might not France and the world have promised themselves from the counsels of those who had presided over such grand prodigies!

After the promulgation of the Constitutional Act of 1793, and of the decree which created the revolutionary government, authority and legislation became every day more popular. An enthusiasm, as sacred as it was new, seized possession of the French people; innumerable armies started up as it were by magic; the Republic became at once one vast workshop of war; youth, matured manhood, and even old age, rivalled one another in patriotism and courage; in a very short time was a formidable enemy repelled from the frontiers, which it had invaded, or which treason had put into its hands. In the interior, factions were quelled and crushed; every succeeding day witnessed the birth of new legislative measures tending to raise the hopes of the numerous class of unhappy poor *(malheureux)*, to encourage virtue, and to re-establish equality on earth. Superfluous wealth was consecrated to misfortune, and to the defence of the country. By means of requisitions (in prints and merchandize) of forced loans, revolutionary taxes, and the boundless generosity of good citizens, provision was made to subsist *fourteen hundred thousand warriors*, and the rest of the population besides, whose

c 3

republican darings the rich proposed to subdue by hunger and destitution.

The establishment of magazines of abundance, the laws against monopoly and forestalling, the emission of the principle, which attributes to the people the right of property in commodities of prime necessity, the laws for the extinction of mendicity, those for the distribution of national succours, and the community of goods, which then reigned *in effect* amongst the generality of Frenchmen, were some of the preliminaries to a new order of things, the plan of which is traced out in ineffacable characters in the famous reports of the Committee of Public Safety, and principally in those which Robespierre and Saint Just delivered in the National Tribune.*

* As long as the present order of things shall endure, the freest form of political government will be advantageous only to those that can live without work. The mass of the people being subjected by their wants to painful and continual labour, and unable either to inform themselves respecting public affairs, or to assist in the assemblies where they are canvassed or discussed, and depending on the rich for their very existence, the latter alone (rich) dispose of the deliberations, which their deceitful governments have the artful plausibility to appear to demand and encourage in the people. Are we to presume that these honest folk forget themselves? How would they act, if the people, taking them at their word, were to moot the question of their own usurped distinctions, and demand of them to descend to their proper level? [How queer the hypocrites would look then!—Bronterre.]

Robespierre's Report of the 18 *Pluviose, Year II.*—" We desire " an order of things, in which all the mean and cruel passions shall " be chained down; all the beneficent and generous passions " awakened by the laws; in which ambition shall consist in the " desire of meriting glory and serving our country; in which dis- " tinctions shall spring but from equality itself; in which the " citizen shall be subject to the magistrate, the magistrate to the " people, and the people to justice; in which the country shall en- " sure the prosperity of every individual, and in which each indi- " vidual shall enjoy with pride the prosperity and glory of his " country; in which every soul shall be aggrandised by the con- " tinual intercommunication of republican sentiments, and by the " wish to merit the esteem of a great people; in which the arts " shall flourish as the decorations of the liberty that ennobles " them; and in which commerce will be a source of public riches, " and not of the monstrous opulence of a few great houses only.

" We desire to substitute in our country morality for Egoism, " probity for honour, principles for usages, duties for courtesies, " the empire of reason for the tyranny of fashion, contempt of vice " for contempt of misfortune, manly pride for insolence, greatness " of soul for vanity, love of glory for the love of money, honesty " for respectability, good people for good company, merit for in-

In order to rightly appreciate the revolutionary government of the French Republic, we must divest ourselves of the prejudices engendered by the political systems which have preceded the revolution, and which,

" trigue, genius for wit, truth for display, the charms of happiness
" for the *ennui* of pleasure, the greatness of man for the littleness
" of the great, a people magnanimous, powerful, and happy, for a
" people amiable, frivolous, and miserable ; in a word, we desire
" to substitute all the virtues and all the miracles of the Republic
" for all the vices and all the ridiculous fopperies of the Monarchy.
" We desire, in short, to fulfil the vows of nature, to accomplish
" the destinies of humanity, to absolve Providence from the long
" reign of crime and tyranny—that France, heretofore illustrious
" amongst enslaved countries, may, by eclipsing all the free states
" that ever existed, become a model for nations, the terror of op-
" pressors, the consolation of the oppressed, the ornament of the
" world—and that in sealing our work with our blood, we may
" at least witness the breaking dawn of universal felicity.
Robespierre again.—Discourse of the 7th Prarial, Year II.—" What
" constitutes a Republic is neither the pomp of denominations, nor
" victory, nor riches, nor transitory enthusiasm ; it is the wisdom
" of the laws, and, above all, probity of manners—it is the purity
" and stability of the maxims of Government."
SaintJust—Report of the 8th Ventose, Year II.—" The wealth of
" the country is in the hands of a great number of the enemies of
" the Revolution; their wants place the labouring people in a
" state of dependence on their enemies. Do you conceive that an
" empire can exist, if its social and civil relations shall depend on
" those opposed to its form of Government? They that make but
" half-Revolutions only dig a tomb for themselves. The Revolu-
" tion conducts us to recognise this principle, that whoever has
" shown himself the enemy of his country can hold no property in
" it. We want still some master-strokes of genius to save us."
" Shall it be, then, to cater for the enjoyments of its tyrants
" that our people sheds its blood on the frontiers, and that every
" family wears mourning for their children? No! Better recognise
" with me this principle—that he alone possesses rights in our
" country who has co-operated in emancipating it. Abolish men-
" dicity, which dishonours a free state. Let the properties of pa-
" triots be sacred, but let the wealth of conspirators be given to
" the poor. The outcast poor are the great powers of the earth—
" they have a right to speak in the character of masters to all
" governments that neglect them."
And at the close of the same discourse—" As regards you! Destroy
" the rebel faction—establish liberty on a rock of brass—avenge the
" patriot-victims of intrigue—make good sense and modesty the
" order of the day—permit not that there shall be one pauper, or a
" single human being in misery, throughout the state. Such is the
" price at which only you shall have made a Revolution, and a
" veritable republic."
Saint Just again—Report of the 23rd Ventose, Year II.—" If the
" people shall love virtue and frugality ; if effrontery shall disap-
" pear from their foreheads, and modesty become the characteristic
" of our citizens ; if the counter-revolutionists, the Moderates, and

in all ages, bequeathed to the earth only calamities and
crimes. The wisdom with which that government prepared a new order in the distribution of goods and
duties, cannot escape the regard of upright minds.
Such minds will discern *more* than the mere expression
of national gratitude in the distribution of lands promised to the defenders of the country, and in the decree
which ordained the repartition, amongst the unhappy
poor, of the goods of the enemies of the Revolution who
were to be expelled from the French territory. They
will see, in the confiscation of the possessions of the condemned counter-revolutionists, not a mere fiscal measure,
but the vast plan of a regenerating reformer. And when,
after considering the care with which these reformers
propagated the sentiments of fraternity and benevolence,
the ability with which they were able to change our
ideas of happiness, and that prudence which kindled in
all hearts a virtuous enthusiasm for the defence of the
country and of liberty, they will further call to mind the
respect accorded to simple manners and good morals,
the proscription of conquests and superfluities. the grand
assemblies of the people, the *projets* of national education, the Champs de Mars, the national festivals—when
they will reflect on the establishment of that sublime
worship, which, by blending the laws of the country
with the precepts of the divinity, doubled, as it were, the
force of the legislator, and armed him with the means
of extinguishing all superstitions in a short time, and of
realizing all the miracles of equality; when, moreover,
they will bear in mind, that by taking external commerce into its own hands, the Republic had snapped

" the robbers, shall roll in the dust: if terrible to the enemies of
" the Revolution, you show yourselves loving and feeling towards
" the patriots; if the public functionaries shall study and labour in
" their closets to work out the well-being of the state, without run-
" ning here and there after shallow renown, and having no other
" witness but their own hearts; if you will bestow lands on all the
" unhappy poor, and take them away from traitor-aristocrats; if
" you will act in this way, then shall I acknowledge that you have
" really made a ' Revolution.' "
The same—Report, 13th *Ventose.*—" Let Europe learn that you will
" no longer suffer that there be one indigent wretch, nor one oppres-
" sor on the French territory. Let this example fructify all over the
" earth—let there be propagated every where the love of virtue
" and happiness. Real happiness is a new idea in Europe," &c.

the root of the most devouring species of avidity, and dried up the most fruitful spring of factitious and artificial wants—when they will consider, that by the requisitions the Republic disposed of the major part of the products of agriculture and industry, and that *subsistence* and *commerce* had already formed two grand branches of the public administration, they will be forced to exclaim, *One day more, and the happiness and liberty of all were ensured by institutions which all incessantly demanded!*

But fate had otherwise ordained! and the cause of equality, which had never before obtained such signal success in the world, was destined once more to succumb, under the combined efforts of all the anti-social passions. Those who had dared the noble task of undertaking so glorious an enterprize had to combat at one and the same time— the infatuating errors of weak men, and the intrigues of dishonest villany, of which they were at last the victims. Some believed, and others feigned to believe, that the revolutionary government, by which the exercise of political rights was partially and momentarily suspended (a mere temporary precaution), did essentially menace the liberty of the nation; the latter party injured the country more by the sophisms with which they deluded and led astray a multitude of honest citizens, than even by the plots they hatched and instigated against the leading reformers. Unfortunately, the nature of an extraordinary but necessary authority was with difficulty comprehended, by minds which had imbibed only the theories of a free and tranquil social order. Forgetful of existing circumstances, they looked to the *end only;* but, incapable of conceiving the means necessary to attain that end, they were easily disposed to look with jealousy and alarm on a form of government, the necessity for which they did not understand. They did not see that an extraordinary or revolutionary authority was indispensable in the actual circumstances of the country, such authority being alone competent to put a nation in full possession of liberty, notwithstanding the corruption which is the consequence of its ancient

Faction, which alarms the people respecting the preservation of its sovereignty. Hebertists.

slavery, and in the midst of the snares and hostilities, in which its enemies, internal and external, never fail to embroil it, by conspiracy and intrigue.

The faction of upstart Egoists, combining with the former, assassinate the friends of equality. Dantonists. The false friends of equality, who had propagated its principles only with the view of improving the opportunities (of the time) to subserve their rapacity, grew pale at the approach of an era when all should bend to the same social level, and submit to the yoke of morals. Some had abused the extensive powers entrusted to them in the departments and with the armies. Others had fixed their hopes in a transfer of riches in favour of the revolutionists, out of whom they desired to form a new privileged class. Others, again, were accused of having received foreign gold as the price of their criminal manœuvres.*

* Hebert and Danton gave their names to two factions, which, though equally inimical to the Revolutionary Government they had aided to establish, differed essentially, both as regarded the tendency of their aims and the characters of the individuals that composed them.

In the ranks of the Hebertists one might count, generally speaking, only the working class—men of labour—upright, frank, courageous, little studious, strangers to political theories, loving liberty from sentiment, enthusiasts for equality, and impatient to enjoy it. Good citizens in an *established* popular Republic, but bad pilots in the storms that precede its establishment, it was not difficult to disaffect them against the prolongation of the revolutionary institution (the necessity of which they did not comprehend) by painting it to them under the colours of a culpable invasion of the popular sovereignty. Neither was there much difficulty in persuading them, that in order to dry up for ever the source of superstitions and of sacerdotal power, it was necessary to proscribe all religious ideas. Nevertheless, such men, more disposed to break through difficulties by *coups de main* than to maturely weigh the utility and consequences of a political crisis, had the same results in view as the wise friends of equality, but they had not, like the latter, formed clear ideas, either of the institutions by which it was to be be won, nor of the route by which it was necessary to arrive at it. It is not to them, however, that we ought to impute the disastrous division in the ranks of equality, and the calamities operated by the faction they belonged to. A responsibility so grave rests entirely with those influential persons who, in the name of the public good, inspired them with unworthy suspicions, and for whose criminal blindness there can hardly be found a just excuse.

The Dantonists have no claim to the like indulgence, because the predominant character of this faction was a compound of vanity, intrigue, audacity, falsehood, venality, and corruption. Its acknowledged chiefs openly professed maxims the very reverse

This faction conspired also against the promoters of democratic institutions. It failed, however, in its first efforts, and had to witness the destruction of some of its chiefs;* but the survivors of the party, rallying to the cry of national justice which threatened them, flattering the enemies of the Revolution of all shades, supported by the deluded patriots,† in whom they excited

of that moral purity upon which the French Government of that epoch desired to base the new Republic. Servile imitators of the profligacy which, before the Revolution, had distinguished the Court and the privileged orders, they combatted the aristocrats of the old regime, only to put themselves in their place,—and they rose against religion, not with the view of emancipating mankind from the yoke of prejudice and superstition, nor of disarming despotism of its most redoubtable auxiliary, but only to disencumber themselves of the sore idea of an all-seeing judge, in order the more tranquilly to abandon themselves to their base passions, and to efface from the human mind the consolatory sentiments of justice, probity, and virtue. The Dantonists considered the Revolution as a game of hazard, in which victory belongs to the most crafty and the most knavish. They had a smile of pity for the words *disinterestedness, virtue, equality*, and did not hesitate to declare, that in the account between France and the Revolution, the advantages of fortune and power enjoyed by the old aristocracy ought, as a matter of course, to pass into the hands of the successful Revolutionists. Accordingly, many that then swelled their ranks have since not been ashamed to borrow the most opposite colours, to flatter all tyrannies in turn, and to abandon themselves to the meanest intrigues, in order to acquire fortune and retain a shadow of power.

By the leaders of these two factions were the most dangerous machinations hatched and plotted; and it was not without grave reasons that the Revolutionary Government (of Robespierre, &c.) accused them of acting in concert with the foreign cabinets then in league against the French Republic.

Whatever may have been the secret understanding of their chiefs, certain it is, at any rate, that the two factions laboured to throw every thing into confusion; and that they both applauded and co-operated in the disastrous events of the 9th Thermidor. They did so, however, under the influence of very opposite motives and ends. The Dantonists wished to disembarrass themselves of an equality that they hated, and of the Republican austerity which bridled their licentiousness, whilst the poor Hebertists acted under the mad impression that equality and the Republic were about to be delivered and consolidated by the result. The latter were soon undeceived. By degrees their eyes opened, and they soon re-attached themselves to the men whose conduct they had a little before condemned, and they subsequently shared the proscription in which every honest man in France was involved by that rotten faction, whose revolting immorality always tended to confound them with the partisans of despotism.

* Danton, Camile Desmoulins, Lacroix, and Fabre D'Eglantine.
† Hebert's party—chiefly well meaning but simple and ignorant operatives.

apprehensions of losing the popular sovereignty, and craftily turning to their account the jealousy which merit ever excites, they contrived to represent the voluntary homage rendered to virtue as the characters of an insupportable tyranny; and by dint of calumnies they succeeded at last, on the 9th Thermidor of the year II, in causing the assassination of the Deputies* to whom the French people were mainly indebted for the vast progress made in the conquest and acquisition of their rights.†

* Robespierre, Saint Just, Couthon, Lebas, &c

† Certain members of the National Convention (Tallien, Freron, Bourdon, Fouché, Rovére, &c.), known by the malversations by which they had polluted themselves in their missions, appear to have been the principal instigators of this deplorable day's proceedings. Alarmed by the punishment of the conspirators (Danton, Lacroix, Chabot, &c. &c.), and by the austere maxims of the Government, they easily communicated their fears to others similarly conditioned; and, by their clamours, roused the confidence and audacity of the enemies of equality.

A thousand different motives of interest, jealousy, vanity, aristocracy, and vengeance, swelled the tempest, which on that day burst on the Republic. One might recognise them by the absurdity of the accusations, by the contradictions of the accusers, and by the ferocity and rancour with which they pursued and proscribed every man that dared to perform his duty in defending the Republican Robespierre.

The secret views of these proscribers were disguised under the vague imputation of tyranny. But a tyrant without treasures, without soldiers, without any other friends than the enemies of tyrants—a tyrant who, far from basely pandering to the multitude by espousing its caprices, had often the courage to divert it, at the risk of losing his popularity, from the seductive schemes which others treacherously presented to it. What is such a tyrant but a creature of the imagination—a fiction of the brain? Folly itself is fooled by the supposition. But, said they, he is the tyrant of opinion. Well, now, the process is judged! the argument decided! the tyranny of Robespierre was, then, nothing else than the power of his wise councils, and the influence of his virtue. He was the tyrant of the wicked—he was a tyrant against all tyrannies.

And how did you prove his tyranny—you who, after his death, were only capable of tearing one another like beasts of prey, and of ruining us? Whilst one party accused him of having sacrificed Danton, another party reproached him with having tried to save him! The very men who the evening before called him the Cato of France, or compared him to Orpheus civilising savage states by his lyre, were those that prepared his act of accusation! On one side he is charged with the crimes of certain Deputies on mission—on the other he is upbraided for the prosecutions which he wishes to institute against them. You gave out that he was rich in the possession of several millions, and France calls him to this day *Incorruptible*; and, besides it is well-known that the sale of his effects, after his death, did not produce more than 450f. in money!

From that moment all was lost! To justify their crime, those who had co-operated in the events of that day were **Virtue is called vice and tyranny.**
obliged to change into heads of accusations, the very principles, conduct, and virtues of their victims. The

You declared him to be devoid of knowledge and judgment, at the same time that you are not ashamed to pretend that he subjected you for fifteen months to his domination. One batch of you called him cruel, whilst another batch reproached him with sparing the lives of the sixty-three imprisoned Girondists! You still talk of his reckless ambition, but you forget to inform the world, abused as it is, by your lying inventions, that had it not been for his heroic counsels the magistrates of Paris, at the head of the majority of the sections, and of the cannoniers, would have inflicted on you the correction you so richly merited. Like scholars in insurrection against their master, you insulted him on his bed of death, and you suffered his bleeding wounds to be envenomed by cuts and stabs with a penknife!
There is no parallel for the madness of those committees who, in imitation of the most furious aristocrats of ancient Rome, armed the people against its defenders, by painting them to it, under ambitious colours, as though they had conspired to re-establish the throne, or aspired to mount it—of those committees who, on the 10th Thermidor, were not ashamed to declare to the Convention that it owed its triumph to the falsehoods by which they had deceived the good and simple inhabitants of the faubourg Antoine. "Mayhap you might not credit it," observed the Reporter of the Committees of Public Safety and General Security, "on the desk of the common hall in which the counter-revolutionary sitting was held, there was a new seal, having for its impression but a single *fleur de lis*; and already in the night time had two individuals presented themselves at the Temple to demand the liberation of its inmates. I ought here to record a trait which marks well the state of the public mind. Secret emissaries had wished to corrupt it in the Faubourg Antoine, but no sooner did the representatives of the people speak to them of the emblems of royalism found in the common hall than the Republican sections rent the air with shouts of indignation!"
Robespierre wishes to confound his accusers—he is silenced! Saint Just is cast into irons at the first words of a discourse which he is prevented from delivering. Couthon is arrested, because he desires to oppose injustice. Lebas is proscribed, for the sole reason that he declares he will not share the infamy of an iniquitous decree. The brother of Robespierre desires to defend him, and he, too, is smitten by a decree of arrest; and David, who had said to Robespierre, "I will drink the hemlock with you," suffered a long imprisonment, and was indebted for his life only to the vain celebrity he enjoyed as a painter. To secure their prompt immolation, you created pretences for yourselves out of the just alarms of the Commune, and from their presence at its last deliberations. But, besides that, you are suspected of having held a snare for them, by yourselves unlocking their prisons, their designs and yours—what they had done, and what you did—the blessings

interested professors of democracy, and the ancient partisans of aristocracy, were found to accord once more.
Certain rallying cries that recalled the doctrines and
institutions of equality, were now regarded as the impure howls of anarchy, brigandism, and terrorism.
Those that in Robespierre's time had been wisely kept in
check for the nation's safety, seized upon authority
again; and to revenge themselves for the humiliation
they had been reduced to, they involved in a long and
sanguinary proscription, together with the sincere
friends of equality, those also who had preached it from
self-interest, and even the very factionists who by
treason, jealousy, or blindness, had so largely and
fatally co-operated in the counter-revolution of the 9th
Thermidor.

promised to us by the times which preceded their death, and the
train of calamities that followed it—all these prove to demonstra-
tion that if they rose against you, never was insurrection more
holy, nor resistance more imperiously commanded.

[Perhaps the history of the world, including France itself, does
not record a more atrocious mass of villanous fabrications than
this brief recital shows to have been set on foot, to compass and
justify the death of Robespierre. Not a word more is necessary
to corroborate all I have stated in the *Guardian* and my other publications, respecting the true character of that illustrious martyr
of equality; but, if further evidence be wanted, the public may
take my word for it, they shall have it abundantly in my forthcoming " *Life of Robespierre*." I shall never cease, if God gives
me life, till I have avenged the memory of this, and of every other
friend of humanity, whom the aristocracy, not content with murder-
ing, have had the additional baseness to consign to the execrations
of posterity, by means of their lying fabrications called "histories." If there be one duty which, more than another, an intellectual man owes to his country, it is to blast the existing literature
of the world, and to damn its authors in the eyes of posterity.
This literature is, from beginning to end, a mass of fraud and
misrepresentation, designed and encouraged to perpetuate the
present cannibal state of society; and is, perhaps, the most
formidable and fatal of all existing obstructions to human progression. It shall not be my fault, at any rate, if the industrious
classes shall continue much longer undeceived as to its real character. It is time that the crimes and machinations of the aristocracy should be placed in such a light as to render it impossible
for them to cheat and mystify mankind any longer.—BRONTERRE.]

From the moment that the Revolutionary Government had passed into the hands of the Egoists it became a veritable public scourge. Its prompt and terrible action, which the virtue of its former directors and their thoroughly popular designs could alone render legitimate, became thenceforward but a frightful tyranny, both as regarded its objects and form. It demoralised everything; it restored luxury, debauchery, effeminate manners, and brigandism; it squandered the national domains, denaturalised the principles of the Revolution, and delivered over to the poignards of its enemies all who had defended it with sincerity and disinterestedness. It was to the maintenance of inequality, and to the establishment of aristocracy, that manifestly tended, at this epoch, the efforts of the dominant party. After having deprived the people of all hope of an equitable legislation, and plunged them into incertitude and discouragement, it was meditating to despoil them of even the feeble remains of their sovereignty.

Much as the friends of equality had desired, before the 9th Thermidor, to see the Revolutionary Government maintained in all its purity,* they longed as much now, to see it replaced by the Constitution of 1793, against which were palpably directed the ma-

The Revolutionary Government becomes a public scourge.

The friends of equality demand the Constitution of 1793, and are vanquished.

* In order to deter the people from all ideas of reform, to disgust it with the exercise of its rights, and to render odious in its eyes its true friends, the old aristocrats and the new applied themselves with peculiar industry, to work on its feelings, by presenting an exaggerated picture of the imprisonments and condemnations which took place, under the Revolutionary Government, antecedently to the 9th Thermidor. They represented them as having threatened indiscriminately all classes of society; and then, applying to a durable state what was only the sad necessity of a state of transition, they laboured to make it be believed that the Order of Equality is neither more nor less than one interminable series of violence, massacres, executions, hatreds, and vengeance. Nevertheless, very little discernment suffices to detect in these declamations the rage and malice of the parties that dictated them; and if men will only judge without passion, they will be forced to agree that love of country and the sentiment of duties the most imperious, determined the friends of equality, after a too long and very disastrous patience, to at last resort to severity against its incorrigible enemies. The justice and necessity of the revolutionary institution once recognised, it is no longer necessary to the question to examine up

nœuvres of the aristocracy. Despairing of the triumph of social equality, they desired, at least, to put the people in possession of their political rights. Such was the

to what point the presiding authority carried the severity of which it was necessitated to make use. The only important matter is to know, whether it answered the ends for which it was instituted. Its province was to establish the reign of equality and the laws, and in this vocation it laboured, without interruption, till the 9th Thermidor of the Year II., either in reforming morals, and the spirit of the laws, or in levelling the obstacles that were incessantly reared up against the execution of so sublime an enterprise. These obstacles lay in the armed opposition of Europe, in the seductions and ever-reviving conspiracies set on foot by a party that had rather perish in the conflagration it had kindled, than bend its haughty head to the level of equality, and renounce its vicious and despotic habits. With such enemies to deal with, the question was not whether they should be punished, but how they were to be exterminated.

Let us call to mind the rapidity with which the plots of the aristocracy against the power of the people succeeded one another since the commencement of the Revolution. From the moment that the Republic was proclaimed, and especially after the insurrection of the 31st May, there was manifested amongst the opposing parties a fermentation so intense, so general, and so characterised, that one might, without fear of mistake, recognise every enemy of reform by his conduct, his manners, and opinions.

For a long time the danger was so imminent that the people would have been justified in thundering down at once upon the class of society it dreaded. The Revolutionary Government did in the name of the people what the people had the right of doing, but it did the business far more usefully. Things were arrived at that pass when it was necessary to choose between the annihilation of certain conspirators on the one hand, and the inevitable ruin of popular rights on the other. The case was one in which we should consider the end, not the means. Was the end just? The severity necessary to attain it was, no doubt, a painful and grievous duty; but then it was the more indispensably necessary, inasmuch as there was neither mercy nor amendment to be expected from exasperated pride. To pretend to establish justice and equality without employing force, amongst a people of whom great numbers had contracted habits and pretensions irreconcilable with the well-being of the rest of society and with the just rights of all, is a project as chimerical as it is seductive in theory. To undertake such a reform, and then to halt at the firmness it requires, is but to avow one's cowardice and want of foresight. It is worse—it is to sacrifice the safety of the whole to the vices of a small number —it is, in fact, to want virtue.

Did antiquity impute as a crime to Lycurgus the sacrifice of some Lacedemonian aristocrats? Did it reproach Brutus for the condemnation of his own children? Has it blamed the more than revolutionary rigour with which Moses himself exterminated without pity all that opposed the success of his institution? Do the oppressors of the earth show any tenderness of the people's blood whenever, in the anguish of their sufferings, the latter break out into resistance against the evils they are made to endure?

motive of the movement of the 12th Germinal of the year III., and of the insurrection in Paris of the 1st Prairial. The ill success of those days redoubled the fury of the enemies of liberty, and greatly augmented the number of good citizens, that were either crammed in heaps into dungeons, or massacred all over the extent of the Republic.*

Revolutions are but the necessary consequences of long careers of injustice. They punish in a moment the accumulated crimes of ages. Why do those that fear them labour incessantly to make new ones unavoidable ? Why did not the parties, that are pleased to exaggerate what they call the excesses of the French Revolution, prevent their occurrence, by the voluntary abandonment of their iniquitous pretensions, which were the whole and sole causes of them ?

There has been a world of declamation on the subject of the numerous arrests, ordered on mere suspicion, and on the brevity of the proceedings instituted against the accused conspirators. But be it observed, that at a time when conspiracies spring out of the intense irritation of passions common to a vast number of powerful and crafty men, it is easy for the conspirators to ripen their murderous projects into maturity without letting the least index of them appear. It then happens that the public danger becomes, all at once, manifest, and that the State is delivered over to general conflagration, before it is possible to acquire material proofs against the guilty parties. At such a crisis, in which every thing announces the existence of imminent perils, is it not prudent, is it not just, to spare the people the hazards of an intestine war, by using severity against the parties whose passions, aristocratic habits, and anti-social interests, manifestly place them out of the pale of the popular sovereignty ? At a juncture of this kind, the salvation of the whole depends on the terror inspired into the wicked, by the rapidity with which the thunder of national justice smites a few guilty heads. It is extremely probably that a single additional act of severity in France, at that period, would have secured to the human race a complete and everlasting victory over its enemies.

But of what use to exhaust arguments to justify the spirit and action of the Revolutionary Government which preceded the 9th Thermidor of the year II.? The instigators of that tragical day have supplied its best justification by the crowd of disasters which they drew down upon the French people. In vain did they afterwards invoke the laws of humanity they had profaned, by violently arresting a salutary action, which was approaching its close, in order to commence another action a thousand times more bloody and terrible, and for the profit, too, of immorality, aristocracy, and royalty.

* The movement of the 12th Germinal was provoked by the prosecutions directed against Barère, Billaud-Varennes, Collot d'Herbois, and Vadier, members of the ancient Committees of Public Safety and General Security, in revenge for the firmness with which they crushed the enemies of the Revolution. The National Convention was convicted by them of having ordered and approved all the acts with which it reproached them ; but so

The prisons of
Paris are the
focuses of con-
spiracies for
equality.

The incarceration of almost all the friends of liberty, and their frequent translations from one prison to another, procured them the advantage of a better mutual acquaintance, and of a closer friendly connexion. The prisons of Paris, and particularly those of Plessis and Quatre-Nations, were at that time the foci of a great revolutionary fermentation. It was there the principal actors in the conspiracy, of which I have proposed to narrate the events, first met together. *Bedon,** *Laujen de Dorimel*, Bertrand (Ex-Mayor of Lyons), Fontenelle, Fillion, *Hannac*, Simon Duplay, *Sombod*, Claude Fiquet, Massart, Bouin, *Moroy*, *Chintrard*, *Glartou*, *La Tilme*, *Vélor*, *Golscain*, *Rivagre*, Julien des Armes, *Laire de la Naitle*, Babeuf, Germain, Buonarroti; the members of the popular commission d'Orange; those of the revolutionary tribunals of Arras, Cambrai, Angers, Rennes, and Brest; those of the revolutionary committees of Paris, Nantz, Nevers, and Moulins; and many other democrats from all the departments, were in detention at the prison of Plessis, in the month Floréal of the year III.

From these abodes of grief issued those electric sparks which so often made the new tyranny turn pale with terror. I know, beyond the shadow of doubt, that the insurrection of the 1st Prarial, in the year III., was, in a great measure, the work of several citizens, in detention

blind was the fury of the aristocrats that then composed the majority of the Convention (the proscribed members of the Gironde had been then restored), that without any regard to their justification—that without making any allowance for the part they had unhappily acted in the events of the 9th Thermidor, and not daring to send them to trial in presence of the people of Paris—it arbitrarily condemned them to deportation.

In Prairial, the citizens devoted to the political system of Robespierre, and the deluded party, that had been maliciously alarmed about the sovereignty of the people (the remains of Hebert's party), were found once more in coalition at the rallying call of the Constitution of 1793, of which they unanimously demanded the immediate execution..

* The names written in italics in the course of this work are the anagrams of the names of parties supposed to be still living.

[The reason of this is obvious. Buonarroti would not expose his old friends to a fresh proscription, or their families to the hatred and persecution of the modern aristocrats of France.—BRONTERRE.]

at Plessis, amongst whom may be particularly named Leblanc, afterwards a Commissary of the Directory at Saint Domingo, and Claude Fiquet.*

* *Bread and the Constitution of* 1793 were at this period the rallying cries of the people of Paris, who were justly alarmed for their rights and for their subsistence. As to the latter (the Constitution) their fears were but too well-founded, for it was to the annihilation of the Constitution of 1793 that the efforts of the ruling party of the Convention then visibly tended.

With respect to subsistence, never had the Parisiens experienced a more cruel famine than this, although the harvest had been most abundant, and the rural districts presented the most flattering appearance. From whence proceeded, then, this frightful famine which cut short the lives of so many citizens? From the retrograde march of the Convention, from the cunning of the aristocracy, and from the avarice of the rich.

For a considerable time before, it had been found necessary, in order to defeat the criminal manœuvres of the aristocracy, seconded as they were, by the avarice of the middle classes, to impose a tax on provisions—to force those that were in possession of them to stock the markets, and maintain by severe measures the circulation of paper-money (assignats) at its nominal value. After the 9th Thermidor, the requisitions and the taxes having been on a sudden interdicted, and the paper money abandoned to the unrestricted speculations of commerce, the price of commodities rose so high that at last there was no possibility of procuring provisions without metallic money. The consequence was, that the mass of labourers, who were destitute of money of that kind, were reduced to absolute starvation in the midst of abundance.

At the very height of the people's sufferings the ruling party never ceased to assure them that their subsistence should be provided for! Its policy was to stuff the people with promises of future abundance and prosperity, on condition of unqualified submission on the part of the latter! Such was the price to be paid for their fatal docility. It is only by the circumstances under which they are established that one can judge rightly of the merit of institutions, and of the intentions of the framers of them.

[In corroboration of the truth of what Buonarroti here states respecting the schemes of the aristocracy and middle classes to subdue the friends of equality by famine, I beg attention to the following passage in Mignet's History of the French Revolution. Mignet was no friend of the working classes, and therefore his testimony is the more valuable in the present instance. Speaking of the events just alluded to, he says:—" They (the assignats) were received with reluctance, and cash, as it was the more sought after, was so much the more carefully *hoarded up*, and the value of paper-money still further decreased. The people wanting provisions, and not having the power, even with assignats, of purchasing them, were *reduced to great distress*; they attributed it to the merchants, to the contractors, to the landlords, to the Government (all with perfect justice), and they called to mind, not without regret, that not long ago they had BOTH BREAD AND POWER

This incontestible fact, placed in juxta-position with
the printed act, which was the signal of the insurrection,
with the demands of the insurgents, and with the political character of the deputies, who supported them,*
are sufficient to wipe away the stain of royalism, which
even patriotic writers were forced to stamp on the principal instigators of that disastrous day, with a view to
spare the blood of the friends of equality, who were
devoted to the most sanguinary proscription.†   So

UNDER THE COMMITTEE OF PUBLIC SAFETY," &c. &c.
Men of England! Social Reformers! Friends of Equality! look
to this. Are your eyes beginning to open now respecting the
real character of Robespierre, and the true design of his government! But wait a little—you shall soon know the whole truth, in
spite of craft and calumny.—BRONTERRE.]

* Goujon, Romme, Soubrany, Duroy, Duquesnoy, Bourbotte,
Prieur de la Marne, Peysard, Forestier, Albitte, &c. &c. The
first six of these were horribly immolated to the fury of the soi-
disant humanity-mongers, who pretended to base their power on
moderation, whilst they were enthroning it on the ruins of public
liberty by making rivers of popular blood flow!

[Are we not here, forcibly, reminded of our Moderates in
England? These villains, who helped our Tories to cause the
destruction of three millions of men in the revolutionary wars, and
who would again shed the blood of half the human race to perpetuate their cannibal and desolating usurpation of the rights of
industry, are incessantly prating about the violence of Radicals,
and endeavouring to persuade the world that all who seek the
overthrow of their fell power are " anarchists," " haters of law
and order," and " sanguinary speculators in a revolutionary
scramble for property." But their days are numbered. The handwriting is on the wall, and (if the people only prove true to themselves) they will not long enjoy their ill-gotten spoils and hellish
ascendancy.—BRONTERRE.]

† My contemporaries are, doubtless, not deceived respecting
the nature of these insurrections. But, posterity, which, not having witnessed the facts, must form its judgment from history, ought
to be apprised that the periodic, and even patriotic, writers have
always had recourse to this subterfuge, whenever the attempts of
the Republicans suffered defeat.

[It may be observed here, that the same well-meaning ruse was
practised by the Parisian journals in all the late Republican movements against Louis Philippe's Government. The intention was
to save the poor Republicans from the consequences of their
failures, and to give the Government a pretext for exercising clemency towards them as the deluded tools of another party's machinations. For this purpose have the Carlists been accused of

general and furious was this proscription, that amongst the citizens, precipitated in thousands into the prisons of Paris, there were many indifferent persons, and not a few that were even opposed to the triumph of the party to which they were accused of belonging.

These prisons were at that time the scene of a spectacle as affecting as it was singularly new. The victims, whom the aristocracy had plunged into them, lived frugally in the most intimate fraternity, honoured one another for their chains and poverty, devoted themselves to work and study, and conversed only on the calamities of their common country, and on the means of bringing them to an end. The civic songs with which, chaunting simultaneously, they made the air resound, caused to congregate every evening around these dismal abodes a crowd of citizens, whom curiosity attracted there, or the congeniality of their sentiments with those of the prisoners.

Manners and occupations of the detained patriots.

It was natural that men of this stamp, burning with patriotism, inflamed by persecution, and confirmed in their common sentiments, by long and frequent inter-communication, should be disposed to hazard every thing to restore the principles of the Revolution, and to attain at last the end of their steadfast wishes. Accordingly were the prisons of that epoch the cradles of those democratic conspiracies which burst forth in the third and fourth years of the Republic.

The immolation of the popular Constitution was at length consummated by the commission, to which had been entrusted the hypocritical task of preparing organic laws for its execution. The *projet* of a new Constitution, proposed by this commission to the National Convention, on the 5th Messidor of the year III., was a subject of deep meditation for the imprisoned patriots. They examined all its parts and provisions with more of ripe consideration than was bestowed upon it in any primary assembly. Behold the opinion they formed of it.

Constitution of the year III., or of 1795.

instigating all the late troubles, and the Government, whose policy it was not to drive the Republicans to despair, found its convenience in appearing to credit and acquiesce in the subterfuge. What devilish shrewd fellows are these upstart tyrants!—BRONTERRE.]

Opinion of the friends of equality on this Constitution.   If the proposed Constitution, said they, could leave any doubts as to the spirit of its authors, they would be effectually dissipated by the report which precedes it. *To preserve opulence and misery*—such is the spirit which pervades every sentence of it. They regarded this work, then, as the final result of the crimes of the egoist or aristocratic faction. Excepting the article which required a property in lands, as a condition of eligibility to the national representation, and another which rendered a man ineligible to a superior office unless he had antecedently filled an inferior one, the *projet* of the commission was adopted, and became the fundamental law of the French nation till the 18th Brumaire of the year VIII.* The most superficial examination suffices to convince one that the conservation of opulence and misery was the base of every part of this new structure.

In the first place, in order to silence all pretensions, and to close for ever all avenues against innovations favourable to the people, its political rights are either taken away altogether, or frittered away by mutilations; the laws are made without its participation, and without the possibility of its exercising on them any species of censure or revision—the Constitution chains to itself the people and its posterity for ever, for it is interdicted to change it. It declares the people sovereign, indeed, (what hypocrisy!) but all deliberation of the people upon it is declared seditious. After speaking confusedly of the equality of rights, it snatches the rights of citizenship from an immense multitude of citizens, and reserves exclusively to persons in easy circumstances the right of nominating to the principal offices of the state. In fine, to perpetuate for ever this wretched inequality, the source of immorality, injustice, and oppression, the authors of this Constitution swept away with the exactest care every institution that tended to enlighten the nation as a whole, as also all that tended to form a Republican youth, to diminish the ravages of avarice and ambition, to rectify opinion, to ameliorate morals, and to rescue

---

* Bonaparte's usurpation.

the mass of the people from the savage domination of the idle and ambitious rich.*

These scandalous violations of our common rights, and this contempt of the principal duties of a popular legislator, were denounced to the French people by Antonelle, in a paper entitled " *Considerations on the Rights of Citizenship;*" and by Felix Lepelletier in his " *Suffrage Explained on the Constitution of the year III.*" Indignation, but not surprise, was the universal feeling at the audacity with which the rulers of the day dared to infringe the declared will of the sovereign people so solemnly put forth, as well as their own recent professions and promises.† The Constitution of 1793 was impudently calumniated; and the doctrine of equality was, by the aid of the most monstrous sophisms, scoffed and vilified by the very parties who, a short time before, had been the heralders and extollers of its justice.‡

* Thanks to the inflexible pride of our *new* lords, it soon came to their own turn to regret the loss, notwithstanding its great defects, of this pet Constitution, to which it might have been possible, with the help of some modifications, to reconcile the friends of equality. But the aristocrats preferred gorging themselves with gold, bedaubing themselves with crosses and ribands, and crouching under the iron sceptre of an insolent and perjured soldier (Bonaparte) to living free and equal with the people; in short, they made of this Constitution the REVOLUTIONARY GOVERNMENT OF ROYALTY.

† In the month Germinal of the Year III., a terrible law, called " The Law of the High Police," condemned as seditious the remonstrances that were raised on all sides against the counter-revolutionary march of the Government; but in order the more easily to assuage the public effervescence, this same law hypocritically menaced with transportation whoever should speak or write against the Constitution of 1793, the prompt execution of which was promised by the Convention on the 2nd Prairial of the same year.

‡ The only care of the Commission appointed to prepare the organic laws of the Constitution of 1793, was to cause this same Constitution to be proscribed, in order to substitute for it another more conformable to the selfish views of the then dominant faction. After having at great length declaimed against the most sacred of the people's rights—that of approving the laws it is to live under— the reporter of this commission proceeds to enumerate the gaps or flaws pretended to be discovered in it. He asserted that the Constitutional Act of 1793 (which, added he, ought to be annihilated, for the sole reason, if there was no other, that Robespierre and Saint Just had laboured in drawing it up), left undetermined the administrative hierarchy, the nomination of generals and ambassadors, as well as the right of declaring war and negociating peace.

Their protests.
Numerous protests against the *projet* adopted by the Convention were transmitted to the primary assemblies by the imprisoned Republicans. Their example, however, was not unanimously imitated by all who then honoured themselves with the qualification of Democrats. In consequence of the events of Prairial, there were found, mixed up with the inflexible Republicans in the prisons, other persons of timid character or indifferent principles, who purchased their liberty by a base submission to the pleasures of the aristocracy; these accepted the new Constitution. Others, despairing of the triumph of democracy, or considering the *then* Revolutionary Government as the most disastrous of evils, or flattering themselves that from the latitude of the Constitutional Order might result some change favourable to the people; or seeing, in the proposed Constitution, the only plank of safety against the threatened return of royalty, and, above all, being apprehensive of personal dangers and persecutions—these also accepted the aristocratic law; but they could not shake the faith of those whom nothing could induce to tamper with the enemies of equality, to the contempt of justice, and to the ruin of the common rights.

Such was the *honest* reporter's statement, in the teeth of the fact that all the points enumerated are determined in articles 54, 55, 69, 83, 107, 118, and 119. [Verily, these Conventionalists could tell a " mighty great lie" as glibly as our own precious representatives on this side the Channel, or as the august Duke of Cumberland himself. That Buonarroti speaks the truth will be found by reference to the Constitutional Act of 1793 itself, which will appear in the progress of this work amongst the justificatory pieces. —BRONTERRE.] On the other hand, the Commission appealed, in support of its opinion, to what it was pleased to call the violence, corruption, and terror, which it pretended had presided over the acceptance of the Constitution now sought to be proscribed. But who will ever bolt the monstrous absurdity, that upwards of 4,000,000 of adult subscribers could have been bought or constrained by violence? Is it not notorious, that at the time this Constitution was accepted, the revolutionary rigour (whose necessity has been since acknowledged) had not been yet brought into play against the enemies of equality, who were free to take part in the primary assemblies, and even to demand in them the re-establishment of royalty? Notwithstanding the manœuvres and stratagems employed to efface the truth, there remain traces sufficiently distinct, by which the severe critic may a future day recognise that this almost unanimous concurrence of the French people proves their adherence to the insurrection of the 31st May (against the Girondists), and the opposition of the parties it was directed against to

The Convention announced the acceptance by the people of the new Constitution. An extreme confusion prevailed in the verification of the votes; and the result of this operation, and of attested

The acceptation of the Constitution of the year III. by the people is a falsehood.

public facts, was, that the voters were very few in number, that a multitude of citizens had been expelled from the assemblies, and that the most outrageously eager acceptors had been those who, having made themselves notorious for their egoism, had been afterwards accused of conspiring for the return of royalty. Let us not lose sight of the distinction (a very real one) of the Egoist party into conservators and aspirers; let us call to mind that the latter had constantly, up to the 9th Thermidor of the year II., copied and followed in, the footsteps of the sincere friends of equality, and had thereby drawn upon themselves the hatred of the counter-revolutionists. The conventional members, who at that time assumed the character of patriots, belonged, almost all, to this latter class.

So far was the hatred of the Revolution carried, that the proscription, which at first had fallen only on its disinterested

Proscription of the Conventionalists.

friends, was destined now to reach the very parties that had first instigated it, and who were unable, by their recent crimes, to erase the recollection of their former appearance of virtue. Respectable people—men of good family—men of the rich middle class—disdained to sit by the side of the old Terrorists, who were loaded with the spoils of the aristocracy. They indiscriminately devoted to the rage of the enemies of the Revolution all the Conventionalists, who were accused of having exercised, or allowed to be exercised, the system of terror; and if they admitted any exceptions, it was only in favour of those that had signalized themselves by their perseverance in defending *the privileges of the " respectable" classes against the seditious pretensions of the un-*

the national will. This will, still manifested for a long time in the interior, and in the armies (Mignet asserts the same), until the people, betrayed by its delegates, disappointed in its hopes, and bereft by assassinations and imprisonments of its most devoted friends and champions, sunk into confusion and apathy, and at length ceased to take any interest in public affairs.

happy poor, whom they qualified by the opprobrious term " canaille" (rabble.)

Hopes of the enemies of the Revolution.
It seems that the execution of the new Constitution, and a new legislative body, excited in the enemies of the Revolution the hope of some participation in power, and in not a few of them the hope of the return of royalty, with which they flattered themselves on every occasion, when the supreme authority deviated from the route of equality, to lose itself in the tortuous path of *egoism*—the cause and effect of all tyrannies.

The People are enslaved by the renewal of the Deputies by thirds.
In order to perpetuate the spirit of the new Constitution, its authors conceived the design of annually renewing the legislative body, only *by thirds*, so as to introduce in the first composition of that body *two-thirds* of the members of the Convention,* to the choice of the electoral bodies. This measure which

---

* All the Deputies that remained attached to the political rights, consecrated by the Constitution of 1793, had been forcibly expelled by the Convention, or cut off by massacre and arrest.

[In corroboration of what Buonarroti states, and as a proof of the horrible system of proscription and extermination adopted by the new Aristocrats against the Democrats after the death of Robespierre, hear what Mignet says. After describing the ferocious proceedings against the Jacobins in Paris, he proceeds,—" In the departments the reaction was much more violent, for there was no authority (alluding to the Convention) to interpose and prevent the carnage with which they were visited. * * * The South became in a peculiar manner the scene of massacres *en masse*, and of individual slaughter. Associations were formed amongst the Royalists, under the names of *Societies of Jesus* and *Societies of the Sun*, who took a dreadful revenge for the sufferings of their party. At Lyons, Aix, Terascon, and Marseilles, they *butchered in prison* all those who took any share in the preceding Government. *In fact, all the South became the victims of another 2nd of September*. At Lyons, after the massacre of the Revolutionists, the men belonging to the societies gave chase to the fugitives, and whenever they met one they immediately, without any other ceremony than the cry of ' Here is a Matavon !' dispatched him, and threw his body into the Rhone. At Tarascon the victims were cast from the top of a tower upon a rock adjoining that river," &c.—Radicals of England ! there is the treatment your friends received in France from the aristocracy and middlemen ! And these monsters talk of Robes-

was dictated by the uneasy anticipations of certain criminal legislators,—this measure, conceived in the design of making the people slaves for ever, was, in the extreme, flattering to the passions of the Conventionalists. Those whose vanity is pleased by the exercise of power—those that dreaded prosecutions for the malversations and apostacies by which they had disgraced themselves—those that had a horror of equality—and those whom even the bare thought of democratic principles alarmed, these and the like were anxiously eager for its adoption.*

pierre's "Reign of Terror!" At the utmost, not more than 1,200 persons perished by the guillotine in Paris, during the two years of Robespierre's greatest influence, and even then he was but one in a Committee of twelve, each of whom was armed with power equal to his own, and the majority of them more severe against conspirators than himself. But what are these 1,200 in two years compared with the horrible picture you have just contemplated? And, remember, the 1,200 put to death by Robespierre (I assume that *he* killed them all) were convicted traitors, that sought to devote France and Frenchmen to everlasting slavery, whereas the thousands, and tens of thousands, and hundreds of thousands, whom the aristocracy and middlemen so inhumanly butchered, were the industrious poor and their friends, who sought nothing beyond a just participation of political rights with the rich. They did not, like their assassins, demand exclusive rights and privileges for themselves. They did not demand to devote the rest of the population to poverty and irredeemable slavery. "Give us our just rights," said they, "and we ask no more." Their doctrine was "Live and let live"—do unto us as we will do unto you—and for seeking to put this doctrine in force were they martyred and murdered in the manner stated! Men of England! when will your eyes open to the truth? Will you not now, at least, ask yourselves how it is, that, while you have heard so much of Robespierre's terrorism, and of the massacres of September in Paris, your honest teachers and instructors have never told you anything of those other massacres practised against the Democrats, a thousand times more atrocious, and a thousand million times more unjustifiable? Shall I tell you the reason? Because the Democrat-sufferers were poor and honest—because the others were rich and "respectable." Believe me, your oppressors set more value on the life of one of their Order than on a thousand such lives as yours; and be assured it will always continue so until you adopt some terrible means of convincing them, that life for life, yours' are as valuable as theirs'. But more of this in my future works.—BRONTERRE.

* This measure, suggested by the aristocratic spirit which pre-

D

In the Convention itself, the false friends of equality, who were as odious to the real Republicans as they were to the Royalists, showed themselves the most ardent partisans in favour of this scheme of renewal. Adopting an artifice, of which they made frequent use, they accused of a conspiracy to re-establish monarchy whatever parties offered any resistance to them; and, indeed, in the present case, those parties were, generally speaking, the same by whom popular institutions had always been rejected.

The fear of playing the game of the Royalists—the selfishness of greedy place-hunters—and the necessity in which the sincere friends of equality found themselves to choose between two factions equally criminal,* exercised a great influence on public opinion; hence resulted a number of suffrages, which, though extremely few in comparison with the population, and very confusedly calculated, were nevertheless sufficient to furnish the guilty Conventionalists with a pretext for giving the force of law to their decrees on the renewal, which public clamour had forced them to submit to the sanction of the people.

dominated in the framing of the Constitution of the Year III., and by means of which they desired to shut out from the new legislative body the old Royalists, as well as the sincere friends of equality, was not attended with all the success that its authors had promised themselves from its operation. Deceived in their expectations, and dreading royalty and the people, by turns, they several times, and from opposite motives, decimated the national representation, to which, impelled by their hatred of equality, they dealt (by one of the most execrable crimes on record) a final blow on the 18th Brumaire of the Year VIII.

* [To circumstances analogous to these have the Whigs of this country been more than once indebted for a triumph over the Tories. The bulk of the English people—at least all the useful and honest classes—abhor both factions; but, having no means of returning men of their own stamp—that is to say, honest Radicals—to Parliament, and when their choice is limited to the two plundering factions, then, as the lesser of two evils, they generally choose Whigs in preference to Tories, just as the French Democrats, to whom Buonarroti alludes, preferred the false but professing Republicans to the avowed and blood-thirsty Royalists. In either case it was but a choice of evils; and, in my opinion, the people made the worst choice on both occasions.—BRONTERRE.]

From the promulgation of this decree arose the agitation, troubles, and, at last, the armed revolt of the Sections of Paris,* on the 13th Vendemiaire of the year IV.;

The friends of equality defend the guilty Conventionalists.

a day on which the greater part of the Conventionalists would have perished, had it not been for the generous devotion of those† whom but a short time before they had betrayed, and delivered over to the enemies of liberty. Their love for their country, threatened as it was with utter slavery, and the hope of seeing spring out of the approaching struggle, a state of things favourable to the cause they cherished, determined a handful of Republicans to defend their recent enemies, by combatting on their side against the numerous army of the Sections. They reasoned thus. If the Conventionalists, said they, who have demoralized the Revolution by calling to their councils a crowd of corrupt men, shall once declare themselves the enemies of these men, they will be forced (for security sake) to join the ranks of the Democrats, and to give in to our wishes. By this reasoning were the most resolute and enlightened induced to take arms, and they were soon joined by others, who were either excited by the desire of vengeance, or by the hope of re-investing themselves with authority. Out of this combination, whose numbers were augmented by the accession of parties similarly circumstanced to the menaced

---

* [This armed revolt was of a very different character from the insurrections in Robespierre's time. The latter, which were chiefly directed by the ardent friends of the working classes, were the insurrections of liberty and justice, against tyranny and oppression. The former, on the other hand, was the rising of the middle classes of Paris against the Convention, for not carrying the counter-revolution far enough. The alleged ground was the provision in the conventional decree for retaining two-thirds of that body in the new legislative assembly. The middle classes opposed this, not because it was selfish and tyrannical on the part of the Convention, but because they wanted to have the choosing of the whole legislative body to themselves, in which case they would have made it entirely Royalist. The proscription of the Democrats by the middle classes, at that epoch, was frightful in the extreme; but all these points shall be more fully explained in my forthcoming " History of the French Revolution."—BRONTERRE.]

† The friends of equality—the true Democrats.

Conventionalists, was formed the armed body which was designated by the name of the " *Battalion of the Patriots of* 1789." * This denomination is very remarkable; it demonstrates how much public opinion was deteriorated since the 9th Thermidor of the year II. ; and proves the extreme rottenness of the Conventionalists, who, though scarcely daring to call themselves Republicans, implored earnestly the help of the friends of equality, to whom they basely feared, at the same time, to incur the suspicion of being reconciled.†

New treason of the Conventionalists.
After the battle of the 13th Vendemiaire, those whom the love of equality had led to victory, claimed from the chiefs of that day's proceedings the fulfilment of the promise they had made to re-establish the rights of the people. Their request was in vain. It was easily seen, by the tone with which the victors recommended an extreme circumspection, that no dependance could be placed on engagements that fear alone had induced them to enter into.

* People have vaunted a great deal of the almost perfect unanimity with which the Revolution of 1789 appeared to have been brought about. Those that have referred the honour of that event to public virtue appear to me to have very imperfectly appreciated the spirit of the Revolution. Figure to yourself the several steps of a ladder crowded with the sons of Ambition (under whose accumulated weight the mass of the people groans beneath), and each aspiring to rise to the degrees above himself. The nobility placed at the summit of the ladder, oppressed all the rest. The destruction of the nobility, therefore, was naturally desired by all ; and, accordingly, against *it* were directed the first movements of the Revolution. It was not virtue, then, but the restless jealousy of the intermediate steps between the nobility and the people that produced this apparent unanimity. Moreover, the working classes having been counted as ciphers by the actors of that epoch, the notable patriots of 1789, were, with very few exceptions, the friends of all abuses, that of hereditary nobility alone excepted.

† At the moment when the first shots were being fired, the Committees of Government were going to propose to the Convention to disarm, and plunge again into dungeons the very Republicans armed for its defence !

[How like this is to the dirty Whigs transporting the poor Dorchester labourers, just after their brothers, the working men of London, had been raising penny subscriptions to present the authors of the Reform Bill with a piece of plate, in token of their gratitude. But such things will always happen till the multitude shall know better how to distinguish their true from their false friends.—BRONTERRE.]

. Whilst the great majority of the Convention were seeking false subterfuges to elude the demands of the friends of equality, those of the latter that were still in captivity never ceased to solicit their companions, already free, to take advantage of their victory, to advance the democratic cause. Uselessly, and worse than uselessly, said they, shall have so much blood been shed, if we let slip the present opportunity, when the friends of virtue are in strength and arms, and when the terrified senators are indebted to them for their lives. They desired that it should be imperiously demanded of the Convention to make void the last elections, to abolish the new Constitution, and to establish forthwith the Constitution of 1793. In conformity with these suggestions they were preparing to demand the nullification of the elections, and the petition, already signed, was about being presented, when the conspiring Deputies of the 9th Thermidor, in concert with the other traitorous Deputies whom the national justice had smitten on the 31st of May, dreading the laws of the people more than royalty, succeeded, by one trick or another, in sowing division amongst the numerous subscribers to the petition, the consequence of which was that the petition was not presented.*

Nevertheless, in consequence of a report of Barras, which unmasked the vast projects of the rebels (Royalists), of whom the Convention itself contained many accomplices, a Commission of Public Safety was appointed, whose presumed intentions rekindled, for a moment, hope in the breast of the Republicans; a hope, however, that was soon frustrated. They believed, in fact, that this Commission was about to propose the nullification of the last elections; but whether this was doing too great honour to the Commission, or whether it was that it suffered itself to be intimidated by the virulent invectives and diatribes of Thibeaudeau, certain it is that

* [Do you not here fancy, my friends, that you see Joe Hume and Joe Parkes, and all the other Whig-Radical humbugs, at work amongst the poor honest Radicals? How many times have the latter been induced to forego active and vigorous measures solely in consequence of the meddling and dishonest interference of these shoyhoys, who appear all the time to be acting in the most friendly and sympathising spirit?--BRONTERRE.]

it did no more than propose paltry palliatives, which remedied nothing; and the Constitution of the year III. was almost immediately put in execution by the Conventionalists, who, more than ever vowed hatred against equality, under the names of terror and anarchy.

Liberty of the patriots.

In the interval which elapsed between the battle of the 13th Vendemiaire, and the amnesty of the 4th Brumaire following, all the patriots that had remained in captivity were liberated. They owed their liberty, however, not to the triumph of the popular cause, but to the mean policy of their enemies. In coming out from their dungeons, where they had sounded the depth of the public calamities, they menaced in their hearts the tyrants that had just broken their chains.

Their straying from their principles.

At this epoch, the persevering friends of equality were deeply afflicted at the depravation, which gliding even into the opinions of a great number of the Revolutionists, threatened the doctrines of democracy with eternal oblivion. In general, the patriots, of whom the greater number act more frequently from impulse than reflection, glorified themselves on the victory of Vendemiaire, counted the nomination of Barras and Carnot amongst the happy events of the Revolution, and found solace for their long misfortunes in the idea of places and favours which they flattered themselves with obtaining. It seemed as if they had forgotten the cause they had combatted for, and that, looking with an eye of indifference on the invasion of the people's rights which had just been consummated, they made the safety of the country to consist in the mitigation of their own calamities.

All the Revolutionists, however, did not participate in these narrow views; for, if the men just spoken of thought, or feigned to think, that it was necessary to trust to time for the reform of the new Constitution, and to prepare the way for such reform by insinuating themselves into public offices, there were others who, alarmed at the stability which the consolidation of the new government, together with the abatement of the Republican energy (every day becoming less and less enthusiastic), were about to confer on the principles of tyranny, believed it to be the duty of the true friends of equality to sound the alarm, and to lead the people once more to the recovery of their rights.

From this division of opinions resulted · Their division. one amongst the Republicans themselves.[*]

That portion of them that had often made the principles of justice yield to their own particular conveniences, took the name of the patriots of 1789; the others, who distinguished themselves by their persevering defence of democracy, were called the *Equals* (les Egaux).

After their liberation from prison, the First meetings patriots, and especially the Equals, anxious of the Equals. about the fate of liberty, sought to unite themselves, and concert plans, to oppose a powerful rampart to the progress of the new tyranny. They assembled frequently in the coffee-houses, in the public gardens, and in the open places; but, as every thing was conducted there with extreme and indispensable circumspection, their general discussions on the state of affairs did not give rise to any prompt and decisive result that might be turned to advantage for the common cause.

At the beginning of the month Brumaire of the year

---

[*] [A similar division, both as regards opinions and persons, has been discernible amongst the Radical party in England since the passing of the Reform Bill. The disciples of Robert Owen, and those who patronize and support the principles promulgated by me in Mr. Hetherington's publications, correspond with the French *Egaux* or Equals; whilst the numerous and motley host of sham and shallow *soi-disant* Radicals, who reject our principles, or are incapable of appreciating them (including knaves and fools of every sort), may be likened to the patriots of 1789. This latter party, who are Radicals but in name, and whom only the accidents of birth and fortune have prevented from being Whigs, Tories, or any thing else, they might profit by, may be thus known. They attach themselves to names and persons instead of to principles; they confine their views almost exclusively to political changes; and, while they incessantly rail against the mere consequences of our social system, they take care to say nothing against the system itself, thereby showing that it is not with the *principle* of evil they quarrel, but with the accident that has made it an evil to themselves personally.—BRONTERRE.]

IV , Babeuf,* Darthé, Buonarroti, *Laurgen de Doimel,* and Fontenelle, exerted themselves to form a centre of direction, at which the scattered patriots might rally, to the end of afterwards acting uniformly to the profit of the

BIOGRAPHICAL SKETCH OF BABEUF.

* Gracchus Babeuf was born at St Quentin, Department of l'Aine. He was a man of sense, well-informed, and indefatigable ; his mind was penetrating and just ; he wrote with clearness, fire, and eloquence.

The French Revolution found Babeuf young, devoted to study, sober, detesting tyranny, and meditating on the means of rescuing his unhappy fellow-citizens from oppression ; he experienced at an early period the necessity of devoting himself for the public liberty. In the beginning of the Revolution Babeuf wrote in the spirit of a freeman against the feudal regime, and against the system of finance, which drew down upon him persecution, and an order of arrest, from the effects of which he was saved by the active solicitations of Marat. At a later period he obtained the post of Secretary to a District Administration, where his discourses and popular writings made him numerous enemies, who had influence enough to get him prosecuted and condemned as a forger of writings or signatures (*faussaire*) ; but the judgment against him was annulled by the Convention, which solemnly declared its injustice. Subsequently, Babeuf got employment in the Bureaux of the Commune of Paris, where he formed a friendly connexion with a great number of courageous Republicans.

After the disastrous events of the 9th Thermidor, Babeuf applauded for a moment the indulgence exercised towards the enemies of the Revolution ; his error did not last long—and he, who had adopted the Gracchi for the models of his conduct, was not slow in perceiving that nothing could less resemble these illustrious Romans than the Post-Thermidorian rulers—the murderers of Robespierre. Greater than if he had never erred, Babeuf owned his mistake, reclaimed for the people its ravished rights, unmasked the parties by whom it had been deceived, and carried his zeal for the democracy so far, that the aristocrats then in possession of the Government lost no time in sending him to prison. From the Gaol of Plessis, where he was at first detained, they transferred him to that of Arras. It was then he got acquainted with Germain of Narbonne, Captain of Hussars, of whom frequent mention will be made in the course of this work, and with several Republicans of the Department of Pas-de-Calais. Amongst these, Babeuf was an indefatigable preacher of popular institutions ; he inflamed their hatred against the new tyrannies ; he familiarised them with the idea of a great revolution in property, and disposed them to form a sort of plebeian Vendée, for the purpose of obtaining by force, what it appeared to him no longer possible to obtain by any other means.

Upon his return to the Plessis, after the insurrection of Prairial of the Year III., Babeuf was entirely occupied with the like projects which his frequent conversations with certain citizens, then imprisoned with him, aided him to mature. It was then he made the acquaintance of *Bedon,* whose real name I regret not

common cause. In the meetings which took place to this effect, several propositions were made; some wished that all the sincere patriots should be incorporated into a sort of masonic association, to act in obedience to certain directors they proposed to appoint over it; others sug-

being able to give—of *Bedon*, who, having passed his whole life in examining the causes of public evils, had seized, better than any body else, the spirit of Robespierre's profound views.

It will be seen in the sequel of this work how the ideas of Babeuf expanded, and how large a share he had in the conspiracy to which his name is attached. This extraordinary man, gifted with eminent talents, the inflexible friend of justice, was constantly disinterested and poor ; a good husband, a tender father ; he was beloved by his family. The courage with which, in the presence of his judges, he appalled the powerful monsters that demanded his head, and the lofty serenity with which he faced the glorious death inflicted on him by the aristocracy, heighten the lustre of his virtues, and shed a sanctity on the patriotic labours of this illustrious martyr of equality.

[Notwithstanding this glowing eulogium—an eulogium so justly earned by the individual, and to which no human being can be entitled that holds other principles than those of Babeuf—there are not wanting villains to vilify and blacken the character of this "noble of nature." I remember reading in one aristocratic account of him, that he was an "insane monster ;" and in another, that during his provincial secretaryship " he exhibited all the little tricks of a low pettifogger !" My readers will, doubtless, stare at these representations, so utterly at variance with facts, and with the whole history of Babeuf's life ; but, be it observed, that the authors of such calumnies would have given the same character of Jesus Christ himself, had his Gospel appeared for the first time at the period to which this history refers. In truth, the doctrines of Babeuf are as nearly as possible (making allowance for different epochs and circumstances) the same that our Saviour preached 18 centuries ago ; while the murderers of Babeuf present just as close a resemblance to the parties that crucified our Saviour. The aristocracy and usurers of France called Babeuf a " bloody fanatic," and his doctrines " anarchical, wild, and desolating." The same character was given of our Saviour by the Jews and money-changers that murdered him, and his religion was denounced by the aristocratic Tacitus as a " destructive superstition (*exitiabilis superstitio*).—[See his Annals, book xv., cap. 44.] Mrs. Woolstonecraft, who knew Babeuf well, declared that she " had never seen any person who possessed greater abilities, or equal strength of character." And this is the " fanatic " and " low pettifogger" of the aristocrats—but wait a little, my friends, and you will see what smash I shall make of the lying histories of these impostors.—BRONTERRE.]

D 5

gested that they might at any moment constitute themselves into a committee of insurrection, by an act signed
individually by each of the members.   As in these
assemblies there was neither uniformity of views, nor the
confidence necessary to obtain a useful result, they could
come to no mutual understanding, and so they soon
ceased to meet.

They did not, however, renounce the two-fold project
of rallying the patriots, and of overthrowing tyranny.
These were imperious wants for every true Republican.
Accordingly, they assembled again a short time after,
for the purpose of establishing a new popular society.
At the first sitting, which was held at the house of
Bouin, there were present, amongst others—Darthé,*

---

* BIOGRAPHICAL SKETCH OF DARTHE.

Augustin Alexander Darthé, of Saint Paul, Department of Pas-
de-Calais, was well-informed, just, bold, constant, active, inflexible,
and very expert in unravelling and interesting in his views the
passions of the parties he had to deal with. He was a law student
at Paris when the Revolution broke out, and he precipitated himself into it, with the zeal of a man who defends truth to desperation,
when once its light shines upon him. In 1789 Darthé took part
in the deliverance of the French Guards, in the taking of the Bastile
(where he contracted an incurable infirmity), and at the siege of the
Castle of Vincennes. He was afterwards member of the Directory
of his Department, and in this capacity rendered to the Republic,
under very critical circumstances, services so important, that he
was rewarded for them by a decree of " bien merité de la patrie" (he
deserved well of his country). Having been subsequently promoted to the office of public accuser before the Revolutionary
Tribunals of Arras and Cambrai, to the severity of which was
owing, in great part, the preservation of this frontier, he approved
himself a true Republican, an incorruptible magistrate, as well as
an intrepid warrior. The Thermidorian proscription, which he
could not escape, found him in honourable poverty. At an early
period, Darthé penetrated, and seconded with all his power, the
benevolent designs of Robespierre ; accordingly, as Robespierre
had shown the greatest esteem for Darthé, the enemies of equality
vowed implacable vengeance against him.

To great intelligence, and a lively passion for true justice,
Darthé united austere manners and a compassionate heart. When
on his trial, before the High Court of Vendôme, he perseveringly
refused to acknowledge its jurisdiction, or to offer any defence—
when condemned to death, his last sighs were for his country.

[With the exceptions of Robespierre, Marat, and a few others,
there is none whose character has suffered more from calumny
than Darthé. If we are to believe the aristocratic accounts of
him, his table-companion was the executioner, and his wit and
conversation all turned upon the guillotine. One caricature of him

Germain, Buonarroti, Massart, Fontanelle, Lindppi, Laurjen de Doimel, Bertrand,* Tismiot, Chintrard, Cha-

says, that when on his mission as public accuser in the North, he would not suffer the cart of basket-work, in which the bodies were brought from the guillotine to be lined, as usual, with tin, because "*he wished that its track of blood should be seen in the streets.*" Another account accuses him of having sacrificed "*whole families to his private malice—of brutal licentiousness—of fraud and rapacity ;*" and so forth through the whole circle of crime. Such are the horrid inventions by which democracy, or (which is the same) common justice has been made so revolting and unpopular with the world.—BRONTERRE.]

* Bertrand, of Lyons, was Mayor of that Commune before the revolt which took place there on the 29th of May, 1793, and again after its forced submission to the laws of the Convention. Bertrand had exhausted an opulent fortune in favour of the Revolution; he was just, loyal (not to the king), generous, full of courage and amenity ; his manners were simple, and candour was depicted on his countenance.

The rich Lyonese were reserving for Bertrand the same fate to which they had devoted his friend Charlier ; their efforts were vain, for the people responding aloud, by sobs and benedictions to the interruptions with which Bertrand reminded them of his sacrifices, and of the services he had rendered the unfortunate, the judges about to immolate him were, on several resumptions of the trial, constrained to adjourn the sentence, and to send him back to his dungeon, where he remained during the long siege of his Commune. On the very day of the 9th Thermidor, the order was issued to seize and transmit to Paris Bertrand, and several other Lyonese Democrats. So strongly were their purity and firmness resented, that their chains were not struck off till after the 13th Vendemiáire of the Year IV.

Bertrand—this ardent lover of mankind, of his country, and of liberty—an austere defender of equality, a popular and incorruptible magistrate, a good son, an excellent friend—this pattern of every virtue was assassinated by the military Commission of the Temple, in consequence of the massacre at the Camp of Grenelle. He was asleep when he was ordered out to execution. This good and virtuous citizen, who had been arrested, without arms, and at a distance from the Camp of Grenelle, would have been (in conformity with the conclusions of the reporter) condemned only to incarceration or deportation, had not the executive Directory hastened to apprise the commission, that it desired his death.

At sight of the certificate of appeal, presented by Bertrand and his companions in martyrdom, the execution of their sentences of death was suspended by General Foissac la Tour, who, having referred it to the Directory, received an immediate order to take no notice of it. A few months afterwards the tribunal of Cassation (to which Bertrand appealed) annulled all the sentences which had condemned them.

[So much for the justice of Barras, the Director, who was one of Robespierre's principal assassins.—BRONTERRE.]

pelle, *Lussorilon*, Lacombe, *Reuf*, *Ulagenoc*, Bouin, and *Sombod*. This interview was very affecting. Our souls re-opened to a hope, which so many misfortunes had almost extinguished. We all swore to remain in union, and to make equality triumph.

The attention of this meeting was directed to the question of ascertaining, whether the establishment of several societies in the different arondissements of Paris would not be preferable to that of a single one. After a long discussion the decision was adjourned to a more numerous sitting, which it was agreed to hold in a place less exposed to the surveillance of the police; it took place in a small closet, situated in the middle of the ancient abbey of Saint Geneviève.

Spirit of the new Government.   Whilst the wreck of the democratic party was endeavouring to reorganize itself as a united body, the Government established by the Constitution of the year III., was laying the foundations of the political system which it constantly adhered to afterwards. The spirit of the Conventional party—that profited by the disasters of the 9th Thermidor—routed the Democrats in Prairial, and triumphed by their aid over the Royalists in Vendemiaire, passed effectually into the men composing the executive Directory; the reduction of that spirit may be thus defined—" *to conserve and to acquire riches and power, to repress the Royalists and Influentials on the one hand, and the Friends of Equality on the other.*"

From the moment of their installation, the five chiefs of the Executive applied themselves to confront the old Royalists with the Democrats, and the Democrats with the old Royalists, so as to fight them one against the other, according as either party obtaining the ascendant, became the greater object of alarm to them.

It favours the re-unions of the patriots.   At the time the patriots were projecting to form themselves into a society, the Government appeared favourable to their views. Being still under a necessity to intimidate the rebels of Vendémiaire, and wishing to force the rich, by the bugbear of terror, to concur in the measures by which it counted upon restoring the shattered finances of the Republic, it secretly instructed its agents to encourage the opening of patriotic unions, although determined to arrest the progress of them, the moment they should attempt to revive the principles of Robespierre's time.

This cheat did not escape the sagacity of the closely-observing patriots, who, having witnessed, on the 13th Vendemiaire, the fruitless squandering of the people's blood, were confirmed in the opinion that nothing of substantial use could emanate from the new Government. *Spirit of the patriots and of the people.*

The democratic party was not numerous, and the mass of the patriots feeble, and scarcely recovered from their fright, were disposed to suffer themselves to be again intimidated at the least appearance of a new persecution. As to the people of Paris, deceived in its hopes, deluded by calumny, and by the underhand plots of Royalism, and of the foreign despots, it had abandoned the Democrats, and languished in profound indifference. There were some that even accused the Revolution of the evils, without number, that pressed them down.

The citizens, assembled in the garden of St. Geneviève, felt the dangers to which the duplicity of the Government exposed those that, by a premature zeal, might dare to make a direct attack on the authority that had usurped the rights of the nation. "Above all," said they, " it is necessary to rectify the ideas of many of the patriots, regain for them the esteem of the people, and restore to the latter the sentiment of its rights and of its force, almost lost to it since Robespierre's death. Meanwhile, it is necessary to cover ourselves with the Constitution, and even with the protection of the Government, up to the moment when we shall be strong enough to attack and destroy it." Thus reasoned the patriots; and it was then resolved to establish the new society on these principles. The necessity of conserving and centralizing its spirit made them discard the proposition for dividing it into several sections, which, though better adapted to elude the vigilance of the police, did, nevertheless, present the inconvenience of being more exposed to diverge from the plan of the institution, and to become the sport *Prudence of the Equals, or Friends of Equality.*

of intriguers, and of the enemies of the Republic. To
this unique society they proposed to invite none but men
without reproach, and capable of being easily and fami-
liarly inspired with the prudence adopted by its founders.

Foundation of the society of the Panthéon. The society was immediately opened in
the ancient refectory of the nuns of St.
Geneviève, of which the patriotic Cardi-
naux, who rented a part of their convent, granted the
gratuitous use; and whenever this apartment was consecrated to meetings of another kind, the society was held in
a vast vault of the same edifice (probably a crypt), where
the dim paleness of the torch-light, the hollow echoes of
their voices, and the constrained position of the persons
present, either standing or seated on the ground, impressed on them the greatness and the perils of their
enterprize, as well as of the courage and prudence it
required. The proximity of this place to the Panthéon
caused the new society to be called by the name of this
temple. The assembly once opened, its numbers rapidly
increased by the accession of a great number of patriots
invited to attend, or induced there by the attractions of
the institution. With these, other individuals insinuated
themselves, who, servilely attached to the members of the
Government, reduced all the duties of the friends of
liberty to the single one of lending their support to the
Government against the Royalists.*

Its organization. At first the society was occupied with
its organization; but such was the exces-
sive prudence or weakness of the greater part of its
members, that there were, in this regard, great obstacles
to overcome. Fearing to offer any resemblance to the
old societies,† their prudence went beyond even the

* [It will be remembered that Buonarroti had just said, that
none but men without *reproach* were to be invited to this society.
By reproach, then, must be understood *moral*, not *political*, delin-
quency; otherwise, these parasites of the Directorial tyranny
could not be admitted. The object of the latter was two-fold—to
canvass support for their masters, who much needed it against
the Royalists, and to act as spies on the proceedings, in case they
assumed too honest or dangerous a character! The conspirators
understood them well, but it was their policy just now to connive
at their baseness.—BRONTERRE.]

† Jacobins, Cordeliers, &c. &c.

shackles forged by the new Constitution against the right of assembling. To have a body of rules—a president, secretaries, minutes (*proces-verbaux*), a form of admission—this, they taught, was to copy too closely the Jacobin model, and to expose their flanks to a new persecution. They came at length to a mutual understanding, and the society had a code of laws, which, admitting neither registers, nor minutes, nor any other condition of admission, than the presentation by two members, rendered all order next to impossible, and threw open the society to the entry of a multitude of doubtful persons, who often perverted its spirit, and excited in it dangerous debates and contests. An orator, and a vice-orator, held the places of president and secretary; and to meet the necessary expenses of the institution, there were no other funds than the spontaneous contributions of the members.

In a short time the society of the Pantheon counted more than two thousand members. In the actual circumstances *Divergences of the Pantheonists.* of the time, and with the regulations agreed to, it was neither prudent nor possible to exclude from it every individual that had not merited being ranked amongst the Equals. It was unavoidable to admit a great number of patriots who had been impeached for some errors, and particularly of that section of them which pretended to restore the democracy, by getting possession of the public functions and offices.

It was easy to perceive the existence of these different elements in the bosom of the society. The Equals made themselves remarkable for their zeal to enlighten the people, and to revive a respect for the doctrines of equality; whilst the patriots of 1789 might be recognized by their eagerness to exercise on the Government an influence favourable to their own repose and interests. The alternating preponderance of these two parties produced contrary movements in the working of the society. The patriots of 1789 frequently determined the assembly to solicit places for the citizens they regarded; the other party laid before it the afflicting picture of public opinion depraved, and of the errors by which the enemies of liberty were labouring to lead the people astray; pointed

out to it the triumph of equality as the only object worthy
of its wishes, and encouraged measures calculated to re-
animate the almost extinguished courage of the multitude, and to rekindle that sacred enthusiasm, to which it
owed so many brilliant victories achieved over every
species of tyranny.

Communication of the society with the people. A commission was charged to propose
a plan of operations, and a prompt and
easy mode of communication with the
people. Placards, entitled " *The Truth to the People
by the Patriots of* 1789," soon attracted public attention to national affairs, without any direct attack on the
authorities, whose vengeance it would have been imprudent to provoke just then. The first effect of these
papers was to bring to the new society a great number
of the working classes, who, as their hopes revived, were
eager to repeat everywhere the numerous truths they
heard proclaimed by us.*

Popular laws. As the end which the founders of the
society proposed to themselves, was to procure speedy succours and consolation for the multitude,
and thereby to merit its confidence, to the end of subsequently employing its physical force for the recovery of
its rights, the commission recommended that petitions
should be presented for the execution of two laws, which
the counter-revolutionary policy of the Government had
all but buried in oblivion—that which promised a thousand millions' worth of national property to the defenders of the country, and that which had been decreed in
the Year II. for the extinction of mendicity.†

Proscription of Babeuf. Whilst they were warily engaged at the
Panthéon in restoring to vigour the prin-
ciples of democracy, whilst other societies were forming
in the same spirit at several points in Paris, and

* I annex to the justificatory, or confirmatory documents given
at the end of the work (under No. 2), one of those placarded appeals which describes in full the state of the French Republic
after the 9th Thermidor, and the cautious prudence that the Equals
were forced to observe in the Society of the Panthéon.

† These two important and highly just and popular laws were
decreed by the Convention in Robespierre's time, and owing
chiefly to the labours and influence of that illustrious reformer.—
BRONTERRE.

aristocratic writers were sounding the alarm against the new attempts of the " *Terrorists*," as they called them, Babeuf resolutely unveiled, in his journal (the *Tribune of the People*), the crimes of the rulers of the Republic, demonstrated the goodness and the legitimacy of the Constitution of 1793, and did not hesitate to signalize *private or individual property* as the principal source of all the calamities that oppress and afflict society. Such extraordinary courage soon drew down upon him a fresh proscription, which he was only able to elude by seeking an obscure asylum in the houses of certain Democrats.*

At the same time a secret Committee was formed at the house of Amar, in the street Clery, to prepare an insurrection against the new despotism, which, more and more, every day, was crushing the French people under its iron arm. The earlier members of the Committee were Amar, Darthé, Buonarroti, Massart, and Germain, who were subsequently joined by *Bedon, Soigne, Felix Lepelletier*, Clément, and Marchand. The intense grief with which they were penetrated, carried the friends of liberty, as it were, by inspiration, to combine their forces against the hateful yoke that weighed down the people. As to the enlightened Democrats, they believed it an imperious duty.

Committee at the house of Amar.

The members of the Committee, assembled at the house of Amar, were unanimous in considering the Government es-

Its opinion of the Government of the Year III.

* Babeuf was, on that occasion, indebted for his liberty to the *Forts de la Halle*. A government officer having presented himself at his house in the street Faubourg, Honoré, No. 29, with an order to arrest him, on account of the incentives to insurrection contained in his writings, Babeuf, after a long struggle, broke loose and effected his escape. The officer pursued him with cries of " *Stop the robber!*" Twice the Forts de la Halle seized him, and twice they let him go again, on hearing the name of the writer who defended the rights of the people. [No mean proof, this, of his great popularity, and of the true feelings and opinions of the then Parisian population.] *Eriddy* and Darthé afterwards gave him an asylum in the ancient Convent of the Assumption.

[The Halle is a fish and vegetable market place in Paris, similar to Billingsgate. It occupies the space included between the streets La Tonnellerie, Marché-aux-Poires, and Piliers-Potiers d'Etain, in the 4th arondissément—it lies in the north east of the city.— BRONTERRE.]

tablished by the Constitution of the Year III. as illegitimate in its origin, oppressive in its spirit, and tyrannical in its intentions. They were all of opinion, that the salvation of the Republic and of Liberty imperiously commanded its destruction.

Before occupying themselves with the means of effecting this, it was the wish of all that each member might be not only convinced of the justice of the enterprise, but that he should also have formed a clear and complete idea of the political system he would substitute for the one whose annihilation was contemplated.* They sincerely desired the happiness of the people; and with this impression, they felt that it was contrary to its (the people's) true interests to rashly expose it to convulsions, the only result of which might be to build up a new tyranny on the ruins of the existing one, to create new privileges, and to favour new ambitions. The Committee was, at first, a sort of political Lyceum, or school, in which, after unravelling the causes of the calamities that afflict nations, they at length arrived at the knowledge of determining with precision the principles of social order the best calculated, in their belief, to deliver mankind from them, as well as to prevent their recurrence.

Never, said they, has the mass of the people attained the degree of instruction and independence necessary for the exercise of those political rights that are essential to its preservation and its happiness. *Individual property the cause of slavery.* The wisest nations of antiquity had slaves, which placed them incessantly in peril; and if we except the Peruvians, the Paraguayans, and some small tribes scarcely known, civil society has never been able to make disappear from its bosom, that multitude of persons who are soured and rendered miserable by the idea of *goods* of which they are destitute, and of which they see or fancy others to be in possession. Everywhere does the multitude crouch under the rod of a despot, or under that of privileged castes, or classes.

---

* A stronger proof could not be offered of their integrity and good intentions. Men that would merely *knock down*, without having clear and just ideas of the edifice they would substitute, are not Reformers, but mere speculators in anarchy. They are either robbers or the tools of robbers.—BRONTERRE.]

And then turning their regards to the French nation, they beheld it, as it were, bound hand and foot by the conquering or upstart Egoists, in bondage to the corporation of the Old Rich and the New Rich.

As to the cause of these disorders, they discovered it in the inequality of fortunes and conditions, and (as the last step of the analysis) in the system of individual property, by which the craftiest, least conscientious, and luckiest, have despoiled, and incessantly despoil the multitude; who, bound down to wearisome and painful labours, ill-fed, ill-clothed, and badly lodged, deprived of enjoyments they see superfluously multiplied for others, and undermined by misery, by ignorance, by envy, and by despair, both in their physical and moral strength, behold in society only a deadly enemy, and lose even the possibility of having a country.

The history of the Revolution came opportunely to the aid of the Committee's reflections. In that history they beheld the class that was rich before, and that which became rich, assiduously occupied in insuring pre-eminence for themselves. They saw in it, that ambitious pretensions went always hand in hand with hatred of work and the desire of riches; that the people's attachment to their rights of citizenship had become less and less ardent, in proportion as the institutions favourable to equality had been assaulted and overborne; and that the whole system of aristocratic policy consisted in impoverishing, dividing, disgusting, terrifying, and compressing the laborious classes, whose cries and remonstrances they uniformly represent as the most active causes of the decay of society. From these observations the Committee were necessarily led to conclude, that the ever-quickening cause of the slavery of nations lies entirely in the inequality of condition, and that, so long as such inequality remains, the exercise of political rights will be little more than illusory for that unhappy class which our false civilization debases below human nature.

To destroy this inequality, then, is the work of a virtuous legislator. Behold the principle which resulted from the Committee's meditations. But how was it to be accomplished? This was the subject of a fresh inquiry. Amar, who had seen the National Convention provide for the urgent wants of the country by the tax on saleable commodities, by the revolutionary contributions, and by requisitions on the rich, extolled this mode of taking away (these are his own words) the superfluity that encumbers the overflowing channels of wealth, to restore it to those that want the necessaries. Others proposed, in turns, the division of lands, sumptuary laws, and the Progressive Impost.

Vices of agrarian and sumptuary laws.

Bedon, Darthé, Felix Lepelletier, and Buonarroti observed, that those legislators who, in order to diminish the ravages of inequality, had had recourse to the division of lands and to sumptuary laws, at the same time that they abandoned the distribution of work, and of its produce (wealth) to cupidity, and competition, had opposed to an impetuous torrent only very feeble ramparts, incessantly undermined, and always overthrown by the action of avarice and of pride, to which the maintenance of the right of property does constantly furnish a thousand means of surmounting all obstacles. The requisitions, said they, the taxes, the revolutionary contributions, were properly resorted to, to meet the urgent wants of the moment, and to defeat the malevolence of the rich ; but they could not form part of the habitual order of society, without assailing its existence : for, besides that it would be impossible to assess them, without risking the taking away of necessaries, they would involve the grave and irreparable inconvenience of drying up the sources of reproduction, by divesting proprietors, to whom they would leave the burden of cultivation, of the necessary incentive of enjoyment, and they would prove insufficient and ineffectual against the silent accumulation of money—an inevitable result of commerce, towards which would be naturally turned the speculations of cupidity.*

---

* The Progressive Impost would be an effectual means of parcelling out the land, of preventing the accumulation of riches, and of banishing idleness and luxury, if the exact estimate of fortunes that it requires did not render the practical application of it extremely difficult. The value of real or immoveable property is easily enough ascertained, but how can you determine the amount or value of money, or credit-capitals, which it is so easy to withdraw from the public sight ? At best, this manner of assessing taxes is

By the law of nature, which makes production depend on labour, this labour is evidently for each citizen an essential condition of the social compact; and as each, in entering into society carries *Equality of labours and of enjoyment the intention of the society.*
with him an equal stake and contribution (the totality of his strength and means), it follows that the burdens, the · productions, and the advantages, ought to be equally divided. They made it, moreover, he remarked, that the end of society is to effectually prevent natural inequalities; that were it even true that inequality of enjoyments had hastened the progress of the really useful arts, it ought to cease now, seeing that any new progress can add nothing to the real happiness of all;

only a preparatory steps towards the evil, but would not go to the root.

[It may be observed here, that Robespierre, who was the author of the Progressive Impost, adopted it only as a means to an end ; and as the best means which the then state of public opinion would sanction, of providing for the wants of the Republic at the expense of the rich and destructive classes. There were at that time, one million, four hundred thousand Frenchmen in arms, and notwithstanding the immense consumption required by so extraordinary a state, and the general interruption of industry necessarily occasioned by it, the people and the armies were well fed and abundantly provided for. What a contrast to the state of France two years after! After the murder of Robespierre, and under the Directory, France, instead of a workshop of war, became a workshop of industry, wealth was abundantly produced, and the harvest was most abundant; yet, never did the French people experience direr distress than then! The workpeople of Paris died by hundreds of famine, and there was hardly a man or woman of them whose effects were not all pawned at the *Mont de Piété*. How is this apparent paradox to be accounted for? With infinite ease, my friends. Under Robespierre the workpeople had power. The Government was in the hands of their friends, and the Conventional Decrees were, in a greater or less decree, all favourable to them ; but when the Usurers and Aristocrats accomplished the destruction of Robespierre, the Government, as a matter of course (for this was the object sought), passed into the hands of the Bourgeoisie, or middle classes. Hoarding and amassing became then the order of the day, and, as a consequence, the people relapsed once more into the old state of misery. The labouring population of a country must be always miserable under a Government of the middle classes.—BRONTERRE.]

and that the equality suggested by their own simple good sense to the first founders of societies, is still more strongly recommended to us by the increase of our knowledge and by our everyday experience of the evils that follow in the train of inequality. Those who reasoned thus, saw in the *community of goods and of labours*—that is to say, in the equal distribution of burdens and enjoyments—the veritable object and perfection of the social state—the only public order adequate to banish oppression for ever, by rendering the ravages of ambition and avarice impossible, and to guarantee to each and every citizen the greatest possible happiness. *Bedon* had composed a work in which he demonstrated the injustice of the right of property, and developed the long series of evils that are its necessary consequences.

Amar appeared smitten, as it were, by a beam of light. At the first enunciation of this system he became its enthusiastic defender ; and no longer thinking of aught else than to justify and propagate its principles, he carried in a short time the heat of his zeal so far as to become its impetuous champion in public. It became an admitted principle in the Committee that the laws of liberty and equality could never receive a useful and durable application without a radical reform in the property system ; it was agreed that the patriots would only appear in the eyes of the multitude a set of restless and selfish intriguers, so long as they would not openly avow themselves supporters of a system suited to guarantee palpably the same advantages to every member of society.

Robespierre the friend of this equality. In developing these ideas, mention was often made of the philosophers, and especially of the men of the Revolution, who had recognised their justice. Of this class was Robespierre and his companions in martyrdom, who, in the eyes of those whose doctrine I have just expounded, had evidently aspired to the equal distribution of burdens and enjoyments. In respect of Robespierre, Amar, who on the 9th Thermidor had been one of his most violent persecutors, acknowledged his wrong, testified his repentance, and only sought to excuse his fault by alleging his complete ignorance of the benevolent views of him whom he calumniated and immolated.

But the ways of truth and justice are Obstacles to its with difficulty perceived by the multitude, establishment. who cannot be persuaded by the same motives that determine minds accustomed to reflect. The philosophers, that desired to effect the happiness of their enslaved, unhappy, and ignorant fellow-citizens, have been generally rewarded by death upon the vulgar accusation of ambition, hypocritically urged against them by the crafty and eternal enemies of equality.*

The Committee did not conceal from itself how disastrous to the common cause and to good morals had been the catastrophe of the 9th Thermidor, and the tragical events that were its consequences. It was aware, that since that period numbers of citizens had abandoned themselves to the most shameful rapacity; nor was it ignorant that the very pettiest proprietors had re-attached themselves with cupidity to their possessions (which, a

* It is difficult to convince the multitude of the danger of innovations, without the aid of that experience which can happen only after they have been acted upon. Accordingly, have the wisest legislators of antiquity been obliged to have recourse to religious fictions, by which they *astonished* the multitude whom they could not *persuade*. This expedient, which, in any case is dangerous, cannot be employed at all with success amongst a people who (whether fortunately or unfortunately, I cannot say) cultivate science and philosophy. With these you can accomplish nothing, unless by the attractions of pleasure, or by force.

[The author explains here (unknown to himself) the cause of the failure of the St. Simonian religion in France. The multitude were too enlightened to believe in it as a revelation, but not sufficiently enlightened to perceive that it was only a new device designed to rescue humanity from " *property*" and its endless horrors. The adage, " a little learning is a dangerous thing," proved equally fatal to St. Simonianism, and those whom it was intended to benefit. With *more* knowledge, the producers in France would have embraced the political economy of St. Simon, while they left the *revelation part* of his religion to sleep quietly in the grave with its eccentric but benevolent author.—BRONTERRE.]

If Christianity had not been disfigured by impostors who deceive in order to subjugate and plunder, it might have proved of vast service to all legislators friendly to their fellow-men. The pure and benevolent doctrine of Jesus, presented, as an emanation of natural religion, from which it differs not, might become the basis of a sage reform, and the source of really social morals. Such morals are irreconcileable with materialism, which influence people to consult in their conduct only their own direct interest, and to make a mockery of all virtue.

little before, they were ready to renounce), from a conviction that all views of general interest had vanished from legislation, abandoned, as it henceforward was, to the most unbridled egoism. It, consequently, felt how difficult it was to substitute immediately, and by a single effort, for the legislation of property, the incomparably milder and more equitable one of *the equality of goods and labour.*

The Constitution of 1793 was a preparatory step to equality. Nothing was further, however, from this equality than the social order established by the Code of the Year III., the confirmation of which was about to take away from the people the exercise of their natural rights. Nevertheless, it appeared to the Committee that in order to lead the people to declare itself upon the constant object of its secret wishes, which the want of enlightenment and proper direction had always heretofore prevented it from attaining, it was necessary to begin with restoring to it its assemblies, its discussions, its deliberations, and the sentiment of its force. The Committee saw in the Constitution of 1793 this preparatory step towards a greater good, and that circumstance, joined to the motives which made the members justly respect it as the sovereign will of the French people, freely and solemnly set forth, determined them to adopt that Constitution as the rallying point of the patriots and the people.

Its faults. Nor did they pretend blindness to the faults of this Constitution—they discovered them principally in the articles of the Declaration of Rights, which, in defining the right of property, consecrate it in all its appalling latitude. Nevertheless, they acknowledged that never before had a work of this kind approached so near to perfection; and they applauded its provisions as opening a vast field for future ameliorations.*

* [If Buonarroti and the Committee had weighed more nicely the terms of the Declaration of Rights, they would have found it more in unison with their ideas than they appear to have thought. When Robespierre proposes to secure to every citizen *whatever property is guaranteed to him by the law,* let it be born in mind that he at the same time leaves the law open to unlimited change at the will of

· On the other hand, they considered that to this Constitution would rally not only the Equals, but also the Democrats, who did not go so far, and a large portion of the people; that all further changes would become easier as soon as the spirit of equality had resumed its energy; and, besides, that it would be hazarding too great a danger to expose themselves to divergences of opinion, at a moment when it was indispensable to unite all the popular forces, in order to attack the common enemy with success.

After a long and serious examination, the Committee reduced the duties of the people to these two cardinal points :— *Rallying points offered to the Republicans.*
1. To re-establish the Constitution of 1793, agreed to by the people, as a fundamental law which frankly consecrates the exercise of its power—a prompt means of arriving at equality—a rallying point necessary to overthrow the existing authority, convicted of tyranny. 2. To prepare, in the distance, for the adoption of a veritable equality, by demonstrating it to the people as the only effectual means of drying up for ever all the sources of public calamity.

The Revolution contemplated being to commence by the destruction of the Constitution of the Year III., the Committee naturally occupied itself with the means *Authority to be substituted for the Government of the Year III.*

the sovereign people; so that if the guarantees of property (established by law) were at any time found mischievous or inconvenient, they might be remedied by the same authority that controlled the law itself. The more Robespierre's Declaration is considered the clearer will appear its perfect adaptation to any or to every social order that the most enlarged and comprehensive benevolence can contemplate. Robert Owen does not go one jot farther than Robespierre's Declaration would sanction. Without the people's consent we have no right to thrust systems upon them (be they ever so perfect in our view), but with their consent all systems should be equally accessible to them. Now, this is the grand point conceded by Robespierre's Declaration, and in that, therefore, consists its surpassing excellence. It is true, the Declaration agreed to by the Convention differs in some respects from Robespierre's, but still it is sufficiently comprehensive to admit of unlimited change in the institution of property. The Conventional Declaration will be found amongst the justificatory documents at the end of this work.—BRONTERRE.]

E

of operation, and with the provisional Government, to be suddenly substituted for the one they sought to overthrow. The necessities of the case, and the very success of the enterprize, evidently required that there should be an interval between the fall of the aristocratic Government and the definitive establishment of the popular Constitution. It was only by the people's force they proposed attacking the usurped authority; and this force they counted on putting in action, only by the ascendancy of truth, by the love of liberty, and by the people's hatred of oppression.

Before I resume (in the course of this work) the subject of the form of provisional authority, by which the conspirators proposed to themselves, to suddenly replace the Constitutional Order of the Year III., I will here briefly expound the several opinions that divided the Committee.

One party proposed to recal the remnant of the National Convention, which they regarded as still existing by right; another party wished to confide the Provisional Government of the Republic to a body named on the spot by the people of Paris, in insurrection; others, again, were inclined to invest for a limited period a single individual, under the title of dictator or regulator, with the supreme power and charge of settling the Republic. By-and-bye will be seen the reasons by which each supported his opinion. Suffice it for the present to state, that the opinion in favour of nominating the Provisional Government, by the insurgents of Paris, was preferred to the recal of the Convention proposed by Amar, and to the Dictatorship suggested by *Bedon*.

Whilst the Committee was ripening its projects, the Society of the Panthéon, and the writings of Babeuf, served it, as levers, for the contemplated movement. To the end of directing their action, it whispered the orators of the Society (which they calculated on making the nucleus of the insurrection), to repress with prudence all premature explosions, without subduing the Society's energy; and it encouraged Babeuf to redouble his zeal against the oppressors, and to summon the people without reservation to the full and complete conquest of its rights.

They were on the point of forming themselves into

sections, to prepare the insurrection, to lay the basis of the provisional legislation which was to follow it, and to reduce to form the definitive institutions of equality, when the demon of distrust interposed to damp the labours of the Committee, which, in consequence, soon dissolved itself. Amar became the object of general distrust; he was equally odious to many of the friends of equality, as to the partisans of the aristocracy. The latter reproached him with the part he had taken in the persecutions against the Girondists, and the severity he had displayed against the enemies of the Republic; the former accused him of having been one of the most violent proscribers of the victims of the 9th Thermidor, towards whom, it was alleged, he had exercised revolting traits of cruelty—they called him vain, imprudent, intriguing, and revengeful. But he had been able to gain the confidence of Darthé and of Massart, and it was owing to them that the other members of the Committee associated with him. Though induced, however, to act with Amar, by their ardent desire to serve the cause of the people, and by the opinion they had of the sincerity of the zeal he manifested, they were soon estranged from him by bitter recollections, by the very eagerness with which he had declared himself for the system of equality, and even by the unjust fear of being betrayed by him.

Dissolution of the Committee.

Héron, who had been one of the principal agents of the Committee of General Security, in the Convention, had, in that capacity, conceived against Amar an implacable hatred; though sick and dying, hardly had he learned the fact of the Republicans placing trust in him, than he hastens to send for Felix Lepelletier, conjures him in the name of the country to warn his comrades against him, and charges him to paint Amar to them under the most frightful colours. The injunction of Héron having been acted upon, the Committee, which, from motives of prudence, had just transferred its sittings to the street Neuve Egalité, was immediately dissolved.*

* Amar had made some pecuniary sacrifices for the democratic conspiracy, towards the success of which he never ceased to contribute, up to the instant when he was implicated in the proceedings instituted against its author.

Other re-unions of the same kind.   There was hardly a true Republican at this epoch that was not a conspirator, or ready to become one, so intensely did they all feel the necessity of uniting, and concerting together the overthrow of tyranny. Thus, no sooner was the Committee just spoken of dissolved, than there were formed other unions of the same kind, in several parts of Paris. In these were observed Darthé, Buonarroti, Massart, Bouin, *Eriddy*, Antonelle, Germain, *De Naumbet*, *Chintrard*, *Ready*, *Tismiot*, Dufour, and Chapelle. These new associations had but a brief existence, partly owing to the surveillance of the police, and partly to a secret influence which tended to draw to another centre the efforts of the Democrats. It was in these assemblies that the project was developed of distributing all the patriots into small obscure clubs, chosen delegates from which were to form district societies, subject to a central committee, which was to have been composed of a small number of tried Democrats, charged with imparting to the whole an uniform impulse.

The democratic spirit bursts forth at the Panthéon.   At the Panthéon it was found extremely difficult to restrain the impetuous bursts of the Society, now become very numerous; against the constitutional tyranny of the Year III. The animated discussions to which the reading of the journals belonging to the different factions gave rise, and the still more exciting ones occasioned by the proposition to demand the execution of the law, which promised to the defenders of the country a thousand millions' worth of national property, as also of another law which authorized the grant of honourable succours to poor citizens, revived in the society the old vigour of the Democrats, and made known to the Government the most devoted and most eloquent friends of popular principles.

Difficult position of the orators of this society.   Though it was admitted, amongst the Pantheonists, that a prudent dissimulation was a necessary precaution to render less difficult the accomplishment of their ends, they could not prevent bold harangues from circulating amongst the members, and occasionally even bursting forth from the tribune of the Society, sometimes through an effect of zeal, and sometimes in consequence of a criminal intrigue to provoke the destruction of this useful institution. Besides, it was impossible to inspire the people with energy without speaking to it of its interests and rights, and the necessity of allowing some latitude to the discussions, combined with that degree of circumspection which was essential to steal a march on tyranny, placed the orators of the Panthéon in a very embarassing position, both as regarded the public interests, and as respected its confidence in the Society—a confidence which it was indispensable to maintain.

Whilst the Society was rousing the attention of the friends and enemies of inequality—whilst its discussions were being repeated and commented upon by the patriotic journals—disfigured, abused, and calumniated by the counter-revolutionary writers—and that the old Democrats were casting some regards of hope towards the Panthéon; the people of Paris were gradually emerging from the indifference into which it had been plunged by a long train of calamities, and there was formed in all the Departments a great number of societies, in secret correspondence with that of the capital, through the interposition of their members admitted into its bosom. *Revival of democratic principles among the people.*

The labours of the Society of the Pantheon were distributed as follows:— *Labours of the Society of the Panthéon.*

Reading of the journals;

Communication of the correspondence of the members;

Collections of money and other relief for distressed patriots;

Measures to restore the liberty of persons thrown into irons by the aristocracy.

Afterwards followed discussions on legislation, and on the proceedings of Government, propositions, and the examining of addresses, to present to the authorities.

From the lively debates that took place, there were frequent opportunities of ascertaining the generous sentiments of the parties that aspired to restore to the people the plenitude of its rights, and the selfish and narrow views of other parties that only aimed at making the Society the pedestal of an odious domination. Amongst the remarkable events that transpired in this Society, the two following merit particular notice.

Distribution to the defenders of the country of a thousand millions' worth of national property.

Previously to the 9th Thermidor of the Year II., two laws had laid the groundwork of a great reform in the distribution of territorial wealth. By the first, a thousand millions' worth of national property had been promised to the defenders of the country. By the second, the goods of the enemies of the Revolution were allotted to distressed patriots.* Almost all the Pantheonists considered the execution of the first as a mere debt of gratitude; but those most devoted to the cause of equality saw in it besides, a first step towards arriving at the vigorous execution of the second, and designed to familiarize the nation with the principle which places in the hand of the sovereign the right of disposing of all property; they felt, moreover, that it was only by discussions of this kind they could awake in the people that energy which had enabled it to work such prodigies, and without which all efforts to establish a reasonable social order would be vain.

Accordingly, the proposition for demanding the effective distribution of the thousand millions was received with transport, and the address containing the demand was at first adopted without any modification. The transmission of it, however, was, at a subsequent sitting, adjourned *sine die*, through the influence of certain agents of the Government, who succeeded in replunging the majority of the members of the society into that state of alarm from which they had just scarcely emerged.†

* Conventional decrees of the 8th and 14th Ventôse of the Year II.

† The national domains, appropriated or mortgaged from the commencement for the extinction of the old national debt, represented for a time by the dividends or annuities on the State, and more recently represented by the paper-money, known under the name of *assignats*, were horribly dilapidated, when, after the 9th Thermidor, it was permitted to purchase them without public auction, by simple contract or subscription, and to pay the price of them in paper which had now scarcely more than a nominal

The boldness with which Babeuf at- Interest of the
tacked, in his *Tribune of the People*, the Society for
Constitution in force, and the members Babeuf.
of the Government, was the cause of the rigorous silence for a long time observed respecting him by the
Society of the Panthéon. Those that approved his
opinions were apprehensive of losing all by precipitation
—the timid ones were afraid to compromise themselves
—the enemies of Babeuf's doctrine had a cautious fear
of giving him importance. At the commencement of
Ventôse of the Year IV., the proscription impending
over Babeuf reached his wife; she was arrested upon a
charge of having distributed the writings of her husband,
but the real motive of the proceeeding was to ascertain
from her her husband's secret retreat. At the mention
of this excess of cruelty the Panthéon resounded with a
thousand cries of indignation; the friends of equality
raised their voice in favour of the courageous Babeuf;

value, since the recent examination and report on the state of the
currency. Hence, as well as from the brigandism of the commissaries for victualling the armies, arose those colossal fortunes, and
that unbridled luxury, which afterwards contributed so powerfully
towards the total ruin of the Republic.

The Pantheonists represented in their address, that if this disorder continued ever so little longer, there would not remain a
single rood of ground to discharge the debt contracted with the
defenders of the country. Already had Robespierre complained,
in his last discourses, of the partiality shown to the rich rentiers
in detriment to the poor, and especially of the Finance Committee,
for suffering to be squandered the mass of national property reserved for the people.

[Do you, my friends, begin to see why Robespierre was murdered? Alas! what a liar is history! Knaves pretend, and fools
believe, that he perished because he was a tyrant, but the knaves
take precious good care not to inform the fools that his death was
compassed by a band of robbers that had forfeited their lives to
the guillotine by their butcheries and peculations in the provinces,
and who, not satisfied with their previous spoliations, wanted
again to swindle the unfortunate people, that had risked their lives
and abandoned their employments in defence of the country, out
of the thousand millions gua anteed to them by Robespierre's law
of the 8th Ventôse, as well as of the property of convicted conspirators, which St. Just's law of the 14th Ventôse assigned to the
unfortunate poor and to distressed patriots. But I must not anticipate—all these matters shall be more fully and appropriately
shown in my forthcoming Life of Robespierre.—BRONTERRE.]

they succeeded in making the Society interfere by petition for the liberation of his wife, and in having pecuniary relief afforded her in her prison.

Schism in the The new enthusiasm with which the
Society of the people received those truths, in support
Panthéon. of which it had lately shed its blood with
so much glory—the spirit of equality which was spreading all over France—this new impulse towards democracy—and, above all, the well-known character of the leaders of the Panthéon—had unchained against this Society all the anti-popular writers of Paris, to whom were joined several orators of the Council of Five Hundred. The Government, which originally applauded its institution, in the design of using it as a bugbear against the Royalists, were already alarmed at its progress and influence. Accordingly, the secret agents of tyranny, seconded by the timidity of weak men, soon paralysed the energy of the Society, by sowing terror in its body. At one time they represented a band of Aristocrats as ready to assail it with armed force; at another they presented to its vision the vengeance of the Government, exasperated by the alleged boldness of its discussions. As to remedies, however, they proposed none but acts of submission and protestations of attachment to the new-established system. Induced by such counsels, the Society was made to propose an address to the Executive Directory, in which, after a thousand base flatteries, it was led to swear fidelity to the Constitution of the Year III. The address was vehemently opposed, but, having been adopted by the majority, it became the ground of an open schism between those that signed it and the sworn Democrats, who preferred the hazards of a fresh proscription to so base a perjury. Assignats—Li-

In the course of its labours, the Society berty of the
turned its attention towards the credit of Press—Juries.
assignats, the liberty of the Press, and the formation of Juries. Such was at that epoch the rapid depreciation of assignats, that wages could not at all keep pace with the rising prices of commodities, which absolutely doubled in one day. The whole of the working population, no longer able to obtain the means of subsistence, and reduced to sell their furniture, tools, and rags of

clothes, were languishing in extreme misery, or absolutely dying of inanition. A petition of the Pantheonists directed the notice of the legislative body to this appalling disorder.

Another petition refuted the sophisms by which certain malignant members of the Legislature had called for restrictions on the liberty of the Press, for the purpose, as they pretended, of repressing the audacity of the Democrats, whom the new Aristocrats hypocritically affected to confound with the Royalists, as though both these parties had in view the same ends.

The new legislation having excluded from the right of being enrolled in the registers of Juries for criminal cases, all who did not pay the electoral qualification, the consequence was that the poorer classes lost all guarantees for impartial justice, and were left completely at the mercy of their natural enemies, the rich. Hence resulted judicial severity for them,—lenity and indulgence for the privileged classes. So dangerous and glaring an abuse was, of course, denounced by the Society, to the people, and to the legislative body, but the latter cunningly remained mute.

Those who, from the outset, had proposed to themselves to make the Society of the Panthéon a rallying point for the restorers of the democracy, kept two points constantly in view—to revive the popular energy, and at the same time to warily avoid offending the constitutional authorities, up to the moment when the general rectification of opinion would permit it to speak out without subterfuge, and would render vain the efforts of the oppressors in power. Consequently, they desired to limit themselves to abstract discussions on the rights of man and of states, without making any direct application to the tyrants of the day; and it was in accordance with this prudence that the Society discountenanced the inconsiderate, and perhaps pretended, zeal of those who uttered grave denunciations against the members of the Executive Directory, and even sometimes threatened insurrection.

Prudence of the Society.

The same motives of prudence made them refuse the admission into the Society of the proscribed Mountain mem-

Exclusion of the Conventionalists.

bers, whom the Government considered, though wrong-
fully, as dangerous conspirators.   Drouet alone was
admitted.*

.In the month of Pluviôse of the Year IV., the great,
concourse of popular men that presented themselves at
the Panthéon—the good spirit of the small democratic
societies, formed in several quarters of Paris—and the
lively interest taken by the people generally in the re-
establishing of its rights, apprized the founders of the
Society that their wishes were beginning to be accomplished, and that the time was come for opening a wider.
field to their operations.   Up to this period, they had
confined themselves to the work of concentrating and
reanimating the most active elements of the Revolution.
At present they felt that the time had arrived for exercising the same influence upon the people of Paris.

Decadary   Seeking to reconcile the indispensable
festivals.   publicity of their sittings with the regulations
of the police, and especially with that prudential caution.
which circumstances required, they began to spread the
conviction that, as their political doctrine was the infallible consequence of the laws of nature, it was as
reasonable as practicable, to present it as the code of the
Divinity—that is to say, as the object of natural religion.

In fact, the practice of a worship which presented the
Supreme Being as the creator, the legislator, and the
protector of equality, offered the immense advantage of
conciliating the class that value Christianity only for the
sake of its morality—those that reject Atheism—and
those that abhor superstition. It was, moreover, founded
on the opinion of philosophers, whom humanity reveres,
and upon arguments impossible to be refuted.   It was
capable of becoming, in the hands of reformers, a most
powerful lever for the establishment of democratic institutions; it was the only means allowed by law of addressing great assemblies of the people.   They resolved,
then, to appear in the public temples, under the name of

* Drouet was the person that caused the arrest, at Varennes, of
Louis XVI.   In the Convention he always ranged himself under
the banners of the democracy. Made prisoner at the siege of Mau-
beuge, in consequence of his burning courage and patriotism, he
was in the dungeons of Austria during the disastrous occurrences of the 9th Thermidor, which he vehemently condemned.

Deists, preaching, as their sole religion, the morality of nature.

And, as it was expedient to accustom the multitude to replace the practices of the Catholic Church by other practices—what the Government itself sought at that time to accomplish by the introduction of decadary festivals—they determined upon celebrating these festivals publicly, and for this purpose to demand a spacious temple from the Executive Directory. The latter, penetrating the design, and apprehending the consequences of complying with this demand, refused it, under the pretext that it was about to occupy itself with the proposed celebration. It became then necessary to hold a clearer language to the Society, and to give a glimpse at those secret views which it would have been indiscreet to reveal to it to their full extent. The intention was to place the Society under the protection of religious forms, in order to enjoy the publicity and places of worship guaranteed by the law to the members of all religious sects. The discussion which took place on this subject was very animated, and was prolonged during several sittings. The authors of the project were obliged to combat the opposition of orators who laboured to prevent its execution, sometimes by recommending a dutiful deportment towards the Government, and sometimes by exhibiting every religious form as the source of a new superstition. At length all obstacles were surmounted, and the Society resolved " to devote the *decadis* * (every " tenth day) to the public worship of the Divinity, by " preaching the laws of natural religion." A commission was charged to rent a place of worship, and to prepare the catechism and rules of the new religion.

About this epoch the Executive Directory conceived a horror of the Society of the Panthéon, whose discussions alarmed the numerous selfish robbers of the capital. The police were accordingly instructed to spy the Hatred of the Government towards the Pantheonists.

---

* [To those of our readers not conversant with the history of revolutionary France, it may not be amiss to state, that, after the formal abolition of the Catholic worship, a Republican calendar was formed, which substituted every tenth day as a day of rest for the Christian Sabbath.—BRONTERRE.]

propositions and conduct of the Pantheonist orators, who had not as yet, in their public conduct, furnished any decent motive of persecution. Nevertheless, their destruction was vowed, and the authorities only waited for a pretext to dissolve the Society, which they already called a den of brigands.

Their zeal. Towards the beginning of Ventôse of the Year IV., the Pantheonists having recovered from their former stupor, were, for the greater part, devoted to the triumph of equality. Instead of inflaming their zeal, the difficulty was to regulate their impulses so as to prevent a premature explosion, which would have proved disastrous. The emissaries, insinuated into the Society by Government, being despised and abashed, and no longer capable of deceiving, sunk into vile informers.

Reading of the work of Babeuf. Dissolution of the Society. The pretext so industriously sought by the Government was offered by Darthé, who, wishing to sound the disposition of the Society, caused some numbers of the *Tribune of the People* to be read to it, in which the persons of the directors, and of certain deputies, were treated with as little ceremony as their oppressive Constitution and tyrannical laws. The reading of these papers was received with bursts of applause; but a few days afterwards * an order was issued by the Directory to shut up the Pantheon, and was executed by General Bonaparte in person.†

* The 9th Ventôse of the Year IV.

† Bonaparte, who then commanded the army of the interior, was the real author of this measure. Having unravelled, by the aid of numerous agents, the secret views of the Pantheonists, he inspired the Directory with fear of them, and obtained the order for their dissolution. He was present at its execution, and caused the keys of the apartment, where the Society held its sittings, to be delivered to himself in person.

By several traits of this nature, the upstart aristocracy was enabled to recognize in this General (already celebrated by the recapture of Toulon from the enemy, and by the proceedings of the 13th Vendemiaire) the man that might one day lend it a solid support against the people; and it was the knowledge thus had of his haughty character, and aristocratic opinions, which caused him to be called from Egypt, before the 18th Brumaire of the Year VIII., to the aid of this party, already terrified at the rapidity with which the democratic spirit was reviving throughout France. Bonaparte was hoisted to supreme power in consequence of the retrograde

Thus, as in all aristocratic governments, there was in that of the French Republic a spirit equally opposed to the authority of an individual, as to the power of the people. The ardour, however, with which the doctrine of the sovereignty of the people had been recently received by the generality of the nation, and preached by even some of the founders of

march impressed on the Revolution by the events of the 9th Thermidor—that disastrous epoch, after which the authority, which governed the skeleton of the Republic, having separated itself from the working classes, had to maintain an incessant struggle against the Royalists on the one hand, and the wreck of the democratic party on the other. It was seen, in fact, to combat this latter party in Prairial of the Year III., to overthrow the friends of royalty in Vendemiaire of the Year IV., to proscribe the Democrats in Floreal and Fructidor of the same year, to pursue the Royalists in Fructidor of the Year V., and to quash and nullify the popular elections in Prairial of the Year VI. In the last months of the Year VII., the popular tempest blowing louder and fiercer than ever, and the armies of the enemy becoming more menacing, the usurpers of the national sovereignty felt themselves pressed between the vengeance of the old regime and the justice of the people, but too much the enemies of equality to have recourse to a capitulation, which they might have easily obtained from the popular party; they preferred exposing themselves to all the chances of military despotism, by delivering on the 18th Brumaire of the Year VIII., the French Republic to the unlimited power of an imperious soldier, whose ambition and audacity they in vain flattered themselves with being able to check.

Thus was it, in consequence of the policy that prevailed on the 9th Thermidor of the Year II., that those who presided over the destinies of France were led to view the war of invasion as a powerful means of absorbing the attention of the nation—of diverting it from the care of its rights—of exhausting progressively the democratic spirit of the armies—of corrupting the citizens—and of furnishing aliment to the ambition of the generals. It is difficult to explain, on any other hypothesis, the conduct observed in Italy and Switzerland, and, especially, that impolitic and criminal expedition to Egypt.

The consulate and the empire were, then, as much the consequences of the war of invasion whence Bonaparte emerged, as of the politics of the interior; these two causes have their common source in the plots of which Robespierre was the victim. Bonaparte might, by the firmness of his character and by the ascendancy of his military exploits, have been the restorer of French liberty; but, the creature of vulgar ambition, he preferred being its last worst destroyer—he held in his hands the happiness of Europe, and he proved its scourge by the systematic oppression he made her groan under, and by that still more terrible oppression of which he prepared the elements, and under which were buried, after his fall, in the name of liberty itself (by the Holy Alliance), so many nations of this part of the globe. The more we reflect on the chain of events, the more must we be convinced that the Counter-Revolution began on the 9th Thermidor.

the new Aristocracy, did not permit the latter party to make a crime of it, in the Democrats, by painting them under their true colours. Accordingly, in order to make them the victims of public hatred, they were obliged to treat them as disguised Royalists, who aspired to bring back the nation to kingly government, by the circuitous route of anarchy, with which they affected to confound democratic principles. This political fraud may be discovered in all the acts of the new usurpation against the popular party;* the Directorial decree which closed, together with the Panthéon, several Royalist unions, that were opened immediately afterwards, is a proof of this; to which may be added other more decisive ones, of which I shall have occasion to speak, when I render an account of the famous, or infamous, law of the 27th Germinal.

No scruples stand in the way of the wicked when they want to destroy disagreeable or troublesome adversaries. It was so in this case. The most disinterested friends of equality were represented to the world as monsters of rapacity and ambition, by the very parties that had spared neither violence nor calumny to retain an authority which had turned their recent poverty to opulence. Similar imputations were lavished in abundance against the Pantheonists by the Directory, whom it accused of having audaciously demanded the Constitution of 1793 and the Dictatorship. As to the latter, the question was never even mooted; and though the Constitution of 1793 was dear to the heart of every member of the Society, the greatest caution was observed to prevent any allusions being made to it at their tribune.

New proscription of the Patriots. This violent act alarmed all minds— even those least devoted to the cause of liberty—and was the signal for a new proscription. A great many patriots were dismissed from the public offices they filled, the events of the Revolution were raked up, and an active persecution

* [It is exactly the same sort of cheat that is practised on the Radicals of this country by O'Connell and the Birmingham " Council," when they represent what they call " ultra-Radicals" —that is, honest Radicals—as " playing the game of the Tories."— BRONTERRE.]

was commenced against the popular writers. Republicans of every shade, from the most impassioned friend of equality to the most moderate patriot—all were indignant at this criminal attack by the Executive Directory, and afterwards by the report of the Deputy Mailhe on the popular societies against the already too restricted right of assembling, guaranteed by the Constitution of the Year III. Tyranny, which in this instance assumed a more than ordinarily menacing and odious character, had the effect of producing against it, a combination of patriots of all shades, and of making them unanimously desire its speedy overthrow. The Pantheonists, dispersed by violence, re-assembled at first in the coffee houses kept by Republicans, and afterwards in the public places when the fine weather returned. Certain writers of the Press inveighed with vehemence against the Directorial Act; others, after the example of Babeuf, seized this opportunity to summon the people more peremptorily than ever to the recovery of its rights. Amongst the writings which then circulated in Paris, there was one remarkable paper, entitled:—" *Soldier, stop and Read,*" *by Felix Lepelletier;*[*] and " *An Address to the French on Associations of the Citizens,*" of which Antonelle was the anonymous author.[†]

Babeuf had not ceased to preach in his *Tribune of the People*, the doctrines of pure equality, and to accuse of usurpation the founders of the new Government, as well as its actual agents and functionaries.

The courage of Babeuf excites numerous enemies against him.

His austere and uncompromising principles had made him shoals of enemies, and disposed several parties against him, including not only those indebted to the supreme authority for favours received or expected, but those who, believing it to be a good policy to feign attachment to the existing authority, in order the more easily to annihilate it afterwards, accused him of rashly divulging what they called the *secret* of the Democrats.

Their distrust was so outrageous that some of them

[*] The plans of organization, alluded to here by Buonarroti, are described more at length in his justificatory documents, the principal of which will appear at the end of the history.—BRONTERRE.]

[†] See justificatory pieces.

resolved to destroy this courageous citizen; they even
tried to excite against him the indignation of the popular
party, by exaggerating his former connexions with the
instigators of the crimes of the 9th Thermidor, and by
maliciously reminding them of his writings against certain
agents of the Revolutionary Government. . Meanwhile,
the decided friends of equality, feeling that comprehensive
political principles, calculated to operate sensibly on the
mass of the people, were the only means of maintaining
and augmenting the popular energy, which the Aristocrats
were labouring to extinguish; and perceiving what services the talents and boldness of Babeuf might render to
the public cause, undertook his defence with spirit and
devotion, and by that means favoured the development
of his plans.

He conceives
the project of
delivering the
people.

To the desire of enlightening his fellow-
citizens, Babeuf had long added that of
actively aiding them to recover their rights.
To this end, he had attached to himself
the ardent friends of democracy, and had endeavoured
to ascertain and direct the efforts made by the Democrats
at Amar's house, in the street Papillon, in the Faubourg
Denis, and in every place where they held meetings.
The habitations of Felix Lepelletier, *d'Eris*, and *Crexel*,
were successively the asylums in which Babeuf, encouraged and aided by Antonelle, Buonarroti, Simon Duplay,
Darthé, *Eriddy*, Germain, Silvain Maréchal, and *Sombod*,
discharged the duties he had imposed on himself, and
ripened his enterprise.

It was not till towards the beginning of Germinal of
the Year IV., that the insurrectional institution of which
I am going to treat, received its existence. There had
been, previously to this epoch, a scheme concocted
amongst Babeuf, Felix Lepelletier, and Silvain Maréchal,
which had at first no other object than that of regulating
the subjects and tone of their political works; it seems
certain that Babeuf, who aimed at directing all the democratic movements to a common centre, contributed,
by the influence of his friends, to effect the dissolution of
the Committees whose labours I have detailed, and many
of whose ideas may be recognized in the acts of the new
insurrectional body.

On the few first days of Germinal, Babeuf, Antonelle, Silvain Maréchal, and Felix Lepelletier, constituted themselves a secret Directory of Public Safety, and conceived the generous resolution of binding to a single point the scattered threads of the democracy, for the purpose of directing them towards the re-establishment of the popular sovereignty.*

Appointment of a secret Directory of Public Safety.

To rally, and place at its immediate disposal all the friends of liberty — to calculate their forces, and to give them an impulse favourable to instruction and to the general deliverance, without at the same time exposing either the conspiracy or its partisans to be compromised by treachery or indiscretion—these were the first cares of the Directory. To give them effect, a plan of organization † was resolved, instituting a chief revolutionary agent in each of the twelve arrondissements of Paris, and intermediary agents to maintain correspondence and communications between the Directory and its revolutionary agents. To this act was added an instruction, in which, after having explained to these agents the motives and justice of the enterprise, the Directory traced out to them the route to be followed in order to guarantee its success.‡ There was in fact, however, no other intermediary agent than *Eriddy*, whose zeal, activity, address, and discretion, were constantly above all praise. Though, according to the established regulation, this agent should know neither the members of the Directory nor their operations, yet the purity of his patriotism, his wisdom, and his fidelity, on all trying occasions, deservedly secured him their unbounded confidence. Of this confidence he availed himself, to determine them to unite to themselves Darthé and Buonarroti, who in their turn obtained the admission of *Bedon.*

Agents and their instructions.

Thus, about the 10th Germinal of the Year IV, there existed a Secret Directory of Public Safety, instituted to restore the people to the exercise of its rights. It was composed of Antonelle, Babeuf, *Bedon*, Buonarroti,

Members of the Directory and their political doctrine.

* See justificatory pieces.
         † Ibid.   ‡ Ibid.

Darthé, Felix Lepelletier, and Silvain Maréchal, and held its meetings in an apartment occupied by *Crezel*, in whose house Babeuf was then a refugee. Amongst these individuals there was no discordance of opinion on the subject of the political doctrine discussed at Amar's house : a perfect unanimity combined them ; they all considered equality of labour and enjoyments as the sole end worthy of honest citizens, and in that end alone they saw a legitimate motive for insurrection. Their theories are so important for the progress of society, for the honour of the French Revolution, and for a knowledge of the true designs of the Secret Directory, that I deem it my duty to transcribe, amongst the justificatory documents of this work, a paper of extracts containing the essence of them. This paper, printed by order of the Secret Directory, is entitled, *"Analysis of the Doctrine of Babeuf's Tribune of the People, proscribed by the Executive Directory for having declared the truth."**

Final object of the conspirators.   Equality without restriction, the greatest possible happiness of all, and the certainty of never losing it by force or fraud—such are the benefits the secret directors of public safety sought to ensure to the French people. Its design was to resume the great work so fatally interrupted on the 9th Thermidor, and after the example of the victims of that disastrous day, to add to the revolution in power and rank, that incomparably more just and necessary one of property and intelligence, whose final result should be, an impartial distribution of riches and knowledge amongst all the citizens.

The people the object and means of the Secret Directory.   And, although the Secret Directory knew that the union of wisdom and authority would be for it a good earnest of success, it was too well convinced of the insufficiency of the best intentioned power, to guarantee a complete and durable success, without the affection and

† Silvain Maréchal was the author of the famous manifesto of the Equals, to which the Secret Directory was unwilling to give publicity, because it approved neither the expressions,—" *Perish the arts, if need be, provided that real equality may remain with us* ;" nor that other,—" *Away at length with the revolting distinction of governors and governed.*" See this manifesto amongst the justificatory pieces.

concurrence of the people, not to place in the latter its chief reliance. Without the support of the people, it felt that all its labours would be fruitless; therefore, to secure *that*, was now its main desideratum.

Before the French Revolution had exhibited to the world the extraordinary spectacle of several millions of men proclaiming, and sealing with their blood, those eternal truths, which, in antecedent times, had been known but to a few philosophers, the design of putting the people in *movement*, by the sole force of these truths, might have appeared chimerical; but this was not the case at the epoch when the Secret Directory was formed. The question, then, was not how to create a new opinion, but how to concentrate and organize that which had already existed so short a time before,* and which calumny and proscription had divided and stifled.

There was a period during the Revolution, when the well-founded hope of an approaching equality, exercising a powerful influence on the hearts of the people, attached them cordially to the new order of things. But disappointed in the attempt, they regretted, after the 9th Thermidor, the sacrifices they had made, and regarding as an *ignis fatuus* the happiness once promised them, began to feel even an aversion towards the Revolution and its champions. This disposition of popular opinion furnished the Royalists with occasion to discredit the Republican system, and the Aristocrats with plausible grounds for inculcating a horror of insurrections, and an indifference to politics. Again, proscription had greatly thinned the ranks of the decided Republicans; the survivors, dispersed by violence or divided by calumny, no longer inspired that confidence by the aid of which they had formerly conducted the people to the conquest of its rights.

In this state of affairs, the Secret Directory which desired to act only *for* and *by* the people, naturally felt that it was necessary, before all things, to enlighten the deluded—to encourage the weak—to lead the multitude to explore the true causes of their calamities—to trace out a uniform plan of conduct for the courageous apostles of

---

* In Robespierre's time.

democracy—and to present to all a single centre of direction. So far from working in darkness like criminal conspirators, the Secret Directory expected the success of its enterprise only from the progress of public reason and the lustre of truth.

What the Society of the Panthéon had been only able to rough-hew, the Secret Directory undertook to complete. The latter possessed the two-fold advantage over the Society, of being less exposed, and of being better able to mature and pursue its plans. The violent dissolution of the Society contributed not a little, by the public discontent consequent upon it, to augment in the Secret Directory the sentiment of its force.

It wishes to establish the Constitution of 1793. Besides the real equality, which it was just and necessary to present to the people as the veritable and legitimate end of the Revolution, it was important to draw its attention to a form of administration proper to preserve it. To this intent, the Secret Directory examined, with more care than had ever been done before, the Constitution of 1793, which at this epoch was the rallying point of all the sincere friends of democracy; and as, at the same time, it discussed the institutions necessary to establish social equality, it was the better enabled to unravel that Constitution's defects, and to discover the supplements it would require.

Its opinion of this Constitution. Like the Committee at Amar's house, our conspirators of the Secret Directory discovered the positive vice of this Constitution, to be in the Articles of the Declaration of Rights which concern property. Respecting the Constitution, *as a whole*, they judged that it could not sufficiently guarantee the people from usurpations by the legislative body, and from errors into which it might be itself drawn. It will be seen, at the close of this work, by what supplements they proposed to prevent these dangers. Notwithstanding these blemishes, the Secret Directory determined to maintain the respect vowed to this Constitution by the Republicans, and this, for two supreme reasons:—1. *The almost unanimous sanction it had received from the nation;* and 2. *The right of the people, consecrated by itself, to deliberate on the laws.* It was in this latter provision, especially, that it saw the distinguishing excellence of the Constitution of 1793, of which all the other parts appeared to it but as articles of regulation. They agreed, then, to take this constitution for a rallying point, and to represent its establishment as the means of attaining that charming equality, of which they, meanwhile, continued to demonstate the justice, to demand the practice, and to develope the fundamental laws. It was not by the aid of a handful of factious persons, excited by a thirst of gain, or by a mad fanaticism, that the Secret Directory pretended to overthrow the ruling usurpation; it desired to employ no other moving principle than the force of truth. The frank and full exposition of the people's rights, and the crimes of its oppressors, was the sole means by which it counted on raising the population of Paris against tyranny, at the moment when public indignation would be fiercest and most general; then, but not till then, would it have hoisted its standard, and given the signal for insurrection.

Truth, the great moving principle of the popular insurrection.

Accordingly, its first care was to labour to convince the multitude, and to make proselytes. To this end, it spared neither discourses nor writings; and to circulate them with more effect, it instituted in Paris a great number of small associations, mutually unknown to each other, but all under the direction of the Democrats, who themselves received their cue and instructions from the twelve revolutionary agents. It is worth observing, in the instructions given to these agents, the precautions by which the Directory of Public Safety endeavoured to guard the Democrats from the consequences of imprudence and perfidy.

Associations of the people multiplied in Paris.

From the outset, the Revolutionary agents were designed to become the levers by which the people of Paris was to dart upon its tyrants. Meanwhile they formed associations, directed popular discussions, circulated writings, and reported to the Secret Directory the progress of opinion, the intrigues of the aristocracy, and the number, capacity, and energy of the Democrats. Nor are we to wonder that its measures applied principally to Paris; it was *in the heart* that it was necessary to

smite the aristocracy, and the immense population
of this commune would have easily impressed its movement, and communicated its fire to the democratic
elements spread all over the Republic.

Choice of the twelve revolu-tionary agents. The choice of revolutionary agents was
a graver operation. Such an important
function could be confided only to men
who combined great activity and great intelligence with
constant love of equality, tried prudence, and the confidence of the people; they were named by the Secret
Directory, according to the votes of a majority, and after
a mature examination of the motives alleged in favour of
each of them by their respective proposers.*

* LIST OF REVOLUTIONARY AGENTS.

ARRONDISSE-MENS.	SECTIONS.	AGENTS.	PROPOSERS.
1	Tuileries, Piques, Champs-Elysées, République.............	*Romaincoksel.*	Babeuf.
2	Lepelletier, Butte-des-Moulins, Mont-Blanc, Faubourg Mont-Martre.	*Denaumbet.*	Darthé.
3	Brutus, Contrat-Social, Mail, Poissonnière	Meneissier.	*Bedon.*
4	Halle-aux-Bleds, Muséum, Gardes-Françaises, Marchés	Bouin.	Buonarroti.
5	Bondy, Bonne-Nouvelle, Nord, Bon-Conseil	*Le Himug.*	Germain.
6	Gravilliers, Lombards, Temple, Amis de la Patrie.............	Claude Fiquet.	Germain.
7	Réunion, Homme-Armé, Droit de l'Homme, Arcis	Paris.	Darthé.
8	Quinze-Vingts, Indivisibilité, Popincourt, Montreuil	Cazin.	Babeuf.
9	Fidélité, Fraternité, Arsenal, Cité	*Adery.*	Darthé.
10	Fontaine de Grenelle, Ouest, Invalides, Unité.	*Rerpino.*	Bouin.
11	Théâtre-Français, Luxembourg, Pont-Neuf, Thermes........	*Sombod.*	{ Babeuf et Buonarroti.
12	Panthéon, Finisterre, Jardin des Plantes, Observatoire	Moroy.	*Bedon.*

From the moment that the supreme authority had quitted the paths of justice, its decrees ceased to have for their support, public opinion and the people's love. Accordingly, they experienced now as much of coldness and resistance as they formerly had of ease and rapidity in their execution. Since the death of Robespierre it became necessary to substitute the resource of force for that of popular affection; it was necessary to intimidate the multitude, whose just resentment was feared by the parties that had usurped its sovereignty. After having surrounded themselves with a crowd of enemies of the Revolution, whose baseness and bad faith were not slow in developing themselves, the moderators of the aristocratic system perceived that their safety could only repose on a prop of bayonets, placed in blind subjection to their creatures, till at last, under pretence of maintaining the public tranquillity, they actually transformed the sanctuary of the national representation, of which the attachment of the citizens had recently constituted the sole defence, into a military camp, which menaced their liberties and their lives.

This army around and within Paris, which in Germinal and Prairial of the Year III., had aided the enemies of liberty to establish their empire, was maintained and augmented by the Constitutional Government; one might perceive at its head, ex-nobles, who were prisoners in the Year II., and generally speaking, men who had given conspicuous proofs of their hatred of the sovereignty of the people. The presence of these numerous forces devoted to tyranny, compared with the state of disarmament to which the Government had (under the twofold pretext of disarming the Royalists and the Terrorists) reduced the people, might possibly discourage the multitude, and dispose it to dread the least opposition.

Amongst the number of obstacles that might oppose the success of its enterprize, the Secret Directory ranged the resistance of the troops, and even the bare contemplation of such resistance by the people, which might prove equally fatal as the reality itself. Accordingly did it apply itself in time to render such obstacle void, by rekindling in the breasts of the soldiers the love of democracy—by reminding them of the mighty interests for which they had shed their blood, and by insensibly weaning them from that servile obedience to their chiefs, which the tyrants had artfully represented to them as an imperious duty. It was, moreover, by the ascendancy of truth that the conspirators desired to inflame the army with hatred of the aristocratic Government, to the end of inducing it to join its forces to those of the people by a unanimous burst of patriotism.

To this intent the Secret Directory <small>Military agents.</small> added successively to the agents of arondissments, military agents, charged with similar functions as the former, to be exercised amongst the battalions stationed at Paris and in the environs. It accorded its confidence

To Fion for the Invalides;

To Germain for the Legion of Police;

To *Sasemy* for the detachments cantoned at Franciade;

To Vannec for the troops in general; and

To Georges Grisel for the camp of Grenelle.

The horrid part played by this Grisel in the *denouément* of the conspiracy, requires that we make known, to the full extent, the circumstances and motives which gave him access to the principal defenders of equality.

Besides the civil and military agents already described, the Secret Directory had instituted superintendants, who examined their conduct, directed their proceedings, and communicated fresh vigour to their operations. Darthé and Germain were charged with this important office. Both had hitherto rendered most signal services to the cause of equality; it was through them that the Directory became more particularly acquainted with what transpired at the popular assemblies, and to them only used it to entrust all difficult commissions, in which they invariably acquitted themselves with a precision and courage, which only profound conviction of right, and a complete devotion to the cause, could inspire.

Darthé, indefatigable and intrepid, expert in imparting the fire of his own soul to those of his auditors—skilful to repress the too precipitate bursts of opinion, and to conciliate its conflicting differences—exerted himself to encourage and bring together the friends of equality, and to discover the parties that could best promote its cause. With these objects it was that he frequented the *Café des Bains Chinois* (Chinese Baths), which was the daily resort of several Democrats, and that he connected himself with Georges Grisel, of Abbeville, at that time a captain attached to the third battalion of the thirty-eighth demi-brigade of the line, encamped on the plain of Grenelle, near Paris.

Grisel, who, like so many others, appears to Grisel. have seen in the Revolution only a great occasion for personal aggrandizement, sought after and courted the patriots. By imitating their language, he succeeded in passing amongst them for an ardent revolutionist; and that step gained, he had not much difficulty in captivating the good will of some Democrats, who introduced him to Darthé, as a person that would prove valuable to their party. The imprudent eulogies lavished on Grisel by his introducers, his own conversations, the ardour with which he volunteered to spread the writings of the Secret Directory amongst the troops, and editing himself an insurrectionary pamphlet tending to provoke insubordination in the army, persuaded the too confident Darthé of the purity of his intentions, and determined him to propose him to the Secret Directory, which needed to have a military agent at the camp of Grenelle. He was nominated to that office, and the instructions relative to his mission were delivered to him by Darthé on the 26th Germinal.

As soon as the agencies it had instituted Democratic were sufficiently organized, the Secret writings. Directory set immediately to work to circulate such writings as it thought would undeceive the people. It was expedient to show the latter that its sovereignty had been usurped by the existing authority—that the Constitution of 1793 was the only legitimate one—that the happiness of the whole could result only from the real equality of all—and that the evils attributed to the Revolution had happened only in consequence of that Revolution having been prevented from attaining its gitimate end. Every democratic pen was put in contribution. Babeuf, in his *Tribune of the People*, developed the spirit of the insurrectional institution, and Simon Duplay propagated the same doctrines amongst

F

the poor and working classes, by means of a small sheet, entitled the Enlightener *(L'Eclaireur).* The Republicans directing the *Journal des Hommes libres* (Journal of free men), also rendered important services to the democracy, by the discussions which they had the boldness to moot on forms of government, and respecting the grand system of equality, the justice of which they caused to shine forth, by inserting the victorious replies of its advocates, in answer to their own objections intentionally put forth for the purpose.

One of the first cares of the Secret Directory was, to mark out, in a positive manner, the rallying points in Paris where the people in insurrection should assemble. This it effected by means of the " *Analysis of Babeuf's Doctrine,*" which was distributed and placarded on the 20th Germinal with immense profusion; and, though the Government endeavoured by its agents to tear down the placards, and intercept the writing from the public eye, such was the impression it made on all minds, that the Aristocrats were driven to the desperate subterfuge of transcribing it into their journals as a master-piece of extravagance and audacity, while the patriots universally made it the subject of their conversations and hopes.

On the 23d Germinal appeared " *Thoughts on our two Constitutions;*" on the 24th was published the letter of " *Freeman to his friend Terror;*" on the 25th was circulated the paper entitled, " *Do we owe obedience to the Constitution of 1795 (or Year III)?*" on the 27th was distributed the " *Tribune's Address to the Army ;*" on the 29th was spread the " *Letter in reply to M. V. ;*" and on the 1st Floreal was put into the people's hands the " *Cry of the French People against its Oppressors.*"*

Misery of the people. The persecution under which the mass of the patriots still groaned, and the ever-growing distress which the working classes experienced, lent prodigious aid to the operations of the Secret Directory. It was at this period that the progressive depreciation of the assignats inducing the merchants to hoard,

* [Such of these pieces as have not been lost, and are deemed worthy of insertion in this work, will be found towards the close of the translation.—BRONTERRE.]

and thereby causing a scarcity of provisions, reduced the labourers either to go without the necessaries of life or else part with their furniture, and even their most indispensable garments, in order to procure specie, with which alone commodities could be purchased.*

This frightful distress, joined to the writings of the Secret Directory, which at once demonstrated its cause and the radical remedy for it, produced so intense and general a fermentation, that very soon the discontent propagated by the secret associations burst forth publicly, and caused the numerous gatherings that were seen towards the middle of Germinal of the Year IV. in the streets, in the open places, and on the bridges of Paris. Then did the usurpers of the popular sovereignty learn with certainty that their enemies were re-uniting in mass, and that the people, while invoking equality and the democratic constitution, uttered regrets for the victims immolated to corruption and aristocracy, on the 9th Thermidor of the Year II., and in Prairial of the Year III.

What was passing in Paris—the opinions, conversations, and discussions of the people and the soldiers—all was regularly transmitted every day to the Secret Directory by the reports of its agents, and by the verbal communications of inspectors admitted to its presence; it used also

Progress of the insurrectionary spirit.

* This revolting invasion of the fortune of the poor, already too straightened, resulted from the suppression of the impost on provisions, and of the requisitions on the rich, two legislative measures, which, before the 9th Thermidor, had precluded the necessity of having recourse to too great an issue of assignats; but since that epoch the subsistance of the public having been abandoned to the speculations of proprietors and greedy contractors, for the most part enemies of popular reforms, the labouring poor were despoiled of the necessaries of existence, which went to augment the superfluities and luxury of the opulent.

[It may be observed here, that one of Robespierre's reasons for guarding against an over issue of assignats was, that the thousand millions' worth of national property, decreed and promised by the National Convention to the defenders of the country, might not be reduced to a nullity by the depreciation of the national money, in which species of currency he was well aware that the base Convention would be but too ready to discharge the claim. A thousand millions of livres in assignats meant something substantial in his time. Two years after it meant something very like nothing at all!—BRONTERRE.]

F 2

to receive information through several Democrats who
had dexterously introduced themselves into the Government police. It was soon perceived by the Secret
Directory that the effect of its inspirations had surpassed
its expectations, and the urgent necessity was felt of concentrating all the means by which it counted upon seconding, directing, and utilitizing the popular commotion, of
which the precursory symptoms were observed by all.

Labours of the
Secret Direc-
tory.
The conspirators assembled almost every
evening in the asylum of Babeuf, with
whom constantly remained deposited the
principal papers and seal of the conspiracy; this seal, by
which the revolutionary agents recognised the orders of
the Directory, bore the words *Public Safety* around a
level surface, probably typical of the ultimate end of the
conspiracy.

During its sittings the Directory examined—
The reports of its agents and draughts of replies ;
The writings to be printed ;
Propositions touching the plan of the insurrection, the
legislative dispositions that should follow it, and, finally,
the institutions and organization of the New Republic.

All the decisions, which the Secret Directory referred
to the plurality of votes, were regularly booked, and
served as bases for the correspondence and preparatory
labours distributed amongst the conspirators. There
was nothing *signed*. Babeuf, whom proscription obliged
to live in concealment, was almost the only person that
drew up the letters and instructions, of which the necessary dispatches were executed by a secretary, and con-
veyed by *Eriddy* to the revolutionary agents.

Authority to be
substituted for
the existing
authority.
After deciding that it should direct the
action of the people against the existing
Government, and towards the establishment of the Constitution of 1793, the
Secret Directory had to resolve another question, which
circumstances rendered a thorny one. It was to determine by what form of authority the people should replace
that whose destruction was contemplated ?

They were convinced that it was neither possible nor
without danger to summon the primary assemblies immediately, to name a legislative body and a government

conformable to the Constitution of 1793. In the first place, it was evident that an interval of some time should elapse between the insurrection and the installation of the new constitutional authority; and it was not less sensibly felt that it would be the maddest imprudence to leave the nation for an instant without a director or guide. Other considerations induced the Secret Directory to think that this interval of time should be longer than what would be strictly required by the elections and the arrival of the new Deputies. These considerations deserve to be developed.

To change the form of public adminis- *Necessity of an authority anterior to the Constitutional Order.* tration was not the sole end proposed to themselves by the conspirators. They desired also—what was by far the most important branch of their mission—to procure useful and durable laws for France. And though the Secret Directory was not ignorant that the mode in which the law is emitted and executed may exercise some influence on the institutions to be established, history, and the experience of the French Revolution, had forewarned it that the certain effect of inequality of condition is to divide the citizens, to create opposing interests, to foment hostile passions, and to subject the multitude (whom it renders ignorant, credulous, and the victims of excessive labour) to a small number of informed and crafty men, who, abusing the preference acquired by their address, apply themselves afterwards only to preserve and strengthen, in the distribution of goods and advantages, the social order that exclusively favours themselves. Hence the Directory concluded, that a people, so strangely elongated from the natural order of things, was but poorly qualified to make a useful choice, and had need of an extraordinary means to replace it in a condition in which it would be possible for it to exercise effectually, and not in mere fiction, the plenitude of its sovereignty.

From this train of reflection arose the project for replacing the existing Government by a revolutionary and provisional authority, constituted in such a manner as to withdraw the people for ever from the influence of the natural enemies of equality, and to restore to it the unity of will necessary for the adoption of Republican institutions.

What shall this authority be ?   Behold a delicate question that was very scrupulously examined by the Secret Directory. The three propositions formerly agitated at Amar's house were reproduced for discussion ; the first was foi recalling the Mountain, or supposed-Radical part of the Convention ; the second, for creating a Dictatorship; the third, for establishing a new body, charged and empowered to consummate the Revolution for the happiness of the people.*

Recal of the Convention.   Amar had proposed in the first Committee to recal the National Convention ; that body, said he, which could not be replaced, but by an authority willed by the people, having been deposed, in virtue of a constitution and laws contrary to its sovereign will, is still the only legitimate authority. Again, continued Amar, the legitimacy of its (the Convention's) decrees depended upon the freedom of the Deputies, guaranteed by the established forms for prosecuting those of its members against whom any grave accusations might be urged ; but certain members of the Convention (Mountainists) were arrested, banished, or despoiled of their political rights, without process of trial or judgment, in Germinal and Prairial of the Year III. Accordingly, the acts of the Convention, posterior to these violences, are null and void ; the establishment

* The experience of the French Revolution, and more particularly the troubles and fluctuations of the National Convention, have, as appears to me, sufficiently demonstrated that a people whose opinions have been formed under a regime of inequality and of despotism, is little calculated, at the commencement of a regenerating Revolution, to distinguish wisely (by its suffrages) the men most capable to direct and consummate it with success. This difficult task can belong only to certain wise and courageous citizens, who, strongly impregnated with the love of country, and of humanity, have long before fathomed the sources of public calamity —have disenthralled themselves from the common prejudices and vices of their age—have shot in advance of contemporary intellects, and who, despising money and vulgar greatness, have placed their happiness in rendering themselves immortal by ensuring the triumph of Equality. Perhaps, therefore, in the beginning of a Revolution, it is of less consequence, even as regards (and for the sake of) the real popular sovereignty itself, to busy ourselves in collecting the suffrages of a nation, than to make the supreme authority fall by the least arbitrary means possible, into hands that are wisely and vigorously revolutionary.

of the Constitution of the Year III., ought to be considered as if it had never happened; and, consequently, *they* are still the veritable delegates of the people, who have not participated in these abuses of power, or who have been the victims of them.

In conformity with this reasoning, Amar proposed to recal to the exercise of the directing power, the members of the National Convention that had been by itself declared ineligible, and those who, having been excluded from the legislative body, had not participated in the usurpation.

Objections.

There were too many and serious charges, however, against these Conventionalists to admit the adoption of Amar's proposition. A great number of them were reproached with the part they had taken in the crimes of the 9th Thermidor; with the proscription of the Democrats under the names of " anarchists," " exclusives," " terrorists," &c. &c.; the breaking up of the popular societies—the return into the Convention of the seventy-three Girondists, and the setting at liberty of all the Aristocrats—the weakness with which they had suffered several of their colleagues to be massacred—the silence they observed on the proposition for changing the Constitution—their great thirst for power—the riches acquired by some of them and, in general, with an extreme pusillanimity in defence of the people's rights.* Could persons impressed with the necessity of confiding the destiny of the country only to men of the greatest wisdom and courage, decide upon recalling to supreme power those who in the exercise of it had merited such grave reproaches? It was ruled by the Secret Directory, that arguments of so much force ought to prevail over the doubtful advantage promised by an apparent legitimacy (in favour of the Conventionalists), by the aid of which it was hoped that resentments might be mitigated and resistences overcome. The Directory, moreover, considered that, relying mainly for the success of its projects on the influence of the Democrats throughout the whole

---

* Though the Secret Directory believed itself instituted to refuse confidence to many of these Conventionalists, it nevertheless paid several of them a well-merited tribute of esteem and respect.

Republic, who, upon all hypotheses, would second the impulse given by those of Paris, it was prudent to throw subtleties aside, and to give a preference to the plan which offered the greatest security against the errors and weaknesses of men clothed with power.

Provisional au-
thority to be
named by the
insurgents of
Paris.

The recal of the Conventionalists thus rejected, the Secret Directory canvassed the proposition for committing to the nomination of the insurgents of Paris, the provisional authority, to which it would be unavoidably necessary to confide the government of the nation. In fact, considering the physical impossibility of collecting at once the suffrages of all the French, it was the only means of rendering to the sovereignty of the people all the homage compatible with circumstances. To this advantage was joined that of a greater probability of a good choice being made, seeing that the men to make it were the same whose devotion to the principles of the new Revolution would have been attested by the courage with which they were about to assume the defence of it.

This system
was in harmony
with the sove-
reignty of the
People.

It was foreseen that the crafty enemies of equality would attempt to excite the inhabitants of the departments against what they would not have failed to call " the usurping encroachments of the brigands of Paris on the rights of the sovereign people." The Secret Directory, who wished to do nothing but what was just, examined this objection—behold how they refuted it.

" When tyranny exists, it is the right and bounden
" duty of every citizen to labour to destroy it. It being
" impossible, however, that all the citizens of a vast
" Republic can repair to the seat of the Authority
" sought to be overthrown, it necessarily devolves on
" those living nearest to, and about it, to take arms
" first; and as it is important that a new authority should
" immediately succeed the old, it belongs to the insur-
" gents to provide that authority. Besides, the right
" of overthrowing tyrannic power being, by the very
" nature of things, consigned to that section of the
" people which lives in its immediate neighbourhood, to
" the same section is delegated, for the same reason,

" the right—which no other section can exercise—of
" replacing it by a provisional authority, as conform-
" able, as actual circumstances may allow, to the prin-
" ciples of national sovereignty."

The next question was, to decide what provisional
form should be proposed to the people of Paris in insurrection. Upon this point there was great diversity of
opinion. Some of the members of the Directory were
for the dictatorship of an individual; the rest preferred
a new body, composed of a small number of tried Democrats. This latter opinion prevailed.

Bedox and Darthé, who proposed the
dictatorship, attached to this word the Dictatorship re-
jected.
idea of an extraordinary authority, con-
fided to an individual, to be charged with the double
function of *proposing to the people a plan of legislation simple, and suited to ensure to it equality, and
the real exercise of its sovereignty ; and to dictate
provisionally the preparatory measures necessary to
dispose the nation to receive it.* According to them,
it being impossible to achieve so bold and important a
task unless by the aid of a perfect unity of thought and
action, it should be conceived and executed by a single
head. In support of their opinion, they appealed to the
example of ancient states, and called to mind the disastrous consequences of *plurality*, of which they had so
many recent proofs in the divisions of the Committee of
Public Safety. As to the dangers of abuse to be apprehended from such a magistracy, it appeared to them that
they might be easily avoided by well ascertaining the virtue
of the citizen to be clothed with such power—by the clear
and legal exposition of the end to be attained by it—
and by imposing limits beforehand to its duration.

By this system the task of the Secret Directory was
reduced to these points : to trace out in a few articles
the object of the reform sought; to fix a limited time to
the new magistracy; to discover the most virtuous
citizen of the Republic; and to procure the adoption of
his plan by the Parisians in insurrection.* The Secret

* To what can we reasonably attribute the loss of the democracy
and of liberty in France, if it be not to the diversity of views, to

Directory, however, judged differently of it.   Not that
it distrusted the soundness of the motives alleged in
favour of the dictatorship, but the difficulty of making
a good choice—the fear of abuse—the apparent resemblance of this magistracy to royalty—and, above all, the
general prejudice against it, which was thought insurmountable, induced it to prefer a body of individuals,
but not numerous, to whom might be entrusted the
same powers, without running the same hazards, and
without having so many obstacles to overcome.

A body consist-
ing of one De-
mocrat from
each Depart-
ment to be pro-
posed to the
people of Paris
in insurrection.

The result of this grave deliberation
was, that after the destruction of tyranny,
the people of Paris should be engaged to
create a National Assembly, clothed with
supreme power, and composed of a Democrat from each department;* and that,
meanwhile, the Secret Directory should
scrupulously search after, and scrutinize the Democrats
to be proposed; and, the Revolution achieved, that it
should continue its labours, and keep watch over the
conduct of the new assembly.

Whilst the conspirators were thus regulating the
major points, they did not neglect the minor ones. They
closely observed every disposition of the people, however
trifling in importance. They lost sight of no means for
ensuring victory on the day of insurrection, which might
possibly prove a day of combat also. In truth, they had
every reason to expect that the army would abandon
itself to the popular impulse; but it would, nevertheless,
be imprudent in the extreme not to take into account
the influence which its aristocratic officers might be able
to exercise over soldiers little informed, and habituated
to blind obedience.

the opposition of interests, to the want of virtue, of unity, and of
perseverance in the National Convention? In my opinion, it is
not in order to preserve, but to establish, equality amongst the
people of a corrupt state, that a strong and irresistible authority is
needed. It may be reasonably presumed, that if in the Year II.,
or the Year III., the French had the wisdom to invest a man of
Robespierre's stamp with a Dictatorship such as *Bedon* and Darthé
proposed, the Revolution would have attained its veritable end.

* The French Republic was then divided into 97 departments.

At the same time that it redoubled its efforts to draw over the soldiers of the Government to the cause of the people, the Secret Directory sought to render the Democrats more than a match for them, in the event of their coming to blows. Its *The Secret Directory considers on the means of rendering the people stronger than the army.* design was to suddenly create a popular army, and to this end it collected information touching the number, valour, and capacity of the Democrats—the forces of the enemy, and the places where the people might be able to provide themselves with arms and ammunition. It procured lodgings in Paris for the Republicans, whom it invited from all parts of France, to reinforce the friends of liberty, and carefully noted the depôts of subsistence (provision warehouses), in order that on the grand day of their redemption the people might not be constrained by hunger to abandon the field of battle, as had happened before, in Prairial of the Year III.

Amongst the patriots of the departments the Lyonese had most particularly fixed *Republicans of Lyons.* the attention of the Secret Directory. There were several of them in Paris that had merited the confidence of Robespierre, and those that remained at Lyons had exhibited such a character that the Directory was warranted in expecting the best services at their hands.

On the 20th Germinal of the Year IV., a violent agitation manifested itself *Great fermentation in Paris.* amongst the people of Paris, of which the criminal factions laboured to take advantage, concurrently with the Democrats.

From that period there existed two principal factions in the Government. The men who, under the banners of *Two factions in the Government.* equality, had craftily got possession of riches and power, and whom I have named "*false friends of equality*," or "*upstart Egoists*," formed that which acknowledged for its chiefs Barras, Tallien, Legendre, Fréron, Merlin de Thionville, Rewbell, &c. &c. The other was composed of the friends of the old Order of Inequality, whom I have comprised under the denomination of "*Conservative Egoists*" or *old Aristocrats*. This latter rallied the remnant of the Gironde, the authors of the new Constitution, and even the Royalists, who promised themselves some advantages from the character which this faction was impressing on opinion, and generally from whatever tended to proscribe equality.   It counted in its ranks Boissy d'Anglas, Larivière, Thibaudeau, Dumolard, Camille Jordan, Lareveillère, Lépeaux, Lanjuinais, Portalis, Pastoret, Siméon, &c. &c.

The first of these factions valued the new Constitution only in proportion as it might maintain them in preeminence; the second anticipated fresh successes from its scrupulous execution.   The former, less numerous, but more enterprising and bold, meditated acts of violence against the latter, whom it accused of aiming at the reestablishment of the throne, and who in their turn (being numerically stronger, but more hypocritical and dastardly) proposed to overwhelm their adversaries by constitutional arms.   It is the character of every aristocracy to repel, at the same time, equality and every other aristocracy whose competition it fears.   All pretexts are good in its eyes for crushing its rivals.   Again, there being nothing which more effectually ruins public men in the estimation of the vulgar than dissoluteness and rapacity, the old Aristocrats exerted themselves to excite by reproaches of this nature, against the friends of equality, true and false, the indignation of the people, which the latter (the false ones) had but too well merited.

The false friends of equality wish to expel the old Aristocrats from authority.   To attacks of this kind the upstart Egoists opposed the mass of persons who had taken any share in the Revolution. They had the dexterity to represent, indiscriminately, all who censured their crimes as so many enemies of the Republic.   They alarmed the Republicans of all shades with the fear of returning royalty; they pretended that the people should waive all considerations of abstract rights, in order to give their whole thoughts to the plots of the Royalists, whose audacity they boasted that themselves alone could repress.   In a word, they set every agency at work to constitute themselves the centre of the popular movement, of which they did not dissemble the approach. According to the tactics of this faction, the insurrection (the direction of which they counted upon seizing to their own profit) was to have no other object than that of driving from the legislative body, and from the Government, the men that offended them, such as Bossy d'Anglas, Isnard, Cadroy, Rovère, Larivière, &c. &c.*

To this end they made the vicinity of the legislative sittings resound with violent declamations against the massacres recently perpetrated in the South of France, the instigation of which they charged *They tried to rally around them the patriots and the people.* upon the opposite party, but of which, however, they had been themselves for a long time the provokers. Hypocritical apostates spread themselves over the public places, to exaggerate the number and criminal designs of the Royalist conspirators, to seduce the people's attention from the crimes of the false friends of equality, and to reinstate the latter in its lost confidence.

Thus the less sagacious Republicans were exposed to incertitude between the seductions of the perjured Revolutionists, and the counsels of the true Democrats.

From this double impulse arose very dangerous obstacles to the labours of the Secret Directory, which immediately felt the necessity of putting a stop to them in some way.

In the force of truth it was, that the Directory once more sought a remedy. It unmasked the wily snare, and the trick was baffled. A number of the *The Secret Directory baffles the deceitful project.*

* By these *traits* it is easy to recognize the faction which triumphed, and that which gave way, on the 18th Fructidor of the Year V. The events of that day were retarded by the inflexibleness of the Republicans, who, wishing to give neither of the factions a triumph, forced them to combine their efforts against Democracy, their common enemy.

[The same would happen in England if there were a popular conspiracy of sufficient magnitude and means to seriously endanger the Government. The O'Connells, Humes, and other sham-Radicals of the country, would seek to put themselves at its head, in order to forward their own ambitious views at the expence of both the parties rising and the parties risen against; but, if they found the insurgents too wise to be gammoned by their palaver, they would then join the Royalists again, or the devil, if necessary, to prevent the real Radicals from succeeding.—BRONTERRE.]

" *Tribune of the People,*" * devoted to the exposure of the crimes of the apostates from the popular party, disconcerted their enemies; and it might be asserted with truth, that amongst the men who had *bona fide* taken any part whatever in the Revolution, there did not remain with them a single partizan; there was breathed but one wish amongst all—it was the speedy destruction of the tyranny established by the Constitution of the Year III.

Committee of the proscribed Conventional-ists.
At the same time the Directory got intimation that *Allinoget, Eudochoi,* Amar, Huguet, and Javogues,† all ex-Mountainists of the Convention, proscribed in the months Germinal and Prairial of the Year III., were concerting measures for putting themselves at the head of the insurrection, which they foresaw, with a view to re-establish the National Convention, and afterwards the Constitution of 1793. These attempts, with which rumour erroneously associated the names of Barrère and Vadier, appeared so important to the Directory, that it deemed them necessary to make them the subject of a serious discussion.

The Secret Directory renders their efforts vain.
Ought the conspirators to give place to the proscribed Mountainists? Ought they to endeavour to form a junction with them? Ought they to oppose their ambitious aims? Such were the questions agitated on this head in the bosom of the Directory.

To the motives which had made it reject the proposition for recalling the Convention, was added, for repelling the Mountain Committee, the well-known anti-democratic views of some of its members, and the extreme weakness of others. But as they had formerly rendered many acknowledged services to the Republic, the Directory was content with recommending the revolutionary agents to engage the people to distrust any movements that might be made at the instigation of the Mountainists. The agents were at the same time en-

---

* See justificatory pieces.
† Huguet and Javogues were assassinated by the Military Commission of the Temple, in consequence of the massacre at the Camp of Grenelle.

joined to watch over their safety, and to prevent the measures which the Government was adopting against them, and of which the Secret Directory received information every day, through some principal agents of the Minister of Police.

The rapidity with which democratic principles were propagated anew; the boldness of the writings which urged the people to a new and salutary Revolution; those numerous assemblies, at which the crimes of the usurpers were proclaimed, and the Constitution of 1793 was imperiously demanded; this concert of wills, inspired as it were with one soul, and revealing a vast plan, the directing hands of which it was difficult to seize; the impatience of the multitude, and the determined boldness of the conspirators;—these circumstances combined, spread terror in the ranks of the enemies of equality, who felt the necessity of suspending their quarrels, and directing all their forces against the incorrigible apostles of the popular doctrines.

The false friends of equality reunite themselves to the old Aristocrats against the Democrats.

In the mean time, a message from the Executive Directory (the Government) came to rouse to action all the enemies of public reform; the Democrats were horribly calumniated in it, and decrees of proscription and death invoked against them. On this occasion, the old hypocrisy, by which it was sought to justify the violent breaking up of the Society of the Panthéon, launched its poisoned arrows with more malignity than ever. The Government, wishing to render the Democrats universally odious, accused them of seeking to plunge the state into a frightful anarchy, in the double design of using it as a means to re-establish royal despotism, and of enriching themselves in the interim by brigandism.*

Message of the Executive Directory against the Democrats.

---

* It is with the same sort of good faith that parties pretended to attribute to Royalism, and to the foreign enemy, the conception of all the great measures by which Royalism was crushed and the foreign enemy vanquished, and that they pretended to treat as disguised Royalists the men whose austerity and disinterestedness attested their sublime devotion to the cause of equality and liberty. This manœuvre, of which the Girondists set the first example, for the purpose of justifying their conduct at the King's trial, and

By the like imputations it was that the Post-Thermidorian Convention had succeeded in imposing upon
France the yoke of the new aristocracy. Nevertheless,
was there common sense in accusing of venality men who
had emerged in a state of poverty from a Revolution,
and from appointments which offered them so many opportunities of enriching themselves?* Did it belong to
those who, after the 9th Thermidor, had practised so
much violence, to stigmatise as anarchists men, the utmost
stretch of whose demands went no farther than the execution of the law which the French people had sanctioned?
The real, the only anarchy, said the Democrats, is in
the pretended laws which, violating the natural rights of
men, condemn nations either to interminable convulsions
or to the lethargy of death. Their uniform conduct, and
the vows they incessantly offered up for the establishment
of a true Republic, were a sufficient answer to the libellous
reproach of disguised royalism which nobody credited.
The Royalists applauded this cheat, which relieved them
from their most formidable enemies, and made them even
conceive the vain hope of attaching them (the Democrats)
to themselves, as auxiliaries against the Directorial
Government.

Solid as were these reasons, they did not confound the
effrontery of the Executive Directory: indebted for its

their hatred of the true founders of the Republic, has been since
brought to perfection by those eunuchs in politics, who, incapable
of those generous movements which save and regenerate nations,
revenge themselves, for the nullity to which they are condemned,
by detracting from the great men whose virtues appear chimerical
to them, through the means of base intrigues, which constitute
their whole stock of political science. To hear these wretches,
you would suppose that the revolutionary action was conceived
and directed by the principal persons who were attainted by it—
that the brothers of Louis XVI. had solicited his condemnation—
that the Royalists who lost their lives on the 2d and 3rd of September were immolated to the profound policy of their friends—
and that the popular enthusiasm which saved France from invasion was the work of those who sought to invade her!!!
Numerous plots were, no doubt, hatched by the European aristocracy against the French Revolution; but to pretend to discover
the traces of them, in what was most ruinous to that aristocracy,
does appear to me the perfection of absurdity.

* Buonarroti was one of these; and, judging by all that is on
record concerning him as a placeman, no human being could be
better entitled to put the question.—Bronterre.]

power to its violation of the people's rights, it thought now only of extinguishing them, and this odious determination extinguished in it all sense of shame. It believed, that by persevering in calumny it would succeed in stifling truth, and flattered itself with being able to rally around itself all classes of citizens, by the frightful colours under which it incessantly painted its enemies.

Nevertheless, this perfidious message revealed one truth which turned many a villain pale. It attested the existence of a courageous association determined upon overthrowing the new constitutional tyranny.

Such was, then, the corruption and baseness of the Deputies, that there was not even one man amongst them that dared openly to defend the rights of the people; with the exception of twelve members, the whole of the Council of Five Hundred accepted with eager haste the disastrous laws of the 27th and 28th Germinal of the Year IV., to which their worthy colleagues of the other Council gave their unanimous sanction on the same day !

Laws contrary to the liberty of speech and of the Press.

These acts, unworthy to bear the name of laws, were a criminal invasion of the liberties of the public. Under their authority any peaceable meeting of the citizens might be dispersed by force as a seditious mob. By these acts, all discussions upon the advantages or inconveniences of different forms of government were made punishable with death. They, moreover, rendered all ameliorations in the constitution of the State next to impossible ; in a word, they tore from the French people—already despoiled of the rights of deliberating on the laws, and of associating in public societies—that of freely expressing their thoughts on national affairs !

From that moment the subaltern agents of tyranny redoubled their audacity against the speakers, writers, and news-agents of the democratic party. The least observations, the slightest murmurs, were distorted into seditious provocations, and furnished pretexts every hour for imprisoning the best citizens ; nay, the array of military force was displayed against peaceable men who frequented the public places, in order to seek in the outpourings of

New persecutions against the Democrats.

friendship some consolations for the grief they felt at witnessing the degradation and misfortune of their country.

Indignation of the friends of liberty.

A sacred rage took possession of all the sincere friends of equality, and impelled them to take the resolution of resisting oppression; they declared aloud that the moment was come for fulfilling the oath—TO LIVE FREE OR DIE!

The Secret Directory calms their impatience.

But the Directory of Public Safety, which had placed itself at the point whence it could measure the forces of its party with those of the enemy, judged that it was not yet time to give battle. Fearing one of those ill-concerted out-breaks, which had contributed so much to establish the Aristocrats' empire, and regarding its enterprise as a last effort, whose bad success would have altogether destroyed the democracy, it could not resolve upon giving the signal of attack, without having prudently co-arranged all the insurrectional elements which appeared to it indispensable for victory.

Although the names of the Secret Directors had a salutary veil thrown around them, their association and their labours were known to all the Democrats. This knowledge, by sustaining their hopes, rendered them docile to the advice addressed to them through the channel of the revolutionary agents, or through that of the " *Tribune of the People*," and of the " *Enlightener*." So long a series of reverses had at length convinced every body that the veritable Republic could not attain its destination of safety unless by the concurrence of all its friends in seconding with confidence the plans conceived, and secretly directed, by a small knot of individuals, who had been resolute enough not to despair of a cause so many times proscribed, and almost annihilated. By the aid of this confidence was the Secret Directory enabled to arrest the premature explosion provoked by the laws of the 27th and 28th Germinal—laws which even the most moderate, compared to the ancient Martial Law. But whilst with one hand it restrained a dangerous outbreak, it hastened with the other to unite together all the threads which were to conduct it to a speedy dénouement and a sure triumph. The slowness that would have encouraged its enemies, divided and damped its friends, appeared to it no less dangerous than an imprudent precipitation. Decided upon promptly saving liberty or perishing with it, it quickened the operations of the revolutionary agents, redoubled its zeal to draw over the army, of which it was not yet sure, and assiduously exerted itself in regulating the forms of the insurrection, and the legislation which was to follow it.

The first object that naturally presented itself for discussion was the manner of effecting the dissolution of the existing illegitimate Authorities, and of disabling the members of them from enterprising any measures against equality. The unanimous design of the Secret Directory was to attain this double end by a great example of justice, capable of terrifying the traitors, and of inspiring with the same salutary dread all future deputies whom the people might honour with its confidence. Revolting treason, and a manifest usurpation, were the crimes of which the members of the two Councils, and those of the Executive Directory, had palpably rendered themselves guilty. Covered with the blood of the best citizens, they had robbed the people of its sovereignty, and had sacrificed the majority of the nation to the criminal pretensions of a handful of insatiable and ambitious rich men. A signal punishment was necessary; but indulgence and oblivion would have succeeded to a day of just and salutary terror, which would have left behind it only the remembrance of a legitimate and too tardy retribution.

Some of the insurrectional measures.

The majority of the Parisians, discontented, uneasy, unhappy, were looking back on the past, and regretted the times which had preceded the 9th Thermidor; they had need, in order to overthrow the tyrants, to be led on by intrepid Republicans, who were themselves awaiting the signal of our conspirators. In this condition of affairs the latter saw that the important point was to withdraw the bulk of the working classes from the influence of the established Government, and to place them exclusively under that of the Democrats; they resolved, accordingly, that on the day of insurrection all the relations existing between the Government and the citizens should be broken—that the people should range themselves under the banners to be delivered by the Secret Directory to persons of its choice—and that to give or execute in the name of the existing tyranny any order whatever, should be on that day a national crime, to be punished with instant death.

Insurrectional   To infuse order into the grand move-
Act.   ment which was preparing, the Secret Directory judged it necessary to declare itself openly at the head of it, and in this capacity to indicate to the people the demands that. they should make, the route they should follow, the obstacles they would have to overcome, and the snares that it would behove them to baffle and defeat.   To this end, after a long and serious deliberation, it adopted the famous *Insurrectional Act*, the publication of which was to have been the signal of the new Revolution.*

Besides, the dispositions having direct reference to the destruction of tyranny, this Act contained the forms of several legislative measures, designed to justify, in the eyes of the people, the benevolent intentions of the Secret Directory, and the legitimacy of its enterprize. Here they are :—

1. A distribution, amongst the defenders of the country and the unhappy poor, of the properties of emigrants, of conspirators, and of the enemies of the people.

2. The unhappy poor to be forthwith lodged in the houses of the conspirators.

3. The gratuitous restitution of the effects of the people pledged at the *Mont-de-Piété* (Government Pawn-offices).

4. The adoption by the people of the wives, children, fathers, mothers, brothers, and sisters, of the citizens that might fall in the insurrection, and abundant provision for them during life.

The distribu-   It would be wrong to consider the pro-
tion of goods   mise of a grand distribution of goods as
ordained by the
Insurrectional   contrary to the spirit of the community at
Act tended to   which it was sought to arrive.   The grand
bring about the   point was to succeed, and the Secret
community of
property.   Directory, which did not adopt its Insur-

* See justificatory pieces.

rectional Act without due deliberation, had felt that to gain that end it should neither practice too much reserve, which might possibly discourage its true friends, nor too much precipitation, which would only swell the number of its enemies. By the promise of distribution the Directory fixed the attention and sustained the hopes of the labouring class, without indisposing those who, whilst they hated the upstart aristocracy, did not, for all that, love equality in fact. To distribute goods did not signify to parcel out the landed property, for wealth consists not in lands but in the fruits they yield; moreover, by distributing the fruits, its promise would have been completely fulfilled; and that was what the Secret Directory proposed to do, after the manner we are going to see.

Immediately after the destruction of tyranny the people of Paris was to meet in general assembly in the Place de la Revolution.* There the Secret Directory would have rendered it an account of its conduct—would have demonstrated to it that all the evils the people complained of were the effects of inequality —would have reminded it of the advantages it was justified in expecting from the Constitution of 1793— and would have invited it to approve of the Act of Insurrection. Afterwards it would have been proposed to the insurgent people to create on the spot a Provisional Authority, charged to terminate the Revolution, and to govern the country up to the moment of putting the popular institutions in activity. *{Assembly of the people of Paris after the destruction of tyranny.}*

In order to obtain from the victorious people a decree conformable to its true interests, the Directory reckoned upon submitting to its suffrages the names of the Democrats it judged most worthy of such high confidence. This new Assembly should have come to contract, in the face of heaven, an engagement to devote itself for the safety of all, and to swear to execute faithfully the orders which it was proposed to prescribe to it by the following decree. *{New National Assembly.}*

" The people of Paris, after having " overthrown tyranny, using the rights *{Decree to be proposed to the}*

* Now called the Place Louis XV.

insurgents of
Paris. " which it has received from nature ac-
" knowledges and declares to the French
" People,—
" That the unequal distribution of goods and of labour
" is the inexhaustible source of slavery and of all public
" calamities.

" That labour is for every one an essential condition
" of the social compact.

" That the proprietorship of all the riches of France re-
" sides essentially in the French people, which can alone
" determine and change the repartition of them.

" Orders the National Assembly which it has just
" created, and in the name of the French people, to
" ameliorate the Constitution of 1793, to prepare the
" prompt execution of it, and to guarantee to the French
" Republic, by wise institutions founded upon the above
" acknowledged truths, an unalterable equality, liberty,
" and happiness.

" Enjoins on the said Assembly to render account, in
" a year at most, to the Nation, of the execution of the
" present decree.

" And, finally, engages itself to enforce respect to the
" decrees of this assembly, if conformable to the above
" orders, and to punish with the penalty due to traitors,
" whosoever of its members shall abandon the duties it
" has just prescribed to them."

We shall see, farther on, by what laws the Secret Directory proposed to itself to fix the destiny of the Republic,
but first let us follow in its developments the march of
the conspiracy, of which it is important to make known
the details.

Insurrection of
the Legion of
Police. Whilst our Directory was silently maturing every part of its great enterprise,
the effects of its inspirations began to be
manifested in the armed bodies stationed at Paris and in
the environs, and particularly in the Legion of Police,
and amongst the grenadiers charged with the guard of
the legislative body.

Nothing alarmed the Government so much as this
spirit of opposition, of which the military had already let
appear numerous symptoms. In that quarter was
vanishing, as it thought, the only rampart which it

flattered itself with being able to oppose to the rage of the people. Thus, after having exhausted every seduction amongst the Legion of Police, it was forced to order away from Paris the two most insubordinate battalions of that body, which, by the law that instituted it, ought never to be engaged in service out of the city. This order, signified on the 9th Floréal, was followed by a formal disobedience, of which the immediate consequence was an increase of agitation amongst the people; indeed, the moment was supposed to be at hand when the existing tyranny might be disposed of on the cheapest terms.

The Secret Directory, which, without having directly provoked the resistance of the legionaries, had nevertheless contributed to elicit it by the maxims it was incessantly promulgating, was also of opinion that the moment of success was near, and although it had not yet in its power all the information it demanded, it would have determined on giving the signal of insurrection, if it had had the certainty of finding in the Legion of Police a sufficient force to repel the first efforts of the Government, and to augment thereby the confidence of the people.

Every engine was set at work to constitute this point of support into a centre of movement, and for a moment the hope was entertained of rendering the insurrection general in the Army of the Interior.* Revolutionary agents were scattered amongst the troops—others held themselves ready to make the people march; a committee promptly formed in the bosom of the Legion of Police, was already in communication with the Secret Directory, through the intermission of Germain; a Manifesto of the Legion to the People, and the reply of the latter,† drawn up in its name by the conspirators, informed all honest citizens of the task they had to accomplish; the Democrars were under arms—everything was about to totter—when the unexpected submission of the insurgent battalions compelled a suspension of the move-

---

* By this name was the army called which, since the 9th Thermidor, was encamped around Paris, to keep the friends of liberty in awe.

† See justificatory pieces.

ment, from an apprehension of drawing irretrievable ruin
on the country.

Its disband-   A decree of disbandment smothered the
ment.   insurrection in its cradle. A considerable
number of the legionaries submitted to it with joy, and
there was but too much reason to believe, that a few
of the dangers to be encountered on the frontiers had
been with many of them the true motives of their resistance, which the republican soldiers had too lightly
attributed to a generous patriotism.

The legionaries   Whatever may have been the probably
become refu-   unknown causes of this insubordination,
gees in the
houses of the   the Democrats derived from it the advan-
patriots.   tage of having at their disposition, by
harbouring them at their dwelling houses, not only the
well-meaning legionaries, but also almost all who proved
refractory to the orders of Government. From this
numerous desertion, was formed the body which the
Secret Directory, counted upon placing in the van-
guard of the insurrectional army. This tumultuous
event redoubled the impatience of the people, whose
impetuosity, every hour increasing, warned the Secret
Directory that the dénouement of the conspiracy
could not any longer be deferred without extreme
danger. Partial movements, fruitless no doubt, were
about to burst forth; and, moreover, the loss of certain legionaries, arrested for having incited their comrades to resistance, seemed inevitable. It was of necessity to prevent false steps, and to break the axe of
authority; these circumstances engaged the Secret
Directory to hasten the movement of the insurrection.
It was then about the 10th of Floréal.

Two things appeared indispensable to our conspirators.
Prudence, without which all success is impossible; and
boldness, which disperses obstacles that none can foresee:
while they took the former for their guide, they made a
constant duty of the latter. Wishing to hasten the
catastrophe—reckoning, in order to put the Parisians in
motion, upon the energy of the Democrats—informed of
the public impatience—sufficiently assured of the friendly
spirit of the troops—and masters of the legionary de-
serters, they bethought themselves of giving the most

suitable dispositions to their forces; and it was to effect this that they judged it necessary to surround themselves with citizens, who united in themselves the love of democracy and experience in military operations. Fion, Germain, Rossignol, Massart, and Grisel, all of them officers or generals, were invited to the presence of the Secret Directory in the afternoon of the 11th Floréal. Grisel was admitted to it on account of the influence it was thought he could exercise upon the camp at Grenelle.

At this assembly were present, Babeuf, Buonarroti, *Bedon*, Darthé, Marechal, *Eriddy*, and the five above-named military officers.* The Secret Directory be-
Politico-mili-
tary sitting of
the 11th Floréal
of the Year IV.
gan by informing these latter of the final object of its labours—the point it had arrived at—and the road which remained to be travelled over. Afterwards it acquainted them with the insurrectional act, of which they approved; and ended by inviting them to deliberate with it on the means to be taken to ensure the triumph of the people.

It was decided that the Secret Directory, while it reserved to itself the conception of every necessary measure, and the supreme direction of the movement, should confide to a military committee the care of preparing the attack and defence, after furnishing it with the necessary instructions and plans relating thereto. The five military gentlemen already mentioned were named members of this new committee, whose first sitting was fixed for the following day, at the house of *Eris*, in the street Montblanc.

In the general assembly already spoken of, Germain had shown himself an ardent Democrat, Massart did not belie the character he had manifested at Amar's house, Grisel played the part of a Republican to perfection, Fion and Rossignol, while they applauded the views of the Secret Directory, only regretted that there were not in its body some of the ex-conventional Mountainists.

In a few hours after this meeting the retreat of Babeuf and the sittings of the Secret Directory were transferred

---

* In convoking this meeting, the Secret Directory infringed the third article of the law which created it; and this fault, without which Grisel could not have known the chiefs of the conspiracy, was the principal cause of the ruin of their projects.

to the faubourg Montmartre, in the house of *Ourecle*, where also the editor of the *Eclaireur du Peuple* was in concealment, who, already acquainted with a part of the conspiracy, had some share in the labours it gave birth to.

Military Committee. Germain was the sole organ through whom the new committee communicated with the Secret Directory. This committee, which a few days after transferred its sittings from the house of *Eris* to that of *Crexel*, near the corn-market, took diligent cognizance of the business confided to it, and submitted on the 15th to the aforesaid Directory the result of its examination.

It is proposed to make the Royalists concur in the enterprise of the Democrats. Amongst the numerous propositions which the conspirators received from all quarters, there were two that attracted particular attention. By the one they were recommended to induce by adroit means, for the overthrow of the Government, the concurrence of the Royalists, who were also its enemies, and whose hopes they should afterwards frustrate by announcing the veritable end of the insurrection. This proposition was rejected, because it was adjudged very dangerous to begin by putting arms into the hands of persons whom it would be soon necessary to combat and because it was felt that their bare presence amongst the ranks of the insurgents would be sufficient to discourage the Republicans, and to destroy in them the confidence they might otherwise accord to the measures of the Secret Directory.[*]

An offer is made to poignard the Executive Directory. By the second, two officers of the Legion of Police[†] offered to poignard, in the same night, the Members of the Executive Directory, about whose persons one of them was on guard with a detachment of patriotic soldiers; their demand was that they might be supported by a body of Democrats, and that the insurrection should be thus commenced:—To facilitate the execution of their project they communicated the word of order. This proposition was also rejected, from the motive that nothing ought to be attempted until the moment when the simultaneous concurrence of all the

---

[*] See justificatory pieces. [†] Peche and Steve.

pre-disposed measures would render victory almost certain. In truth, grand dispositions were being made— the new legislative edifice was making progress every day—the active patriots were ascertained and classified —the Insurrectional Act, and the standards around which they were to rally, were marked out and distributed to the agents—public impatience was at its height.

But, besides that the Military Commission had not as yet declared itself upon the means to be employed to operate every where simultaneously the grand commotion of the people, the Secret Directory was still unprovided with money, of which it had need to subsist certain parties very useful to it, but bereft of fortune, and it had not been able to provide the powder necessary to ammunition the insurgents.

Want of money was, perhaps, the most characteristic feature of our conspiracy. The love of money was judged criminal *The conspirators despised money.* by the conspirators, and the Secret Directory never sought to procure from the contributions of the conspirators anything beyond what was necessary for the printing of its papers, and the support of a few indigent Democrats it employed. Nevertheless, means of this kind were indispensable, either to buy over certain agents of tyranny, or to furnish the Democrats with occasions to flatter and undeceive the deluded soldiery. Some steps were taken to obtain a little, but the largest amount at the disposal of the Secret Directory was two hundred and forty francs in specie, transmitted by the Minister of an allied Republic—it was seized by the agents of the police, who introduced themselves on the 21st Floréal, into the place where the conspirators were assembled.

How difficult it is to do good by such means only as reason approves! How much it costs an austere Republican to relax the duties which reason imposes, and to employ men by whom these duties are disregarded, unless he would see his endeavours frustrated, and become the witness of fresh miseries! Such was the painful situation in which the members of the Secret Directory found themselves placed since the creation of the Military Committee.

Rossignol and Fion solicit the co-operation of the Mountainists with the Secret Directory.

Germain was not slow in perceiving that Rossignol and Fion did not frankly adopt the system of the Secret Directory. Strongly attached to the Mountainist Deputies, they saw with dissatisfaction that the latter did not form a part of it; very soon they became so possessed of this desire as to afford grounds for suspecting their devotion to the cause in the event of its not being complied with. The Mountainists in question were the Conventionalists proscribed after the 9th Thermidor, whom we have seen assembled in Committee, with a view to the re-establishment of the Constitution of 1793, and whose ambitious endeavours the Secret Directory had judged it necessary to obstruct and fetter. According to Fion and Rossignol's opinion, the motives which had caused the secession of these Mountainists were of no weight; their private affections weighed more with them than political considerations, and they appeared convinced that the presence of these old legislators would produce a magic effect—would efface the conflicting shades of Republican opinion— would propagate the insurrection rapidly, and overcome all resistance in the departments. A great many citizens participated in this opinion, and even had Fion and Rossignol been without imitators, the advances that had been made to them, and the services that were expected from them, especially by reason of Rossignol's influence over the inhabitants of the faubourg Antoine, were sufficient to induce the Secret Directory to take their advice into consideration.

The Mountainists aim at seizing the leadership of the insurrection.

Meanwhile, it was reported to our Directory that the Mountainist Committee, to which Robert Lindet had just joined himself, so far from having lost sight of the object for which it was formed, calculated upon its accomplishment through the assistance of the movement prepared by the Democrats, of which it hoped to assume the leadership, by making its members appear in the midst of the insurrection, and exhibit themselves to the people as their only representatives.

On the other hand, Drouet, celebrated *Drouet is linked* for his devotion and courage, was ac- *with the con-* quainted with Babeuf's projects—was *spirators.* intimately connected with Darthé—and desired likewise a revolution favourable to equality; the Secret Directory accordingly reckoned on using his popularity as a lever of the insurrection. But Drouet was no stranger to the doings of the Mountainists, his old colleagues, and he appeared to incline in favour of blending the two conspiracies into one.

At last Germain came to complete the *Incertitude of* perplexity of the Directory; he manifested *the Secret Di-* intense anxiety respecting the intentions *rectory.* of Fion and Rossignol, and seemed alarmed at the obstacles about to be raised up by the ambition of the Mountainists, whose designs had just been confided to him by Ricord and by *Allinoget,* who had, at the same time, proposed to him a coalition with the Secret Directory in formal terms; he had no doubt as to there being a mutual understanding between them and the two before-mentioned members of the Military Commission.

Bedon, who had always taken an active part in the labours of the Secret Directory, could not listen unmoved to the proposal of a coalition with the Mountainists, whom he reproached with the calamities which oppressed France. "Will you sully," he exclaimed, "your noble " enterprise, by inviting to the glory of saving liberty the " parties who, through ambition or vanity, or jealousy " or ignorance, have been its ruin? Are there not " amongst them the very men who, by assassinating on " the 9th Thermidor the most resolute and firmest sup- " porters of the country, restored to the aristocracy the " power it had lost, and resuscitated the almost extinct " hopes of the Royalists? Can you forget that they " were the first to sharpen the poignards of the counter- " revolutionists against the friends of equality? Beware " how you give them the least influence; they will only " make use of it to deceive and divide the Republicans. " Would you speak respectfully of Robespierre and his " companions in martyrdom? These Mountainists will " lavish upon you the epithets ' *exclusives,*' ' *drinkers* " *of blood,*' ' *dictatorials,*' and ' *satellites of tyranny !*'

" Would you render homage to virtue, to morality, to
" the divinity? They will stigmatize you as *fanatics,*
" *moderates, sophists!* Would you give wise counsels
" to the people? They will pretend that they are the
" sole depositaries of the power to foresee all, to direct
" all! With them you will experience nothing but coun-
" teraction and discord. It will be told you, that they
" were only deluded on the 9th Thermidor; in my opi-
" nion they will never agree to that. I am willing that
" they should be pardoned—that their faults should be
" forgotten; but, at the same time, let them be reduced
" to eternal silence. And why? Because it is impos-
" sible to march with them in the ways of truth and
" justice."

The impossibility of inducing these Mountainists to
concur in any way for the re-establishment of the public
welfare, appeared so evident to Bedon, that he inclined
to believe a complete inaction would be preferable to
the proposed coalition. This idea of renouncing the
conspiracy was displeasing to the Secret Directory; and
so exasperated was one of its members at it, that he so
far forgot himself as to accuse Bedon of pusillanimity.
The altercation that ensued was, however, soon ap-
peased; but the impression produced by it entered deep
into the minds of the conspirators. They felt more
strongly than ever how much prudence was required to
prevent the best Democrats from being sacrificed without
any advantage to the people, upon whom a failure would
only draw down increased oppression.

It was not dissembled that the result of a coalition
with the Mountainists would be a state of things less
favourable to the reforms sought; but their daring boldness, and, above all, the opinions of Fion and Rossignol
seemed to be obstacles capable of clogging every wheel
of the conspiracy. The faults of the Mountainists, and
the frightful evils that had resulted from them, incessantly occurred to the friends of the conspirators, and it
was a point confessed, that from the free determinations of
these ex-Conventionalists, no such thing could be expected as the establishment—so much wished for—of an
impregnable, indefeasible equality.

To persist in the conspiracy, whilst at the same time

renouncing this equality, would have been only to avow themselves inconsequential and ambitious; to burst the threads of the conspiracy at the moment when every thing betokened a speedy success, would have been to render themselves criminal in the eyes of the patriots, and of posterity; it was necessary then to persevere in the first resolves, and elicit from circumstances the course most favourable to the popular cause.

After a long and animated discussion, the Secret Directory adopted the proposed coalition, and resolved at the same time to take great precautions to restrain the ambition of the Mountainists, and to compel them to concur in the execution of its designs. *It resolves to coalesce with the Mountainists.*

After the explications that had been given, the conspirators, by adopting the coalition, would be pledged to re-establish the National Convention—that is to say, the section of that body which Amar regarded as the only one legitimate, and still existing by right; if that were done without any modification, France would be at the mercy of those against whom such heavy reproaches lay. To avoid so great a misfortune, the Secret Directory decided that the recal of the Convention should take place only on condition that the Mountainists would consent to the following preliminaries :—

1. To superadd to the National Convention, composed exclusively of the proscribed Deputies, a Democrat from each department, to be named by the insurgent people upon the presentation of the Secret Directory. *Conditions of the coalition.*

2. To cause to be executed without restriction, and on the spot, the provision of Article 18 of the Act of Insurrection.

3. Unqualified submission to the decrees which might be passed by the people of Paris on the day of the insurrection.

As soon as this resolution was taken, Germain was authorised to conduct on the following day a member of the Mountainist Committee to the Secret Directory, which immediately transferred itself to the house of Tissot, in the street Grande Truanderie, where it had formerly held some of its sittings.

A messenger from the Mountainist Committee is presented to the Secret Directory.

On the morning of the 15th Floreal, Germain conducted to the Secret Directory, Ricord, a messenger from the Mountainist Committee. He was received by an address* in which he was informed of the state of affairs—of the motives which had caused the rejection of all thoughts of a coalition with his brethren of the Committee—and of those subsequent ones, in conformity with which that coalition was at length agreed to. The Act of Insurrection was read to the Mountainist Deputy, and a discussion forthwith raised as to the changes to be made in the article concerning the Provisional Authority, which it was indispensable to create. It was spontaneously agreed that the proscribed members of the National Convention should be recalled to the supreme power; but the messenger was, at the same time, given to understand, that all negociation would be broken off, unless the Mountainists would give irrefragable guarantees of their popular intentions. They spoke to him without reservation or ambiguity, and declared to him that they had little confidence in his colleagues of the Committee, against whom very serious objections were urged.

It was impossible for Ricord to justify the whole of his colleagues; amongst them, to use his own words, there were some that did not merit the people's censure. The three aforesaid conditions were explained to him, to which was unanimously added—

The suspension of all laws and decrees passed since the 9th Thermidor of the Year II.

The expulsion of all the restored emigrants.

Refusal of the Mountainists.

Ricord consented to all on condition of receiving the ratification of his colleagues. The following day he came to announce their refusal. According to the ideas of the Mountainist Committee, the immediate and only effect of the insurrection ought to be the re-installation of about sixty proscribed Conventionalists, in whom an unqualified and blind reliance should be placed, as regarded all consecutive measures. The adjunction of a Democrat for each department was

* See justificatory pieces.

repelled by the Mountainists as a criminal invasion of the national sovereignty, of which they pretended themselves the sole depositaries; the orders which the Directory desired to have prescribed to them by the insurgents, were, in their estimation, but so many encroachments on the rights of the French people, whom it belonged to them alone to represent; they had no objection to putting the people in possession of the lodgings and goods promised by the Act of Insurrection, but they would be understood to concede that point on political grounds only, not as though they were executing an order or acknowledging a right, but as performing a mere act of generosity; in fine, they offered the members of the Secret Directory to nominate them upon the Executive Council which they proposed to establish.*

The reader will doubtless be pleased to Reply of the Se-
know the answer which was returned to cret Directory.
the Mountainist messenger. Here it is. " In yielding
" our concurrence in the provisional re-establishment of
" a part of the Convention, we understand ourselves to
" serve only the people. The sole recompense we aspire
" to is the complete triumph of Equality. We will
" combat, and expose our lives, to restore to the people
" the plenitude of its rights, but we do not comprehend
" how persons can pretend generosity towards the mas-
" ters of every thing. If you sincerely desire to co-
" operate with us in the great enterprise which engages
" us, be cautious how you announce propositions and
" propose terms, which may cast suspicion on your in-
" tentions. Several of your colleagues have betrayed
" the interests of the people; and we should be infinitely
" more reprehensible than they, were we to abandon the
" country again to their passions or weaknesses. It is
" inconceivable how it should be necessary, in order to
" re-establish the sovereignty of the people, to employ
" the very instruments that caused its ruin. It is to

* [The palpable selfishness of these demands attests the true character of these ex-Conventionalists; and when it is considered that they constituted the most meritorious part of what was called the Mountain party in the Convention, we can be at no loss to comprehend the real motives and authors of the crimes of the 9th Thermidor.—BRONTERRE.]

" those from whom the nation expects the destruction of
" tyranny, that it necessarily delegates the right of
" adopting the provisionary measures indispensable. Our
" object is not to annihilate one oppressive Government
" in order to substitute a no less oppressive one in its
" room. It is good to pardon error; but it would be
" criminal as well as foolish to confide anew the destiny
" of the country to the parties by whose errors it has
" been ruined. Better perish by the hands of the pa-
" triots, who, indignant at our inactivity, will be war-
" ranted in accusing us of pusillanimity and treason,
" or by those of the Government, which will at length
" obtain cognizance of our projects, than to place the
" people again at the mercy of those who, on the 9th
" Thermidor, immolated its best friends, and who after-
" wards basely suffered the Republicans to be proscribed,
" and the democratic edifice to be demolished."

Upon retiring, Ricord promised to communicate to
the Secret Directory the definitive resolution of his
colleagues.

Alarms of the   Whilst this negociation was passing
patriots.   between the Secret Directory and the
Mountainist Committee, the patriots were being alarmed
and discouraged by sinister rumours; the principal conspirators were exposed to suspicions and calumny, and
the calm which had succeeded to so intense a fermentation was generally considered as the precursor of new
calamities. These fatal presentiments insensibly worked
upon the revolutionary agents, who had been recommended to restrain premature outbreaks, in order to get
time to arrange for simultaneous action; beginning to
be themselves disconcerted, they sent word to the Secret
Directory that any further delay would lose it the confidence of the men most decided to take the field.

In order to dissipate all fear, the Directory resolved to
discover frankly to its agents the position it found itself
in, and the obstacles which marred its progress;* but,
before the circulars intended for them had been transcribed, it was apprised that the Mountainists had just
agreed to and subscribed its propositions.

* See justificatory pieces.

In fact, Darthé reported, on the 18th Floréal, to the Secret Directory, that in a meeting, at which he was present, the Mountainist Committee had, after a

Coalition of the Secret Directory with the Mountainist Committee.

violent debate, consented to the adjunction of one Democrat for each department, to the engagements promised in favour of the unhappy poor, and to the execution of the decree, which it was purposed to demand from the people of Paris in insurrection. He related, at the same time, that the objections spoken of by Ricord had been triumphantly refuted by Amar, and particularly by Robert Lindet, who, after justifying the distrust of the Secret Directory, spoke largely on the necessity of impressing on the Revolution a character veritably popular, without which, as he observed, it is but a mere game of parties. This news was instantly communicated to the agents, and from that moment there was nothing thought of but to hasten the denouement of the conspiracy.

During the negociations which took place between the Mountainist Committee and the Secret Directory, the communications of the latter with the

Certain points relative to the insurrectional movement.

Military Committee were very frequent; they continued to be agreed upon the following points :—

That the insurrection should take place by day.

That generals acting under the orders of the Secret Directory should lead the people against its enemies.

That the insurgents should be divided by arrondissements, and subdivided by sections.

That the arrondissements should have chiefs, and the sections sub-chiefs.

That all allegiance to the existing authorities should be dissolved, and every act of such nature punished with instant death.

The better to understand one another,—in order to establish a perfect confidence amongst all the chief actors, and to secure harmony in all the measures to be taken, a general assembly of the Directory and the two committees, on the principle of the recently concluded coalition, was arranged for the evening of the 19th, at the house of Drouet, near the *Place des Piques.*

Treason of
Grisel.
By the side of so many generous defenders of the rights of humanity, there was one infamous hypocrite, who, in order to ruin the cause they were devoted to, had maliciously borrowed their principles and language. This monster was Georges Grisel.

Whether with a view to open a road to fortune for himself, of which his knowledge of the levelling projects of the conspirators would have precluded all hope, or whether with the immediate intent of serving tyranny, Grisel exerted himself to conciliate the confidence of the Democrats. After having engaged Darthé to communicate to him the instructions destined for the military agents, he spared no pains to confirm the favourable opinion conceived of him; admitted afterwards to a sitting of the Secret Directory, and named a member of the Military Committee, he showed himself the most outrageous and impatient Democrat amongst them; he wished, in fact, to know every thing, and aimed at nothing less than to disembarrass tyranny for ever of its enemies, by crushing all the friends of equality at a single blow. To this end, he disclosed to the Government all the thoughts and designs of the Democrats.*

He denounces
the conspirators
Having at length ascertained the principal conspirators, and a part of their plan, he denounced them on the 15th Floréal to the Government, to whom he engaged to deliver them up, together with the papers of the conspiracy. To this trait of perfidy Grisel subsequently added fresh ones every day; most assiduous in his attendence at the Military Committee, he pressed his confiding colleagues to make haste—he smoothed away difficulties—suggested measures—and never forgot to confirm their courage by painting in exaggerated colours the devotion of the Camp of Grenelle to the democratic cause. Agreeably to information given by Grisel, orders were dispatched by the Government to surprise the conspirators on the 18th, at a meeting which it was supposed would take place on that night at Ricord's house. The officers of Government repaired thither, but there was nobody to be found.

* See the letters written by Grisel to the Insurrectional Directory, amongst the explanatory documents or justificatory pieces.

New measures were forthwith taken to invest the house of Drouet on the following night, where the traitor knew that the conspirators were to assemble.

In fact, this meeting was held from half-past eight o'clock to a quarter before eleven.   The parties present were Babeuf, Buonarroti, Darthé, *Eriddy*, Fion, Massart, Rossignol, Robert-Lindet, Drouet, Ricord, *Allinoget*, and Jarogues. Grisel also repaired thither. Perfidious villain! he came to sell his generous associates to *tyranny*; and while in waiting for their executioners, he actually embraced them, applauded them, and lavished upon them pledges of the most implicit devotion without betraying a blush!

Assembly of the conspirators at Drouet's house.

The conspirators assembled at Drouet's house felt themselves in the most perfect security; the ardour of their sentiments, and the sacredness of their cause, banished all distrust—the assurance and verbosity of Grisel diverted all suspicion from that quarter.

The Secret Directory, through the mouth of one of its members, explained the motives which had determined it to constitute itself the centre of the efforts of the Democrats against the upstart tyranny. "Remember your oaths," said the orator to the conspirators—" call to mind the
" evils produced by the forgetfulness of the principles
" which you have sworn to seal with your blood. The
" moment is come for fulfilling your engagements. We
" must to battle. The triumph of the noblest of causes
" —the liberty of the French people—the confidence
" with which it honours you—the fury of its enemies and
" your own safety impose upon you the imperious duty.

Report of the Secret Directory.

" Never was conspiracy more legitimate—more holy.
" The question we have to decide is not a choice of
" masters. Not one of us aspires to fortune or power.
" Traitors oblige us to take arms, and it is for the exist-
" ence—for the liberty—for the happiness of our fellow-
" citizens, that an army of liberators, secretly organised
" by us, awaits but our signal to thunder down upon
" this handful of perfidious tyrants who oppress the
" people.

" Until we commenced operations everything was
" inert and despairing. After the fruitless victory of the

" 13th Vendemiaire aristocracy had no obstacle to en-
" counter. The greater number of Democrats, despairing
" of liberty, were upon the point of making their peace
" with odious oligarchs, who are gorged with the blood
" of your friends.

" At our call hope revived, and France put forth her
" energy once more ; and already, thanks to the inde-
" fatigable zeal of so many courageous Republicans, the
" people, burning with impatience, invokes aloud the
" signal for combat.

" All the good are known to us ; the wicked tremble.
" On the day that you will appoint for action, the arms
" of which tyranny has essayed in vain to despoil you,
" will be found in the hands of your brethren. You
" have willed that the Revolution we are preparing should
" be complete, and that the people should no longer
" have to content itself with a mere speculative liberty,
" and a mockery of equality. Equality real and legal
" —behold the grand character which is to distinguish
" your sublime enterprise from all others that have pre-
" ceded it.

" All difficulties are vanquished. The love of country
" has united us all. The conditions subscribed to by
" those of our former national representatives, and the
" dispositions of the Act of Insurrection unanimously
" resolved, will announce and guarantee to the people
" the justice and utility of its insurrection.

" Time urges—every moment is precious—public im-
" patience is extreme ; let us not endanger the loss, by
" too long a delay, of an opportunity which it might
" never again be possible for us to recover. We implore
" you—

" To add to the measures already adopted any others
" that you will judge necessary.

" To determine the moment for beginning the insur-
" surrection. We shall perish in the conflict, or, by
" victory and equality, terminate for ever so long and so
" sanguinary a revolution."

Robert-Lindet demonstrated the justice of the insurrection, justified the recal of the Convention, and insisted
at great length upon the necessity of impressing upon
the approaching revolution, by the practice of the strictest

equality, a character peculiar to itself, and absolutely and unequivocally popular.

"For my part," said Grisel, "I answer to you for my brave comrades of the Camp of Grenelle; and to let you see how much I take to heart the triumph of holy equality, I will inform you that I have found the means of abstracting from my aristocratic uncle the sum of 10,000 livres, which I destine to be applied to the providing of refreshments for the insurgent soldiers."

The new Act of Insurrection was once more approved by the Conventionalists, who promised to repair on the day of rising, with their colleagues, to the place which the Secret Directory might appoint, for the re-installation of the Convention, and to yield a sincere concurrence in the execution of the measures resolved, and of the decrees which the people in insurrection might pronounce. *Renewed adhesion of the Mountainists.*

Massart, in the name of the Military Committee, rendered an account of the bases of the plan of attack, which had appeared to it most conformable to the views of the Secret Directory. Agreeably to the Committee's opinion, the twelve arrondissements of Paris, united in three divisions, were to be led by as many generals against the legislative body, the executive Directory, and the staff of the army of the interior. The first platoon was to be composed of the most ardent Democrats; and such was the public impatience that a rising, *en masse*, of all the working classes, at the call of the revolutionary agents, and of the active friends of equality, was regarded as a matter of easy execution. Massart added, that before deciding upon the moment of insurrection, the Committee had need of some fresh information respecting the number of the Democrats, and of the capacity of some of them, as also respecting the arms and ammunition, of which it would be necessary to seize possession at the commencement of the action. The assembly then resolved— *Report of the Military Committee.*

"That the Secret Directory should "accelerate the dénouement of the con- "spiracy. *Resolution of the Assembly.*

"That it should give its agents instructions conform- "able to the plan of the Military Committee.

" That the assembly should meet again two days after
" to hear a final report upon the state of things, and to
" fix the day of action."

The Police in-   Hardly was the assembly dissolved,
vest the resi-   when the Minister of Police, followed by
dence of Drouet a detachment of infantry and cavalry,
penetrated by open force, and in contempt of the laws,*
into the apartment of Drouet, where he hoped to seize
the conspirators; but he found there only Drouet and
Darthé, whom he did not think it prudent to arrest. An
order, either badly conceived or badly given, thus frustrated
for the present the sinister designs of the reigning tyranny.

Grisel restores   But this event, which ought to have
confidence to   inspired the conspirators with distrust,
the conspira-   only served to increase their fancied se-
tors.   curity. Grisel, who had been able to
convince them of his honesty, dissipated their alarms and
persuaded them that all new precautions were unnecessary. At first, the Secret Directory attributed to treason
the danger it had run; and in the investigation which it
hastily instituted to discover the author, it fixed its
suspicions for a moment upon one of the sincerest friends
of the popular cause. Germain had not assisted at the
meeting at Drouet's house, and this absence, which was
unavoidably caused by the persecutions directed against
him by the Government, excited against him some suspicions, which were soon, however, dispelled by the
recollection of his morality, his uniform behaviour, his
sacrifices, and his frankness. All further distrust was
dissipated by a course of argument suggested to Darthé
by Grisel himself—" If there had been a traitor,'' said
he, " amongst the conspirators, he would have at once
conducted the police to Drouet's house, where we were
yesterday evening, or to the place where we were all
assembled on the 11th, because the papers of the conspiracy are deposited there;† that not having taken

* The then existing Constitution (that of the Year III.) forbid
domiciliary visits at night time.

{† Grisel declared afterwards, before the tribunals, that he had
not been able to recollect the place where the meeting of the 11th
was held. Thus did the villain turn his very ignorance to the
profit of treason and perfidy.—BRONTERRE.]

place, we ought to conclude that there is no treason amongst us, and that the movement of the police is only the effect of some suspicions it entertains, or of the extraordinary surveillance imposed upon it." Thus was every alarm dissipated, and the Secret Directory judged it useless to adopt any precautions by which it would have been so easy to avoid the calamities that soon after overwhelmed it.

In pursuance of the orders of the Secret Directory, there was held on the evening of the 20th a new meeting, at which were present Darthé, *Eriddy*, Germain, Fion, Rossignol, Grisel, and all the agents of arrondissements. The object of this meeting, which took place at Massart's house, was to consult each of those citizens, who were all men of tried experience, as to the best means of making the insurrectionary movement explode simultaneously, and of ensuring its success; as also to learn from each agent an exact account of his resources in men, arms, ammunition, and devotion to the cause. *Meeting of the agents at Massart's house.*

Claude Fiquet, agent of the sixth arrondissement, suggested the propriety of barricading the faubourg Antoine, in order to protect the dissolution of the troops encamped at Vincennes, if they were well-intentioned; or to prevent them from penetrating into the city, if they were hostilely disposed. *Propositions of the agents.*

Paris, agent of the seventh arrondissement, rendered account of the plan of attack proposed by a general whom the Secret Directory had engaged him to consult; he explained how the Executive Directory might easily be arrested, and proposed that the conspirators should take possession of the subterraneous avenues of the Luxembourg, through which its members might otherwise escape the hands of popular justice.

Cazin, agent of the third arrondissement, recommended that the communication between the faubourgs Antoine and Marceau should be secured by a bridge of boats; and that the insurrectionists should, from the commencement, occupy the heights of Montmartre,*

*[These heights lie to the north-west of Paris, and command the whole town, particularly the aristocratic parts in the *quartiers* of the Thuilleries and Palais Royal.—BRONTERRE.]

either in order thence to thunder down upon the Aristocrats who might resist, or to serve as a rallying point in case of experiencing any serious check.

Sombod, agent of the eleventh arrondissement, desired that the insurrection should take place on a day when the decade (Republican sabbath) might fall on a Sunday, in order to facilitate the concourse of the workmen still attached to the forms of Christian worship, and those who had renounced it. He proposed to make use of women and children to break the ranks of the soldiers, and to entice them to amalgamate and make common cause with the people.

With respect to public opinion, the revolutionary agents repeated what they had told the Secret Directory, namely, that the impatience was general and extreme, and that the fall of tyranny was certain, unless the soldiers should decide to put the people to the sword ; in this case they counted upon the numbers and courage of the Democrats, seconded by their maturely concerted military dispositions.

The Military Committee demands from them fresh instructions. Nevertheless, the instructions given by the agents did not appear sufficient to the Military Committee, which, desiring more precision, wished that the citizens destined to play so important a part in the insurrection should be consulted, in order that there might be no mistake as to their intentions. These new reports were to be put into Massart's hands, to be by him communicated to a general assembly, appointed the following morning at Dufour's house in the faubourg Poissonière.

Whilst the agitation, still on the increase, was causing a general presentiment of an approaching shock, the Secret Directory was measuring in silence the forces it had rallied, combining the movements to be impressed on them, and maturing the plans by which it proposed to itself to obtain the grand end of the Revolution—that is to say, the equal distribution of goods and labour.

Forces of the Democracy. In casting its regards around, it saw itself at the head of an army composed of a vast number of ardent friends of the Revolution, rallied by its exertions for a common end, and impatient to grapple with tyranny; of ex-officers who had been in authority before the 9th Thermidor—of the cannoneers of Paris, famed for their Democratic spirit—of disbanded officers—of patriots from the departments, which it had invited to Paris, or which had fled thither to escape persecution—of military men in detention, either for patriotism or for insubordination—of the grenadiers of the legislative body—of nearly all the Legion of Police, and of the whole corps of Invalides.*

Moreover, it perceived great disaffec- Discontent and tion amongst the soldiers encamped impatience of the people. around Paris, and heard murmurs in every quarter from the labouring classes, whose indignation was bursting forth without reservation in the secret societies, and in the immense gatherings which took place every day in the open air.

Besides, it was the general conviction that the zeal of the Proletarians,† the only true supporters of equality, would redouble when they saw executed, from the very outset of the insurrection, those engagements so many times postponed, by which their hard lot was to be ameliorated; and the Secret Directory felt the greater confidence in its forces, from the circumstance that its agents, whilst describing the people's vehement impatience, boldly demanded of it the signal of battle.

* We may, without exaggeration, reckon at *seventeen thousand* the men then in Paris who were in readiness to commence the insurrection, without counting the very numerous class of workmen, whose discontent and impatience were breaking out in all directions. Behold the calculation on which the Secret Directory based all its determinations :—

Revolutionists of Paris	4,000
Members of the Old Authorities	1,500
The Democratic Cannoneers	1,000
Disbanded Officers	500
Revolutionists of the Departments	1,000
Grenadiers of the Legislative Body	1,500
Military Men in Detention	500
Legion of Police	6,100
Corps of Invalids	1,000

Democrats ready to commence action.... 17,000

† [Proletarians (so called from the Latin word, *proles*) means the multitude who, possessing no fortune or property, have only their offspring (*proles*) to offer as a guarantee for their attachment to the state.—Bronterre]

Force of the reigning tyranny.   By the side of its own list the Directory had placed in view the forces which the reigning tyranny could oppose to it. It was aware that armed bodies, however apparently weak, might obstruct the popular movement—that the Royalists would, in all probability, assume the defence of the Government it hated, in order to escape the law of equality, which was still more odious to it—that the great bulk of the rich, who exclusively commanded the National Guard, would rather die than witness the triumph of Democracy—that the greater number had arms, and that Government would provide the remainder with them.

Resources of the people.   On their side, the conspirators had at their command the arms and ammunition with which the grenadiers of the legislative body and the legionaries were provided ; and they counted upon seizing those deposited at the armorers and gun-smiths, at the chief places of the sections, at the Thuilleries, at the Feuillans, and at the Invalides, with the help of the most resolute of the citizens, and by the connivance of the men appointed to guard the magazines. They reckoned besides upon the artillery of the Camp of Vincennes, which was devoted to them, and expected the troops would join the people—that the sudden explosion of an immense population would strike the partizans of tyranny with terror, and that the people would find a powerful auxiliary in the cowardice so natural to the rich favourites of fortune, upon whom the Government founded its principal hopes.

The Director Barras offers his services to the conspira-tors.   Was it in order to escape the just resentment of the people ? Was it to favour the conspirators, or with a view to ascertain their designs, that the Director Barras had a long conference, on the 30th Germinal, with Germain, the accredited agent of the Secret Direc-tory ?—a conference in which Barras sounded Germain upon the causes of the popular effervescence so strongly manifested ; and that, on the evening of the 20th Floréal, he made an offer to the principal conspirators (using Rossignol and Louel as his organs) to put him-self, with his staff, at the head of the insurrection or to place himself as a hostage in the Faubourg Antoine? They who would give these facts an interpretation favourable to Barras's honour, would have at the same time to explain why he did not apprise the parties to whom he testified so much interest and confidence on the 20th, of the denouncement which had been made against them on the preceding 15th Floréal.*

After having rendered an account of the Democratic forces at Paris—after having collected the opinions of the most enlightened patriots, and heard the report of the Military Committee, the Secret Directory considered it a duty to trace out a plan of insurrection, to the end that all operations might tend uniformly to the same point, and that the enterprize might not fail for want of prudence.

It had been long since admitted that it would be expedient to open the insurrec- tion by the public announcement of an Insurrectional Directory, around which all should rally, and whose impulsion all should obey. This announce- ment was to be made by the promulgation of the Insur- rectional Act, agreed to in concert with the Mountainist Committee. In this Act, as well as in all others to

Order of the insurrectional movement.

---

* A fact posterior to our conspiracy seems to throw a light upon this mystery. After the violent dissolution of the Secret Directory and the imprisonment of several of its members, some other De- mocrats undertook to break their irons, and to continue their great work. To these, two friends of the Director Barras introduced themselves, and persuaded them that the latter participated in their aspirations, and desired to effectually second their efforts. It was owing to their counsels that the project was formed of making the Democrats fraternize with the soldiers of the camp of Grenelle, in conjunction with whom they were then to invade the Executive Directory, in order to operate the desired Revolu- tion. These promises made in the name of Barras by his friends, a sum of about 24,000 francs distributed by them, and the pro- testations of certain officers of the camp, did, in fact, determine the Democrats to present themselves there in a body, without arms, crying *Vive la Republique*, and singing patriotic hymns. But instead of the fraternity promised to them, they found mas- sacre and death. Who laid these traps? Who desired to destroy the democratic party at a single blow?

[My readers may learn from this single anecdote the true cha- racter of the Thermidorian assassins of Robespierre. Barras, the true author of this ambuscade, had been appointed chief of the counter-revolutionary forces of the Convention on the night of 9th Thermidor.—BRONTERRE.]

appear during and after the insurrection, the Secret Directory assumed the title of "Insurrectional Committee of Public Safety," with the view of restoring the forms under which the Robespierrians had prepared the way for equality before the 9th Thermidor, and to avoid all analogy to those which the aristocracy had instituted.

The distribution of the insurgent army into three divisions had been adopted. Three generals were to command them, under the orders of a general-in-chief, subject to those of the Insurrectional Committee; subordinate to each general of the division were to be placed chiefs of arrondissements, and to the latter again, chiefs of sections, which in like manner were to be subdivided into platoons, with appropriate leaders.

With respect to generals, the views of the Committee were fixed upon Fion, Germain, Rossignol, and Massart. The chiefs and commanders of platoons, marked out by the same Committee, were to present themselves to form the ranks of the people, at the moment when the proclamation of the Insurrectional Act, the tocsin (alarum-bell), the trumpets, and the shouts of the friends of liberty, would have summoned it to the reconquest of its rights.

The popular army being thus composed, the next step was, by the aid of the insurrection, which it was expected would be general amongst the labouring classes, to direct it against the reigning tyranny, whose forces it was to combat. Columns of it were to march on the legislative body, on the Executive Directory, on the staff officers, and on the hotels of the Ministers, in order to support the Republicans charged with arresting the usurpers. The best disciplined sections, and those least armed, would have been directed towards the depôts of arms and ammunition, and particularly towards the camps of Grenelle and Vincennes, where there were no more than 8,000 men, and even these, it was believed, were ready to join the people.

To hasten this junction, it was proposed to employ the display of a grand force as well as the language of persuasion; orators were to remind the soldiers of the crimes of the Government, and of their duties towards their country; the women were to present them with garlands and refreshments; the Invalides to invite them to follow their example. If the worst happened, preparations were made for barricading the streets—for showering upon the troops torrents of boiling water mixed with vitriol, besides stones, slates, tiles, and bricks.

The rest of the popular army was to be employed in guarding the entrances to Paris—in maintaining communications between the different bodies of the people—in protecting the provisions intended for the city—in preventing all anti-popular gatherings—in intercepting all aristocratic correspondence—in checking all attempts at pillage, and in executing the orders of the insurrectional authorities.*

Unforeseen accidents, like those which caused the disasters of Prairial, might possibly render doubtful the success of the enterprise, if measures were not taken to prevent them. Accordingly, did the Insurrectional Committee consider of the means of abundantly provisioning all the places where the people was to assemble, and it was principally with this intent that it had decided upon installing in each section, from the outset of the insurrection, three members of the Revolutionary Committee, which was in activity up to the 9th Thermidor, and whose duty would be to instantly place at the disposal of the insurgent citizens, whatever meat and drink they might require, by seizing the provisions deposited at all the public and private stores, and to execute on the spot the first offices of kindly relief promised by the conspirators to the unhappy poor.

For the purpose of giving the people a sensible idea of the new Revolution, and of strengthening its zeal, the Insurrec- {Lodging and clothing for the poor.} tional Committee proposed to publish, during the insurrection, two decrees, by virtue of which the poor should be immediately clothed at the expense of the Republic, and on the same day lodged in the houses of the rich, to whom should be left only the accommodation indispensable in that way.

* It would be wrong to confound the regular distribution of lodging and clothes with pillage, which is opposed to all amelioration by the irreparable losses it causes to society, by the new inequalities it produces, by the demoralization it fosters and feeds, and by the difficulties it opposes to the reception of good laws.—It belongs to laws alone to re-establish equality.

It is right to make known the idea formed by the Insurrectional Committee of the public sentence to which it desired to subject the most guilty of the people's enemies, that is to say, the members of the two Councils, and those of the Executive Directory. The crime was manifest—the penalty was death—a grand example was necessary. Nevertheless, this example should bear the stamp of rigorous justice, and of a profound feeling for the public good. It was agreed that the insurgent people should have read to it a full and detailed account of the treasons it had been the victim of, and should be invited to except from proscription those of the accused, in extenuation of whose political faults excusable error might be pleaded, or simple and popular manners, or some brilliant service rendered to equality during the insurrection. According to some opinions in the Insurrectional Committee, the condemned were to be buried under the ruins of their palaces; which ruins were to be left in that state as a monument to the latest posterity of the just punishment inflicted on the enemies of equality.

Every measure of attack and defence was about being signified to the agents of arrondissements, and to the generals the Committee was upon the point of naming. From the happy termination of the insurrection was necessarily to flow a new order of things, some substrata for which it was necessary to lay beforehand, in order to prepare for the most urgent wants; the Insurrectional Committee had made them the subject of its meditations. We have seen how, previously to its coalition with the Mountainists, it counted upon getting established, by the people in insurrection, the new Authority and the rules of its conduct. To the changes rendered necessary by this coalition, the distrust, excited by the equivocal course of the Mountainists, caused others to be added.

To triumph over tyranny would have been nothing, unless there were a certainty that it would be replaced by guides animated with the purest love of equality. It was necessary to have men whose doctrines, morals, and entire life were in perfect harmony with the institutions they were summoned to create.

According to its first system, the Insurrectional Committee was certain that the spirit which animated it would pass effectually and fully into the new National Assembly, and in that consisted the strongest guarantee it could offer the people of the approaching establishment of equality, and of the popular Constitution of 1793. But from the moment it was decided to recal a part of the Convention, the Insurrectional Committee believed it to be its duty to fortify the people against the seductions of the new authority. The reproaches which it urged againsts the Mountainists sufficiently prove that it was far from reposing confidence in them.

The equivocal conduct of the Mountainists renders new precautions necessary.

To the old grounds of distrust, the recent conduct of these Conventionalists added new ones. The Committee had been struck by the subtility with which they endeavoured to evade the proposed adjunction, by the haughtiness they carried into the discussions, and by that aristocratic pride which made them call the restitution of the people's rights a gratuitous concession. Moreover, it was informed that manœuvres were being clandestinely practiced, with a view to elude the conditions agreed upon, and to make the supreme authority of the Republic fall exclusively into the hands of the Mountainists. The Committee was now so strongly convinced of the impossibility of these Mountainists effecting any good, that it regarded as an unpardonable crime the least movement, which by delivering power into their hands would be only substituting one tyranny for another.

They considered then of the means of forcing the recalled Conventionalists to abide by their promises, and to throw no obstacle in the way of an effective and permanent equality. It was by the people that the conspirators had hoped to overthrow tyranny. It was by the ascendancy of truth that they had obtained the support of the people, and it was now again by the aid of truth and the people that they resolved to baffle the new machinations.

Notwithstanding the provisions of the Insurrectional Act, by which a part of the National Convention was recalled to the exercise of power, the Committee wished

The dispositions of the insurrection were to be sanctioned by the voice of the people.

H

that it should be re-established by the express will of the people in insurrection; that by the same authority should the stipulated adjunction be solemnly decreed, and the additional Deputies named. It wished, besides, that the same people should order the magistrates in authority before the 9th Thermidor to instantly resume their functions ; that it should confirm all the insurrectional dispositions, prescribe the prompt execution of the decrees of the Committee concerning the lodging and clothing of the poor, and directly instal the new Convention after having pronounced the grand decree already spoken of.

To this effect, the Insurrectional Committee had recommended its agents to direct all their cares to produce, immediately after the overthrow of tyranny, a concourse of all the citizens round the place where it would hold assembly. There the Committee would have rendered account to the people of all it had done to break the new yoke imposed on the nation, and demanded of it the decrees it might judge necessary for the safety of the Republic. The discourse which one of the members was to pronounce upon that grand occasion was actually drawn up, and was about to be submitted to examination.

Discussion on the participation of the Insurrectional Committee in the new authority.

A very delicate point was maturely discussed in the Insurrectional Committee. The question was to determine what part its members should have in the exercise of the new authority. Its intention was to speak to the people without reservation or equivocation, and to pay the most striking homage to its sovereignty. Had it deemed it necessary, to the complete success of the insurrection, to be temporarily invested with the whole national power, it would not have hesitated to demand it. But every institution of this sort having been previously rejected, it remained only to examine whether it would be expedient to recommend the people in insurrection to institute a numerically small body, authorized to propose legislative measures to the new Convention, whose decrees it would execute, or whether it would be more expedient to commit this important care to the Convention itself. Whatever might have been the decision of the Insurrectional

Committee, it would be still necessary to ask itself whether the success of the new Revolution did not require that its members should exclusively compose the contemplated body in question.

There having been no resolution come to in this respect, I can only record the arguments by which the Committee had compared the advantages and inconveniences of the different plans proposed for adoption.

It will occur, in the first instance, that the conversion of the Insurrectional Initiative into a permanent, and necessarily very extended power, would expose the members of the Insurrectional Committee to the suspicion of having ambitious and interested views; it was feared that inculpations of this kind would, by the readiness with which they are credited and propagated, only obstruct their march, and leave them no time to realize the good proposed. And it was asked, whether the presence of the conspirators in the new Convention, their intimate union, and the general confidence bestowed upon them, would not suffice to impart to the laws the spirit of their enterprize, and to raise to the supreme executive power magistrates worthy of exercising its functions?

On the other hand, the Insurrectional Committee saw but few men in whom purity of principle was to be found united with courage, with firmness, and the intelligence necessary to reduce them to practice; it felt how dangerous it would be not 'to leave the completion of so hazardous a work to those who had had the boldness to commence it, and it dreaded the duplicity of certain persons with whom it was about to find itself in competition. After having long hesitated, our conspirators had almost decided upon demanding from the people a decree by which the initiative and the execution of the laws should be exclusively confided to them.

Several of our projects remained imperfect; many useful undertakings were cut short by the treason which delivered over to the vengeance of the aristocracy the men whom circumstances had carried to the head of the Democratic Party; and the history of their conspiracy might be terminated here, were it not necessary, in order to give a thorough knowledge of their designs, to throw some light on the picture they had formed to themselves of the probable state of the nation immediately after the insurrection—on the final results to which they aimed, and on the means they counted upon employing to attain them.

View of the probable state of Paris during the insurrection. In the midst of the consternation with which so radical a Revolution would have smitten aristocrats of all shades, and of the joy which changes of so popular a cast would have excited amongst the numerous class of operatives and unhappy poor, was the new Convention to spring up, composed of about *one hundred and seventy* thorough Democrats and Equalitarians, all of them irrevocably pledged by the principles of their lives, and the aspirations of the surrounding people, to lay the foundation of a solid and enduring equality. By the side of it, the Insurrectional Committee, seconded by the magistrates installed by the insurrection, would have presided, at least provisionally, over the execution of the Act which was to put the citizens in movement; at its call the enormous mass of Parisian poor would have been suddenly transferred from their cells and garrets into healthy and commodious habitations. The unhappy poor would have been supplied with clothing, and their goods and furniture in pledge at the pawn-offices would be gratuitously restored to them. At the same time diligent care would have been taken to ensure abundant subsistence; the principles of the new Revolution would have been explained to the citizens in the assemblies to be forthwith re-opened;* a numerous popular guard would have repressed the ill-intentioned, and facilitated every operation that might be adjudged necessary to the consolidation of the new system.

It is impossible to determine exactly to what extent the display of physical force might have been necessary; the conspirators desiring to carry the day at any price, were determined either to vanquish or to bury themselves under their country's ruins. Unless in case of resistance, the severity to be employed would not have exceeded the punishment of the principal usurpers, and

* The same as in Robespierre's time.

the arrestation of certain dangerous persons, of whom the Insurrectional Committee had lists drawn up.

To the preparatory steps judged necessary to overthrow the scaffolding erected by the new aristocracy, it would have been necessary to add those others which appeared best calculated to render the Revolution of Paris common to the whole Republic, and to establish throughout the institutions of equality and popular sovereignty.

From the first moment of its appointment, the Insurrectional Committee had *The departments.* made the departments and the armies the subject of its meditations; it had circulated its writings in all quarters; the Democrats were everywhere apprised of its projects, and everywhere prepared to co-operate. There was in the hands of one of its members a voluminous correspondence which indicated the places were the Democrats were in force, and the men in whom most confidence could be placed; information was received from all sides stating that the Revolutionists, abandoning the shades of opinion that had hitherto divided them, were rallying one and all to the standard of pure equality.

With respect to the armies, the Committee was well aware how difficult the commissaries of the Convention had found the task of stifling amongst them, after the 9th Thermidor, what they called the *spirit of anarchy and insubordination;** neither was it ignorant that the Constitution of the Year III. had raised murmurs throughout whole armies (*avait fait murmurer des armées entières*); it was informed that the soldiers obeyed with repugnance the commands of the officers that succeeded those destituted after the 9th Thermidor, and that amongst the chiefs, of whom some corresponded with it, there were several that still remained strongly

---

* [Even Mignet (an historian devoted to the middle classes) admits this. "During these occurrences," he says, " the intelligence of the Revolution of the 9th Thermidor reached the armies. They were entirely Republican, and apprehensive lest the fall of Robespierre should carry along with it that of the popular Government; they heard it, therefore, with marked disapprobation," &c. —BRONTERRE.]

attached to the principles of democracy.* It was, moreover, authorised to reckon upon the co-operation of
certain Conventionalists, whom the Executive Directory
had sent on a mission to the armies of the Republic.
Furthermore, it was likely that the example of Paris
would give an impulse to the people of all France, which
a subsequent knowledge of the truth would have rendered irresistible. By way of spreading amongst the
soldiers this knowledge (upon which the Insurrectional
Committee founded its principal hopes), commissaries
were to have been dispatched to them, and proclama-
tions † addressed, in unison with those by which it was
in preparation to announce to the French people the
news of its redemption.

Legislation of   Whilst meditating the overthrow of
equality and in- tyranny, the Committee had never ceased
termediary laws to occupy itself with the definitive legislation of equality, and with the intermediary laws by
which it was to be gradually attained. In relation to this
important branch of its labours, there were (at the moment when part of the papers of the conspiracy were
seized) certain memoirs and projects deposited with one
of the Committee, in a place which the police could not
discover; unfortunately these documents were almost all
destroyed in consequence of the sudden consternation of
their authors, and I have been only able to procure some
fragments which were deposited elsewhere. With the
help of these fragments, and the remembrance retained
by several persons of the facts and discussions they
were witnesses to, I will endeavour to give an approxi-
mate idea, but as substantially exact as possible, of the
object and intentions of the conspirators. I will first
explain the civil and political state to which they desired
to gradually conduct the French people. I will afterwards relate some of the temporary institutions by which
they counted upon preparing them for, and leading them
to that state.

---

   * They were not yet covered with the spoils of Italy, of Switzer
land, of Egypt, of Germany, and Spain.
   † See the spirit of these in one of them inserted amongst the
justificatory pieces at the close of this work.

From the decree which the Insurrectional Committee was to demand of the people of Paris, was to emanate a new social order.* In the first place it was there implicitly acknowledged that individual property, so far from emanating from the law of nature, is but an invention of the civil law, and may, like it, be modified or abolished; in the next place, it was there laid down as a principle, that the proprietorship of all the wealth comprised within the national territory is one and indivisible, and belongs inalienably to the people, which alone has the right of repartition, as regards its enjoyment and usufructuary possession.

The proprietorship of all wealth is one and indivisible. It belongs to the people.

Assuredly the proclamation of these truths would have been very agreeable to the multitude, whose sufferings and slavery are always inevitable consequences of the contrary system; nevertheless it would have been only a cruel derision to acknowledge the principle, unless measures were assiduously taken to apply it in such manner as to produce practical consequences of utility to mankind.

The principle once recognised, that the right of regulating, for the general good, the distribution of wealth and of the labours which produce it, belongs to society: and that from 'the inequality of this distribution flow, as from an inexhaustible source, all the calamities which afflict nations; it follows that society should provide that this inequality be destroyed never more to return.

It remains then to be decided, whether the remedy for these evils ought to be sought in modifications of the right of property, or in its total abolition.

It has been seen, in the course of this work, by what motives the conspirators had been determined to adopt, as the final object of their enterprise, the proscription of individual property, and by what means they reckoned upon attaining it; by establishing the community of wealth and labour—the sole means of drying up for ever the source of all inequalities, and of extirpating all prejudices, as well as all the evils derived from them. Instructed by the lessons and by the examples of the great

* For this decree, see pages 117, 118.

men of antiquity, and of the Revolution, and encouraged
by the dispositions lately manifested in France, they had
conceived the design of giving new manners to the
French, and of constituting them into a people passion-
ately attached to their country and laws; happy at home:
loved, respected, and imitated abroad.

Right of every
one to a happy
existence. The
obligation of
labour equal for
all.

In this social state, private riches disappear; and the right of property is
replaced by that of each individual to an
existence as happy as that of any other
member of the social body. The gua-
rantee of this sacred right becoming the principle of
all institutions, rests in the obligation imposed upon each
member of the social body to take a share of the labour
necessary to insure the maintenance, the prosperity, and
the conservation of society—an obligation which, being
derived from the law of nature (which has given to all an
equal right to happiness), is consequently equal for all.

Agriculture and
arts of the first
necessity.

The first and most important occupations of the citizens ought to be those
which assure them subsistence, clothing,
and habitations, and have for their object agriculture,
and the arts subservient to the cultivation of the soil, to
the construction of edifices, to the making of furniture,
and the fabrication of stuffs and cloths. And, as all
lands are not equally suited to the culture of the same
products, one of the principal cares of the public administration ought to be to establish in each canton, the
productions and works most conformable to the soil and
climate, and the most favourable to abundance and
equality.

Distribution of
the citizens.

Thus, as all lands cannot produce with
equal fecundity every species of commo-
dity, in like manner all persons cannot be usefully employed with several sorts of works. To the end that
society may derive from the equal and moderate labour
of each of its members, all the advantage that it ought
to expect from it, and that habit may diminish its difficulties, it is necessary that occupations be distinct—
that each have his state or calling—and that those, for
example, who cast metals, be not obliged to work wood,
to weave stuffs, &c. Thence arises in the system of

community of goods and labour, the necessity of distributing the citizens into several classes, to each of which the law allots a particular sort of work, according to the wants of the country, and in accordance with the supreme principle of equality.

This distribution takes birth in the houses of public education, of which we shall speak anon. The magistrates charged *It takes its source in public education.* with their superintendence cause to be executed therein all branches of work ordained by the laws, and attach to each of them the number of *élèves* (pupils) proportioned to the wants of the public, at the same time consulting the capacity and peculiar bent or turn of each pupil.

The grand object of this general activity, from which none may withdraw themselves but those whom old age or infirm- *Abundance the object of general labour.* ities render incapable of it, is to provide in superabundance the things necessary for all; and to furnish them with those articles of pleasure not disapproved by public manners. Whatever is not communicable to all, ought to be severely retrenched.

In the Order in question, the works necessary to the subsistence and pleasures of the people are functions, the regulation *Labour is a function regulated by law.* of which is prescribed by the laws, in order that they may never degenerate into fatigue—that they may cause the least possible pain—that they may not fall heavier upon one citizen than another—and that all may be called and encouraged to take part in them, by custom, by the love of country, by the attractions of pleasure, and by the approbation of public opinion. Thus, whilst the greater number would be occupied in labouring, sowing, reaping, and putting up in the granaries, some would be constructing and repairing houses, public edifices, roads, harbours, canals : others again would superintend the breeding and preservation of animals ; the latter would prepare and employ the thread, the wool, the hides ; the former would manufacture the furniture, vehicles, shipping, or work the metals, &c. &c. The duration and severity of the labours would be regulated by the law, which, while it spared the weak, would excite the strong by the encouragement of opinion, and by the praises of the magistrates, so that all might find themselves subject to duties equally proportioned to their strength, and to the rudeness of the labour they might have to perform.

Mitigation of painful labour.   Fearing that the diversity of occupations might produce for certain classes too sensible an increase, or surfeit of labour, it was considered—1st. That it would be expedient to call in the sciences to soften the labour of man, by the invention of new machines and the perfecting of old ones.* 2d. That it would be right to charge, in turn, all the able-bodied citizens with the more repulsive occupations, the disagreeableness of which, it was hoped, would be progressively but rapidly diminished by a masculine education, and by the assistance of mechanism, chemistry, and the physical sciences in general.

Probably it would have been found convenient to distinguish the works of strict necessity into *easy* and *painful*, and to oblige each citizen to exercise one of one class, and one of the other. Probably it might have been also just to establish another division of citizens, according to age, for the purpose of proportioning the weight of labour to the increase and diminution of strength; for, in matters of this kind, equality ought to be measured and determined less by the intensity of the labour required than by the capacity of the labourer.

* It is only in the system of community that the use of machines can prove a real benefit to humanity, by diminishing the labours of man, while, at the same time it augments the abundance of things necessary and agreeable. At present, machines, by superseding a vast deal of manual labour, have only the effect of depriving multitudes of men of bread, for the advantage of certain insatiable speculators, whose gains they augment.

[Buonarroti, it will be perceived, takes the same view of machinery that I have so often endeavoured to elucidate in the *Poor Man's Guardian, People's Conservative,* &c. He would have been more correct, however, had he added to the greedy speculators he alludes to, that infinitely larger mass of the community, which may be comprehended under the two-fold class of *idle* and *uselessly-employed;* that is to say, those who do nothing for their living, and those who do only what is useless or mischievous, such as lawyers, priests, stockjobbers, and the great majority of profit-hunters of every sort, nine-tenths of whom are not wanted by society for the purposes of distribution, &c. &c.; these, and the ilke, are the parties that chiefly profit by the present use or abuse of machinery.—BRONTERRE.]

From the impartial and universal division of labour—from the reduction of occupations to those alone which are necessary to all—from the most advantageous use of animals, and from the perfecting of instruments and machines, flow two consequences infinitely favourable to the happiness of the species. 1st. The useful employment of all the land, and the multiplication of things truly useful. 2d. The removal of idleness, and thereby a great mitigation of individual labour.

All having equally contributed towards the fertilization of the land, and to preparing its productions, it is but palpable justice that all should participate equally in the enjoyments resulting therefrom, and to which Nature has attached the conservation and happiness of the species. To the end that partiality should not disturb the social tranquillity, it is necessary that all the productions of the land, and of industry, should be deposited in public magazines, whence they should issue, to be distributed equally to the citizens, under the superintendence of the magistrates, responsible for such impartial distribution.

Equality of enjoyments.

If the society thus instituted were limited to the scanty territory of a commune or district, its administration would be a matter of extreme simplicity,* for its inhabitants would have a right to only the things produced within it. But in an immense Republic, composed of several millions of men, who constitute its strength, and insure its durability, the proprietorship of the riches of each of its parts belongs to the entire people, and the inhabitants of each section have an equal right to the consumption and use of the commodities and products of all the rest; the districts which

* By dividing the grand national proprietorship into as many partial proprietorships as there might be small communities, each of them would be able to procure the necessaries it might be in need of, only by the exchange of its own superfluities. Those which, on account of the sterility of the soil, or the inclemency of seasons, might find themselves without superfluities, would have to experience the inconveniences and evils of scarcity. Thus would vanish that general fraternity, and immense reciprocity of succours, which it was intended to establish; and the selfish and chicaning spirit of traffic, which would have soon presided over the deliberations of all those communities, would not be slow to awake once more the old cupidity in the hearts of the citizens.

yield a superfluity ought to furnish the less productive ones with what is necessary. Thence arises in the administration of a very extended society a certain complexity which is extremely puzzling to persons who consider the thing superficially; but at bottom the whole affair is one of simple calculation, susceptible of the most exact order and regular operation, since cupidity being deprived of all aliment, by the establishment of the institutions in question, there would be no longer any occasion to fear the losses which incessantly cause, under the existing order of things, the competition of rival chiefs, and the plunder of their subordinates.

Advantages of community applied to a very extended country.　Besides, the greater the extent of territory a community embraces, the stronger is the guarantee it offers to each part of that territory against dearth and scarcity of every kind. Moreover, from such great and frequent intercommunication of men and things, ought necessarily to spring up a feeling of happiness, of fraternity, and of devotion, so general and so strong, that it is to be presumed no human force could either invade such country nor destroy its institutions of equality, once they were firmly established.

Equal distribution of riches.　So numerous an association of men, scattered over so vast a territory, requires another species of function, without which the fraternal bond that links together all parts of the Republic would be broken, and the superfluities of one district be rendered useless to itself and to the rest. These functions have for their object the transfer of the products of land and industry from places where they exceed the wants of the inhabitants to those which are deficient. They are of two sorts. 1st. A superior magistracy compares the riches of the whole with the wants of each part, points out the commodities to be deported, and the places whence they are to be taken. 2d. Inferior officers superintend and effect the transport.

By-and-bye we shall see by what channels the supreme administration of our Republic would have been able to easily provide for an uninterrupted communication between all its parts; for the present we shall only observe, that in this order of things the inhabitants of barren countries, whose extreme fatigues would never have yielded other than extreme poverty, would behold themselves consoled for the labours they had bestowed, and invited to participate in the riches of more productive soils.

With respect to transport, the Insurrectional Committee was of opinion that society ought to consider it not merely as an indispensable means of providing the inhabitants of one district with the surplus products of another, but also as a happy occasion for strengthening the love of country, by bringing home to every individual the knowledge of its beauties, of its institutions, and of the benefits of the equality to be established by the laws; consequently, they wished that every citizen capable of work should be called in turn to this function, as also to those of courier, bearer of dispatches, &c. Let my readers bear in mind that I have not before me all the documents to which the conspirators had committed their most secret thoughts; I cannot, therefore, develop in detail all the parts of the edifice they proposed to construct, but am limited to a mere report of such outlines as my memory may furnish, with the aid of the few fragments I have been able to recover. The considerate reader will accept this as an apology for the imperfect manner in which I must necessarily treat this part of my subject.

Such are the vicious habits we have contracted, such is the multiplicity of artificial wants we have inconsiderately created, that it is to be presumed there would still be a necessity to draw from foreign countries some of the more important commodities that France does not produce; at all events, it would have been necessary to send abroad for those which the medical profession derives, more or less, from all climes. The people being sole proprietor of all wealth, it belongs only to the people to treat with foreigners for the mutual exchange of superfluities. Besides, a traffic of this kind could not be entrusted to other than responsible magistrates, without refalling into the evils inseparable from private or individual property, and exposing the state to a new corruption. It

thence follows that all commercial relations with foreigners ought to be subjected to the supreme direction
of the Republic.*

Usufructuary right. It also follows, from these principles,
that the system of community once es-
tablished, a citizen could never acquire over anything
what is called the right of property ; he would have only
the right of using, or a usufructuary right to whatever
objects or goods he became possessed of by the actual
delivery of the magistrate.   In this Order of Economy,
the right of property vests always in the Republic,†
which may at all times dispose of every thing not consumed or destroyed.

This regimé once established, the satisfaction of
future wants is effectually guaranteed, by the labour of
all being made subsidiary to them, and by the natural
desire of each and all to have what is good.   There
would be no longer any reason to be greedy of riches ;
all motives for being anxious about the future would
cease, and thus the most prolific source of the cares and
vexations which gnaw the heart of civilised man, would
be for ever dried up.   Under the existing order of things,
two painful feelings incessantly haunt the labouring man,
and, generally, persons of small income—the fear of poverty from the infirmities of old age, and apprehensions
for the condition and fate of their offspring.   In the
system of community these corroding feelings would be
unknown.

The aged and infirm.   To the obligation of labour imposed on
the strong, correspond the right to a
happy existence at all times, and that of being exempted
from labour, and unburdened with care, whenever the infirmities of age, or the weakness of the organs, render
labour painful or impossible.   Thus, in the Order of

---

* There exists corruption in society whenever the elements that
compose it are divided by diversity and opposition of interests. A
nation may be always pronounced corrupt whenever there exists
in the bosom of it a class of persons who have formed to themselves pretensions irreconcilable with the well-being of the
whole, or of the other component parts.

† That is to say, the absolute empire or faculty of disposing at
its pleasure. *Jus utendi atque abutendi* (the right of using and
abusing).

Community, the repose and tender treatment of the aged and infirm are placed in the rank of the principal duties of society. In return for these good offices, the Republic would receive lessons of experience from the old, and make them subjects of emulation for the young; they were destined, in fact, to become the guardians of morals and of the laws, the censors of public manners, and the conservators of virtue.

One of the effects of these institutions would have been, I think, to attach the citizens so strongly to them, that the love of country would have become their predominant passion. By education, the legislator would have been able to render all affections of family and kindred subordinate to this sentiment; he could have rendered it so intense and active, that the truly fraternal union of all Frenchmen would, in all probability, have been its happy and astounding consequence. This reflection constituted the delight of our conspirators, and was the animating soul of all their projects. I remember one occasion, when, in the midst of a discussion on the advantages and inconveniences of family ties, the proposition was formally made to forbid children to bear the name of a father that had not distinguished himself by great virtues.

Thus, what was to embellish the declining years of old age would have also strengthened the virtue of the young, and from this reciprocity of advantage, joined to the happy effects of an education in common for all, at the public charge, the country would have derived an augmentation of power from every increase of its population —an augmentation progressive and sure, as there would be no moral cause to retard it.

Everything in this social order favours the multiplication of our species. The system of community does away with those obstructions which now frequently prevent the legitimate intercourse of the sexes; it gives to the soul a tranquillity at present unknown to us, it fortifies the body by a mild and varied activity, and augments the productions useful to all by banishing luxury and idleness.

Propagation of the species encouraged.

Superiority of this institution over those of the ancients. It was by similar ways that the most celebrated legislators of antiquity qualified their respective fellow-citizens for the enjoyment, in different degrees, of liberty and happiness. Lycurgus, in particular, had nearly attained the end of society marked out by nature. But the law of nations practiced by the ancients, and perhaps, also, an unjust egoism or selfishness had introduced into all their institutions an inhuman usage, with which the system of our conspirators would never have sullied itself —I mean the practice of holding slaves. The community sought by us would have this honourable distinction in its favour—that the liberty to be established by it would not, as in Greece and Rome, be the privilege of a certain class or classes, to be enjoyed at the expense of the servitude of the rest.

New repartition of the population. Since the inequality of fortunes has condemned one portion of the people to overwhelming toil, and another portion to a demoralizing inaction; the country parts have retained comparatively few inhabitants, often insufficient for the wants of cultivation, but always crushed under the weight of excessive fatigue. The supernumerary population has crowded into cities, either to dissipate there in voluptuousness the riches produced by the country people, or to procure an easy living by subserving the pleasures of the rich, or through the complication of the public administration.

In verging towards equality, society should necessarily witness the breaking up of those huge gatherings of human beings, which are destructive alike of morals and population. Those capable of work should necessarily return to the country to lighten the burden of their rustic brethren. The industry of towns would go to embellish the lives of the country people who feed them. The simplicity of the new Government would render unnecessary the myriads of clerks and placemen who are now abstracted from agriculture and the useful arts; and the maintenance of order being dependent on the due discharge by each citizen of his respective functions, it would be no longer compatible with those tumultuous gatherings in towns, amongst which it is so easy to hide one's actions from public observance and censure.

No longer a capital—no more great cities*—the country would be gradually but rapidly covered with villages, built in the most healthy and convenient places, and located in such

Decay and disappearance of great cities.

* If I mistake not, the existence of large cities is a symptom of public malady, and an infallible forerunner of civil convulsions. The nucleus of them is formed of overgrown proprietors, large capitalists, and opulent merchants; around whom congregate a multitude of persons who subsist on their expenditure, by purveying for their wants, by flattering their tastes, by lending themselves to their caprices, and by pandering to their vices.

The more populous a city is, the greater is the number we meet of servile domestics, of abandoned women, of hungry writers, of poets, of musicians, of painters, of loose wits, of comedians, of dancers, of priests, of intermeddlers and interlopers, of thieves, and of vagabonds of every sort.

From the perpetual exchange of services and wages, there is engendered in one class the habit of authority and command; in the other classes, that of submission and servitude. The latter, while they crawl and cringe to the former, do, at the same time, contract their dissolute morals, their airs, their disdainful pride and manners; they also accustom themselves to exercise a vulgar authority over those less favoured by fortune than themselves, in imitation, no doubt, of their masters. Both one and the other scorn real happiness; they desire to be rich, powerful, and preferred, and, above all, to appear so.

Those sumptuous palaces, those vast gardens, those costly varieties of furniture, those brilliant equipages, those numerous and flaunting liveries, and those riotous saloons, which constitute, as they say, the ornaments of great cities, make fatal impressions on the minds of all whose regards they attract. On the one hand, they inflate the minds of the possessors, and dispose them to see in those deprived of them so many malignant enemies, whom jealousy and misery are incessantly urging to despoil them of their possessions, and to revenge themselves for the state of humiliation and destitution to which the rich have reduced them. On the other hand, the excluded parties either get their minds perverted by covetousness, and envious hatred; or rendered abject and degraded, they become the degenerate props of ambition and tyranny. All such luxuries and possessions occasion real misery, both to the possessors, and to those desiring them, for while the former are tormented by ennui and suspicions, the latter are gnawed by an envious longing for imaginary goods, of which more happy mortals (as they fancy) are in possession.

The parties who go to seek in great cities distraction of thought, pomp, and homage, are such as need not to labour, having already thrown upon other people's shoulders their proper share of the common burthen which nature imposes upon all alike. Accordingly has the task of those remaining in the country parts exceeded the limits of nature, and the labours of agriculture and of the necessary arts of life, have become more and more subjugating and painful The evil always making progress, at length attains

manner as to communicate easily one with another, by
means of roads and numerous canals, which it would be
in every respect the general interest to open and construct.

that last desperate stage when the condition of the labourer and
artisan, scarcely differing from that of the galley-slave, is at
length despised and abandoned.   Every peasant then turns his
regards towards the great city, and hies thither, if he can, in
quest of those advantages of which his imagination exaggerates
the allurements. The folly once committed of going there, he
must now live there. Examples are seductive ; the multitude of
wrong-doers protects vice from censure, the senses get inflamed ;
what at first appears repulsive, assumes by little and little the
complexion of *bon ton* and " knowledge of the world"—very soon
are money and applause preferred to duty and virtue; by dint of
being supple and polished, he becomes hypocrite, liar, and knave ;
and if fortune smiles, he attains his wished-for elevation, when
without being happy, he appears so, or becomes a mark of ambition to be envied or imitated by a crowd of imprudent creatures,
who fling themselves into the jaws of misfortune by false reckoning and illusions.

Nevertheless, the number of competitors, attracted by riches,
pleasures, and dissipation into large towns, goes on increasing to
the point, when the majority of them, reduced to slender salaries,
exhausted by excesses, and overburdened with children, are at
length confounded with that multitude of wretches who wound
the sight and afflict the heart, in every country where there are
large cities.

Agriculture and the arts of first necessity, being the true nu-
tritive supports of society, it is to the scene of these occupations
that men are called by nature to live, whether it be to till the soil,
or to furnish the agriculturists with commodities and with recreations.

To the evils immediately resulting from inequality, there is
added a multiplicity of others, by the extent of territory, the cen-
tralization of Government, the enormity of taxes, public debts,
the luxury of banquets, and the deceitful splendour of courts.
These and the like are inseparable from those grand capitals,
" where the women," says Jean Jacques Rousseau, " no longer
believe in honour, nor the men in virtue."

In proportion as these living masses of humanity extend in
bulk, in the same proportion do they suppose progressive inequalities of fortune and condition ; and, as public misery and discontent augment with inequality, wherever these crowded populations have place, there are the causes of discord and convulsion
most rife, and there, also, are most obstacles to be overcome
before real liberty can be established.

People complain of the imposture of priests, of the violence of
military men, of the duplicity of courtiers, and of the perfidy of
spies—let us complain rather of the monstrous inequality which
renders them all necessary. How should any one expect that,
without deceiving and terrifying, an appearance of peace could be
maintained amongst this motley multitude of persons, who are
impelled by their very morals, institutions, and laws, to envy,
hate, and combat one another ?

It is to be presumed, that all considera- Simplicity of tions yielding to the supreme law of the habitations. equality, the sumptuous mansion and towering castle would give place to the salubrity, commodiousness, and prosperity of all the habitations, disposed with an elegant symmetry, both to please the eye and facilitate the maintenance of public order.

As there would be no longer palaces, Magnificence of neither would there be any miserable the public ruins, such as now constitute the greater edifices. number of habitations. The dwellings would be simple, and the magnificence of architecture and of the arts, which set off and heighten its imposing grandeur, would be reserved for the public magazines, for the amphi-theatres, for the circuses, the aqueducts, bridges, canals, public places, the archives, the libraries, and, above all, for the places consecrated to the deliberations of the magistrates, and to the exercise of the popular sove-reignty.

In a well-ordered society nothing would escape the searching mind of the legislator; in a veritable republic nothing should run counter to the principle of equality, which is at once its end, bond, and strength; let its citi-zens only once begin to taste the sweets of equality, and

These capitals, which inequality engenders, and in which are forged the elements of all revolutions—these capitals, which have so often been the instruments, were also at times the focuses of liberty; they might still be made to render effectual aid towards establishing a real social order, provided wise and upright minds could attain the directing power of their movements, and were afterwards able to make their unwieldly bulks disappear, by scattering their inhabitants over the country, to be better employed for themselves and their country.

[How dear old Cobbett would have enjoyed this philippic of Buo-narroti against the vices of city life! Who does not recollect some of that able writer's descriptions of the "Wen," as he used to call this metropolis. Buonarroti, however, possesses this advantage over Cobbett—that he tells the whole truth, while Cobbett tells only a part. The taxes and the tax-eaters were all that seemed to trouble Cobbett. Buonarroti takes a wider and juster view of things. Without assigning a pre-eminence of mischief to any one class in particular, Buonarroti shows what must inevitably be the vices of all city populations—vices which can be no otherwise remedied than by the application of some such principles as those inculcated in his book.—BRONTERRE.]

soon will every department of civil life be most easily moulded and harmonised upon that principle.

Furniture and clothing.
The same rules are applicable to dress and furniture. It is essential to the happiness of individuals, and to the maintenance of public order, that the citizen should habitually find in all his fellow-countrymen equals, brothers; and that he should nowhere meet with the least sign of even apparent superiority, the precursor of despotism and servile submission. Equality and simplicity do not exclude elegance and propriety. There might be, for instance, different colours and forms to distinguish the different ages and occupations; and there is no reason why the citizen should not wear a different costume at the assemblies and festivals, from his ordinary one in the workshop. The girls, too, might be differently attired from the grown women; and it might prove useful, as well as pleasing, that the youth, the adult, the old man, the magistrate, and the warrior, should have each a peculiar and appropriate costume. Indeed, with respect to dress in general, the Insurrectional Committee was of opinion that the main point to consult for was health, and the development of the organs; for fashion and frivolity it had no sympathies. It desired, also, that the French people should adopt a costume to distinguish them from all other nations.

Happy consequences of this reform.
To appreciate fully the utility of so great a change, the readers of this work ought to bear well in mind the train of reasoning by which the Committee demonstrated to itself the justice of its enterprize, and felt encouraged to persevere. If, it observed, the only object of regard be that class of men who, by their riches, their talk, their wit, their dissipation, and their insolence, engross the whole of public attention, and call themselves the sound and interesting part of the nation, it must be owned that such persons will have many privations to experience in the transition from the old to the new life of the social body. Those amongst us who have been led, by a vicious education, to contract disastrous habits, will necessarily view with uneasy astonishment the regeneration they must have to undergo. But if, on the other

hand, we consider the state of oppression, of misery, of suffering, of drudgery, and bondage, to which the great majority of our fellow-citizens are reduced—if we reflect that the rich man does not taste a single pleasure which is not wrung from their toils and privations—we shall be convinced that every advance towards equality prevents the recurrence of an infinity of afflictions, and opens an immense field to the benedictions of emancipated millions, which, though less noisy, cannot be counterbalanced by the selfish murmurs of a handful of corrupt usurpers, whom, for their own true happiness, as well as for that of the whole Commonwealth, and of all posterity, it is necessary to lead, by consent or force, to more reasonable sentiments.

The labour necessary to the mainte- Non-productive nance of society, equally distributed occupations. amongst all its valid members, is for each of them a duty, the fulfilment of which is rendered imperative by the law. Nevertheless, there remains in the life of man a long interval of time, the occupancy of which ought not to be abandoned to voluptuousness and ennui. It is upon the wise and free employment of this time that the happiness of the citizen depends, and consequently the liberty, prosperity, and duration of society. To fortify the soul by giving vigour to the body—to close without restraint all the avenues to corruption—to shed a charm upon every moment of life—to develope the enthusiasm of virtue, and to render his country the dearest of earthly abodes to each citizen—such are the grand effects that a legislator truly popular would elicit from the occupations, by which he might contrive that this interval of life be freely filled up.

It would be idle to attempt introducing a taste for such occupations into a country where corrupt institutions render the love of riches the principal spring of human action, and place the talent of acquiring them in the rank of honourable qualities. Were the attempt made to ally them to the spirit of avarice and traffic, they would immediately sink into utter contempt; and the man who, to accomplish such a task, should neglect the care of his own affairs, would pass for an incorrigible dupe, and inevitably carry about him the penalty of his good intentions.

Good manners.   Those occupations which have for their object the exercise of the body, the cultivation of the mind, general instruction, the scientific use of arms, military evolutions, the rendering honours to the Divinity, the apotheosis of great men, public games, the celebration of festivals, the perfecting of useful arts, the study of the laws, the public administration, and the deliberations of the people, differ from the other occupations spoken of in this—that they are neither indispensable for man's existence, nor, for the most part, commanded by the law. They ought to be taken up voluntarily, and without constraint. To obtain a good result from them, the skilful legislator attaches the people to them by their own free choice. And here, the master-piece of policy consists in so modifying the human heart by education, by example, by reasoning, and by the attractions of pleasure, as to cause it never to form any other desires than those which tend to render society more free, more happy, and more durable. When a nation reaches this point, it has good manners; then are duties, the most painful, discharged with alacrity and pleasure. A spontaneous obedience is yielded to the laws; the limits imposed on our natural independance are regarded as blessings; reasonable propositions encounter no opposition, and there prevails throughout the body politic unity of interest, of will, and of action.

There took place in the Insurrectional Committee, a few days before its violent dissolution, a long conference on this department of the new institutions, all the circumstances of which I regret that I am unable to report. To acquit myself, however, in the best way I can of the duties I have imposed on myself I shall state all that remains of it in my memory, but without attempting to fill up the breaks of the argument, lest I might substitute my own thoughts for those of the Committee.

Education the source of manners.   According to the conspirators' plan, the mould of national manners lay in the common education, which they placed under the immediate direction of the Republic. They would be afterwards confirmed in the civic assemblies, where the young people would have found the same sentiments, the same opinions, and the same usages, which they had been taught to love in the early days of life. I will speak of this education after I shall have given a more complete idea of the superstructure of which it was to be the eternal base.

We have seen that the employments indispensable for the preservation of society, ought to be so distributed amongst the different classes of workers, that each would have its own department. But there are other employments to which it is expedient, for the maintenance of liberty, that all the citizens should be invited to take part in turn— viz., such as appertain to the administration and defence of the Republic.

Works not subject to division of labour.

The Insurrectional Committee was of opinion that equality and liberty could not be maintained in society unless all the citizens participated in the construction of the laws, were all equally eligible to be charged with a share of the public administration, and were always ready to carry arms for the defence of the country and the laws.

Direction of public affairs, and defence of the country, common to all.

If, observed the Committee, we allowed to grow up in the State a class of persons exclusively versed in the principles of the social art, of law-making, and of Government, it would soon find, in the superiority of its knowledge, and in the ignorance of the rest of the citizens, the secret of creating for itself distinctions and privileges. By exaggerating the importance of its services, it would easily succeed in making itself be regarded as a protecting power, necessary to the country; and, colouring its audacious designs with a pretended regard to the public good, it would, by degrees, usurp the popular sovereignty, and talk all the time of liberty and equality, the same as though it were not reducing the deluded people to the worst of all servitudes; the worst, because it would be an apparently legal and voluntary one.

Dangers to be apprehended from a class exclusively instructed in the art of governing.

The exercise of legal power not above the capacity of any citizen.

The primordial laws are not sufficient for a state; they cannot foresee every thing, nor be adapted to all times and circumstances, and new ones will be frequently required to preserve the spirit of the institutions, as well as to provide for unforeseen cases. Moreover, it belongs to the nature of man to ameliorate his works by experience; and in order that the end of society be completely attained, it is necessary that its practical results should be from time to time applied by the laws to the improvement of the public administration. If a permanent legislative power be necessary to a state—if this power can, as we shall presently see, reside only in the whole people—it becomes one of the most important duties of the founder of a Republic to place all the citizens in a capacity to exercise it; that is to say, to give the people the means of being really sovereign. The enlightened decisions of the people on general objects could never run counter to equality, or to the well-being of society (since no people would knowingly legislate against themselves); but to be and to continue enlightened, they should be formed under a régime in which equality exists in the fullest sense of the word.

From this fundamental duty emanate for every citizen three species of occupations, which, by the importance of their object, the attention they require, and the elevation they give the mind, would charm a great part of life. These occupations consist in the conservation and propagation of the principles of the social institution and laws, in the necessary training to learn them, and in exercising them. I shall speak elsewhere of the magistracies charged with the public education and instruction, as also with the training of youth; at present I will confine myself to describing the career intended for the young people after they had quitted the common halls of education, through which all should pass.

Age and capacity required for having the right of Suffrage.

Of all social rights, there be none more important than those which relate to the formation of the laws, for by them it is that society lives and moves; next in importance come the functions of the magistrates charged with the execution of the sovereign will. These rights cannot be exercised, nor these functions properly discharged, unless by well-informed, experienced, and prudent men. Thus, according to the plan of the Insurrectional Committee, the legislature was to prescribe the age under which no man could participate in the sovereign power or in the magisterial authority: it was even proposed to interdict from the exercise of civic rights all who could not furnish proofs of their capacity; but the fear of thereby affording a pretext for the exclusion of a vast number of citizens, made the Committee reject it, and the more determinedly, because its members were convinced that, real equality once established, the multiplicity and opposition of interests would be annihilated, and the art of government so simplified, as to be brought within the capacity of anybody and everybody.

In coming out of the halls of education, the youth of France would not have been inconsiderately thrown into the Comitia;* it was expected they should first attend them for some time in silence, and in a place marked out for the purpose, in order to learn the forms and order of debate, and to acquire habits of gravity and decency. It was also desired that, before being invested with the most precious of all social rights, that of voting for the laws, the young people should frequent unions, wherein it would have been lawful for every one to speak his opinion; there they would have heard men deeply versed in the science of law, and perused such books as the Republic would have provided for the purpose. Moreover, they should not have arrived at the exercise of the suffrage without having served a certain time in military affairs at the camps; the youth would have been constantly in the presence, as it were, of their country, which, never losing sight of their future destination, would have cherished and enlightened them in the knowledge of its benefits, of its laws, and of their duties.

* [An assembly of the whole Roman people to give their vote upon anything was called *comitia*; in these assemblies, every thing which came under the power of the people was transacted, such as electing magistrates, passing laws, declaring war, &c.— BRONTERRE.]

I

The rights of citizenship are acquired by consent.

The Committee regarded as a great vice the custom of placing in the rank of citizens all who happen to be born in a country, without any deliberation on their part, thus presuming a consent which ought to have so great an influence on their future lives. It was considered, that the submission of every one to the laws of the society of which he forms part, ought to be the result, formally expressed, of a free and enlightened will. For this purpose, it thought of establishing a solemnity, by which the reciprocal engagements of society towards the citizens, and of the citizens towards society, would have been formally verified.

On stated days, young men of the requisite age, and after completing the degrees of civil and military instruction prescribed by the laws, should have come to demand of the assembled citizens the inscription of their names on the register. After the deliberation of this assembly, the nature of the social compact would have been explained, the rights it confers, and the duties it imposes on the candidates, who would have been called upon to declare whether they consented to become a part of French society on the conditions they had just heard, and in which they had been instructed by their education. The recusants, if any, would have been forthwith banished for ever from the Republic, and accompanied to the frontiers, after being provided for a certain time with the necessaries of life. As to the others—those consenting to the conditions—they would have contracted a solemn engagement with the sovereign people, by virtue of which they would have received the tokens of their new condition. Clothed by the magistrates in the costume of the citizens, they would have been saluted as French citizens, and their names inscribed in the civic register borne with pomp in the midst of the people; then would each new citizen have been presented with a military coat and a complete suit of armour with his name engraven thereon, to the end that the fear of being dishonoured by losing it, might render him more resolute in battle, and engage him to defend at the cost of his life whatever his country confided to his care.

From his inscription on the civic regis- *Popular assem-* ter till death, each citizen would have *blies for the* been summoned without fail to the assem- *exercise of so-* blies in which the people was to exercise *vereign power.* its sovereignty. It will be seen by the developments, I propose to give of the doctrine of our conspirators respecting the form of Government which was to be the final result of their success, that these assemblies would have met for the following purposes :—

To discuss—to admit or reject the laws proposed to the people by its delegates.

To deliberate on the laws demanded by a certain number of citizens, or by other sections of the sovereign (people).

To ascertain and promulgate the laws approved by the whole people.

The same development will also make *Formation and* known the occupations to which the elec- *action of the* tion of magistrates, their installation, and *Government.* functions, would have given place. The essential point was to render these occupations agreeable and sought after; and this our reformers hoped to accomplish by education, by the carefully-cherished remembrance of the unnumbered evils from which equality had delivered Frenchmen, and by the esteem and gratitude with which the laws, manners, and public opinion, would have honoured those who devoted themselves to the public administration.

It would have been an object to em- *The public as-* bellish the localities of these assemblies *semblies are oc-* with every thing that the arts, Majesty, *casions of re-* Order, and Liberty, present as most at- *laxation and* tractive. If, moreover, we consider that the confusion caused now-a-days in such meetings by the clashing of interests, which often makes them degenerate into tumultuous mobs, would have been unknown in our assemblies; if we reflect, besides, that from the simplicity of our political system, all persons would have been able to appreciate the utility of these assemblies, we shall retain the conviction that, real equality once established, they would necessarily become objects of interest, of relaxation, and of useful emulation.

Every citizen is a soldier.   The aggression of foreign powers being a thing always possible, the defence of the country against invasion is an essential part of the wisdom of laws; for the best internal institutions would offer no safeguard to a people unskilled in war, against the attack of an unjust and warlike neighbour. But if, on the one hand, arms are useful to the Republic, they become, on the other, very disastrous to it, when habitually and exclusively confided to a part of the citizens. These, seduced by the temptation of booty, or by a false glory, often turn them against the liberty of the other citizens, to the advantage of ambition and tyranny. To prevent so dangerous an abuse, it is good policy to give arms to all the citizens, and to render all equally skilled in the use of them. Besides being a preservative against the danger just spoken of, the Republic would find in such institutions the advantage of being better respected by its neighbours, and the no less valuable one of accustoming the citizens to legal obedience, and of increasing their vigour by fatigue, and by the contempt of pain and death.

The children to be brought up in the love of country and of true glory.   Accordingly, so soon as the children would have acquired strength, they would have been habituated to military works. In speaking of early education, I shall explain how it was intended to inspire them with firmness and courage. I shall only observe here, that according to the views of the Committee, the effect of the institutions relating to this point would have been to preclude the introduction of young people into social life until inured to discipline, and to the privations of the camp, inflamed with love of country, and burning to serve it.

The youth constantly encamped on the frontiers.   In proportion as the new institutions would have augmented the defensive force of the nation, in the same ratio would they have inspired it with sentiments of justice towards foreigners, and with aversion for conquests. An agricultural people without money, and without luxury, having no other soldiers than citizens, and enjoying the sweets of equality, of liberty, and abundance, has neither the wish nor the power to take up arms to oppress its neighbours, or to prolong war, after being engaged in it in self-defence. Nevertheless, its respect for the laws of nations being no security against the restless projects and ambitious designs of its neighbours, it ought to be on its guard and prepared. Its army, composed of all the able-bodied citizens, would soon punish the audacity of invaders; but is it not wiser to stop them on the frontiers, to preserve the country from the ravages of an invasion, and to give the nation time to fly to arms? Accordingly was the Committee of opinion, that in the then political state of Europe, and until reason and liberty might have made new conquests, it would be necessary to keep the youth of France constantly encamped, or cantonned on the borders of the Republic. Before entering on the chapter of military education, it is right to throw a glance or two on the formation, force, and movements of the National Army.

We have seen that it was to be composed of all Frenchmen capable of bearing arms. The laws had determined the age at which this capacity is presumed to begin and end.

All the citizens, distributed into bodies of equal force, are ready to march at the voice of the country in danger. There is in military life a time exclusively devoted to obedience; the chiefs are named for a time by the people.* Some members of

Military order.

---

* The perpetuity of military grades is, if I mistake not, one of the greatest scourges of public liberty, and by it it is that a certain despotism raises itself on the ruin of the laws. Officers, formerly good citizens, seeing themselves placed for life above the common soldier, insensibly separate their interests from those of the people, create out of the services they have rendered the country titles or licenses for arrogating to themselves distinctions, treasures, and power; they no longer carry arms, except in the sense in which one exercises a profession or trade, and they end by forming in the state an aristocratic body, which, to please its chiefs to whom it owes every thing, accredits the doctrine of blind obedience, and labours to stifle in its subordinates even the remembrance of their rights.

It is the interest of tyranny to persuade the people that war cannot be made with advantage, unless by those who make it the exclusive business of life. That is an error belied by all experience. The souls of freemen have a spring of action within them more powerful than all the rules of tactics. A united and wisely-instituted people will always know enough of the art to confound the audacity of its enemies, and will find old men and

the Committee believed it would be useful to call the civil magistrates to the superior functions of the army. We shall revert to this opinion when we speak of government.

Occupations of which the Military Order is the source. In time of peace the Military Institution would tend to prepare the citizens for the fatigues and manœuvres of war, to strengthen man's physical and moral constitution, and to open to the people a vast field of amusements and emulation. Frequent assemblies would be formed, to enter the names of the new defenders—to elect and proclaim the chiefs—to execute military evolutions—to assist in the exercises of running, riding, and swimming, &c.—to form grand encampments—to distribute the prizes and triumphal honours decreed to zeal and valour.

Levy of the whole people easy to execute. Thus far military functions agreeably fill up a part of the void left in human life, unclaimed by its necessary occupations, of which they derange neither the distribution nor harmony; but war arriving, they immediately pass into the rank of works essential to the maintenance of society, whose wants are then considerably augmented.

To the authority charged with the supreme executive power, it belongs to summon the citizens to the common defence, and to mark out, agreeably to rules established by law, the divisions that are to march when the concurrence of all is not necessary. The lists, the arms, the habiliments, and the military instruction being always

---

magistrates of sufficient experience to direct its military operations.

There is Sparta—had she irremovable officers? Had the Greeks, who bid defiance to the countless army of Xerxes, perpetual chiefs at their head? In the glorious days of ancient Rome had they commanders for life? Was it not with armies of peasants and shepherds that the Swiss, the Dutch, and the Americans repelled the troops of their oppressors, though disciplined, fashioned to blind obedience, and commanded by professional officers? A handful of rude Corsicans constantly beat the disciplined soldiers of the Genoese aristocrats, and for a long time resisted a numerous and well-regulated army of Frenchmen. In short, it is to soldiers without experience, and to new chiefs, that France was indebted, at an epoch, when she marched with rapid strides to liberty, for the prodigies of valour, by which the servile soldiery of all the despots of Europe was repelled and defeated.

in an effective state on all points of the Republic, the levy or rising of the whole people presents no more difficulty than the march of a single regiment. Where is the nation that can oppose to its enemies so formidable a force?

However, if the whole or a part of the people take up arms, and remove to a distance from home, productive labour being necessarily suspended or diminished, there will result a lack of the ordinary materials of consumption, unless a wise administration can find in the ordinary course of society preservatives against unforeseen accidents.

These accidents are not confined to the ravages of war, and the suspension of industrial works; there are some which human prudence can neither foresee nor prevent—such are inundations, parching droughts, hail-storms, and that sterility with which frequent revolutions smite lands rendered fruitful by the hand of man. For the want of good social institutions, flourishing countries are oftentimes depopulated by these and the like events, and what is far more distressing to every honest mind, a season of scarcity causes the labouring classes to die of misery, not through any real lack of food in the country, but because the workpeople, who are then in less demand, cannot reach the high price to which the rich raise commodities and provisions, the latter of which they alone have been able to accumulate during years of abundance.

Unforeseen accidents and precautions.

Where a people is equitably governed, the goods and the evils ought to be equitably shared amongst all its members. The scarcity of things necessary for use, ought, whenever it happens, to make itself be felt equally everywhere; but before coming to privation, every precaution, rendered practicable by the ordinary fertility of the soil, and by the activity of the inhabitants, ought to be exhausted.

The labour of all the valid citizens would, no doubt, produce far beyond the wants of the public, since, even under the existing order of things, there are so many idle people, and so many useful things converted into superfluities. To obviate unforeseen accidents then, it is only necessary to gather up, and preserve the super-

abundance of fertile years, now-a-days almost entirely
dissipated in frivolous customs, which, by flattering
pride, vanity, and depraved tastes, render us wicked and
unhappy.

From its ready knowledge of the state of production
and demand, the Supreme Administration deduces the
arrangements necessary to guarantee everywhere a sufficient supply of provisions, and to provide also for the
unforeseen wants of the future. As matters stand now,
nothing is more rare than exactness in such surveys, because every one, believing himself less exposed to adversity in proportion as he piles up, endeavours by false
declarations to withdraw his substance from the public
charges. But in our system, where the sole proprietorship of the country replaces individual properties, it being
impossible for any man to be tranquil as regards the
future, unless the Republic be rich, and able to ad-
minister and distribute with equity the fruits of the common labour, the same anxiety, which now causes men to
think only of themselves, invites them to approach one
another, to mix together, to lend mutual succours, and
to communicate to one another without mystery or
fraud their wants and their resources. Let all the circumstances, said the Committee, be duly weighed, and
it will be seen that the advantages of the social state are
almost annihilated by the introduction of private property, and that it is only when that institution shall have
been abolished, that each individual will feel how much
he is interested in the well-being of all his associates.
The science of government, which the collision of so
many opposing interests renders at present so very in-
tricate, is reduced by the system of community to a simple
calculation scarcely beyond the capacity of an ordinary
shopman. By means of grand depôts, replenished in
times of abundance, our Republic would have provided
for unforeseen accidents; upon the least appearance of
external danger, the subsistence necessary for the armies
would have been abstracted from the depôts, to be
transported to the places where the troops were mus-
tering.

Under the existing order of things, whenever we want
to prepare for war, our greatest difficulty is not to direct

the movements of the armed bodies, but to assemble them and subsist them.

If we succeed so far as to overcome in some degree the resistance opposed to us by effeminacy and selfishness, a great deal remains still to be done in the way of raising money, which is contributed with reluctance, and in ensuring provisions of every kind, either by direct purchase, which the sudden rise of prices and the inevitable peculations of agents render very burdensome, or through the medium of contractors, whose insatiable and crafty cupidity nothing can satisfy. Sometimes, indeed, the fear of a foreign yoke kindles, at least for a time, the love of country, and favours the raising of extraordinary contributions, but it is only by inflicting a disastrous wound on agriculture and industry, that the means are procured for repelling foreign aggression.*

In the political system of our conspirators all these difficulties disappear. The provisioning of the armies is always at hand, and the armed bodies always ready at a moment's warning to march to the frontiers, without any necessity for the citizens to make the least retrenchment in their mode of living; their numbers remaining the same, the consumption of the whole is not increased, wherever that consumption may take place.

Nevertheless, if a second or third cam- Extraordinary paign were necessary, since the mass of resources. labour necessary to be done, and the number of consumers would remain undiminished, whilst a part of the citizens was engaged in non-productive occupations, there would ultimately result in the provisioning department, a *deficit* which might become a cause of calamities and disorder. To remedy this, a new application of the principles of equality furnishes new resources. Since the citizens engaged in war bear a burden to which nothing can possibly be added, it is just that, by a fresh repartition of the common industry, an increase should take place in the labour of those who do not take arms. A half-hour or a hour's additional work per day would be the *maximum*

---

* [The reader will please to bear in mind, that Buonarroti's argument applies to a continental and agricultural country. In an insular country, like Great Britain, the dangers and difficulties to which he alludes exist in a comparatively small degree.—BRONTERRE.]

of the burden which the most calamitous war could entail on the people. " Let there be shown to us," exclaimed some of the conspirators, " any other social order in which such grard effects are produced, by means so simple and of such easy execution."

Precautions against the abuse of war. From the facility with which a people, living under such institutions, would be able to develope its strength, it would be wrong to conclude that it would be therefore disposed to disturb the quiet of its neighbours. On the contrary, the presumption is that it would impose restraints on itself, either to prevent precipitation and injustice in the declaration of war, or to direct the conduct of its warriors during the existence of hostilities. Probably, such a people would never wage war, unless to repel invasion, or to support a neighbouring power unjustly oppressed. Content with the riches of a fertile soil, and containing in its bosom neither beggars nor rogues, for what purpose could it be tempted to dispute with its neighbours for productions which it neither required nor would know how to dispose of? Agricultural, simple, happy, and attached to the manners, and to its laws, the love of pillage would be as foreign to it as the passion for conquests; and its commercial institutions could never expose it to espouse the quarrels of its merchants—a race of vampires that would be unknown to the country.*

It was thought in the Insurrectional Committee, that the law ought to forbid all offensive wars, and oblige the army to await on the territory of the Republic the attacks

* Peace being the most desirable of objects after liberty, it is useful and just to have recourse to arms only when the latter is menaced. Except in this case, the most successful war is but a crime against humanity, and a source of evils to even the conqueror himself. History informs us that military glory was most frequently the footstool of tyranny. The necessity of bridling the military spirit by laws and manners, is rendered greater by the circumstance that conquest and pillage corrupt the citizens, drive the vanquished to despair and vengeance, taint public opinion with a false ambition under the names chivalry and honour, and elevate above the laws rebel chiefs, who dare to exercise upon the country the despotism to which they had fashioned the soldiers, under pretence of disciplining them. These traitors, aided by the passion for money and distinctions, which they craftily foment in their imprudent companions in arms, sow everywhere the seeds of corruption, proscribe virtue, insolently proclaim themselves the saviours of

of the enemy; the intent was to preserve the nation from the corruption which the spoils of victory draw in their train; that all individual booty should be interdicted, and that every soldier should be obliged to carry to the public depôt whatever might fall into his hands. It was well understood, however, that the best security against military licentiousness would be found in the contempt entertained for the treasures of slaves—a contempt which the general education would have engraved on all hearts. In the tent—in the field—in the midst of battle, the citizen soldier would have had no other passion than the love of equality and of country, and no other guide than the laws.

To the love of their Republic the conspirators united that of humanity, to the Respect for the law of nations. well-being of which all their projects fundamentally tended. Had their wishes been fulfilled, it would not have been their fault if the same spirit of equality and of justice, which was to reign amongst the citizens, did not direct the conduct of the Republic towards foreigners. They desired that the French people, considering itself as a member of the great human society, should contribute, by its wisdom and by its example, to ensure universal peace, and to procure respect in all places for the rights which nature has accorded to all men alike.

Occupations having for their object the administration and defence of the State, are not less essential than those which contribute to satisfy the wants of men, because without them internal order could not be maintained, nor external dangers prevented. Besides, they are duties for all, since, if they were otherwise, they would soon cease to have for their sole object the public interest. Those of which I am going to speak differ from them in this—that while no less necessary for the preservation of liberty, and for the happiness of society, they are neces-

---

the nations they are loading with chains, and after having outraged humanity, and made a mockery of all religious ideas, they carry their effrontery to such a pitch, as to place their criminal usurpations under the protection of the Divinity and of justice.

[What an admirable portrait of the insolent usurper Buonaparte, who used at one time to sign himself " citoyen sans culottes !"—BRONTERRE.]

sarily more fruitful of good results, since, instead of being
commanded, they are voluntary, and sought after—make
pleasure a source of virtue, and fortify the sentiment and
love of equality.

Advantages of frequent meetings of citizens. The Committee desired, that in the
Republic, the citizens should do in common
whatever was to be done. The presence,
it observed, of a numerous and incorruptible public, checks
the secret impulses of selfishness, makes the want of
mutual co-operation more sensibly felt, and fosters in
the heart of each the desire of obtaining the general approbation, by punctuality in the discharge of his duties.
If relaxation or recreation be the object, it is in the very
genius of equality to value pleasure only in proportion as
it is shared by all. Thus, have free people frequent
assemblies, while slaves have none. The amount of
happiness in a state increases in proportion as public
amusements are more preferred, and, as there exists a
less disposition to shut oneself up, and become insensible
to the sufferings and to the ennui of the multitude.
Under a wise legislature, the events of nature, of life,
and of society, are rendered so many occasions for instruction and amusement. By the one, he invites the
attention of the citizens to the works of the Divinity,
and to the wonders of the social system. By the others,
he celebrates the virtues of great men, and excites an
ambition to imitate them. At one time he inflames
courage, at another he kindles the love of equality; and,
by incessantly occupying the soul with sublime objects,
he preserves it from those appetites and corrupt passions
which enervate and deprave it.

Four classes of assemblies. The Insurrectional Committee distinguished, if I mistake not, four classes of
the people. In the first, it ranged those who had for
their objects the exercise of sovereign power, of the
judicial functions, and of the public administration. I
have already alluded to it, and shall revert again to the
subject, in rendering account of the form of Government. The assemblies of the second class had reference
to the military order, of which I have spoken. To the
third belonged exclusively the assemblies destined for
instruction. I will say more of it, in treating of educa-

tion, and the development of the intellectual faculties. Finally, by those of the fourth class, the Committee proposed to nourish and strengthen the love of virtue in the hearts of the French people. I shall attempt a brief description of the ideas formed by the Committee on these points.

It began by turning its eyes to the most re- Festivals. markable events of civil life, and judged it to be conformable to the spirit of its institutions to make such events the subjects of so many popular festivals. *The union of the sexes, the presentation of new born infants, the entrance of children into the houses of education, the departure of the youth for the frontiers, their return, and admission to the rank of citizenship,*—all these and the like events would have given place to public solemnities celebrated in every part of France. In case of war, *the departure of the warriors, the rendering of honours to the defenders of the country fallen in battle, and the triumphs to be decreed to the most valiant,* would have given occasion to other festivals, calculated to exalt the soul, and to preserve the martial spirit of arms.

Other assemblies were destined by the Assemblies of Committee to foster the desire of appro- censorship. bation, and the fear of public censure. At certain prescribed times, a species of censorship would have been exercised on the conduct of the citizens, and principally on that of the magistrates. We have seen that the consent of the people would have been necessary for the enrolment of the youth on the civic register. The same sort of ceremony would have been required for the honours to be decreed to old men, and for according to the dead a glorious memory. According to the views of the Committee, the old men should have played a grand part in the Government of the Republic, either by enlightening the deliberations, or by watching over the preservation of morals; or finally, by directing the education of youth. Distinguished by a particular costume, and by a marked place in the public assemblies, they had collectively the initiative of opinion (right of speaking first) on all propositions made to the people. Important functions, and the principal influence over the censorship, were reserved to them; and, by yielding to them a filial respect full of deference, as their due reward for a life without reproach, the public deliberations were preserved from levity, and from the precipitate rashness of immatured experience.

Judging of the public functionaries.   Our conspirators desired, also, to institute tribunals of opinion, to which all the magistrates, on the expiration of their offices, would have been amenable. No magistrate could have been called to a new office unless his behaviour in the preceding one had been approved.

Judging of the dead.   And, to the end that something might always remain to be desired, or feared by the citizens, even by those most covered with glory, it was in contemplation to naturalize in France a custom of ancient Egypt, by which the lives of the dead were subjected to an examination, which accorded or refused them the honours of sepulture, according to their admitted deserts. Places embellished by nature and art were to be consecrated to receive the mortal remains of good citizens. Monuments erected by the people to the most worthy, and the inscription upon them of the names and virtues of all, would have transmitted to posterity a vast field of instruction and of patriotism; and the old men to whom would have been confided the guardianship of these sacred precincts, would have invited the whole nation, by their example, to render a useful homage to the memory of deserving men.

Anniversaries of memorable events.   Festivals would have been consecrated to celebrate the memorable events which had most contributed to establish and consolidate equality. By placing before the people's eyes the causes which gave rise to them, the circumstances by which they were accompanied, and the good or evil which were the consequences of them, it would have been made to pass through a course of national history, of morality, and politics; and it would have learned to know the rocks upon which the lack of wisdom might expose the vessel of the Republic to be wrecked and dashed to pieces.

Games and spectacles.   It was also a wish that some of these events should be represented, as it were in living action; and, in that case, what advantages might not the legislator have derived from poetry, from music, from dancing, and painting, to engrave profoundly on the heart the sentiments sought to be inspired? By the aid of rewards decreed by opinion, he would have rendered highly honourable courage, agility, temperance, modesty, the love of labour, and all the physical and moral qualities which are the ornaments and the supports of equality, and of liberty. It seemed to the Committee that these amusements, in which all the people do not share, ought to be severely retrenched in a well instituted state, through fear, as it observed, lest the imagination, released from the surveillance of a severe judge, might soon engender monstrous vices so contrary to the happiness of all.

All the institutions and republican manners intended to be created and pre- Divinity and
immortality of
the soul.
served would have found a last and important support in the religious ideas, the seeds of which were to have been implanted in all minds by the laws and by education. The French Republic, acknowledging no revelation, would have adopted no particular worship; but it would have established equality as the only dogma agreeable to the divinity, whose beneficent works would have been proclaimed by popular solemnities, and it would have strongly engraved on the hearts of good citizens the hope of a happy immortality.*

---

* It was thought in the Committee, that the only dogmas on which a regenerated society would be really interested in maintaining the belief, are the existence of a Supreme Being and the immortality of the soul, because, said they, it is important that the citizens should acknowledge an infallible judge of their thoughts and of those secret actions, which no laws can reach, and that they should be firmly convinced, that an eternal happiness will be the necessary consequence of their devotion to humanity and to their country. As to worship, they wished it to be limited to respect for the social compact, to the defence of equality, and to certain public festivals. All pretended revelations would have been disavowed by the laws the same as other public maladies, the seeds of which it was necessary to gradually extirpate. Meanwhile, every one would have been free to follow his own religious vagaries, provided public order, general fraternity, and the authority of the laws, were not disturbed. Such was the religious doctrine of the principal defenders of equality during the French Revolution, such was that of Robespierre, who owed, in a great measure, to the courage with which he defended it, the bloody proscription of

Bond which
unites all parts
of the Republic.
What appeared to the Insurrectional Committee the most difficult point in the social order intended to be established, was the maintenance of that sacred bond which holds in

which he was the victim. The infatuation of the Atheists, the errors of the Hebertists, the immorality of the Dantonists, the humbled pride of the Girondists, the dark plots of the Royalists, and the gold of England, disappointed, on the 9th Thermidor, the hopes of the French people, and of the human race.

[There was no period of the French Revolution in which the career of an exalted and benevolent legislator was rendered more painful and perilous than during the fanatic orgies of the Atheists, towards the close of 1793 and in the beginning of 1794. The hatred of the old superstition, inspired by the recollection of its countless crimes against liberty and happiness, became so furious and indiscriminating, that, in their rage to extirpate all traces of it, many of the inflamed patriots plunged headlong into the opposite extreme of Atheism. Not content with destroying all vestiges of the Catholic worship, and proscribing its priests, the fanatic multitude was impelled to make war on the Divinity, by denying his existence, and seeking to make a religion of Atheism itself, under the form of a sort of demi-pagan worship, instituted in honour of reason. This popular madness, which went to confound the Deity with the crimes committed in his name by sacerdotal impostors, occasioned the bitterest sorrow in the more enlightened friends of equality. One of the objects of the Revolution was to establish liberty of conscience, but the Atheists outvied even the fanatics of the old religion in persecution and intolerance. They broke open the churches, demolished the altars, stripped the clergy of their vestments, and, adding barbarous insult to cruelty, paraded asses in the robes of the priests, and presented the chalice to them to drink in derision of the ceremony of the mass. Robespierre witnessed these disgusting orgies—these outrageous invasions of liberty, with horror and indignation. He saw that they were calculated, not only to degrade France in the eyes of the world, but what was of more immediate consequence, to produce sympathy, and a consequent reaction, in favour of the priests and superstition. The Convention having decreed the worship of Reason, at the instance of the Commune, which encouraged the atheistic party, Robespierre denounced the extravagant and persecuting proceedings of the leaders of that body, and, at his suggestion, the Convention declared the existence of the Deity, and re-established the freedom of worship and opinion. The speeches and conduct of Robespierre on these occasions were of the sublimest character. At the risk of his popularity, he opposed himself to the phrensied excesses of the multitude, and, though he detested

compact union all classes of the Republic, and causes each of them so far from regarding itself as a separate whole, independent of and indifferent to the fate of the rest, to feel that its prosperity depends on their's, and

the Catholic worship, he defended its priests, because he saw the rights of conscience invaded in their persons. On the same principle that he would have resisted the persecution of the Atheists by the priests, he now resisted that of the priests by the Atheists. One of his discourses on this topic is worth reciting here, if it were only to show his love of justice and the real magnanimity of his character. " No," he observes, "it is not religious fanaticism " which ought, at this time of day, to fill us with most alarm. Five " years of Revolution—a Revolution which has crushed and de- " molished the priesthood, attests its impotence. Fanaticism has " fled before reason; but once more pursue it with loud yells, and " lo! it will return again to plague you.

" And what other effect can result from this extraordinary and " sudden heat with which, as appears to me, it has been warred " against for some time?

" With what right do obscure individuals, hitherto unknown in " the career of the Revolution, obtrude themselves to seek in the " midst of events to usurp a bastard popularity, to seduce the best " patriots into false measures, and to fling amongst us firebrands of " trouble and discord? What right have they to disturb the " liberty of worship in the name of liberty, and to attack fanaticism " by a new fanaticism? With what right dare they to degrade " the solemn homages rendered to pure truth into eternal and " ridiculous farces? Why should they be permitted to thus sport " with the dignity of the people, and to attach the rattle of folly to " the sceptre of philosophy itself?

" It has been supposed that, by accepting the late offerings of " civism, the Convention had proscribed the Catholic worship. No! " the Convention has not made that false step. Its intention is to " maintain the liberty of worship it has proclaimed, and, at the " same time, to repress those who would abuse it, with a view to " disturb public order. It will not suffer the peaceable ministers " of religion to be persecuted. * * * The priests have been " denounced for saying mass. * * * The man who " would prevent them from it is more fanatic than he who says the " mass.

" There are men who would go further still—who, under pre- " tence of destroying superstition, wish to make a sort of religion " of Atheism itself. Every philosopher—every individual—may " adopt upon that point whatever opinion he pleases. Whoever " would make it a crime in him to do so is a madman; but the " public man—the legislator that should adopt such a system

can be preserved and increased only by a harmonious
communion of the whole in will and action.

There are in every extensive country some fertile spots
where the soil furnishes an abundant superfluity, and

" would be a hundred times more insane still. The National
" Convention abhors it. The Convention is not a maker of books,
" an author of metaphysical systems ; it is a political and popular
" body, commissioned to cause to be respected, not only the rights,
" but the character of the French people. It is not in vain that
" it has proclaimed the Declaration of the Rights of Man, in pre-
" sence of the Supreme Being.

" It will be said, perhaps, that I am narrow-minded—a man of
" prejudices—nay, perhaps, a fanatic. I have already said, that I
" speak neither as an individual, nor as a systematic philosopher,
" but as a representative of the people. The idea of a Great Being,
" who watches over oppressed innocence, and punishes triumphant
" crime, is a purely popular one.   *   *   *   I have been, since
" I left college, but an indifferent Catholic ; I have never been
" either a cold friend or an unfaithful defender of humanity. I
" am in consequence more strongly than ever attached to the
" moral and political ideas which I have just expounded to you.

      " *If God did not exist it would be necessary to invent one.*"

" I address myself to a tribune where the impudent G—— dared
" to make it a crime in me to have pronounced the word *Provi-*
" *dence.* And at what a time ? When with ulcerated heart, and
" bleeding spirit, I sought to elevate myself above the impure
" crew of conspirators by whom I was surrounded, by invoking
" against them the vengeance of heaven, in default of the popular
" thunder.   *   *   *   *   *   *   *   *   *
" This sentiment is engraved on all pure and feeling hearts ; it
" was at all eras the animating spark of the most magnanimous
" defenders of liberty. Thus, long as there shall exist tyrants, a
" sweet consolation will be ever present to the hearts of the op-
" pressed ; and, if ever tyranny should revive amongst us, where
" is the energetic and virtuous soul which would not in secret
" appeal from its sacrilegious triumph to that eternal justice which
" seems to have written in all hearts the decree of death against
" all tyrants. It seems to me at least that the last martyr of liberty
" would exhale his soul with a sweeter sensation by reposing upon
" this consolatory idea."

Notwithstanding the noble sentiments of liberty breathed in this
discourse, so strong was the current of atheistic fanaticism at the
time, that it was generally denounced in the clubs as anti-popular,
and counter-revolutionary. The more ardent but less reflecting patriots fancied they saw behind the theism of Robespierre a lurking

others where it yields hardly enough for the wants of the inhabitants. In the system of community the advantages of union are easily enough felt by the latter of these parties, but how are you to prevent the districts most favoured by nature from regarding as onerous their association with the less favoured ones, and from aiming to remain, by a violation of the law of equality, in possession of a more commodious existence. Perhaps the institutor of a new people might see, in the possibility of this disorder, a motive for extending or contracting his territory; or the object might perhaps be gained by varying the productions in such a manner that each commune would have something to expect from the others; but it is chiefly by the reciprocity of benefits, and by the knowledge of the advantages of social order, that the bond in question may be rendered indissoluble. When the inhabitant of the south shall know how useful to him are those of the north, by the enjoyments they procure him, by the importance of the district they defend, and by the fraternal sentiments engendered in them by the conformity of manners and laws, he will feel his soul aggrandized, he will admire the social mechanism by which so many millions of men conspire to render him

desire to restore superstition and priestly power. It was in allusion to this speech that a *ci-devant* bishop, then a deputy on mission, was heard to deliver himself at a popular tribunal of the following execrable words :—

" The priests are miscreants. I know them better than anybody " else, since I have been their colonel. Woe to you, people! un- " less you wage against fanaticism a war of extermination.

" Robespierre himself shall answer to the revolutionary patriots " for the fanatic discourse which he pronounced at the Jacobin " Club, on the 1st Frimaire last."

My readers may infer from this what a hard card Robespierre had to play at that epoch. Execrated and conspired against by the Aristocrats on the one hand, and accused of *moderantisme* by the clubs on the other, it is astonishing how he was able to maintain his ground so long. The misfortune was, that the people of France were not then sufficiently enlightened to appreciate such a man as Robespierre. • In times of great excitement, the most fatal of calamities is popular ignorance. A revolution should never be attempted until the people are first well instructed in a knowledge of their rights and duties.—BRONTERRE.]

happy, and he will be convinced that, for the very sake
of this equality which he cherishes, it is necessary that,
overstepping the limits of his commune, it should comprise the whole extent of the Republic.*

Communica-   Nothing is more calculated to give
tions between   birth to, and to cherish these sentiments,
the citizens.   than frequent communications between
the inhabitants of different parts of a state : they redouble
their zeal by proving to them the eagerness of all to
serve the country. At present, merchants do, for the
purpose of enriching themselves, what ought to be done
for the general good, for the sake of instruction, and in
order to improve ourselves. But the selfish spirit of
trade being stifled under our system, by the proscription
of individual property, the legislator who does not wish
to circumscribe his Republic within the precincts of a
city, ought to supply it with means and motives for useful
and agreeable intercommunication amongst the citizens.
The transport of provisions, the transmission of orders,
the functions of Government and war, require a great
number of citizens to traverse the country ; that is not all.
To the communications of duty we must add others,
incited solely by love of the pleasures of mind and heart ;
and methinks there is no better way to encourage, and
make them be sought after, than by the frequency and
variety of public festivals.

Festivals.   Each commune, each department, would
                    have its particular festivals ; the more general
ones would have been celebrated only near the seat of
Government. Others would have alternately embellished several points of the Republic, which should have

---

* The real or tacit compact upon which society reposes, necessarily includes the application in common, or the clubbing together
of all the strength and all the powers of individuals ; for otherwise,
these being found from the beginning unequally divided, the compact
would operate all to the advantage of some and to the detriment ot
others.

From this fundamental convention it results, that the territory,
however extensive, is entirely the original property of the
people occupying it. Now, by the people not wishing to treat
one party more favourably than another, is necessarily understood this—that when it fully exercises its rights, the unequal
production or equal works should be compensated by an impartial
distribution.

the honour in turn of attracting the regards of the entire nation.*

By such institutions it was that the Insurrectional Committee thought liberty Necessity of an authority. might be solidly founded, and that by a gradual change of manners the French might be rendered happy, united, beloved, respected, and invincible. Nevertheless, the cares of our reformers would have been insufficient, if they had not looked to the means of preserving their work from the attacks of force and corruption, as well as of successively ameliorating it. Whatever might be the wisdom of institutions, they would soon totter, and in their fall break down the established equality, if the legislator did not give them a guarantee more active than the efforts of egoism ; there is no more effectual one than the combination of all the individual forces into a single grand general one, always ready to bring back to the rule of the common interest whosoever might deviate from it—it is the creation of the political body.

But this force may be itself dangerous and hurtful to liberty, unless placed in subjection to the will of the sovereign The legislative power resides in the people. people, and directly emanating from it. It is necessary, then, that the declaration of the national will, or the law, should be the work of the people itself. Accordingly, it was to the people that the Insurrectional Committee desired to consign the care of maintaining, by the acts of its will, the grand principle of equality.

Though primitive institutions be wisely conceived, they can neither foresee all the dangers and all the future wants of society, nor provide by anticipation for all the circumstances in which society may find itself. Our Republic would have therefore required, like all political incorporations, a successive legislation, and consequently a permanent legislative authority, which, as we have already seen, should reside only in the people

* The Divinity, the grand phenomena of nature, the useful arts, the virtues, political revolutions favourable to humanity, and the great men who have served and honoured it, were subjects which these festivals would have engraven on the minds of the people, and of which the first idea had been furnished by the decree of the National Convention, passed in consequence of the memorable report of Robespierre on religious ideas.

After settling the foundations of the social economy suited to maintain equality, the Insurrectional Committee applied itself to devise means by which the principle of the sovereignty of the people might be at all times secure from violation, that is to say, to dispose things in such a manner that no obligation could be imposed on the people without its *bona fide* consent, that it might have no difficulties or obstructions in emitting its will, and that it might carry into its deliberations all the maturity desirable. In order to attain this end, it was necessary to determine the elements of which the people is composed, the forms to be observed in eliciting the expression of its will, and in ascertaining its decisions, and the precautions requisite to force the magistrates to submit to them.

Before I render account of the projects of the Committee relative to the public authority—an account as faithful as the lapse of time, and the feeble and sole resource of my memory will permit—I ought to premise that they, one and all, tended to ensure the execution of the fundamental dogma—*the people deliberates on the laws*, consecrated by the Constitution of 1793, of which it forms the distinguishing character; for the rest, I by no means give these projects as points definitely determined upon.

The people, observed the Committee, is the totality of the individuals living as brothers under the same political laws, and as nature makes the happiness of individuals, and the durable tranquillity of society to depend on equality of rights, there cannot exist within the body of the nation a single individual having more or less than his proper share, without there being thereby sown a seed of disorder and dissolution. Consequently, all the inhabitants, who having arrived at the age when the intellectual faculties are developed, consent to live in the country, and to submit to the decrees of the sovereign people, are, *ipso facto*, citizens and members of the legislative power.

Foreigners.   In treating of the views of the Insurrectional Committee on external commerce, I have said that the direction of it was to have been confided to magistrates. This arrangement was adopted, not only as being in conformity with the principle of community of goods, but also as a safeguard against the contagion of pernicious examples which might otherwise enervate the force of manners, and the love of equality, the only guarantees of the rights and happiness of all. Thus, between France and its neighbours, there would have been raised up, as it were, barriers bristled with obstacles—obstacles not insurmountable, however, for the love of humanity would have opened them to the persecuted friends of liberty, to the benefactors of nations attracted by the desire of knowing French institutions, and to all men weary of bondage, who might come with pure hearts to seek in our Republic the asylum of equality and happiness.*

No pains would have been spared, however rigorous, to keep away all persons who would introduce frivolities and foreign fashions; the curious would have been subjected to rude tests (of their good faith), and to a severe surveillance; and with respect to those honestly aspiring to the rights of citizenship, the law would have required that the National Act conferring them should be preceded by

---

* This precaution in regard to foreigners was dictated not by a malevolent spirit of isolation, but by the desire of better discharging the offices of humanity and fraternity, which all states reciprocally owe to one another. The first of these duties is that which binds a people to aid others in the recovery and defence of their natural rights; and the Insurrectional Committee thought that the French Republic ought, above all others, to acquit itself of this duty, by displaying the brilliant example of a powerful institution founded upon equality and liberty. According to its view, so great a blessing could not be communicated by force of arms, either because invasion carries with it the idea of conquest and domination, or because the accents of fraternity do not harmonize well with the violences which follow in the train of war. Wishing, then, to render effectual the grand example that was preparing for the world, it was important to carefully ward off from the new social order every thing that might retard or prevent its establishment; and consequently to rigidly exclude from the French territory that crew of foreigners which hostile Governments would not have failed to pour in upon it, under the colours of philanthropy, for the perfidious purpose of sowing discord and creating factions in it. Besides, the experience of the Year II. was too recent not to make the necessity of caution be felt. A perfectly free intercourse would not have been held with foreign States before they had adopted the political principles of France. Until then the latter would have seen only dangers for herself, in their manners, in their institutions, and particularly in their Governments.

a long and scrupulous noviciate. Where there is a numerous people spread over a vast territory, it is not possible to convene all the citizens to a single assembly, so as to collect the national will simultaneously at once. Hence the necessity of regulating in a uniform and commodious manner the sections into which the whole people is distributed, and to discover a prompt and easy means of comparing their wishes, without incurring the risk of seeing them misconstrued or outraged. The Committee believed that this end would be attained by means of the three following establishments:—1. The assemblies of Sovereignty. 2. The Central Assembly of Legislators. 3. The body of Conservators of the National Will.

The two first are consecrated by the Constitution of 1793; the third was to be the object of a supplement, which the Committee judged necessary.

Assemblies of the Sovereignty. To form the Assemblies of Sovereignty, the Republic would have been divided into arrondissements, as extended as the convenience of meeting might permit. There would have been held in each arrondissement—

The Assembly of Sovereignty, composed of all the citizens;

A Senate, composed of old men named by the aforesaid Assembly;

A President and Secretaries chosen by the same Assembly;

An ornamented and commodious amphitheatre for the Assemblies of the People—archives or records—Officers commissioned to convoke the meetings, and to maintain order in them.

Central Assembly of Legislators. The Central Assembly of Legislators was composed, conformably to the Constitution of 1793, of Delegates directly named by the people, with the double mission of proposing laws and of passing decrees to ensure the execution of them, and to direct and watch over the Government. By a remarkable difference between the provisions of the aforesaid Constitution and the projects of the Insurrectional Committee, the legislators would have been, in certain cases, responsible for their opinions.

The Body of the Conservators of the   Conservators
National Will was a new institution, des- of the National
tined to collect the Acts of the Sovereign Will.
Assemblies, and to proclaim the will of the Sovereign.
It was, moreover, projected to constitute this body into
a species of tribuneship, charged to see that the legislators
might not, by abusing the right of passing decrees, make
any encroachments on the legislative power. I do not
recollect that any steps were taken with respect to the
number of Conservators, and the duration of their functions, but I remember very well that it was agreed to
engage the people to take them, by immediate suffrage,
from the body of the senators.

This point settled, two ways of forming   Formation of
the law were contemplated—it might the law.
originate either in the Central Assembly of Legislators, or
in any of the Sovereign Assemblies. In the first case,
the Central Assembly addressed to the Sovereign Assemblies its projects, with the exposition of its motives. The
results of the popular deliberations were then transmitted
to the Conservators, who proclaimed the will of the
nation, by publishing the votes of each fraction of the
sovereign whole.* In the second case, any Assembly
of the Sovereignty might propose a new law, or the

* According to the Constitution of 1793, the tacit acquiescence
of nine-tenths of the primary assemblies of one-half the departments, and one over, is equivalent to a general consent. The object
of this arrangement was not to fatigue the people by too frequent
assemblies; and the provision itself was a consequence of the
right of individual property, guaranteed by the declaration of
rights which precedes that Constitution. This right being abolished, or considerably abridged, the danger of seeing the people
diverted from public affairs, by the care of its own private affairs,
disappears; and greater strictness is justly required in the proofs
of national consent, the presumption of which might often be
founded upon a silence resulting from ignorance and criminal
manœuvres. It would be absurd to fear the multiplicity of political
assemblies in a country where equality simplifies legislation, especially if we reflect that the acts which do not legislate on general
matters are not laws.

[It would be instructive and amusing to see a comparative estimate of the trouble and expence of British legislation in juxta-
position with that which would be necessary under Buonarroti's
system. My own opinion is, that the O'Connell and Raphael
squabble, arising out of the Carlow election, and the late Dublin
Election Commission, have conjointly cost more time, trouble,

K

repeal of an old one—the same proposition being made
by the majority of the nation, the Conservators communicated the result to the Legislators, who were bound
to put it into legal form, and thus submit to the people's
approbation the law demanded by itself.

Guarantee
against en-
croachments of
the Assembly of
Legislators.

Should it have happened that the Assembly of Legislators encroached on the
sovereign power, by passing, under the
form of decrees, any legislative acts contrary to the existing laws, the action of
the conservators would have become necessary to provoke the judgment of the people. With regard to this
action there prevailed in the Committee some diversity,
or, at least, some incertitude of opinion; for if all acknowledged the necessity of raising up a rampart against
the precipitation or ambition of an assembly clothed
with a great authority, they were not all agreed as to
the extent of power which it was expedient to confer on
the conservators. Some were of opinion that their intervention should not exceed a simple appeal to the
people; others thought it advisable to authorise them to
suspend, until the decision of the sovereign power, the
operation of the decrees objected to.

Division of the
Authority of
this Assembly.

All was vague and undecided in this
respect, except the fear of usurpations on
the part of the Central Assembly—a fear
so strongly felt, as to give rise to the project for dividing
this Assembly into two sections, one of which was to
have its functions limited to the drawing up of laws,
whilst the other, retained within constitutional bounds
by the Conservators, would have directed and comprised
the Government.

Advantage of
several organs
of legislation.

It will be readily perceived, that the
distribution or diffusion of the sovereign
power amongst so many Assemblies, has
a great advantage over its concentration in a single body,
which is more liable to become the sport of factions and
of a false eloquence. The inconstancy and precipitation

and money, than seven years' legislation would under the projected regime of the conspirators, if once fairly established.—
BRONTERRE.]

so often urged against Democracies, are no longer to be dreaded in a system where the deliberations pass through so many stages before being converted into laws. This manner of forming the law is, in these respects, preferable to all others—that it has simplicity of manners and uniformity of interests for its supports, and that, by the already cited institution of senates, it offers the securest possible guarantee against human errors.

The sovereign power belonging of right to the people, it cannot, without destroying itself, submit its acts to any will, nor ever acknowledge any superior. Its truly *The people ought to adopt precautions against errors.* legislative decisions are necessarily dictated by upright intentions, but being composed of men, and man being fallible, it may be deceived. It is, therefore, prudent, and to its interest, to take precautions to guarantee itself from errors.

Behold why, if it is contrary to the imprescriptible rights of people to dispossess them of the exercise of sovereign power, either by condemning them to silence, or by submitting to a particular sanction the acts of their will, it is just and necessary for the maintenance of these same rights, to surround the people with lights and councils, to the end that they may pronounce only enlightened and useful decisions.

These supports the Insurrectional Committee found in nature, and after the *Senates.* example of ancient legislators, it found them in the experience and prudence of old age. It desired that an Assembly of Sovereignty might not be legally able to deliberate without having first heard the opinion of its Senate, whose functions were limited to advice, after which the senators should have voted with the citizens. It has been seen that the Conservators would have been selected from the Senates, and it was proposed to also extract from them a Council of Ancients, charged with the sole function of enlightening by its advice the Central Assembly of Legislators.

Nevertheless, it was admitted, that time alone could give to this institution *First formation of senates.* its utility and its efficacy. It was felt that the same force of habit which would one day attach old men to

the institutions of equality, attached them then as now
to the illusions of hereditary monarchy, to the errors of
superstition, to the false fascinations of property, and to
the precepts of a servile morality. The senates sought
to be established were to be the conservators of equality
and of democratic manners, and of these the majority of
modern old men know neither the one nor the other.
Besides, these bodies should have been in the commencement the propagators of the new order, of which they
would afterwards become the guardians. Accordingly,
the Insurrectional Committee calculated on composing
the first senates only of the citizens most distinguished
for virtue, zeal, and attachment to the new institutions.
After a certain time they would have united to themselves whatever old men were most estimable, and most
agreeable to their respective arondissements.

Inviolable prin-   It appears from the preceding remarks
ciples.   that, in the eyes of the Committee, happiness and liberty depend much more upon the maintenance of equality, and in the attachment of the citizens
to the institutions which establish it, than on the distribution of the public administration. There was in
their Republic an *Institution of the State* and a *Constitution of Authority*, and in each are fundamental
points which the people itself can neither violate nor
modify, because they cannot be touched without instantly dissolving society. Such are, in the first,
rigorous equality; and in the second, the *popular
sovereignty*. The inviolability of these dogmas would
have been solemnly recognized by the law which was to
authorise resistance and insurrection in case a part of the
citizens should attempt, in misconception of these dogmas,
to arrogate to itself the right of enslaving the rest.

Rectification of   Excepting these cardinal points of na-
theConstitution   tural right, all the rest was subordinate to
the will of the people, which might modify and change at
pleasure the authority established by itself. To render
homage to this doctrine, and at the same time to preserve the Republic from the dangers of intrigue and
tumult, it was wished that the assemblies of sovereignty
should be periodically convened to consult on the constitution, and that in case they should demand any

changes in it, a small number of sage persons should be charged to propose in regular form the changes demanded. It was also desired that, at fixed periods, the state of the nation should be investigated by special commissioners, who should propose to the people the proper measures for extirpating whatever abuses they might have discovered to exist.

To appreciate the advantages to be derived from a legislative power thus constituted, it is necessary, above all, to recollect that a people without property, and without the vices and crimes it engenders, without commerce, without money, without imposts, without finances, without civil processes, and without poverty, could not feel the want of that multiplicity of laws under which the civilized societies of Europe groan.

Few laws suffice for a people in the enjoyment of equality.

Before terminating what relates to the sovereign power, I deem it useful to remark, that the supreme direction of agriculture and the arts would have been one of its principal prerogatives. The general rules laid down by the laws would have been developed by the central assembly, and put in practice by the executive authority, of which I am about to treat.

The direction of agriculture, and of the useful arts, is one of the principal prerogatives of the sovereign power.

If every precaution is taken that the will of the people be at all times known, if the delegates authorized to prepare and proclaim its decrees are happily placed in a state of impotence to substitute their own for them, it only remains to constitute the authority charged with the execution of them, in such a manner that the magistrates may in no case be able to constrain the citizens to obey any other wills than those of the laws, and that their conduct may furnish a permanent lesson of good manners and patriotic devotion. In enforcing respect to the people's will, the magistrate should be clothed with the full powers of the nation; but he should experience every possible difficulty and obstruction the moment he deviates from that will, whether from error or prevarication.

Executive authority.

Causes of its goodness. An administration such as I have described is the result of the mode of nominating its members, of their number, of the distribution and duration of their functions, of the surveillance exercised over them, of the accounts exacted from them, of the penalties and rewards awarded to them, and, above all, of the national manners and enlightened attachment of the citizens to their country and laws.

Supplement to the Constitution of 1793. It seemed to the Insurrectional Committee that the provisions of the Constitution of 1793, relative to the Executive Council, were good, though insufficient. It applauded the article which limits its action to the execution of the laws and decrees, and that, also, which makes the Council responsible for their non-execution. It approved the separation, established by that Constitution, of the *administrative* functions of the Council from its concurrent jurisdiction in the *judicial* functions assigned to the tribunals, and it adhered also to what the Constitution ordained respecting the number of supreme magistrates and the duration of their power, but it deemed it expedient to determine a mode of investigating their conduct, of assigning a penalty to each infraction of their duties, of regulating the forms to be observed in awarding them the praise or blame they might merit, and of instituting prompt and ready means for prosecuting delegates and supreme magistrates accused of infidelity to the people.

Nature and object of the different magistracies. The safety, defence, and, in the system of the Committee, the very subsistence of the people, imperiously require that the impulse given by the first or supreme depositaries of the laws, should propagate itself rapidly and uniformly to the very extremities of the Republic; it is, therefore, necessary that the country should be, as it were, embraced by long chains in every direction, of which every link responds instantaneously to the movement impressed at the central point. These links are the magistrates, instituted to remind the citizens everywhere of their true interests, and to provide for the wants of the people, as directed by the laws. There is, then, in the

Republic, a graduated scale of magistracies, descending by divers degrees of jurisdiction from the Executive Council to the inferior officers, who form the point of contact between the sovereign power and each of its subject parts. A similar scale, but altogether judicial, re-ascends from the inferior magistrates appointed to verify and prosecute infractions of the laws, up to the supreme tribunal, whose province is to maintain uniformity of legislation throughout the whole. One class of magistrates direct productive occupations, and regulate the impartial distribution of the wealth accruing therefrom—others maintain harmony among the citizens. Some watch over the defence of the state, and implant in the soul the seeds of courage and virtue; others let fall the severity of the laws on those that infringe them. By some the weak are protected, and the deluded set right.; by others are aliments incessantly supplied to feed the love of country, by liberty, by majesty, and by the propriety and gaiety which they cause to reign in the public meetings and festivals.

It would be as tedious as it is unnecessary to enter into all the details of this social order, the bases of which are laid by the Constitution of 1793; it institutes on the one hand, tribunals, and on the other, intermediate administrations, and municipal bodies, under whom are placed other subordinate magistrates to regulate the national economy.

To these same municipal bodies was the military Order attached, which they were commissioned to form and superintend. It was desired that the superior posts of the army should be occupied by civil magistrates, to the end, said they, " that war be never made, except in the spirit of the Government and people—to render all collision between the army and the people impossible—and that there might be less to fear from the ambition of generals." Leaving the judicious reader to follow all the ramifications of authority, which flow as so many consequences from the foregoing principiples, I will confine myself here to the explanation of the means by which it was hoped that so great a number of magistrates would be restrained within legal bounds. In fact, no nation had ever so many magistrates, without

Uniting the civil to military functions.

taking into account that, in certain respects, every citizen would have been a magistrate, keeping watch for himself and others ; it is certain that public functions would be very much multiplied, and, consequently, the magistrates very numerous. The aggregate, or totality of functions, being composed of every action necessary for feeding, clothing, lodging, educating, informing, governing, and defending the people, every citizen, so to speak, is, or has been, a functionary. The difference between the functions, in which all participate, and those assigned by the laws to particular magistrates, consists in this— that the latter have exclusively for their object to direct and protect the rest. We call them public functions.

The magistrate not more expensive than the common citizen.   It would be wrong, however, to feel any alarm at so great a number of magistrates, who almost all restricted to the work over which they preside, have no other authority than the example of a greater activity, or else are drawn from the class whom age exempts from painful occupations. Not one of them costs the Republic more expense than the simplest or obscurest citizen.

Simplicity of manners a guarantee for the fidelity of magistrates.   It is a grand prodigy of social order when the magistrate, appointed to apply the laws of a great people to one of its fractions, attracts to himself, by conforming strictly to those laws, the esteem and love of this fraction, to such degree that he can displease it, or become unpopular, only by violating the law himself. If such prodigy be within the compass of realization, it is only where simplicity of manners gives to all parts of the state the same spirit and the same interests ; and that was precisely the end to which the efforts of the Insurrectional Committee tended.

Graduated scale of magistracies.   In its view, the people was the creator, the superintendant, and the support of its magistrates. Wishing to spare it the regrets of an ill-placed confidence, the Committee had turned its regards to such laws by which nobody could be raised by popular suffrage to magistracies of the higher order, without having given proof of a great love of equality, and without having successively passed through all the inferior magistracies of the same class. This provision, which the Committee by no means extended to the exercise of sovereign power (in which the people should be left unlimited liberty), appeared to it to unite to the advantage of calling to the more important functions only men of matured experience, that of better preserving the spirit of reform, which, for the rest, could only attain complete success by the abandonment of vanity, pride, and avarice, and by a happy change in the morality and manners of the citizens.

Here naturally recurs the observation which has been made in speaking of senates. Honest old men are calculated to preserve equality when once established; they are incapable and dangerous when the question is only to establish it. To found a Republic belongs only to such disinterested friends of humanity, and of their country, whose reason and courage have shot in advance of the reason and courage of their contemporaries. The spirit of the Republic, when established, forms that of the citizens and of the magistrates; but at the commencement it is only the wisest and most ardent instigators of reform who can create the popular Republican spirit. It was, therefore, a point resolutely agreed on by the Committee, that the magistracies, composed at first, and exclusively of the best Revolutionists, should not be subsequently renewed by the full application of the constitutional laws at once, but only gradually and partially in proportion to the progress of national regeneration.

In commencing reform, the magistracies ought to be confided to Revolutionists only

Those of my readers who have followed me thus far have been able, I trust, to form a sufficiently clear idea of the political principles of our conspirators, and of the instrumentality by which they proposed to apply them to the French Republic.

Nobody, I presume, will do them the injustice of supposing that they entertained the mad hope of putting these principles into practice by, as it were, the magic stroke of a wand, or by an act like that of creation. They did not dissemble the objects they had to vanquish, but they were convinced that the reform they projected was the only means

Gradual march.

of founding a vigorous and durable Republic; and they saw in the progress of public spirit—in the reviving activity of the revolutionary elements—in the coalition of the various classes of Democrats*—in the extreme discontent of the people, and in the courage of the devoted citizens, sufficient materials to commence, and to consolidate by degrees, the revolution of which they had laid the foundations.

Education the means of consummating and conserving reform.

Amongst the means to be imagined for making head against ambition and avarice, for inspiring new manners, and for fully calling into play the natural goodness of human nature, there is one which, though slow in its effects, is infallible, if the Reformers of a state know how to employ it to its full extent : it is education.   Education once placed in the hands of the Reformers, would have completely changed the face of the country, by rendering the love of country, and the principles of liberty and equality sacred.   The grand edifice once raised, it belonged still to education to ameliorate it, to fortify it, and to render it immortal.   We should here, therefore, consider education in two points of view—first, as a conservative institution in the hands of the Republic when founded, afterwards as a means of regeneration in those of the Reformers.   An age passes whilst our sentiments and intelligence are being formed and modified by the action of all that surrounds and operates upon us; in this action consists our education; it makes us good or bad, wise and humane or the contrary, citizens or brigands.

Society ought to direct education.

As society cannot be free, happy, and flourishing, but by the sentiments and strength of its members, there is nothing clearer than the right it has to watch directly over all that may exercise on their education any influence whatever, it is its duty to do it, because thereon depends its own future destiny.

Separation of the sexes.

From the natural division of our species arise two branches of education, one for

---

* The Hebertists, or deluded Democrats, and the Robespierrists, or enlightened Democrats, were, at this time, coalesced and rallied under the same banners.

males, the other for females. The end which society ought to have in view is the same for both, but the differences made by nature between the sexes apprise us that we cannot, without running counter to her laws, employ indiscriminately the same processes of training for each. It is moreover important to the vigour and conservation of individuals, that the development of the passion of love, which is accelerated by early intercourse of the sexes, should be retarded. It is, therefore, expedient that they should be brought up separately. According to the views of the Insurrectional Committee, education ought to be NATIONAL, IN COMMON, EQUAL.*

National—that is to say, directed by the laws, and superintended by the magistrates. Education being to complete the work of reform, to maintain and consolidate the Republic, the latter is the sole competent judge of the instructions and habits which ought to be given to youth. Besides, the principal object of education ought to be to engrave profoundly on all hearts the sentiments of general fraternity, to which the exclusive and selfish régime of families is directly and abhorrently opposed. Education is national.

In common—that is to say, simultaneously administered to all children living under the same discipline. It is essential that the young people should be early accustomed to see in all their fellow-citizens only friends and brothers—to intermingle their pleasures and sentiments with those of others, and to find their own happiness inseparable from that of their In common.

---

* Michel Lepelletier, who had the glory of sealing with his blood the rising Republic, had also that of being the first of the men of the Revolution to conceive a plan of education to be *national, in common,* and *equal.* This plan, an eternal monument of the virtue of its author, was unfortunately made to reconcile itself with the miseries which flow in such abundance from individual property—that true Pandora's box of ills—and, consequently, it had to comprise qualifications and exceptions which considerably abridged its advantages. Lepelletier proposed to bring up children in common, from five to twelve years old, and to deliver them thenceforward to their families. Was it not to be feared, that the impressions still feeble at that age, might be in great measure effaced by the false opinions and bad examples, of which the youth, thus flung into a whirlpool of vices and prejudices, should have necessarily experienced the influence?

companions. Communities of education are the images of the great national community to which every good citizen ought to refer his actions and his enjoyments.

Equal. *Equal*—because all equally beloved children of their country—because all have the same rights to happiness, which is necessarily disturbed by inequality—because from inequality of education would inevitably flow the worst political equality, and consequently a return of the old evils.

Education is directed by an eminent magistracy. To form an adequate idea of the projects of the Insurrectional Committee in this respect, let us figure to ourselves a supreme magistracy, composed of old men who had grown grey in the more important functions of the Republic, directing, by the aid of inferior magistrates, all the establishments of education, assuring itself, by inspectors chosen from its own body, of the execution of the laws and of its orders, and having under its eye a seminary of teachers, whose training it has in charge.

Cares of infancy. In the social order conceived by the Committee, the country takes possession of every individual at birth, and never quits him till death. It watches over his first moments, secures him the nourishment and cares of his mother, keeps out of his reach every thing that might impair his health or enervate his constitution, guarantees him against the dangers of a false tenderness, and conducts him, by the hand of his parent, to the national seminary, where he is to acquire the virtues and intelligence necessary to make him a good citizen. They wished to establish, in each arondissement, two houses of education; one for the boys, the other for girls. Places with good air, the country parts at a distance from towns, the vicinity of rivers would have been preferred.

Natural differences of the two sexes. The duty of man, who is designed by nature for movement and action, is to nourish and defend the country; the woman's part is to give birth to vigorous citizens. The latter, weaker than men, subject to the inconveniences of pregnancy, to the pains of childbirth, and to the evils which are the after consequences of them, and gifted with charms which exercise so powerful an empire over the other sex, appears destined for the less rude and noisy operations of life, and seems to have received as her natural portion of duty, to soften the ills of humanity, and to give to the practice of virtue its highest and sweetest reward. It follows, from these indelible differences, that the education of the two sexes cannot be altogether the same. Let us speak first of that of boys.

According to the ideas of the Insurrec-tional Committee, the national education was to have three objects in view:—1. The strength and agility of the body; 2. The goodness and energy of the heart; 3. The development of the understanding.

Objects of education.

The health and strength of the citizens are conditions on which essentially depend the happiness and safety of the Republic. These are acquired and preserved by the action of the organs, and by banishing the causes which disturb the animal functions. Thence the necessity of fatigue, of exercise, of sobriety, and temperance. The youth which form their country's hope ought, therefore, to be exercised in the most laborious works of agriculture and the mechanical arts, to be habituated to the most difficult movements, and to live in the strictest frugality. Military manœuvres, coursing, riding, wrestling, pugilism, dancing, hunting, and swimming, were the games and recreations which the Insurrectional Committee intended for the rising generation. It wished that sloth and idleness should be banished from the national houses of education, and that effeminacy and love of voluptuous pleasures might not find a single avenue to glide into the hearts of the youth of France.

The body.

The houses of education were to be distributed into as many separate apart-ments as they would have comprised dif-ferent ages. Here,—rooms for dining in common; there workshops, where each pupil should be trained in the art which was the object of his preference: on the one side extensive grounds, where the youth might be seen at one time engaged in the works of agriculture, and at another lodged in military fashion under tents; on the

Arrangements of the houses of education.

other side, gymnasiums for manly exercises, besides amphitheatres for instruction.

The heart.   From the ever-varying occupations of our youth, they should necessarily contract sentiments analogous to the principles of the state. They would have been accustomed to refer to the country—the mistress of all—every beauty and perfection they witnessed, and to attribute to her sacred laws, their health, their well-being, and their pleasures. Living constantly together, they would soon learn to commingle their happiness with that of others, and removed from the contagion of self-interest and ambition, as well as convinced by experience, and by what they heard, of their country's tenderness towards them, the desire of serving it, and of meriting its approbation, would have become the ruling principle and spring of their actions. Every precaution would have been used to guard the youth from forming ideas of superiority and self-distinction. There being nothing in those abodes of innocence and of peace to awake the passions of avarice and power, a burning love of equality and of justice would have been so effectually blended with the earliest sensations of our young people, that every virtue inspired by our institutions, and recommended in the name of a beloved country, would have become thoroughly familiar and dear to them.

Arts and callings.   Shall the human mind be left to rove without guide and without curb through the vast fields of imagination? Shall it be left to introduce into society, under pretence of polishing and ameliorating it, an infinity of factitious wants, of inequalities, of disputes, of false ideas of happiness?—or shall limits be imposed on industry, by banishing from the houses of education, everything that is not strictly necessary to the well-being of the Republic? Our Committee, wishing to deliver their fellow-citizens from the constraints of superfluous wealth, and from the love of enjoyments, which enervate men, and are of no value, except on account of the distinctions of which they are signs, had unanimously determined to restrict, in the houses of education, the works of art and handicraft to such objects as are easily communicable to all. It desired that the pretended elegance of costly furniture and clothing should give place to a rustic simplicity. Order and propriety, it observed, are wants of mind and body, but it is expedient that the principle of equality, to which every thing must yield, should proscribe those pomps and delicacies which only flatter the silly vanity of tyrants and slaves.

With regard to speculative knowledge, the Insurrectional Committee, warned by the sages of antiquity, instructed by some true philosophers of modern times, and convinced that nothing is less conducive to a nation's happiness than to shine and get itself talked about, wished to divest false science of all pretext for escaping its share of the common duties —of all opportunity of flattering pride—of deluding credulous honesty—and of seducing the passions with the idea of an individual happiness foreign to that of the rest of society. They saw in the abolition of property that also of our voluminous jurisprudence—the despair alike of those who study it, and of those whose interests it pretends to defend ; they were stoutly decided upon throwing overboard all species of theological discussion; and they felt that the cessation of salaries would have soon cured the mania for displaying small wit, and for book-making.

The learning of the citizens, said they, ought to make them love equality, liberty, and their country, and place them in a condition to serve and defend it. It is then, necessary, they added, that every Frenchman should be able to read, speak, and write his own tongue well, because, in so vast a Republic, written signs are the only possible means of intercommunication between its parts, and because upon them the other sciences depend ; that the science of numbers should be familiar to all, because all may be called to guard and to distribute the national riches ; that every one should be trained to reason correctly, and to express himself with brevity and precision ; that nobody should be ignorant of the history and laws of his country—of history, because it will make known the evils the Republic has made cease, and the blessings it has given birth to—of the laws, because by the study of them, each citizen will be instructed in his duties, and become capable of exercising the magistracies, and of taking part in public affairs; that all should be acquainted with the topography, natural history, and statistics of the Republic, in order to have a just idea of the power which protects them, and of the wisdom of the institutions which make all the parts of so vast a body to contribute to the felicity of each individual; that to embellish the public festivals all should be skilled in dancing and music. Such was pretty nearly the course of education destined by the Committee for the youth of France; to that Committee it was an object of predilection, because they considered it the most solid foundation of social equality, and of the Republic.

Thus inured to fatigue, exercised in agriculture and the useful arts, provided with useful knowledge, the young people would have insensibly become the hope and consolation of all the citizens, who would have found in them a great source of comfort during their hours of labour, and of agreeable and inspiring delight in the public festivals.

No more domestic education—no more paternal sway; but, for the individual authority thus taken from fathers at home, the law would have compensated them with authority a hundred fold greater in common. The senates, of which mention has been made, were to become in each arrondissement, the guardians of the houses of education, and under their direction, the women also would have been invited to watch over the education of girls, to be also brought up in common till the period of their marriage.

Education of girls.   To the end that the state should comprise only robust and hardy citizens, a good constitution should be ensured to those whom nature destines to give citizens to the state; it is, therefore, necessary to invigorate their bodies by fatigue, by labour, and by exercise. Active motion and occupation, said the conspirators, are the grand springs of Republican education. They concur with the absence of property and distinctions, to weaken the inclination to coquetry, and to check the too early impulses of sexual passion.

The girls, they continued, will be brought up to the less laborious works of agriculture and the arts, because work, which is the common debt of all, is also the curb of the passions—the desideratum and charm of domestic life; they will be chaste, because chastity is the guardian of health, and because it seasons and makes love wholesome; they will love their country, because it will be an object with them to be loved by the men, and they will, consequently, participate in the studies calculated to make them admire the wisdom of its laws; they will be engaged in singing national hymns to embellish our festivals; in fine, they will take part, in the people's presence, in the sports of the boys, in order that gaiety and innocence may preside over the first emotions of love, and be the happy forerunners of approaching unions.

It is impossible for me to enter into all the details of so new an institution, of which the Committee had scarcely sketched the plan. For the rest, it suffices to know that the grand end of the education, *national*, *common*, and *equal*, was to form vigorous citizens, who would have served the Republic with devotion, from the habit of behaving well, and for the pleasure of contributing to the prosperity of so fond a country.

In the system of the Committee, the young people passed from the houses of Military education. education to the camps established near the frontiers; there, always ready to repel external aggressions, they would be perfected in the military art; there, living in a perfect community of work and enjoyments, they would have acquired, by fatigue, by application, and by frugality, the requisite qualities for obtaining, on their return home, the exercise of the rights of citizenship. On the success of the first essays of this kind depended, as the conspirators thought, that of their projected reformation. That alone, said they, will suffice to establish equality; for that alone will prove the existence of manners, and of Republican opinions, which the existing generation can adopt but very imperfectly.

In order the better to preserve the spirit of the new laws, and the principles of Assemblies of instruction. public morality, assemblies of instruction were to have been opened, where it would have been lawful for each citizen to explain to the public the precepts of Republican morality and politics, and to converse on national affairs. Near these assemblies the magistrates would have established printing-offices and libraries.

In this order of things, printing is the Liberty of the most active means of communication, and press. the best rampart against any usurpation of the sovereignty of the people. It alone can render the citizens of a vast state equally competent to pronounce ripely on the projects of law submitted to them; it alone gradually ameliorates public order; it alone baffles the machinations of ambitious men. But individual property being abolished, and all pecuniary interest become impossible, it is necessary to adopt means for deriving from the press all the services to be expected, without risking the again calling in question the justice of equality, and the rights of the people, or delivering the Republic to interminable and disastrous discussions. On the subject of the liberty of the press, the following articles had been submitted to the examination of the Insurrectional Committee :—

1. No one may promulgate opinions directly contrary to the sacred principles of equality, and of the sovereignty of the people.

2. All writings on the form of Government, and on its administration, are to be printed, and sent to all the libraries upon the demand of an assembly of sovereignty, or of a prescribed number of citizens, above the age of thirty.

3. No writing about any pretended revelation whatever can be published.

4. All writings are printed and distributed, if the conservators of the National Will shall judge that their publication may be useful to the Republic.

In speaking of education, we have seen that the Insurrectional Committee intended to prevent the refinement of the arts and the study of the sciences, from introducing into the Republic effeminate manners, false ideas of happiness, dangerous examples, and incentives to pride and vanity. This article was, like a great many others, discussed again and again, and the discussion was not exhausted when the Committee was forced to renounce its enterprize.

By the progress of the arts, it was *Advantages of* sometimes argued, indispensable labours *the arts and* may be mitigated, communications by *sciences.* land and by water may become easier and more rapid, and new enjoyments may be added to the mass of the common enjoyments. And what would the arts be, continued the speaker, without the sciences which fix the theories of them, and illustrate the practice? By the sciences, diseases are often cured or prevented. They teach man to know himself; they preserve him from religious fanaticism, put him on his guard against despotism, charm his leisure hours, and elevate his soul to the highest virtues.

But considering things under other as- *Evils which* pects, there were seen to spring from the *flow from them.* refinement of the arts, a taste for superfluities, disgust at simple manners, the love of voluptuousness and frivolities. It was feared that men, devoting themselves to the sciences, would imperceptibly form for themselves out of their acquirements, real or supposed claims to distinctions, to superiority, and to exemption from the common burdens; and that the opinion entertained of their knowledge would, by feeding their vanity, engage them at last in disastrous enterprises, against the rights of simple and less informed persons, whose honesty they would deceive by the aid of an hypocritical and dangerous eloquence. To the weight of these reflections was joined that of the opinion of Jean Jacques Rousseau, who had said, on the authority of history, that never were morality and liberty found united with a brilliant state of the arts and sciences. During the discussions which frequently took place on this subject, it was observed that the greater part of the evils for which the arts and sciences were blamed, being caused by the thirst for gain, which now tempts people to make professions of them, it was probable they would disappear, and that the number of artists and professors would greatly diminish, once the establishment of community had annihilated poverty, and destroyed the possibility of subserving avarice. With respect to the following points which had been proposed, the Committee came to no determination :—

1. No study or profession gives a right to exemption from the common labours of society.

2. There shall be regularly appointed magistrates to preserve and to increase the existing stock of human knowledge.

3. Such young persons as may have given proof of great natural talents shall, upon quitting the houses of education, be sent to those magistrates to pursue their studies under their direction.

Objections. Such are the faint outlines of the civil and political order towards which the efforts of the Insurrectional Committee were directed. The objections against it rest partly on the alleged injustice of its projects, and partly on the presumed impossibility of putting them in execution. As to the injustice, we have, in the course of this work, placed our readers in a situation to form their own judgment upon it. As regards the impossibility of execution—the vulgar objection of all whom the slightest reform alarms—we will only observe, that when a just idea has been formed of the state of France during the two first years of the Republic, every thinking person must be convinced that the devotion of the French people to the cause of equality, and their confidence in its leaders, were then so great that there was no democratic institution whatever which they would not have adopted with enthusiasm. Those happy dispositions were, it is true, greatly weakened by the frightful event of the 9th Thermidor;* but they still continued to manifest themselves strongly, during the labours of the Insurrectional Committee, and even a long time after. Besides being natural to the people, they are always ready to show themselves whenever the causes cease which keep them down, and in fear of declaring themselves. Obstacles to real Radical reform never come from the majority of citizens; they always arise from the depraving influence of those who have found the secret of throwing upon others their proper

* The results of that day were the more disastrous, inasmuch as they reduced to despair of the happiness of their country, and of humanity, vast numbers of persons who had previously elevated themselves to the highest pitch of virtue.

share of the general labour. Reduce this corrupt minority to silence, and all the rest of society will applaud you, and second you with all their force. For the rest, the Committee, I repeat, far from pretending to give us complete equality at once the day after the insurrection, (though resolved to neglect no means of accelerating its establishment), did not consider itself to be in a condition to determine the epoch of its commencement. It felt the necessity of proceeding gradually, according to the progress of opinion, and the success of its first measures of which I am about to render account. Indeed, had it only founded upon a solid basis its proposed system of *education in common*, it would have done a vast deal for humanity.*

* What the Democrats of the Year IV. were unable to execute in France, a generous man has recently essayed, by other means, to put in practice in the British Isles and in America. Robert Owen, the Scotchman, after having established in his own country, and at his own expense, some communities founded on the principles of *equal distribution of enjoyments and of labours*, has just formed in the United States sundry similar establishments, in which several thousands of people live peaceably under the happy régime of perfect equality.

By the counsels of this friend of humanity, the co-operative society established in London has been for some time at work, propagating the principles of community, and demonstrating, by practical examples, the possibility of their application.

Babeuf attempted to combine a numerous people into one single and grand community; Owen, placed in other circumstances, would multiply in a country small communities, which afterwards united by a general bond, might become, as it were, so many individuals of one great family. Babeuf wished his friends to seize on the supreme authority, as by its influence he hoped to effectuate the reforms they had projected; Owen calculates on success by preaching and by example. May he show to the world that wisdom can operate so vast a good without the aid of authority! May he, above all, be spared the grief of seeing his noble efforts fail, and furnishing, by an unsuccessful experience, the advocates of equality with an argument against the possibility of establishing, in any manner, a social equality, to which violent passions oppose so formidable a resistance, and which, as appeared in our time, could only be the result of a strong political commotion amongst civilized nations.

[When Buonarroti penned this remarkable passage, he neither knew the failure of the Owenite experiments in America, nor the successive breaking up of the various co-operative societies established in London and throughout Great Britain. If success depended on individual merit, on generous zeal, on indomitable perseverance, and an unquenchable desire to make man free and happy, at all sacrifices to the individual himself, unquestionably

First measures of the Insurrection.   The first cares of the insurgents, after victory, would have been to conciliate the good opinion of the people, to place all offices of authority in the hands of persons thoroughly

the experiments of Robert Owen would have succeeded. But alas! the materials to work upon forms as essential an element in the calculations of success, as the skill of the architect. Robert Owen brought to the task the necessary skill, but the demoralizing effects of our institutions left him no materials to work upon For my own part, while I admire both Babeuf and Robert Owen and agree, generally, with both as to the *end* sought, I am obliged to dissent from both as regards *means*. The points in which I agree and differ from them will be found in the following article of mine, which appeared some weeks ago in the *Twopenny Dispatch*:—

" It has been intimated to me, that in consequence of my having expressed generally a concurrence in the political and social principles of Buonarroti, as promulgated in this work, an impression has gone abroad that I am for a *community of goods and labour*, to be established by force, if necessary. It has also been insinuated, that my design in sending forth the work, is to instruct the British people in the arts of conspiracy and insurrection. I ought not, perhaps, to notice such silly imputations, but, as it is not my habit to disguise or qualify my principles, let me, once for all, explain what they really are, to prevent further misconception.

" I am for LIBERTY and EQUALITY; meaning by these terms precisely what they are defined to be by Mr. Augustus Beaumont, in his excellent prospectus to the *Radical* newspaper, namely—" *An equal opportunity to every man of obtaining all the advantages of society; no one having a monopoly, and each exclusively enjoying the produce of his own industry and intellect!*" The first step towards this equality, is the extension of the franchise to all classes alike, without restriction or qualification, other than what would apply equally to all members of the social body, such as age, sanity, and moral fitness, &c. Therefore, the first article in my creed is *Universal Suffrage*, alias, the equal participation of all in forming the laws and institutions of the country. As to the ballot, short parliaments, equal representation, and so forth, they are mere accidents or contrivances for securing the valid use of the franchise. They are not rights, but arrangements for the due exercise of rights, and being the best at present familiar to us, I am for having them, at least till better ones be discovered and agreed upon. Some such guarantees for good voting will be always necessary, so long as the laws are not *directly made or approved by the people themselves*, as was the case with the Athenians and Romans, and as was provided in France by the famous Constitution of 1793. By that

devoted to the principles of the new Revolution, and not to leave the well-known enemies of equality any time for concerting the plots to which, it was certain, they would resort.

Constitution the representative body could only propose bills and discuss them, after which they should be transmitted to the Primary Assemblies to be approved by the people : otherwise they were not *law*. The authors of that Constitution were too well acquainted with the encroaching spirit of representative bodies to trust them with the whole legislative power. To the people alone was that most important of all functions reserved. Hence, they had little need of ballot-boxes, or short parliaments, though, indeed, to make assurance doubly sure, they made annual elections one of the articles of the Constitution. If it rested with me, no Parliament—no matter how elected—should have the power of passing laws. I would provide, as the Democrats of France did, that that power should reside in, and be inalienable from the people. Parliaments are good and necessary to originate and discuss laws —to collect the evidences necessary to adjust the details of them, and, finally, to put them into shape and form ; but as to *passing* them, that is quite another question. The moment a people lets that power out of its hands, farewell its rights and liberties. Even with universal suffrage it is almost impossible to recover them. The temptations to abuse are too great for any Parliament to withstand. Hence there has hardly ever existed a representative body that has not, at some time or another, prostituted its mission to sinister ends. Even in Republican America the representative chambers are little better than gangs of smooth-tongued lawyers and profit-mongers, who make all the institutions to favour their own class. Witness the recent chartering of the United States' Bank by the legislature of Pennsylvania. Would that have happened, if the law were referred to the people for approval ? I apprehend not. At all events, if I had my way, the people's sanction should be essential to every law ; and if I have not hitherto broached the doctrine, it is only because I would not distract the people's attention by new projects, especially as I deem universal suffrage sufficient to gradually give us all we want. The best fundamental law ever promulgated to man was the French Democratic Constitution of 1793, which was voted by nearly five millions of adult Frenchmen. Had that Constitution survived, how different would be the condition of France now ! It is my firm conviction, that had Robespierre and his friends lived to execute it, there would not be now one pauper or one oppressor on the French territory, nor probably in Europe. To this end was it drawn up by its framers, and it was solely owing to its pre-eminent fitness to attain such end, that the brigands of the Convention conspired

Proclamation to the French people.

For this purpose, the Committee had resolved the plan of a proclamation to the French people, of which one of its members was in the act of writing the first sentences, when

to Burke it after the death of Robespierre. It was a fatal error of the Revolutionists of 1830 not to have proclaimed it at Paris during the three glorious days. Should there be ever another successful popular commotion in France, the insurrectionists ought to proclaim it instantly, and see that it was speedily executed. How grievously do we Radicals feel the want of some such rallying point in England.

"Buonarroti was a great admirer of the Constitution of 1793—so am I; but Buonarroti thought it did not go far enough, because it did not proscribe individual commerce and private property. There I differ from Buonarroti. If all men are placed equal before the law—if the means of acquiring and retaining wealth are equally secured to all in proportion to the respective industry and services of each, I see no objection to private property. Every man has a right to the value of his own produce or services, be they more or less. If one man can and will do twice the work of another man, he ought certainly in justice to have twice the reward. But if his superior strength or skill gives him the means of acquiring more wealth than his neighbour, it by no means follows that he ought, therefore, to acquire a right or power over his neighbour's produce as well as his own. And here lies the grand evil of society—it is not in private property, but in the unjust and atrocious powers with which the existing laws of all countries invest it. If a man has fairly earned a hundred or a thousand pounds' worth of wealth beyond what he has consumed or spent, he has a sacred right to the exclusive use of it, if he thinks proper; but he has no right to use that wealth in such a way as to make it a sort of sucking-pump or thumbscrew for sucking and screwing other people's produce into his possession. Sir John Cam Hobhouse, for example, has 60,000l. in Whitbread's brewery. Now, supposing Sir John to have earned that money honestly, he has a right to use it, and live upon it, while it lasts; but he has no just right to make it the means of sucking 5,000l. or 6,000l. additional every year out of the public, without a particle of labour or industry on his part. He has no just right to employ his money in usury or speculation. His money should not be allowed to grow money, as cabbage grows cabbage, or weeds grow weeds. To employ money in that way is not to use the right of property, but to practise robbery. Every shilling which Sir John Cam now derives from Whitbread's brewery is a shilling *not earned*, but a shilling *filched from the public*. Sir John does nothing for it, and the people get no return, or equivalent. I do not imhe was seized by the satellites of tyranny.* By this proclamation was to be placed before the people's eyes, the long tissue of crimes, by means of which equality and the rights of the citizens had been indignantly outraged;

pute this as a crime to Sir John. The fault is not in him, but in the laws and institutions of the country, which have established such modes of acquiring wealth. Sir John does no more than what is uniformly practised in trade. He takes advantage of his "capital," and of the poverty that surrounds him. He says to the hungry man, come and labour for me, create fresh wealth for me, and you shall have a small share of your produce to keep you alive. You ought to have the whole, I know. There ought to be institutions which would enable you to get and retain the whole, but as no such institutions exist now, you must either starve or submit to my terms. " Hunger makes every thing sweet but itself." The labourer can stand any thing before hunger. Hence Sir John grows richer and richer every day, without earning any riches at all, while HE who produces the riches grows poorer and poorer, as age diminishes his strength, till at last he dies in poverty and in the workhouse. Such are the effects of wealth as now administered. They result not from property, but from robbery —they are not rights of property, but wrongs on industry—they spring from bad laws—from depraved institutions. These laws and these institutions, instead of protecting industry from dishonest cupidity, have utterly sacrificed the former to the latter. The employers of labour and the exchangers of wealth are alone considered in the laws. The producers and active distributors are only thought of as slaves or criminals. Enormous fleets and armies are kept up to protect the merchants' gains. Enormous gaols and penitentiaries are kept up for the poor. Thus are the labourers forced to pay, not only for the protection of those that plunder them, but for the very instruments of their own torture and misery. Buonarroti considers all these results inseparable from private property. So did Babeuf—so did thousands of the French Democrats of 1793—so do Robert Owen and his disciples of the present day. I think differently. I will never admit that private property is incompatible with public happiness, till I see it fairly tried. I never found an objection urged against it, which I cannot trace to the abuse, not the use, of the institution. Assuredly, if men are allowed to acquire wealth by all manner of nefarious means, and to afterwards employ that wealth more nefariously still, there must be public ruin and misery; but I deny that these are the necessary

* Here are the words—" The Insurrectional Committee of Public Safety—The people have vanquished—tyranny is no more —you are free...." Here the writer was arrested and carried off.

L

the proclamation was then to show that the causes of
the public calamities—the same which had occasioned
the Revolution, and which the Revolution had not yet
uprooted—were all to be traced to social inequality, and

effects of private property. Usury, for instance, has destroyed all
the nations of antiquity, and is now undermining all modern states;
but is usury essential to private property? I deny it. But, then
it is necessary to, and inseparable from, commerce. I deny that
too. It is, certainly, inseparable from commerce as now conducted; but I deny that an enlightened Government, representing
all classes, would allow commerce to be conducted as it is now.
I assert, that such Government would place commerce and manufactures upon a totally different footing from the present, and make
the land the common property of all the inhabitants, and that, without any real or material injury to the existing proprietors. I hold,
and I am sure I can prove, that such a dispensation of things is
within the power of an enlightened Legislature, fairly representing
all classes. I have no space to argue the question here; but,
assuming that I am right for the present, why should we conclude
that private property is the inevitable cause of the evils alluded to,
until the institution be fairly tried and tested?

" But, if I hold these opinions on private property, let it not be
supposed that I am opposed to the system of community. On the
contrary, I hold that system to be the ultimatum of social progression. I hold it to be the grand prize destined by our Creator
for the human race, whenever it shall prove itself worthy of it by
the perfection of moral and intellectual science. Were it possible
to induce all men to renounce individual and selfish interests, and
to combine their powers for the common advantage, I am enthu-
siast enough to believe that the human race might be as far raised
above its present state as it is now above the meanest animals—
that it would, in fact, attain a degree of prosperity and happiness
of which not one mind in ten thousand is now capable of forming
an estimate. But the elements of such community do not at present exist. It requires opinions and habits utterly incompatible
with the existing laws and institutions of property. To obtain the
prevalence of such opinions and habits, we must first have property
upon a just and legitimate foundation. Whenever that is done, we
shall witness the spontaneous formation of communities, without
the necessity of either law or force to establish them. The difference between Buonarroti's ideas and mine, is this:—
Buonarroti would establish community by force; I would leave it
to establish itself spontaneously, by first preparing the materials
through a radical reform of the laws of property. It is the right of
every man to have the produce of his labour secured to him by
law—it is not his right to compel any other man to co-operate with

its resulting vices; to propose to the nation the conduct
of the people of Paris as the model to be universally
imitated, to boldly invite the French nation to equality,
and to enter into a solemn engagement to ensure it to

him in forming communities. The latter is the spontaneous work
of wisdom. Laws can have nothing to do with it, further than to
prepare the materials, and encourage it by sympathy and protection.
I have no doubt that had the Constitution of 1793 been established
in France, it would have led to the magnificent results anticipated
by its benevolent framers. That Constitution was wise and just
in not making community of property an elementary principle.
The National Convention had no right to say to Frenchmen—you
must all club your means and resources, you must live in community, and work and enjoy on equal terms. That would be to subject the whole to the opinions of a sect; and hence do I differ
from Babeuf and Buonarroti, in preferring Robespierre's Declaration in favour of private property to their proscription of the institution. If people choose to renounce private property, and live in
community, they have a right to do so; but they have no right to
compel others to the same course. The system of community
must, as I observed before, be the spontaneous growth of wisdom.
The Constitution of 1793 neither ordained it nor proscribed it. It
contented itself with laying the foundations of a just and natural
order of things, leaving it to time and wisdom to develope the advantages of community. I know not whether my readers have
seen the work of Mr. Etzler, lately published in America, and re-
published in London by Mr. Brooks, of Oxford-street. If people
would know the advantages of community let them read that book.
It is entitled, " Paradise within the Reach of all Men," and though
some of its statements appear extravagant, it is impossible to deny
the truth of its general principles, or of the particular facts and
experiments detailed in it. Why do I mention this book? Because, believing that the system of community must be the work
of wisdom and knowledge, not of force or law, I believe Etzler's
book to be one of the best that ever appeared for the purpose. Had
Buonarroti's conspirators seen that book, 'it would have been a
powerful lever in their hands. It would, most likely, have induced
them to limit the objects of the insurrection to the restoration of
the Constitution of 1793, in the hope that time and knowledge
would soon render that Constitution effectual for the working out
the great ends developed by Mr. Etzler.

" To conclude—I am for *Liberty and Equality*, as defined by Mr.
Beaumont. I am for *Equal Laws and Equal Rights*, and consequently for Universal Suffrage, that being the first step necessary
to the attainment of them, as well as the most familiar to the
English people. I am for new property laws—not laws to abolish

L 2

all, with the help of a few months of calm, of courage, of patience, and of docility.

The same proclamation would have erected into a principle of legislation the decree of the Parisian people

private or individual property, but to place it upon a just and righteous foundation; securing to every man what is legitimately his own, but preventing him from employing his wealth to the detriment of others.

"In fine, I am for community, provided it be adopted voluntarily, and without injury to those who prefer the individual competitive system. The former I *demand* for the people as a right. The latter I only *wish* for as a good which deserves the best consideration and attention of all who seek to be happy, and who would live without care for to-morrow."—BRONTERRE.

BUONARROTI'S DEFENCE OF OWEN AND BABEUF.

Several objections have been urged against the system of Owen, which apply equally to that of Babeuf. Let us record them, and the answers which demonstrate their futility.

1st Objection.—The physical differences which exist amongst men do not permit, in the distribution of labour and of the objects of consumption, that perfect equality which is the end of community.

Answer.—In this case, equality ought to be measured by the *capacity* of the workman, and by the *want* of the consumer, and not by the *intensity* of the work and *quantity* of the objects consumed. The man who possessing one degree of strength raises a weight of ten pounds, works equally hard as he who, having a quintuple strength, raises a weight of fifty pounds. Again, the man who, to appease a burning thirst, drinks a bottle of water, does not enjoy more than his fellow man who, with a less ardent thirst, swallows only a small pintful. The end of the community in question is equality of enjoyments and of labour, and not that of the things to be consumed, or of the task of the labourer.

2nd Objection.—The unequal quantity of objects of the same kind, as fruits, vegetables, dairy produce, viands, drink, liquors, &c. &c., would introduce into distribution a real inequality, which would engender jealousy and altercations, and would convert society into an abode of discord and endless enmities.

Answer.—People reason thus, only because they judge of men brought up under a system of perfect fraternity *after themselves*, whom bad institutions render vain, jealous, and enemies of one another. It is unjust towards the Author of nature to suppose that men are naturally prone to envy, hate, and tear one another for the sake of a fruit, or for the sweet scent of a flower—while fruits and flowers abound around them. Remove individual property from men, and you will calm their most fatal passions, and at the same time rid them of almost all means of self-injury. Besides, could not the petty inequalities in question be rendered still less sensible by casting lots, or by distributing the bad and good alternately to each? In morals, in politics, and in economy, equality is not mathematical identity: it is not altered by petty differences. Good sense and the spirit of

in insurrection, and would have consecrated the Constitution of 1793 as the ultimate term of the new political regime; without prejudice, however, to certain supplements to be added, and the previous establishment of

equality and concord, smoothed away in Sparta all those feeble difficulties, which, even now, do not trouble the peace of numerous families, of boarding-houses, and of military barracks.

3rd Objection.—If society charged itself with providing for the wants of each and all, nobody would feel the necessity of working to procure his subsistence, and a man naturally inclined to idleness would abandon himself to a general indifference, which would render all labour impossible.

Answer.—Every well-constituted man has need of motion, and to dissipate ennui he seeks work, towards which he shows a repugnance only when it is excessive, and when he gets more than his due share by having the burden thrown upon him exclusively. Neither of these cases can apply to community, where all being workers, the task of each is the mildest possible.

To these motives of activity ought to be added the conviction which all would feel of the necessity of labour, the disgrace with which public opinion would brand the lazy man, and the severity of the law, which would punish voluntary idleness with such pains as are now inflicted on thieves.

4th Objection.—For the same reason there would be no more progress made in intellectual and industrial pursuits.

Answer.—The frivolous productions which the stimulant of a paltry salary elicits, and which have no value but in the eyes of vanity and laziness, would disappear never to return. Surely there could be no harm in that. But, undoubtedly, it would not be the same with respect to studies and researches, tending to strengthen the love of country, and to ameliorate the condition of all. To these people would devote themselves with unexampled ardour, inasmuch as they would generally have more leisure, and be encouraged by public gratitude, and by the attraction of wisely-decreed honours, which would be at all times the spring of grand actions and of inventions truly useful.

5th Objection.—The mechanical régime and minutiæ of community would make a sort of friary of civil society, and be injurious to liberty.

Answer.—Monks, whether they have property or beg, do not apply themselves to any agricultural or industrial occupation; whilst, in the community of Babeuf and Owen, every one serves the country by his industry. Monks practice celibacy; but in community there is no renunciation of the conjugal union. Monks yield a blind obedience to their chiefs; but in community we are subject only to the law in the formation, modification, and abrogation, of which all have a share. The lazy monks make the air resound with useless prayers, whereas under the system of equality we render to the divinity the only worship worthy of it, by the exercise of true charity. In fine, monks are constrained to conform all their actions to a severe rule; the men of community, on the contrary, have, with the exception of a few hours work a day, the disposal of their time according to their inclinations and pleasure.

To decide whether liberty of action is more respected in the

institutions, without which the most popular Constitution will ever be a body without a soul, exposed to the
fury of every faction.

The following are some of the dispositions by which
this proclamation was to be followed :—

The immediate dissolution of all the existing civil and
judicial authorities, and the outlawry of every individual
who should dare to exercise the functions belonging to
them.

The immediate re-establishment of executive commissions, of departmental and district administrations, of the
municipalities, the revolutionary committees, the justices
of the peace, and the criminal tribunals, the same as
they were all before the 9th Thermidor of the Year II.

An order to all citizens who exercised, at that period
(9th Thermidor), any functions whatever in the aforesaid

system of community, or in that of individual property, it suffices
to consider that, under the latter, the majority of the population
being, by necessity, subjected to long and painful drudgery, is
always more or less deprived of the free use of its will, even while
the law seems to insure to them its enjoyment. There will assuredly exist more of this liberty in a country where all work three
or four hours per day, than in that where four-fifths of the population are constrained to labour ten or twelve hours per day, in
order that the remaining fifth may wallow in voluptuousness, and
get depraved by sloth and luxury.

6th Objection.—The life of community would make society retrograde to the state of barbarism.

Answer.—The absence of the arts and sciences, united to gross-
ness of manners, and violence of character, constitute what is
commonly called *barbarism.* Now, nothing of that sort would be a
necessary consequence of community, such as Babeuf and Owen
have conceived it. This community, so far from excluding the
studies and industry which really contribute to the happiness and
maintenance of society, would encourage them, by common interest, by public opinion, and by leisure to pursue them. The
sciences and arts, no longer supplying aliment to avarice and
vanity, would soon get released from all that is neither true nor
of general advantage. Again, the education in common, and the
uninterrupted interchange of succours and benefits, would engender in the feelings that fraternity which softens the manners, and
tempers the impetuosity of character. By the suppression of
misery and of meanness—inevitable consequences of individual
property—would be banished from society that dissimulation and
hypocrisy which now make it a field of battle, a veritable hell on
earth. People would be good without disguise or artifice, and
proud without brutality. So far from re-falling into barbarism, we
should then discover the possibility of attaining, by the establishment of community, a durable happiness, and a real and perfect
civilization.

authorities, to resume them instantly, except where there was a legitimate impediment.

Exclusion from all public employment, under pain of death, of every individual known to have augmented his fortune in the exercise of any public function whatever.

Publication of the Insurrectional Act throughout the whole Republic.

Application to the whole Republic of articles 1, 2, 18 and 19 of the said Act.

Seals to be put on all the national chests, &c.

Abolition of all direct imposts, and of patents (to date from the 1st Vendemiaire of the Year IV.), in favour of those citizens who, occupied in the works of agriculture and arts of the first necessity, had barely simple necessaries for themselves and families.

The whole of the direct contributions thus rescinded to be levied on the rich on the plan of the progressive impost.

These contributions to be gathered in kind.

Payment in kind of the timber of the national estates.

Establishment of public magazines in each commune, and of grand military magazines within twenty leagues of the frontiers, covered by the armies.

Every citizen to be invited to present to his country clothing materials for its defenders.

An order to the municipalities to see that no part of the territory remain uncultivated.

The estates of all proprietors neglecting to cultivate their lands according to the custom of the country to be forfeited to the people.

Suspension of the sale of national effects, or property.

Immediate abolition, in the interior of the Republic, of all salaries paid in money.

The public agents to be supplied with what was necessary, in kind, according to their proved wants.

A similar provision to be made for the indigent families of the defenders of the country, and for all aged or infirm poor.

The rich to be exhorted to yield, with a good grace, to the imperious voice of justice, to spare their country the necessity of convulsions, and themselves a long train of calamities, and to restrict themselves to simple living, by a generous abandonment of their superfluities to the people.

A general amnesty—including oblivion of all acts and opinions contrary to equality—in favour of those who, within a given time, should evince, in an unequivocal manner, a sincere return to truth, and to patriotism.

Return to prison, under pain of outlawry, of all persons who had been in detention on the 9th Thermidor of the Year II., unless they complied with the exhortation to restrict their wants to what was necessary, in favour of the people.

Revocation of all decrees passed since the 9th Thermidor, in favour of emigrants, or those accused of emigration, of conspirators, or their heirs.

Arrest of all persons known to have executed, or provoked, since the 9th Thermidor, the assassination of the patriots.

These were but the commencement of the grand reforms projected by the Insurrectional Committee; it was no more than the forced transfer of authority to popular hands.

The Committee, calculating on preserving after the Insurrection a useful influence over the deliberations, occupied itself with a plan of operations immediate and preparatory to the definitive legislation at which it desired to arrive. I shall give a faint idea of it.

Commissary Generals. There would have been immediately dispatched into the departments, and to the armies, Commissary Generals taken out of the new Convention, invested with ample powers, commissioned to vanquish all resistances by the force of the Republicans, authorised to employ severity and indulgence as circumstances might require, armed with power to eject from office, to send to trial, to reward; bound to declare before entering into office the state of their fortunes, and responsible for their conduct to a special tribunal erected expressly to receive accounts of their behaviour, and to punish whoever might have perverted the object of their mission.

Normal Seminary. The Committee regarded as a most important object, the immediate formation, near the Insurrectional Authority, of a Normal seminary,

to which the citizens of the departments should come
to imbibe the principles of the new Revolution, to penetrate themselves with the spirit of the Reformers, and to
learn to direct, by public persuasion, the execution of the
laws which were to change the face of the nation.

To the Commissary Generals was to be Public spirit
confided the important care of enlightening and popular so-
and of uniting the Republicans, and espe- cieties.
cially of imparting to them the views and spirit of the
directors of the Insurrection; they were to attach them
by the wisdom of their measures, by the warmth of their
zeal, by their disinterestedness, and by their irreproachable manners.   Like true apostles, they would have
spread the light of equality in every commune, and particularly in the popular societies which were to be opened,
so that public opinion might, as it were, light the way
before the reforming acts of the legislature.

Five projects of revolutionary decrees were submitted
for discussion to the Insurrectional Committee, at the
moment of its dissolution—to wit: 1. Regarding the
POLICE; 2. The MILITARY; 3. On EDUCATION; 4.
ECONOMY; and 5. On NATIONAL FESTIVALS.

By the vigour of the *Police Decree*, it Decrees of Po-
was intended to terrify and disconcert lice.
those who might be tempted to renew the scenes which
deluged the Republic with blood after the 31st of May,
1793.   Such was the end sought by the interior camps,
by the general armament of the citizens, and by the new
formation of the National Guard.   All who were not
interested in the complete success of reform were to be
reduced to the most complete impotence.   Accordingly,
every man who did not serve the commonwealth by some
useful employment, would have been excluded from it.   In
fine, it was contemplated to make even the discontented
concur in facilitating the execution of the general plan,
by forcing them, however reluctant, to seek in it their
only means of safety.*

From the *Military Decree* was to re- Military decree.
sult a sort of republican education for the
youth who could no longer receive its benefits in the

* [This is more fully explained in No. 28 of the justificative
pieces.---BRONTERRE.]

L 5

houses of education; this decree contained amongst many other articles the following:—

Every Frenchman performs active service in the army from the age of twenty to that of twenty-five.

No one can exercise a command in the army, unless he has carried arms as a simple soldier during ... years.

The soldiers concur in each corps, in the nomination of their chiefs, who are to be periodically removable.

Military payments to be no more made in money. The Republic distributes daily a military ration to each individual composing the army. It lodges, clothes, yields an equal supply of light, firing, washing, and maintenance to all the defenders of the country.

The military ration is the same as that of the public functionaries.

The defenders of the country live in common under the direction of their chiefs, and according to the rules to be established.

Individual pillage is forbid. Every defender of the country promises, before entering on the campaign, to carry to the administrators of the army whatever he may legitimately take from the enemy. After extraordinary fatigues, the soldiers who endured them, receive a more copious distribution of provisions.

Insubordination is punished with death. The same penalty attaches to generals and officers who are found guilty of robbery, drunkenness on duty, rape, gaming, contempt of the laws, violence and arbitrary acts towards those under their command.

There shall be established in the armies, employments, studies, and festivals.

The Republic decrees rewards for gallant and brilliant exploits.

Every citizen is trained to the use of arms and to military evolutions.

Decree on Edution.   The *Decree on Education* was designed to put in immediate execution the plan of which we have spoken. In fact, no pains were to be spared in the training of infancy, which, having no formed habits, was in a disposition to contract whatever it might be desirable to impart to it. Every difficulty in that department reduced itself to this—to vanquish the

repugnance of certain families, and to find a sufficient
number of men capable of directing houses of education
in the spirit of the projected reform.   The first obstacle
we hoped to overcome by the influence of the Republicans, by the .enthusiasm about to be awakened by the
propagation of the principles of equality, by the immediate comfort which this measure was to bring to the
indigent class, and by the evidence of the advantages
which it was about to ensure to the children.

As to the intelligence, morality, and capacity of those
to whom was to be confided the direction of the houses
of education, we calculated on securing them by the help
of the Normal school, where we were to employ in
forming them, the time necessary to accommodate the
people to the new system, and to arrange the places
where the youth was to be brought together.   Let us
succeed, said the Insurrectional Committee, in inducing
the young people and the soldiers to contract an affection
towards the manners of equality, and the most important
part of our mission will be accomplished; for, in a few
years, these young people and soldiers will compose
the great bulk of the nation; however, not to render
useless the good dispositions which the national education
will have given them, let us not suffer them to find, on
entering society, any social order opposed to its effects.
Let the destruction of the spirit of individual property
commence simultaneously, and march in front of the
progress of the youth and of the army, in the doctrines and in the manners of equality.   To this end it
was, that the Committee designed the *Economical
Decree*.

This decree embraced every part of the Economical de-
public administration : agriculture, arts, cress
commerce, navigation : the finances, and public works,
came within its province, and were destined to receive
new life from it.

It is understood, that the establishment of the grand
and perfect national community was the ultimate object
of the labours of the Committee.   Nevertheless it would
have been very cautious in making it the object of a
social order, immediately after its triumph, and of com-
pelling opposing parties to take part in it; all individual

violence, all innovation not ordered by the laws, would have been interdicted and punished. The Committee was of opinion that the legislator ought to act in such a way as to determine the mass of the people to proscribe property from necessity and from interest.

But how induce such numbers of persons, depraved by idleness, by factitious enjoyments, and by vanity, to desire a state of simplicity to which they had opposed so sharp a resistance? By establishing through the laws, replied the Committee, a public order in which the rich, while they keep their wealth, shall find no more abundance pleasures, or consideration than the rest of society. Let us, it added, enable all industrious men to enjoy, in return for a very moderate labour, and without wages, an honourable and certain competence, and soon will the bandage fall from the eyes of the citizens led astray by prejudices, and by the routine of fashion. It will then happen that the proprietors of wealth, or of its representative money, forced to offer a superior workmanship to the commodious and gratuitous maintenance of the public works guaranteed by the Republic, and to expend the greater part of their incomes in costs of culture, preparations, and imposts—no longer able to procure themselves any extra pleasures, or services; oppressed under the weight of oppressive taxes, shut out from the administration of affairs, deprived of all influence, despised, forming in the state only, as it were, a suspected class of foreigners, they will either emigrate, by disposing of their effects, or will hasten to seal, by their voluntary adhesion, the pacific and universal establishment of the community.*

Let us invite to join us, added the Committee, the small proprietors, the less prosperous shopkeepers and tradespeople, the journeymen, the labourers, the artizans, all the unfortunate persons whom our vicious institutions condemn to a life surcharged with fatigue, with privations, and with pain; let them be born again unto humanity; let the country forthwith guarantee to all who will frankly consecrate to it their faculties and

* To rightly comprehend this passage, it is necessary to read, in connexion with it, the fragment of the Economical Decree, inserted amongst the justificative pieces under No. 29.

their labour, a commodious living, secure from reverses, and relieved from the apprehensions and cares, which are no less the effects of possession than of poverty; let us create from this moment a grand national community; let us endow it with an immense territory; let us incorporate with it all the real estate, over which the nation or the communes have rights to exercise; let us confer on those who will make over to it an absolute surrender of their persons and property, the imprescriptible right to every thing that constitutes a prosperity such as all may participate in; let us see that this prosperity be real and immediate; let us prevent coxcomb witlings from coming to disturb it by sophisms and exaggerations; let us force all the ramifications of authority to march in the sense of equality; let us receive into the country's bosom all who seek an asylum in it with good intentions; let us dry up every source whence pride might still derive the means of displaying before the people the illusions of a deceitful pomp; let us render gold more onerous to its possessors than sand and stones; let us strike the first blows with boldness and firmness, and then leave to man's natural desire of happiness and to wisdom, to complete, by progressive changes, so sublime an enterprize.

This preparatory operation once consummated, the nation would have existence only in those participating in the community; but every thing inclined the Insurrectional Committee to think that the community would soon amalgamate itself with the entire nation, by the successive returns of the defenders of the country, by the incorporation of the possessions of non-participators deceased, or retired abroad, and by the happy change of opinion, which would have been the infallible consequence of such a reformation. The day would have soon arrived when obligation and restraint might be, without danger, substituted for exhortations, example, and the force of necessity. Then and from that time the word *proprietor* would begin to signify something barbarous or outlandish to the French.

In speaking of the assemblies of the people, we have made mention of national festivals, and of the principles upon which

Decrees respecting the national festivals.

the Committee reckoned upon instituting them. The same spirit reigned in the Revolutionary project which it discussed a short time before its dissolution. Those festivals would have been numerous and varied. All the days of rest would have been devoted to them. In the Committee's opinion, it was of sovereign importance to the cause of equality to keep the citizens incessantly exercised—to attach them to their country, by making them love its ceremonies, its games, its amusements—to banish ennui from all their leisure moments, and to cherish and fortify, by frequent intercourse, sentiments of fraternity amongst all parts of the Republic.

Upon the consolidation of those institutions, and especially of those which the Economical Decree was to establish, depended, as the Committee thought, the accomplishment of the Revolution and complete exercise of the popular sovereignty. In other words, that the day on which the people should enter into the peaceable enjoyment of equality, would have been that on which it would be able to exercise, in all its plenitude, the right of deliberating on its laws, as consecrated by the Constitution of 1793.

Partial and successive execution of the Constitution. Till then the sovereign power was to be rendered to the people only gradually, and according to the progress of the new manners. The authority of the Senates, tempering by different combinations (during the progress of the Reformation), the influence of the mass, would have preserved it from the troubles and dangers to which old habits, and the snares of the wicked, would have infallibly exposed it.

Numerous details are effaced from my memory; it has preserved only the recollection of the more prominent features, and an idea sufficiently clear of the successive and simultaneous progression of the institutions and of the Constitution. It will be easily felt that the Insurrectional Committee itself could neither foresee all the measures which circumstances might have rendered necessary, nor determined beforehand the epoch when the mission of the reformer would have been completed.

Who could calculate all the resistance of alarmed

passions? Who could predict to what extent the external enemies of the Republic would have multiplied their efforts against the new Reformation, which, undoubtedly, would have been more odious to them than all preceding ones? Its calculations and foresight must have necessarily depended on the celerity with which the democratic opinion resumed its former ascendancy. We can only be certain, from the well-known views of the conspirators, that, so far as *they* were concerned, foreign hostilities would not have been prolonged a single day, either through the ambition of conquest and domination, or the jealousies of commerce.

So many and such vast efforts, to which some merit will not be refused, were frustrated by the treachery of Grisel. Aided by the wiles of this perfidious villain, the oppressors of France succeeded in arresting, on the morning of the 21st Floréal of the Year IV., the greater part of the chiefs of the conspiracy.* Babeuf and Buonarroti were seized, in the midst of some papers, in the chambers where they had passed the night, meditating and preparing for the insurrection and subsequent reforms. Darthé, Germain, Eriddy, Drouet, and several others, were arrested at the same time at Dufour's house, where they were met together to fix the day of the popular movement. The army of the interior, under

Arrest of the conspirators.

---

* At this epoch commenced the brilliant campaign of Italy, which paved the way to supreme power for an audacious soldier (Buonaparte). Thenceforward the love of liberty began to give place, in the hearts of Frenchmen, to that of military glory, and to the passion for conquests, which subsequently proved the most active cause of their reverses, and total subjugation under the Holy Alliance. Judging from all appearances, the success of the conspiracy, of which we have just given the history, would, by snatching the Government from the weak and corrupt men who exercised it since the 9th Thermidor, have restored to the Republic the vigour of its first years; and it is to be presumed that the French people, thus escaping the aristocratic complots under which it afterwards sunk, would have been saved from the ambition of Buonaparte, and from the disastrous consequences of those distant expeditions, of which the allied sovereigns took such plausible advantage to replunge France under the yoke of its old masters (Bourbons), by unchaining against her (by the aid of insidious promises of liberty) the several nations, whose jealousy was roused by the dazzling success of the Revolution, and which were soured against us by the evils of a war of invasion and of spoliation.

arms, protected the Government expedition against the Democrats; and the Parisian people, who were made to believe that it was only robbers that were going to be arrested, stood motionless spectators of the imprisonment of the conspirators, whose chains they some time after vainly endeavoured to break.

[As some of my readers, not conversant with French history, may not understand the Republican dates used in the course of this work, I have thought proper to insert here the new French calendar adopted by the Convention. It will be perceived that the Republican year begins on the 22d of September, that being the day on which the monarchy was formally abolished in France, and (by a curious coincidence) the day also upon which the autumnal equinox falls. Thus nature appeared just then to conspire with politics, in giving *eclat* to the new Revolutionary æra.—BRONTERRE.]

NEW FRENCH CALENDAR,
FOR THE YEAR, COMMENCING SEPTEMBER 22, 1792.

New French Names of the Months.	English.	Terms.	Duration. Days.
AUTUMN.			
Vindémiare	Vintage Month	Sept. 22 to Oct. 21	.. 30
Brumaire	Fog Month	Oct. 22 to Nov. 20	.. 30
Frimaire	Sleet Month	Nov. 21 to Dec. 20	.. 30
WINTER.			
Nivose	Snow Month	Dec. 21 to Jan. 19	.. 30
Pluviose	Rain Month	Jan. 20 to Feb. 18	.. 30
Ventose	Wind Month	Feb. 19 to March 20	.. 30
SPRING.			
Germinal	Budding Month	March 21 to April 19	.. 30
Floréal	Flower Month	April 20 to May 19	.. 30
Prairial	Pasture Month	May 20 to June 18	.. 30
SUMMER.			
Messidor	Harvest Month	June 19 to July 18	.. 30
Thermidor	Hot Month	July 19 to Aug. 17	.. 30
Fructidor	Fruit Month.	August 18 to Sept. 16	.. 30
SANS CULOTIDES, AS FEASTS DEDICATED TO			
Les Vertus	The Virtues	Sept. 17	.. 1
Le Genie	Genius	Sept. 18	.. 1
Le Travail	Labour	Sept. 19	.. 1
L'Opinion	Opinion	Sept. 20	.. 1
Les Recompenses	Rewards	Sept. 21	.. 1
			365

* They were subsequently re-named, *Jours Complementaires* (complementary days.)

The intercalary day of every fourth year was to be called *La Sans Culotide*, on which there was to be a national renovation of their oath,—*To Live Free or Die.*

The month was divided into three *Decades*, the days of which were called, from the Latin numerals—

1. Primidi
2. Duodi
3. Tridi
4. Quartidi
5. Quintidi
6. Sextidi
7. Septidi
8. Octodi
9. Nonodi, and
10. Decadi, which was to be the day of rest.

PART I. CONCLUDES HERE.

PART II.

CONSPIRACY FOR EQUALITY,

CALLED

BABEUF'S CONSPIRACY.

TRIAL AND JUSTIFICATIVE PIECES.

CRIMINAL PROCESS.

THE imprisonment of the conspirators, Imprisonment. and the announcement of the conspiracy, produced a variety of sensations; affliction and amazement amongst the oppressed classes—yells of horror and ferocious joy amongst the upper and affluent classes, who uttered howls of death against the " *Babouvists.*" The numerous papers seized with Babeuf, enabled the aristocracy to discover the means of annihilating the party it dreaded.

Immediately were the dungeons of the Abbaye filled with the accused, who were dragged there amidst demonstrations of the most intense interest for their fate, lavished upon them by the people and the soldiery. For several days the crowd blocked up the streets adjacent to that prison; but the accused were soon separated, and those who appeared most compromised were put *au secret* in the towers of the Temple! Almost all of these expected to perish immediately by the sentence of a military commission: Drouet saved them from that fate.

By the Constitution of the Year III., a Drouet suspends the axe Deputy could not be sent to trial, except ready to smite upon an accusation of the legislative body, them.

and by a High Court of Justice, the jurors of which were at the choice of the Electoral Assemblies of the Departments. Several months were required to form this extraordinary tribunal, which could not hold its sittings near the commune where the Government resided. Drouet, one of the accused, was a Deputy, and the judgment of the rest was necessarily suspended, until it might be known whether Drouet could carry with him to his tribunal those whose accomplice he appeared to be. Two days after his incarceration Babeuf addressed the following letter to the Executive Directory :—

G. BABEUF TO THE EXECUTIVE DIRECTORY.

Paris, 23 *Florèal, Year IV.*
of the Republic.

Babeuf's letter to the Direc- tory.   " Do you consider it beneath you, " Citizen Directors, to treat me as one " *Power* with another ? You have now " seen of what a vast confidence I am the centre ! You " have seen that my party can very well balance yours'. " You have seen its immense ramifications, and I am " more than convinced that the discovery has made you. " tremble. Is it for your interest—is it for the interest of " the country- -to give an *eclat* to the conspiracy you " have discovered ? I think not. What would happen if " it were brought out in broad day ? that I should play " the most glorious of all parts ; that I should demon- " strate with all the greatness of soul—with all the energy " which you know to be mine—the holiness of the con- " spiracy of which I have never denied that I am a " member. Leaving the base and beaten path of dene- " gations, which vulgar criminals resort to to justify " themselves, I would develope great principles, and " plead the eternal rights of the people with all that " advantage which arises from an intimate knowledge of " the beauty of the subject. I would, I say, demonstrate " that this could be no process of justice, but of the strong " against the weak—of the oppressors against the op- " pressed and their magnanimous defenders. You might " condemn me to deportation or to death, but my sen- " tence would be immediately reputed as that which " powerful *guilt* pronounces upon *feeble* virtue. My

" scaffold would figure gloriously beside those of Barne-
" velt and Sidney. Would you, and on the very morrow
" of my suffering, prepare altars for me, by those on
" which at present the Robespierres and the Goujons
" are revered as martyrs? This is not the way by
" which governments and governors can secure them-
" selves.

" You have seen, Citizen Directors, that you gain
" nothing by having me in your hands. I am not the
" whole conspiracy—far from it. I am but a single link
" in the vast chain which composes it. You have all
" the other links to dread as much as me. You have
" proof, however, of the great interest which all the rest
" take in me. In striking me you would strike and
" irritate the whole against you! You would exasperate,
" I say, the whole democracy of the Republic; and that,
" you know, is not so trifling a matter as you had at
" first imagined. Remember, it is not at Paris alone
" that it has its strongholds. Observe, that at every
" point of the Departments it exists in equal vigour.
" You would better comprehend me, if your officers had
" seized the *great correspondence* from which those lists
" have been formed—of which you have seen only a few
" fragments. It is in vain that you wish to extinguish
" the sacred fire—it burns, and will burn! The more it
" appears to go out at certain moments, the more it
" menaces to burst forth again into a sudden flame of
" powerful and terrific explosion.

" Would you undertake to completely deliver your-
" selves from that vast *sans-culottide* sect which is yet
" far from having declared itself vanquished? Suppose,
" even the possibility of crushing us, in what posi-
" tion would you afterwards find yourselves? You are
" not yet in the position of that Government which, after
" the death of Cromwell, deported some thousands of
" English Republicans. Charles II. was a king, and
" (whatever may be said of you) you are not kings yet.
" *You need a party to support you; but once remove*
" *the patriots, and you stand unprotected and alone*
" *against Royalism.* What, think you, would be the
" consequences to yourselves, if pitted alone against the
" Royalists? ' But,' you will say, ' the patriots are as

" ' dangerous to us as the Royalists—perhaps, more so.'
" You are mistaken. Mark well the character of the
" enterprise of the patriots; you will not discover in it
" any intent against your lives, and it is a calumny to
" have published it. For myself, I can answer to you,
" they never desired it; they wished to march by other
" ways than those of Robespierre; they did not wish for
" blood; they wished only to force you to acknowledge
" that you have made an oppressive use of your power—
" that you have stripped it of every popular form and safe-
" guard; and they wished, therefore, to recover it from
" you. To this determination they would not have come,
" had you, as you seemed to promise after Vendémiaire,
" put yourselves in train to govern popularly. I, myself,
" in the early numbers of my paper, wished to open the
" door to you; I told you by what means you might
" cover yourselves with the benedictions of the people.
" I explained how it appeared to me possible that you
" might make disappear whatever the constitutional
" character of your Government offers in the way of
" contrast to true Republican principles.
" Well!—there is yet time. The upshot of this last
" event may be rendered profitable and salutary for
" yourselves and for the commonwealth. Disdain not
" my opinions and conclusions, when I urge that the
" interests of the country, and your own, consist in not
" giving celebrity to the present affair. Methinks I
" have already perceived in you a disposition to treat it
" *politically*. In so doing you will act rightly. Do
" not suppose me interested in making these overtures;
" the frank and singular manner in which I avow my
" guilt, in the sense imputed, lets you see that I am
" not actuated by weakness. Death or exile would be
" for me the road to immortality, whither I am prepared
" to march with a heroic and religious zeal; but not
" my proscription, nor that of all the Democrats, would
" advance your ends, or ensure the safety of the Re-
" public. I have reflected that, on the whole, you were
" not at all times the enemies of this Republic; you have
" been even honest Republicans. Why should you not
" be so still? Why may it not be supposed that you,
" who are but men, were only betrayed into temporary

" error, like many others, by the inevitable effect of
" exasperations different from ours, into which circum-
" stances have thrown you? Why, in short, may not
" all of us concede some part of our extreme opinions,
" and embrace a reasonable compromise? The patriots,
" the mass of the people, have their hearts already ul-
" cerated—ought you to rend them still more? What
" would be the final result of such a course? May not
" these patriots deserve that, instead of aggravating their
" wounds, you should think of curing them? You can
" begin the work whenever you please, because in you
" resides all the power of government. Citizen Directors,
" govern popularly!—behold all that these same patriots
" demand of you. In thus making myself their organ,
" I am sure they will not belie my representations—I am
" sure they will throw no obstructions in my way. I
" see but one wise course for you to take—declare that
" there has been no serious conspiracy. Five men, by
" showing themselves great and generous, have it this
" day in their power to save the country. I will engage
" that the patriots will then cover you with their bodies,
" and you will no longer stand in need of whole armies
" to defend you. The patriots do not hate you, they
" have hated only your unpopular acts. I will give you,
" on my own account, a guarantee as extensive as my
" perpetual frankness. You know what influence I
" have over that class of men. I will employ it all to
" convince them that if you identify yourselves with the
" people, it is their duty to make common cause with
" you.
" It were fortunate should the effect of this simple
" letter be to pacify the interior of France. By prevent-
" ing any *éclat* upon the affair of which it treats, might
" not *that* also be prevented which impedes the peace
" of Europe? (Signed) " G. BABEUF."

It had been for a long time evident— Blindness of the
and the discovery of the conspiracy had Government.
just furnished fresh proofs of it—that the proscription o.
democratic doctrines had caused a great division among
the old friends of the Revolution, and that it more and
more inflamed the zeal of the people to defend it. This

state of things, augmenting the chances in favour of the
Royalist party supported by foreign influence, ought, methinks, to have moderated the pride of the chiefs of the
upstart aristocracy, and to lead them to adopt some modifications of the law, which, by attaching to them the
Democrats, and through them, the people, would have
spared the Republic the subsequent struggles so disastrous to it, and themselves the calamities which ultimately overtook them.* Such was the object of
Babeuf's proposal, which he urged as much for the sake
of sparing his friends, as in order to restore to the Republican spirit its expiring vigour.   But can alarmed
pride hearken to the councils of prudence? The new
Government shut its eyes, and disdaining to wisely re

* [There is something so very childish in this remark of Buonarroti's, that one is at a loss to reconcile it with his general
shrewdness and knowledge of human nature. The *worst* that was
likely to happen the Executive Directors, from the triumph of
Royalism, was the loss of their power, which they might, at any
time of danger, commute for something substantial, in money or
lands, as Barras subsequently did when he struck his clandestine
bargain with Buonaparte to facilitate that usurper's success;
whereas, had Babeuf's party triumphed, the *best* that could happen
the said Directors was to have the precarious and perilous honour
of serving the Republic without plunder or estates, and under the
awful surveillance of the "Insurrectional Committee."   What
value the murderers of Robespierre would have set on such *barren*
distinction, Buonarroti ought to have known too well not to see
the impossibility of their forming any connexion with the Equalitarians or Democrats.   And, as to what he says of the subsequent
struggles and disasters of the Republic, what cared Barras and Co.
about them, so long as they could feather their own nests? Men of
that stamp regard the calamities of their country about as much as
did Lord Castlereagh or Major Sirr, the life of an United Irish-
man, in 1798; and as well might the modern Whig party of England
be expected to fling themselves into the arms of real Radicals like
myself, by way of escaping the Tories, as the upstart aristocracy
to which Barras belonged, be expected to unite with the Robespierrists, in order to make head against the Royalists.   Between
the Royalists and the upstarts it was only a question of *dividing the
plunder*, which might be easily settled; but between the upstarts
and the Democrats it was a question between *plunder* and *no
plunder at all*, which, manifestly admitting of no adjustment, rendered the parties irreconcileable to one another.—BRONTERRE.]

trograde even one step, which would have gained it the
affections of the people—affections it never had—it impru-
dently gave way to a blind rage, which, in contempt of
good sense and public opinion, it pushed to the extent
of imputing Royalist intentions to citizens who abhorred
the very name, and of proscribing in their persons the
only men from whom the Republic could reasonably expect a sincere and necessary devotion.

The revolutionary Aristocrats thought only of momentarily profiting by a victory they owed to an infamous treason, to crush the party which condemned
their usurpation. Articles of impeachment were drawn
up against Drouet, and he was sent before the High
Court of Justice, whose sittings were fixed to be held at
Vendôme.

No accused person, said the Constitu-　The Constitution of the Year III., *can be withdrawn*　tion is violated.
*from the jurisdiction of the judges whom the law as-
signs to him, by any commission, or by any privileges
other than those determined by an anterior law.*
Nevertheless, a law *posterior* to the discovery of the
conspiracy, decided that the Deputy (Drouet) should
drag his co-accused with him before the High Court,
which was not the tribunal assigned to them by law.

Again, said the same Constitution—*there is for the
whole Republic a Tribunal of Cassation* (Court of
Appeal) *which pronounces on the final judgments of
all other tribunals.* The aforesaid law, however, ordered that the judgments of the High Court, which was
notoriously a tribunal, should not be subject to appeal.
These provisions, contrary to the letter of the Constitution, were attributed by Drouet's associates in misfortune
to the fear entertained by Government of a public debate
in presence of the people of Paris, and were considered
as the effects of that animosity which, subsequently
bursting forth during the discussion, made one furious
legislator exclaim, *there is no need of such precautions
in favour of seditionists;* and another, no less enraged,
*too much time would be required if, in proceeding
against factious criminals, all the legal forms were to
be observed.*

M

Accusation. Fifty-nine citizens, of whom seventeen were *contumacious*, were put in accusation at Paris, many upon unpardonably slight grounds. At the same time, spies were on the watch all over the Republic to hunt out pretences, however trivial, for swelling the number of accused, of whom the rulers of the day flattered themselves that the High Court would make a complete hecatomb. Cherbourg, Arras, Rochfort, Bourg, and Saintes furnished each its contingent of accused, but all such manifestly utter strangers to the affair that a shadow of reproach could not be urged against them.

Evasions. Whilst they were getting up at Paris the tragedy to be played at Vendôme, the Parisian Democrats were agitating to deliver their companions. Drouet effected his escape from the Abbaye by the aid of a Republican turnkey, but the escape of the prisoners in the Temple, which had been concerted with the soldiers placed to guard them, miscarried for want of necessary accord in the plan.

Pache was the only man out of prison that openly embraced, in a printed paper, the opinions and cause of the accused. Some periodic writers opposed a feeble barrier to the torrent of invectives which burst upon the prisoners, but they did it without skill or courage, sometimes by denying palpable facts, at other times insinuating that the Government had secretly instigated the conspiracy; at no time did they dare to start the question of the legitimacy of the conspirators' enterprise, or justify their real intentions.

Translation of the prisoners to Vendôme. In the night of the 9th Fructidor, of the Year IV., all the accused in detention at Paris were transferred to Vendôme. The staff of the place had them minutely searched in its presence, and placed them itself in *barred cages*, constructed for the express purpose of exhibiting them, like wild beasts, as a spectacle to the enemies of equality, and to the deluded people whom the latter excited against them. The convoy traversed Paris in the midst of a numerous army, and was escorted all the way by a strong detachment of *gendarmerie*, and by regiments of cavalry. The women, daughters, and sisters of the accused, had frequently to endure the inclemencies of the atmosphere and the gibes of the Aristocrats. The prisoners themselves had a deal to suffer from the brutality of the officer who commanded their escort; but they had reason to be proud of the reception, full of sympathetic regard, which they experienced from the municipal administrations of Chartres and of Châteaudun.

At Vendôme there was expressly prepared for them a tribunal and a spacious court-house, in which the accused present were locked up for the night of the 19th Fructidor. Antonelle and Fion, arrested subsequently to the impeachment—as also the accused from Rochfort, Cherbourg, and Arras, entered there in succession sometime after. Troops of every description guarded with strictest severity the approaches to the prison, as well as the entrances to the town, to which a specific law for the occasion interdicted all access nearer than ten leagues round. The intention was to ward off from the debate every species of publicity.

The time which elapsed between the arrival of the accused and the opening of the sittings of the High Court, was employed by it in constituting itself, in giving notice of the *contumacious*, in forming the jury, and in judging the demands and exceptions taken by the accused against the Court's jurisdiction. The latter availed themselves of the time to protest, to agree on the challenges which they had the right to exercise, and to concert and prepare their defence.

By the unconstitutional decrees already spoken of, a wide field was opened for protests on the part of the accused. Several of them, in denying the competence of the High Court, surmised the possibility of raising between it and the legislative body a contest which might lead to events favourable to the popular cause. Vain hope! The Hight Court declared itself competent.   *Protests.*

Upon the totality of the jurors named by the electoral assemblies, the accused had the right of exercising thirty challenges. This was a very grave operation, as upon it might depend the fate of a great number of the prisoners. By help of   *Challenges.*

M 3

some imperfect and frequently erroneous information, collected in the departments, the accused agreed, after deliberating together, upon the names to be rejected. Thirty of the accused distributed the privilege amongst themselves, in such manner that each might challenge one name. The elections of the Year IV., however, having in many places been made in the absence of the Republicans proscribed, or violently expelled from the assemblies, and under the influence of the enemies of the Revolution, it was impossible to leave on the list of jurors only true friends of liberty. Force was to content itself with the less bad. Amongst those who merited an entire confidence, some were excluded by the Tribunal as relations of emigrants—others, sacrificing to fear, feigned illness, and were excused; three were present at the trial.

Courageous avowals of Babeuf. From the moment Babeuf was deprived of liberty his first thought was to avow the conspiracy, and to maintain its legitimacy. The legitimacy is demonstrated in his replies to the Minister of Police, who demanded whether he had intended to overthrow the Government, and if he had combined with certain parties for that purpose? Here are his answers:—" Convinced in my heart that the " existing Government is one of oppression, I would have " done all in my power to overthrow it. As to my ac- " complices, they are all the Democrats of the Republic; " it is no part of my duty to name them. Being questioned by the same Minister respecting the means he counted upon employing, he replied, " all the means " legitimate against tyrants." And a little after:—" It " is not my business to give the details of the means " attempted to be employed. Besides, they did not " depend on me alone. I had but a single voice in the " Council of Tyrannicides."

Interrogated some days afterwards by the foreman of the jury, he replied thus, to the imputation of his being the author of the conspiracy:—" I attest, then, that too " much honour is done me, in decorating me with the " title of Chief of the Conspiracy; I declare that I had " not ever more than a secondary part in it—a part " limited to what I am about to tell. I gave my sanction

" to this conspiracy, because I believed it legitimate;
" because I believed, and believe still, that the existing
" Government is supremely criminal—an usurper of au-
" thority, a violator of all the rights of the people, whom
" it has reduced to the most pitiful destitution, to the
" most deplorable slavery; guilty, in short, of treason to
" the national sovereignty; and that I believed, and do
" still believe, in the soundness of the principle, that it is
" the rigorous duty of all free men to conspire against
" such a Government; accordingly did I voluntarily
" consent to aid, with all my resources, the chiefs and
" leaders of a conspiracy which was formed against it."
And after having established the part he had played in
the conspiracy, he added :—" Behold details which,
" no doubt, will destroy the absurd supposition that I
" was chief of the conspiracy, and that, founded on the bare
" circumstance that I was found, at the moment of my
" arrest, with a portion of the papers of the conspirators
" about me. I repeat the fact, without meaning thereby
" to extenuate my culpability; I only desire to act
" honestly, and not to appear in a more brilliant character
" than I merit—a character that is not mine. I consent,
" however, after that acknowledgment, to endure the
" severest penalty awarded against the crime of plotting
" against oppressors; for I still own, that as regards in-
" tention, no one has conspired against them more reso-
" lutely than myself. I am convinced that it is a crime
" common to all Frenchman, at least to all the virtuous
" part—to all that are not wedded to the frightful system
" of founding the happiness of a very small number upon
" the degradation and extreme misery of the mass; I
" declare myself fully convicted of the crime charged,
" and I declare that it was the crime of all the conspi-
" rators whom I served."

During the long preparatory examination taken by the
foreman of the jury, the principal accused in detention
were kept constantly shut up. It being impossible to
concert matters with Babeuf, who was deemed the best-
informed of the affair, the other conspirators, through
fear of contradicting themselves or of compromising one
another, were to consign to him the care of giving explanations, and to keep themselves within the limits of a

rigid circumspection. Some failed to recognise their own handwriting—others imagined stories—Darthé all along protested against the legality of the procedure.

Had it not been for the weakness of Pillé, arrested with Babeuf and Buonarroti, his handwriting, and that of several of the accused, would have remained unknown. Foolishly fearing that the numerous copies he had made of the Acts of the Insurrectional Committee, whose secretary he had been, would draw down upon his head the accusation of having dipped actively in the plot, he hastened to declare what he had done and seen, and to make known the authors of the manuscripts he had transcribed. This prisoner, whose timid conduct produced fatal consequences, played the part of a simpleton in prison and during the trial, with great skill. In presence of the High Court, he pretended that a malevolent spirit had driven him to Babeuf's house. He declared that one might have a compact with a demon, either to be protected by him or to hurt somebody, and demanded to speak, to give, as he said, some details! Not one of the accused, really compromised, quailed or staggered before the capital and impending danger which menaced them. All remained unalterable in their attachment to the doctrines they had defended, and resolved to seal them with their blood. Nobody was compromised by their declarations.

Firmness of the accused. Upon their arrival at Vendôme they had already agreed to renounce all concealment, all evasions, all denegation; to avow the conspiracy, and to offer no other defence than demonstrations of its legitimacy; they considered they owed this last testimony to the justice of their cause, and to their country a memorable example of perseverance and of firmness.

Others of the accused, less compromised and more prudent, were alarmed at this plan of defence, and set about preventing its execution, " If you avow," said they to their comrades, " the reality of the conspiracy, " will the jury be able to declare it not proven? Could " there possibly be amongst our jurors four persons so " hardy as to dare justify your intentions, or reply by a " pious falsehood to the questions of fact which will be

"submitted to them? That were to presume too much
"of men elected at a period of corruption and per-
"versity. If the conspiracy is declared real, will you
"not involve in your destruction us who are your friends,
"and those numerous Republicans who are already ex-
"posed to calumnies and persecutions. Be cautious of
"putting the virtue of our judges to a too severe a
"proof, and offer them at least a pretence for acquitting
"you."

Whether it was that these remon- Modifications
strances made the principal accused fear of the defence.
that a fatal division would burst forth during the proceedings, or that they shrunk back from the idea of wounding their country by injuring their friends, or finally
that they opened their hearts to their own preservation,
the first plan was rejected, and it was agreed that the
formal conspiracy should be denied; that its end should
be hypothetically defended, and that an attempt should
be made to give plausible explications of the documents
seized, and of the facts proved.

Nevertheless, the testimony of the informer detailed
particulars, and was precise; and even though he stood
alone as to the main point of the accusation, he was so
strongly corroborated by the numerous and overwhelming
writings of the accused, that it seemed impossible, all
political considerations apart, for any honest man to
deny. after the slightest examination, the reality of the
conspiracy. From that moment, the gravely-compro-
mised prisoners proposed to defend themselves by maintaining that the concert pretended to have been established had not existed, and that, even had it been real,
it was clear of all criminality, whether arguing from the
want of means, or because, on the most unfavourable
hypothesis, the final aim attributed to them was legitimate and founded in right.

What the conspirators were preparing Antonelle.
for the debates, Antonelle executed beforehand for public opinion. This generous citizen made
then the noblest use of his talents and of his wealth.
Although no legal presumption was raised against himself, he frankly espoused the cause of his incarcerated
friends; by numerous writings he disposed the public to

favourably receive their defence, and from the depth of
his dungeon he unsparingly accused the Government,
rendered homage to the Constitution of 1793, justified
the intentions of the conspirators, and dared almost to
declare himself their accomplice. At this calamitous
epoch, nearly all that there was of energy in the Republic was locked up in the prison of Vendôme.   There
the accused mutually encouraged one another to serve
the people, by showing an example of unflinching firmness, and they lived in the most democratic fraternity.
The shades of difference remarked between the Equals
and the Ex-Conventionalists, did not prevent their harmony from being complete; it increased every day by the
comparison and mutual conciliation of their opinions,
as well as by the fidelity with which each discharged his
duty before the tribunal.   In the evening Republican
songs, in which all the prisoners took part, re-echoed in
the distance; and the inhabitants of Vendôme, attracted by
sympathy and curiosity to a neighbouring hill, frequently
mingled with them their own voices and applauses.

For men who had dared so much in favour of a cause
they were devoted to, the fate of the Republic was necessarily the permanent subject of their conversations
and anxieties.   To one and the other, new aliment was
supplied by another horrid calamity. Hardly had the
accused arrived at Vendôme, when they were apprised
of the fatal event of Grenelle, where, in consequence of
a murderous ambuscade, the bulk of the democratic
party lost their lives in a generous attempt to liberate
the imprisoned patriots, and to re-establish the rights of
the people.   By this horrible butchery, the power of the
Aristocracy was increased by all the strength lost to the
Democrats.*

* This unfortunate affair of Grenelle is thus described by
Mignet :—" Their partisans made a last attempt. In the night of
the 7th September (23d Fructidor), about eleven o'clock, they
marched to the number of six or seven hundred, armed with
sabres and pistols, against the Directory, which, however, they
found defended by its guards. They then proceeded to the camp
of Grenelle, which, from the supposed understanding between
themselves and it, they had hopes of gaining over. The camp
had retired to rest when the conspirators arrived. When the
sentinels demanded ' Who goes there?' they replied ' Long live
the Republic ! Long live the Constitution of 93!' The centinels
immediately gave the alarm. The conspirators, relying upon the

Shortly after, some Royalist conspirators, emissaries of the proscribed dynasty, and surprised in the overt act, were treated with a scandalous indulgence by a great part of the Legislature, which openly protected them, as well as by the Military Commission which tried them. About the same epoch, the tribunals charged to try the *contumacious* of the 13th Vendémiaire (Royalists),* declared *not proven* the conspiracy which that day deluged the city of Paris with blood. This judicial compliance displeased the Ministry. *I fear*, said one of its members, *that it will prove a bad example for the prisoners of Vendôme; it is breaking the ice for their escape.* It was of our conspirators, indeed, that the Government most desired to rid itself.

At last the debates were opened on the 2d Ventôse of the Year V. There were forty-seven accused present; eighteen were tried in their absence, being contumacious.† Babeuf, Darthé,

Opening of the judicial debates.

---

assistance of a battalion of the guard which had been reduced, marched towards the tent of Malo, the commander, who ordered his men to sound to horse, and his dragoons, who were half-naked, to mount. The conspirators, surprised at this reception, made but a feeble resistance; they were put to flight, leaving a number of dead, and many prisoners, on the field of battle. This unfortunate expedition was almost the last of the party; at each successive defeat it lost its energy and its leaders, and at length acquired the secret conviction that its reign was at an end. The enterprise of Grenelle proved a very disastrous affair to it; for, besides its losses in the engagement, it suffered considerably before the military commissions, which were as fatal to it as the revolutionary tribunals had been to its enemies. The commission at the camp of Grenelle, at five times, condemned thirty-one of the conspirators to death, thirty to transportation, and twenty-five to imprisonment."—BRONTERRE.

* Persons refusing to appear in a court of justice, when summoned, are called, in the French language, "*contumaces.*"— BRONTERRE.

† *The accused present* were—Babeuf, Darthé, Germain, Blondeau, Cordas, Frossard, the widow Mounard, Buonarroti, Sophia Lapierre, Goulard, Mugnier, Massard, Raybois, Fion, Cochet, Nayez, Boudin, Jeanne Breton, Vadier, Laignelot, Toulotte, Lambert, Lamberté, Pottofeux, Morel, Dufour, Moroy, Clerex, Amar, Philip, Cazin, Nicholas Martin, Taffoureau, Drouin, Roy, Pillé, Breton, Didier, Antonelle, Antoine Ficquet, Ricord, Thierry, Adélaïde Lambert, Vergne, Duplay the father, Duplay the son, Crepin.

The accused absent were—Drouet, Lindet, Vacret, Claude Ficquet, Guilhem, Chrétien, Monnier, Reys, Manessier, Mounard, Baude, Bouin, Parrein, Bodsom, Lepelletier, Rossignol, Jorry, and Cordebar.

Buonarroti, Germain, Cazin, Claude Ficquet, Bouin, Fion, Ricord, Drouet, Lindet, Amar, Antonelle, Rossignol, and *ten* others, had really an active part in the conspiracy; *five* had indirectly taken part in it; all the rest had been absolute strangers to it, and were dragged before the High Court only through the rage of the ruling party, who meant to use this tribunal for the extermination of the democracy.

A numerous armed force guarded the tribunal; each prisoner was placed between two gendarmes. The court was spacious, and the enclosed space reserved for the public was always crowded with people, who frequently applauded the accused—never the accusers. We had a great many advocates; these prolonged the debates by the numerous incidental objections they raised—sometimes even thwarted the views of the accused, whose intentions they never dared to justify. The true defenders of the cause were Babeuf, Germain, Antonelle, and Buonarroti, The generous women who had followed the accused from Paris were never absent from the sittings of the Tribunal.

Darthé. Amongst those of the prisoners most seriously compromised, Darthé alone, more consistent than the rest, persisted in his protest. Never would he recognize the jurisdiction of the Court, or its right to try him. He persevered to the end in refusing to answer questions, or give explanations, and suffered himself to be condemned without a defence. After reiterating his first protest before the jury, he delivered the following words:—" For myself, if Providence " has ordained my career to close at this epoch, I shall " terminate it with glory, without fear, without regret. " Alas ! what could I regret ? When liberty succumbs— " when the edifice of the Republic is piece by piece " demolished—when its name is become odious—when " the friends, the adorers of equality, are pursued in " exile, wandering over the Republic, delivered to the " fury of assassins, or to the agonies of the most fright- " ful misery—when the people, a prey to all the horrors " of famine and poverty, is despoiled of its rights, de- " graded, vilified, despised, and languishes under a yoke " of iron—when this sublime Revolution, the hope and

" consolation of oppressed nations, is no longer but a
" phantom—when the defenders of the country are
" everywhere overwhelmed with outrages, naked, de-
" fenceless, maltreated, and crushed under the most
" odious despotism—when, in return for all their sacri-
" fices, for their blood shed in the common defence, they
" are treated as miscreants, assassins, and brigands, and
" their laurels of victory changed into the cypress of
" death—when Royalism is everywhere audacious, pro-
" tected, honoured, rewarded even with the blood and
" tears of the unhappy Republicans—when fanaticism
" has again grasped its poignards with redoubled fury—
" when proscription and death hover over the head of
" every virtuous man, of all the friends of reason who
" have taken any part in the great and generous work
" of national regeneration—when, to crown the climax
" of horrors, it is in the name of what is most sacred,
" most revered on earth, in the name of sacred friend-
" ship, of revered virtue, of honourable probity, of be-
" neficent justice, of gentle humanity, nay, of the
" Divinity itself, that the brigands drag desolation,
" despair, and death in their train—when profound
" immorality, horrible treason, the execrable informer,
" the infamous perjurer, unqualified brigandism and
" assassination, are officially honoured, proclaimed, and
" qualified with the sacred name of virtue—when all social
" bonds are broken—when France is covered with fune-
" real crape—when she will soon offer to the affrighted
" traveller's eye only piles of dead bodies, and smoking
" deserts—when, in short, there is no longer a country
—then, then, *is death a benefit*.

" I will bequeath to my family neither opprobium nor
" infamy. They shall be able to cite my name with pride
" amongst the defenders and martyrs of the sublime cause
" of humanity; I attest it with confidence; I have tra-
" versed the whole revolutionary sphere without taint or
" blemish; my career was never once sullied by mean-
" ness or corruption; never did the idea of crime or
" baseness tarnish my soul; launched young into the
" Revolution, I supported all its fatigues, I bore all
" its dangers without a murmur—without any other
" enjoyment than the hope of once seeing founded the

" durable reign of equality and liberty; solely occupied
" with the sublimity of that philanthropic enterprise, I
" devoted myself to it with the most perfect self-abne-
" gation; personal interests—family affairs—all were
" forgotten, neglected, for it; my heart never throbbed
" but for my fellow-creatures, and for the triumph of
" justice."

Counter-revo-lutionary spirit of the national accusers.

From the outset the national accusers
displayed a most rancorous hostility, not
only against the accused, but also against
every thing done in favour of democracy
during the Revolution. First, laying down as an admitted
fact, the existence of an imaginary faction of " *malignant
beings, monsters heretofore unknown, hypocrites without
religion or morals, ambitious, revengeful, furious, calumniators, homicides, children of anarchy, born in its
bosom, strangers to every other element, incessantly
invoking it, and never smiling but at its approach,*" &c.
—they attributed to that faction all the commotions and
acts of the Revolution, and blushed not (before a word
was heard in their defence) to identify with it the accused
whom the High Court was just going to try for their
lives. Such, to believe these accusers, had been the in
fluence of the said faction, that it was impossible for their
auditors to make out what events of the Revolution they
honoured with their approbation; according to the definition they gave of a legitimate insurrection, one should
necessarily conclude, that in their hearts they did not
except from their anathema against the great movements
of the nation, even that of the 14th of July, which was
the only one they appeared to applaud.*

It was not difficult for the accusers to prove, by the
help of the numerous papers seized with the accused, the
concert which they qualified with the name of criminal
conspiracy; but as to the intention—an essential element

* [By the taking of the Bastile, which happened on the 14th of
July, the Government passed from the partisans of absolutism to
the friends of constitutional monarchy, and the result was the
middle class Constitution of 1791. The subsequent movements
of the 10th of August and 31st of May, having been in favour of
republicanism and democracy, were naturally hated by the. upstart Aristocrats of the Directorial Government.—BRONTERRE.]

of crime—they endeavoured to prevent all discussion upon it, and in the little they said of it, they denaturalized truth by hazarded suppositions and inductions of the most absurd kind. Their constant aim was to render the accused contemptible and odious, and to prevent them from convincing France that their views were benevolent, that their opposition to the Constitution of the Year III. was legitimate, and that their projects had been just and conformable to general interests. What must we think of those accusers who, charged to prosecute, in the name of the Republic, the authors of a project not executed, permitted themselves to justify the conspiracy and armed revolt which caused to flow, on the 13th Vendémiaire of the Year IV., the blood of several thousand citizens, and of which the final object was to re-establish Royalty?

In concert with the accusers, the judges, wishing to confine the debate to the mere matter of fact, several times interposed *Impediments made to the defence.* their authority to interdict all discussion, even hypothetical, on the part of the accused, touching the main object of the conspiracy, as well as all examination of their papers, notwithstanding that these papers were represented in the indictment as the principal, and almost the only means of the conspirators. Thus, a tribunal, apparently designed to be the bulwark of national rights, and to curb the force of power, was, in fact, but the instrument of those, who, in contempt of the sovereignty of the people, had seized the supreme authority by violence and stratagem.

Although those of the prisoners gravely implicated had abandoned the idea of formally avowing the conspiracy, they *The accused defend the Revolution.* persisted in defending its principles. The Revolution was, in their view, a *sacred thing*. They were conscientiously faithful to the popular sovereignty, and to the Constitution of 1793, which consecrated it. Proud of what they had done to re-establish them, they felt honoured by their chains and by the danger that menaced them.

A violent irritation—the necessary consequence of the opposition manifested between the views of the accusers and the sentiments of the accused—repeatedly burst forth, sometimes in the virulent declamations of the public Minister, sometimes in the partial interruptions of the Court, and frequently in the impetuous sallies and protests of the prisoners.

Was it possible for those noble spirits to listen cold-bloodedly while the founders of the Republic were being calumniated, and whilst the firmest supporters of equality were represented as devoid of talents, courage, and morality? Could they, without retaliating, hear the hired accuser impute vile and interested motives to men, the greater part of whom had a thousand times exposed their lives for the country, and who had emerged from public functions in an honourable poverty?—men against whom there was not raised, in the course of so long a procedure, a single voice to reproach them with even the semblance of an infamous act? Throughout the debates the accused never belied their character. On every possible occasion they rendered brilliant homage to the Republic, and to equality. They several times victoriously refuted the political sophisms of the accusers, and at almost every sitting made the vaulted roofs of the Court re-echo to their Republican songs.

The traitor.   The traitor, by whom the confiding men he had flattered, inflamed, and caressed, were denounced and delivered up. GRISEL! figured in the list of witnesses, amongst whom were some other police spies, who, struck with horror at his atrocious conduct, constantly refused to sit near him during the trial.

The prisoners had hoped to set aside this witness, for the law forbade the informer to be heard in evidence in cases where the information of the crime is pecuniarily rewarded by the law, or when *the informer may in any other way profit by the effect of his information.* In the opinion of the accused and their advocates, the word *may* expressed a possibility *without limitation,* and comprised such rewards as the informer of the conspiracy might reasonably expect from Government.

The expedient hit upon by the national accusers, to extricate themselves from this embarassing argument of the accused, excited universal laughter. They had the impudence to maintain that the term informer was not applicable to Grisel; because, said they, having made his first declaration to the Directory, and not to an officer of judiciary police, he was but a simple discloser (*révélateur*)!

This subterfuge was not successful; nevertheless the Court, having ruled that *He is a witness.* the signification of the word *may* was to be limited to *advantages accruing, of right,* to the informer in consequence of the informations, ordered, to the great scandal of many persons, that Grisel should be heard.

In support of the prosecution, there were about five hundred documents presented in evidence, and several sittings were occupied in handing them to the accused for recognition, or in verifying, by expert witnesses, those attributed to the prisoners who did not make answer, or were *contumacious.*

All manner of conjectures were ex- *Tumult.* hausted to ascertain, in a document to which the accusers attached great importance, certain words which Babeuf had covered with a great blot of ink, in flourishing his signature to it, at the house of the Minister of Police. The fastidious discussion which took place on this subject occasioned violent invectives on both sides, and ended in a frightful tumult. The sitting was abruptly adjourned, amidst cries of the accusers, the advocates, and the accused; the latter, as they retired, chaunted with vehemence the couplet of the Marseillais hymn, "*Tremblez tyrans, et vous perfides!*" The Court prepared a minute of the whole, on which the legislative body passed to the order of the day.

In consequence of a reproach addressed by the accused to the President, the accusers complained that there was a design, by crowding incident upon incident, to indefinitely prolong the debates. "So many indignant voices," said they, "arise against the slowness of this Court's proceedings!"—"What, are these voices so "multiplied?" exclaimed Babeuf. "Friends of the "people! you guess them; they are but the yells of "that caste audaciously called *respectable*, which is "but a speck in comparison with the mass, but which

" has the egregious insolence to pretend to be the whole;
" to live, without doing anything, upon the extorted
" sweat of the millions—to count as nothing the mass
" exclusively useful—to massacre them, to starve them,
" in return for the incessant employment of their arms,
" of their skill, and of their industry. Such, Repub-
" licans, is the true character of this handful of vam-
" pires, whose voices, we are told, are raised against the
" slowness of the operations of men who have come
" prepared to immolate us. Such are the parties whom
" there is so much eager haste to please. Respectables,
" you will be satisfied! Only read the first day's pro-
" ceedings in this affair to be convinced how well you
" are served. And you, the essential and major part of
" the people—*you* will see how you are treated in the
" persons of those who have not abandoned your in-
" terests. You, also, friends and advocates of the people,
" companions in glory, you have heard it; it is the
" *Golden Million* which demands your crucifixion. You
" do not distinguish amidst the yells of the devouring
" horde—you do not recognize the voices of those four-
" and-twenty millions of oppressed citizens whose noble
" cause you have to sustain. Alas! no. They groan
" in silence, loaded with irons, despoiled, naked, sinking
" from inanition, addressing their homages and sighs to
" the names of the glorious martyrs who have preceded
" us in the career of establishing public felicity, of which
" they have bequeathed to you the sublime apostleship,
" in the same manner as you will transmit it to other
" just spirits, as zealous, and, perhaps, more fortunate,
" than you and your predecessors. Virtue never dies:
" she is imperishable. The tyrants abuse themselves
" in their atrocious persecutions; they destroy only the
" body—the perishable dust. The virtuous man's soul
" only changes its mortal envelope; when one is dis-
" solved, it passes into and animates other beings, in
" whom it continues to inspire generous movements,
" which never leave any repose to triumphant crime.

 " After these last reflections, and after all the innova-
" tions which I see each day introduced to accelerate my
" holocaust, I give my oppressors all the facilities they

" desire; I abandon the useless details of my defence;
" let them strike without further delay; I shall repose in
" peace in the bosom of virtue."

Grisel spoke during two sittings, and Deposition of
related circumstantially all he had done the traitor.
to find out, second, deceive, and betray the accused.
He spoke truth, saving some additions dictated by
vanity, and by which he succeeded at times in contradicting himself.   But, though he could not be regarded
as a liar, people were not the less revolted at the effrontery with which he paraded his perfidy, and the
stratagems by means of which he had gained the good
will of the persons he was plotting to destroy.   By a
natural movement of indignation, Antonelle painted to
the life the traitor's hypocrisy, and stamped upon his
forehead the ineffaceable seal of infamy.

In speaking of certain accused, Grisel had said,—" I
" see here only agents; not one of them was the real
" chief of the conspiracy.   There were men behind the
" curtain who made these move and act at their
" bidding."   This sentence wrung from Germain the
following phrases :—" Ah! since we are not victims
" enough for you, go to the banks of the Aude, and
" drag from under the sand that covers it the carcase of
" my wife; go and dispute its prey with the worms, less
" worthy than you to devour it; fling yourself, like a
" famished tiger, upon my mother; join to the abomina-
" ble feast my sisters and their children; tear my son
" from the feeble arms of his nurse, and grind his tender
" limbs under your cannibal teeth.   Our sixty families
" offer you the same unsightly ministry.   Go—set about
" it; go.   What! does not this allurement tempt you?
" Ah! no doubt, it is because you still dissemble."   The
words with which Germain ended his eloquent defence
are not less remarkable :—" I await your verdict," said
he, " without fear or weakness; whatever it may be,
" why should I fear it?   If I am to die, liberty never
" had a more devoted martyr; if I am to live, she will
" never have a more resolute defender."

Grisel had spoken of the insurrection Babeuf justifies
of the 1st Prairial of the Year III., as- the insurrection
cribing it to the " *anarchists*," a deno- of Prairial.

mination under which he affected, in imitation of his masters, to comprise all the sincere friends of equality. " Prairial!" exclaimed Babeuf, " epoch of terror, tragic, " but sacred and revered days!—days which never recur " to the thoughts of virtuous Frenchmen, without exciting " tender regrets and sorrow—the remembrance of the " greatest crimes, the recollection of the most generous " efforts of virtue, as well as of the deepest calamities of " the people. Prairial!—days disastrous, but immortal, " in which the people and its faithful delegates so nobly " performed their duty; on which its traitor-deputies, " its famishers, its assassins, the usurpers of its sove- " reignty and of all its rights, capped the climax of " atrocities, such as no history offers the like example ! " You alone of the Convention—oh Gracchi! immortal " Frenchmen !—you were generous; you alone had the " courage to declare yourselves the supports and de- " fenders of the people. There were but you whose " entire devotion sustained its too just demands—*Bread* " *and the Laws !** Goujon, Duroy, Romme, Soubrany,

* [The rallying cry of the people during the Prairial Insurrec- tion was " *Bread and the Constitution of 1793.*" *Bread*—because the Parisians were literally dying of hunger, the *maximum* having been suppressed for the benefit of the profit-hunters and mono- polists ; and the *Constitution of 1793*, because all the then schemes of the Convention manifestly tended to Burke it, the starvation itself being intended for that purpose. " *Give the people a good famishing*," said the usurers, " *and they will soon forget the Con- stitution to look after bread.*" The monied vampires were too cunning to use these words, but that was the palpable language of all their acts, and the aim of their assassin organs in the Con- vention. A bloodier or baser confederacy of human devils never existed than the majority of the Convention at this epoch. They were just the sort of fellows that would have passed a New Poor Law Act, or a Coercion Bill, with as little ceremony as they murdered Robespierre, after worshipping him during fifteen months with adulation so fulsome and abject, that he was at last obliged to complain of it in the public papers. The perfidious manner in which the People's Constitution was shortly after Burked, under pretence of preparing organic laws for its execu- tion, is proof enough that the insurrectionists ot Prairial knew well what they were about, when they united the cry for the *Democratic Constitution* with that for *bread.*—BRONTERRE.]

" Duquesnoy, Bourbotte—illustrious victims!* You,
" whose names, for ever celebrated, have already re-
" echoed in this place, where they shall still re-echo
" more than once again!—you, whose manes we inces-
" santly honour by our daily hymns!—you, whose noble
" constancy in irons, and before your hangmen judges,
" will serve as an example to us to endure the longest
" and direst captivity!—you, in fine, whom the mis-
" creants have massacred, but whose courage they could
" not make flinch even for a single day! Glorious
" martyrs, intrepid champions of sacred equality!—you
" rescued liberty, the sovereignty of the people, all the
" principles which guarantee happiness, from the dis-
" grace of being immolated without a courageous re-
" sistance. It belonged to us to replace you, after your
" fall; fallen like you, it is now our duty to imitate you,
" and to appear before our persecutors, unflinching, un-
" conquerable like you; and it is the duty of every true
" Republican to honour the epoch in which you died,
" the victims of the most execrable enemies of the
" Republic." Here the Court compelled Babeuf to be
silent.

About this time, some police bloodhounds came to
depose against certain workmen, accused of having, since
Babeuf's arrest, formed a combination to deliver him
and execute his projects; these abandoned men, amongst
whom was seen a coiner of false money, released from
prison for the express purpose of being used as a spy,
had encouraged, by their concurrence, the very men
against whom they appeared as witnesses.

In the midst of so many perverse beings, Generosity of
appeared two unfortunate young men, two witnesses.
who, by their misfortunes, their generosity, and courage,
made the spectators shed tears of tender affection. Jean
Baptiste Meunier and Jean Noël Barbier, both soldiers,
had been condemned to ten years' imprisonment in irons

---

* [The unflinching bravery of these noble-minded Deputies is
best attested by the fact, that the instant they were condemned
they deliberately inflicted death on themselves by a single blade,
which they passed in succession from one victim to another, in
front and in contempt of their assassins.—BRONTERRE.]

for circumstances relating to the insurrection of the
Legion of Police.   Before the Military Commission that
tried them, they had been inveigled into certain admissions implicating some of the accused at Vendôme; it
was to confirm these admissions that they were transferred to this latter place.   But far from answering the
expectations of the accusers, Meunier and Barbier boldly
disavowed what they had had the weakness to confess,
and preferred exposing themselves to a new condemnation, as false witnesses, to uttering a single word against
the men on their trial before the Court.   They did more:
they bowed respectfully to the accused; greeted them
with Republican hymns; called them friends of the
people; and demanded to participate in their glory!
Such extraordinary virtue was rewarded by a fresh condemnation to irons..... What times!....

Defence.   None of the accused was more crippled
in his defence than Babeuf, in conse-
quence of the resolution which had been taken by common consent to deny the conspiracy.   Amongst about
five hundred documentary proofs—almost all of them
seized with himself, and containing in black and white
the organization, plan, acts, and correspondence of the
Insurrectional Committee—there were more than a hundred in his own hand-writing; the information was
throughout against him; five long sittings were occupied
in his examination.

How was it possible to give to the numerous facts, resulting from these documents, and corroborated by the
informer, any explications how little soever plausible?
The principal accused, however, made the attempt;
they sometimes even succeeded partially, but on the whole
they obtained no other advantage than that of putting
more at ease those of the jurors who already participated
in their opinions.   In this respect, their defence was but
an incoherent tissue of subtleties, which their hearts disavowed, and to which they submitted only from considerations for their companions in misfortune.   The
true defence of these accused is fully comprised in the
avowals they made of their democratic doctrines, in the
solemn homage they rendered to the Constitution of
1793, and in the perseverance with which they hypo-

thetically justified the object of the conspiracy. This conspiracy was all comprised in the Act creating the Insurrectional Directory, which the accusers called an *usurpation of sovereignty*; it was on this document that the accusation mainly rested. Babeuf justified its motives, intentions, and means of execution.

" This is not," said he, " a trial of individuals—it is " that of the Republic; in despite of all who hold a " different opinion, it must be treated with all the gran- " deur, majesty, and devotion which so all-powerful an " interest demands.....This act," continued he, " be- " longs to any and every Republican, and all Republicans " are implicated in this affair; consequently it belongs " to the Republic—to the Revolution—to history : my " duty is to defend it." A moment after, comparing his actual position with that of the non-imprisoned Democrats—" Genius of Liberty !" he exclaimed, " what " thanks ought I not to render you for having placed " me in a position in which I am more free than all " other men, from the very fact that I am in fetters ! " How grand is my position ! How beautiful my cause ! " it permits me exclusively to use the language of truth. " ....In the midst of my chains my tongue is privileged " beyond all others of the countless number of oppressed " and unhappy citizens, for each of whom the tyrants " cannot, as for me, erect a prison for an abode. They " are suffering, harassed, pressed down, overwhelmed " under the most poignant distress, crouched under the " most odious subjugation, and, to complete the atrocities " of despotism, they are no longer permitted to complain. " ....At any rate, if our country is doomed to perish " in those of her children who are implicated in this " affair, let it be recorded that, in dying, they have not " betrayed her—that they have courageously professed " the maxims of their mother....I address myself to the " virtues; they alone can vouch that we are just; if " there were no more but these (virtues) to hear my " voice—oh ! indeed, it would only remain to prepare " the scaffold."

But when Babeuf spoke with affection of the Constitution of 1793—when he began to enumerate the violences by which that Constitution had been torn from the people, the national accusers commenced a torrent of invectives against the accused, and pretended that they were still conspiring against the Government. So Babeuf was immediately condemned to silence again.

Buonarroti also undertook to justify this document.[*] He said that the body it created had no other object than that of propagating democratic doctrines; he maintained that even had this body prepared legislative draughts of measures to be submitted to the people, whose discontent was notorious, and every moment expected to explode, it would have done no more than an act of prudence, in nowise contrary to the laws; and then assuming the hypothesis, that the Secret Directory might have wished to provoke the people to examine the form of Government, he demonstrated that such provocation is the right of every citizen in every country ruled by a constitution, which, like that of the Year III., acknowledges that the sovereignty resides in the universality of the citizens.

At a later stage of the proceedings Babeuf adroitly recurred to this object, and by the help of some prefatory remarks, suited to bespeak the ear of the Court, he was enabled to speak aloud—" to rouse the real people from " their slumber—to provoke the reign of happiness, the " reign of equality and liberty, abundance for all, liberty " for all, the prosperity of all—behold the aspirations of " those pretended insurrectionists, who have been painted " in such horrifying colours to the eyes of all France." Touching afterwards on the *means*, he made it appear that in reality they reduced themselves to the operating a revolution in opinion, a general movement of mind, the effects of which, he thought, had been exaggerated by the authors of the Act creating the Insurrectional Directory. " For, added he, very judiciously, " it is but " too evident, that a moral revolution being the necessary " result of the conversion of the majority of men, and of " their renunciation of all the passions which subjugate " them, is not an affair, whose execution by the sole " means of apostolically preaching virtue, can be easily " comprehended. Since the first existence of instructors

---

[*] See No. 4 of the justificative documents.

" among nations—of generous men devoting themselves
" to teach the maxims of supreme reason, and to point
" out the ways of true justice, we have witnessed little
" success attending their efforts, and we have seen nearly
" all of them fall victims to their benevolence !"

He did more; he proved that when the people is
oppressed, insurrection, even partial insurrection, is just
and necessary; and supporting his argument by the
authority of Mably, he completely refuted the lethargic
doctrine of the national accusers, who said—" Insurrection
" is legitimate only when sanctioned by the universal
" participation of the citizens," as much as to say—*never !*

Twice was Babeuf asked to name his accomplices,
and twice did he reject the proposal with horror. With
the like indignation did he scout the system of falsehood
by which some of the accused and an advocate wished
to defend themselves, by attributing the conception of
the conspiracy to the Government, and by representing
the agents of authority as having provoked its most dangerous acts. For example, when the Court was canvassing
the Insurrectional Act, on the subject of which Ricord
had exclaimed—" it is Grisel himself who has drawn it
up"—" No," replied Babeuf sternly, " *he has not drawn*
" *it up; it is not a document that should make its*
" *author blush, and Grisel is too great a miscreant to*
" *have drawn up such an Act.*"

All the documentary proofs were handed in by the
accusers in the exact order in which they had really been
framed, and when tied together as a parcel in their
consecutive form, they offered an easy clue, of which the
accusers naturally availed themselves, to deduce the
veritable history of the conspiracy.

Conformably to their previously co-arranged plan of
denying the conspiracy, the accused made great efforts
to sever the connecting chain of documentary evidence,
of which the accusers had shown the true and consecutive order. This they attempted to do by referring their
respective papers to isolated causes, to fortuitous circumstances, and to distinct epochs. In analysing those
papers, they let no opportunity escape of avowing their
democratic principles, of justifying them, and of showing
that the Constitution which then ruled France was not

the one which the French nation had given itself. Thus, in explaining the draught of an address to the soldiers, of which he was the author (see justificative pieces), Buonarroti described why he had actively served the French Revolution; developed, in spite of the interruptions of the Court, his reasons for defending the Constitution of 1793; accused the Government of usurpation and tyranny, and pronounced an eulogium of the designs and acts of the Revolutionary Government. "The "oath," cried he, "which I took to defend the code "unanimously sanctioned by an immense people in the "days of its union and glory, cannot be effaced from "my heart; and the fidelity which even slaves have "been seen to preserve towards their masters, I have "preserved to a magnanimous people, which generously "received me in its bosom, and adopted me, in its days "of liberty, as a constituent part of its solemn will."

It was not without intense emotion and excitement that a multitude of citizens, belonging to Vendôme and its environs, attended every day the sittings of the High Court. Those vehement attacks so often reiterated against the Government; those pressing argumentations from which the accusers seldom emerged victorious; the lively attachment of the prisoners to the rights and interests of the people, and their bold and frank defence of the most popular events of the Revolution; those noble youths who, called from their irons to give evidence for the Government, not only refused to speak, but absolutely rendered homage to the men they were dragged to appear against; those devoted families who travelled from Paris to witness the struggle whose issue they awaited with trembling;—these, and the like circumstances, had inspired the spectators with an ardent interest in behalf of the accused, an interest which was every day augmented by the articles of a journal printed in the place, and by the conversations of the inhabitants, who were almost exclusively occupied with what was passing in the Court.

To these friendly dispositions was soon superadded the desire to rescue the most implicated of the accused from the dangers that menaced them. On one side, secret attempts were made to induce a part of the soldiers who guarded them to make an insurrection in their favour; they did not succeed. On the other hand, it was in contemplation to favour a clandestine escape. By the help of some instruments, furtively introduced into the prison, the accused in a few days opened a large breach in the walls, through which those most implicated were on the point of escaping from their executioners, when the inconsiderate conduct of some of the prisoners alarmed the vigilance of the guards, and thus all hopes of flight vanished.

About thirty heads were devoted to death in the long address delivered by the national accusers at the close of the debates. The documents seized were so numerous, and so conclusive, that it was most easy for them to establish the truth of the information, and to prove the reality of the conspiracy. They were not equally successful in demonstrating its criminality.

Hostile discourse of the national accusers.

The accused had repeatedly maintained that, even supposing there had been a conspiracy, there was nothing criminal in it, seeing that the Constitution, against which it was directed, being subversive of the sovereignty of the people, and not having been accepted by the people, was, therefore, *not the veritable law*. To this paramount and decisive point the accusers made no reply, but taking their stand upon the *fact*, they affected to treat as irrelevant to the question, the *legitimacy of intention*. Throwing aside the gravest argument of the accused, they amused themselves with combatting those which appeared weakest, and, above all, they aimed at terrifying timid minds, by painting, in exaggerated colours, the means of execution, by a calumnious exposition of the intentions of the accused, and by a fantastic picture of the consequences of their projects, falsely deduced, of course. Nothing, in fact, appeared more extravagant than the conclusion, in which it was dogmatically asserted, that the practice of the popular sovereignty and of equality should necessary eventuate in the devastation, depopulation, and desolation of France, and by consequence, the circuitous, though insensible, return of royalty.

It would be as useless as fastidious to report minutely

N

the strained interpretations given by the accused to the
documents opposed to them, the denegations by which
they repelled the allegations of the informer, and the
slight contradictions into which the latter fell for want of
memory, or through the vanity of appearing more sagacious and cunning than he had really been. The information was true on the whole, the conspiracy had been real,
and if the principal accused denied its existence, it was
only by a pious falsehood, from which they did not promise
themselves any success, and of which they were in their
hearts ashamed.

Answers of the   But what ought not to be lost to his-
accused.   tory is that part of their general defence
in which were discussed the principles of the public
rights of Frenchmen; here the Revolution was justified
in its utmost tendencies to equality and to the sovereignty of the people. We shall give a brief recapitulation of it, to make known the sentiments in which the
accused persevered to the last moment of their lives.

In the system laid down by the accusers and the Court,
the function of the jurors was limited to examining
whether any offence had been really committed against
the Constitution of the Year III., the legitimacy of which
they pretended to prevent the accused from discussing.
The more implicated of the conspirators, however, persisted not the less in developing and justifying the principles they so ardently professed, because they believed
them true, and conducive to the well-being of all. In
this course alone they saw their veritable means of defence
in the eyes of the people, and of popular jurors.

Appeal to the   In the first instance, they addressed
patriotism of   themselves to the virtue of the jurors, in
the jurors.   order to awake in their souls a noble
sentiment of independence; they endeavoured to convince
them that the sublimity of their mission imposed upon
them the duty of ascending to first principles, of lifting
their minds above the Constitution of the Year III., of
submitting the origin and essence of that Constitution to
a rigorous examination, and of taking as guides to their
decisions the real rights of the people, and not the pretended ones of the existing authority, which, in reality,
had not been created by the people. " This affair,"

said one of the accused, " is not an ordinary process.
" The power of the accusers, the weakness and obscurity
" of the accused, ought to command the scrupulous
" attention of the high-jurors to considerations altogether
" foreign to the ordinary course of tribunals. It will
" not be in vain, citizens, that the oppressed will appeal
" to your consciences against the cruelty of their op-
" pressors. The holy enthusiasm of liberty will not in
" vain invoke at your hands respect and justice for those
" sacred principles to which we owe the destruction of
" privileges, the fall of the throne, and the progress of
" public reason towards equality of rights. The mission
" confided to you by the people is to *defend the rights*,
" and not to adapt any formula of jurisprudence to sub-
" serve schemes of ambition and folly. Representatives
" of the people ! be the people itself—to give expression
" to its will, it is necessary that you should feel with its
" heart !"

Before undertaking to demonstrate that the veritable
law of Frenchmen was the Constitution of 1793, and
that the Constitution of the Year III. was but an act of
spoliation and violence, the accused endeavoured to
neutralise the horror with which the national accusers
had laboured to envelope the democratic law, as well as
those who remained faithful to it, by the exaggerated
picture they drew of the severity of the Revolutionary
Government with which they affected to confound it.

" You are constantly reminding us,"
said the accused, " of the measures of   Justification of
" 1793; but you throw a veil of silence   the Revolution-
" over what led to the unhappy necessity ary Govern-
                                           ment.
" of employing them. You forget to remind France of the
" innumerable treasons which destroyed the lives of
" thousands of citizens; you forget to remind us of the
" terrific progress of the war of La Vendée, of the trea-
" sonable surrender of our frontier towns, of the revolt of
" Dumouriez, and of the perfidious protection he found
" in the bosom of the Convention itself; you forget to
" remind us of the unheard-of cruelties with which the
" the ferocious Vendeans tore limb from limb, and made
" expire, in the midst of the most refined torments, the
" defenders of the country, and all who showed any

" attachment to the Republic. If you evoke the manes
" of the victims of a deplorable necessity, produced
" by the incessant and augmenting perils of the country,
" we will meet you by exhuming the piles of French
" corpses massacred by the counter-Revolutionists at
" Montauban, at Nancy, in the Champ de Mars, in La
" Vendée, at Lyons, at Marseilles, at Toulon.   We will
" awake the shades of a million of French Republicans
" slaughtered on the frontiers by the partisans of tyranny,
" who are incessantly conspiring with it in the very heart
" of France; we will put in the balance the blood shed
" by your friends, through cold and callous calculations of
" selfishness, to weigh against that which the patriots
" have shed with regret in the generous transports of
" national defence, and in the exaltation of their love of
" liberty.....Is it *us* or *liberty* that the national accusers
" are instructed to prosecute?....Their malignant ran-
" cour will serve our cause, and the high-jurors will
" doubtless detect, in their one-sided representations,
" and in the hypocrisy with which they outrage history,
" and heap upon the heads of the accused, events
" utterly foreign to their case, that secret and rank-
" ling vengeance which the enemies of the Republic,
" more adroit than we, have vowed against its intrepid
" and too-confiding friends."

Having concerted with the intent to overthrow the
Constitution of the Year III., in order to replace it by
that of 1793, and with the design of invading private
property by establishing a community of goods—these
were the two grand heads of accusation, against which
the prisoners had to defend themselves. " Assuredly,"
said they, " we love the Constitution of 1793; we love
" it, because it guarantees to the people the inalienable
" right of deliberating on the laws; we love it, because
" it was solemnly, and almost unanimously, accepted by
" the French people."

Eulogy of the   " Assuredly," they added, " we still
Constitution of   " consider that Constitution to be the real
1793.   " fundamental law of France, because
" that of the Year III. has robbed the people of the
" effective right of sovereignty, and because it is false
" that the French people have accepted it."   The rea-

sons and numerical calculations by which the accused
demonstrated the truth of their assertions were so overwhelming, that after a long argumentation on both sides,
the accuser Viellart acknowledged himself defeated, in
pronouncing these words—*For the rest, I consent.*

" Is it alleged," continued the accused,   The accused
" that we have invoked the attention of maintain the
" the people to this extraordinary infrac- legitimacy of
" tion of its rights? In that, we have the conspiracy.
" done no more than use the right of speech and of
" writing, which the Constitution of the Year III. itself
" guarantees to all Frenchmen. Furthermore, if it be
" pretended that we have conspired to re-establish, by
" consent or force, the Constitution of 1793, which we
" regard as sacred—as the palladium of public liberty—
" our answer is, that, in the first place, the act of con-
" spiring (which we deny) is not proved, and the want
" of means of execution alone suffices to set aside all
" presumption of a dangerous and criminal conspiracy.
" But even if we had really conspired with the design
" and means of re-establishing the Constitution, of 1793,
" we should have only obeyed the dictates of a pure
" conscience, we should have only obeyed the veritable
" law of France, we should have only done what every
" true citizen ought to do, we should have only, in fact,
" fulfilled our oaths, which, in binding us to that Con-
" stitution, bound us to liberty, to the sovereignty of the
" people, and to the Republic."

Whilst the accusers and Court pretended that the
jurors should confine themselves to the simple question,
whether the prisoners had conspired against the Constitution of the Year III., the accused represented that if,
at all hazards, the fact of the conspiracy was to be decided against them, still their conspiracy was not a crime,
since the authority against which it was directed, not
having been sanctioned by the people, was an illegitimate
one. It was to the fact of this illegitimacy that the accused most earnestly solicited the jury's consideration.

As to the design of establishing a com- Community of
munity of goods, it was unnecessary for goods defended
the accused to discuss it at any length, by Babeuf.
because the papers containing the successive plans of

legislature not having been seized, and nothing of the kind having transpired in Grisel's presence, this part of the accusation was very feebly established. Nevertheless, Babeuf, who had often made this community the subject of his writings in the *Tribune of the People*, did not fail to speak of it; he expounded his democratic opinions on that point, and justified them by reason—by depicting the evils entailed upon society through the contrary system, and by a host of imposing authorities, which had propagated the same doctrine. " *Private pro-* " *perty*, said he, " *is the source of all the calamities on* " *earth.* In preaching this doctrine, long since pro- " claimed by philosophers, I desired to attach to the " Republic the people of Paris, who are wearied of " Revolutions, discouraged by misfortunes, and almost " *royalized* by the plots and schemes of the enemies of " liberty."

Peroration of Babeuf.   Babeuf thus terminated his long de- fence :—" If the axe of tyranny menaces " my head, its lictors will find me prepared : it is glo- " rious to die in virtue's cause.....The verdict of the " jurors is about to resolve this problem—Shall France " remain a Republic,* or shall she, after being the prey of " the brigands who dismember her, degenerate once more " into a monarchy? Citizen jurors, will you condemn men, " the sole guide of whose conduct has been the love of " justice? Will you accelerate the counter-Revolution, " and precipitate the fall of the patriots under the " poignards of triumphant royalism? However, if our " death be resolved upon—if the fatal knell has tolled for " me, I am long ago resigned. Incessantly a victim " throughout this long Revolution, I am grown familiar " with torture. The Tarpeian Rock is ever present to " my sight, and Gracchus Babeuf is but too happy to " die for his country. Well! all things considered, what " is there wanting to console me? Could I ever expect " to end my career at a brighter moment of glory? I

* Four years after this epoch there no longer remained a vestige of it.

[The trial took place in 1796. Before the close of 1799 Buona- parte was master of France, and the Constitution of the Year III. was no more!—BRONTERRE.]

" shall have experienced before my death, such sensations
" as have rarely accompanied that of men who have
" immolated themselves for humanity.....The power
" which was strong enough to hold us so long in op-
" pression has failed in its efforts to destroy our fame.
" We have lived to see the pen of truth engrave on the
" page of history facts which shed honour on our names,
" and which will brand our persecutors with eternal
" infamy. Yes! history will engrave our names in cha-
" racters of glory. And who are the men with whom I
" am associated as a culprit? It is Drouet! it is Lepel-
" letier!....Oh, names dear to the Republic! Such
" are my accomplices! And you, my friends, who sur-
" round me hard by on these benches, *who are you?*
" I recognise you—you are almost all founders—firm
" supports of this Republic; if you and I are condemned:
" ah! I foresee, we are the last of the French—we are
" the last of the energetic Republicans. The reign of
" Royalist terror begins—its daggers will soon penetrate
" everywhere. Is it not better for us to reap the glory
" of not having survived servitude—of having died to
" save our fellow-citizens from it? O my children
" (here a flood of tears came to his relief)! I have but
" one bitter regret to express to you—it is, that having
" burned with a holy desire to bequeath you liberty, the
" source of all happiness, I leave you a prey to every
" calamity. I have no earthly good to bequeath you!
" Not even my civic virtues, my profound hatred of
" tyranny, my ardent devotion to the cause of equality
" and liberty, my intense love of the people—not even
" these can I now wish to bequeath you—for they would
" be a fatal legacy. What use could you make of them
" under the royal despotism which, to a certainty, is
" about to establish itself? I leave you slaves! and this
" reflection is the only one that will rend my soul in its
" expiring struggle. It would be my duty, indeed, to
" advise you to bear your bonds with more patience than
" your unhappy father did, but even of that last sad
" office I feel that I am incapable!"

To the first questions submitted to the Questions on
deliberation of the jurors, and which con- the facts.
cerned only the *fact* of the conspiracy, and the par-

ticipation in it of each of the accused, the Court, at the
request of the foreman of the jury, added some others,
touching the provocations (written or verbal) to re-establish
the Constitution of 1793.   This addition produced in
the terms of the indictment a change the more illegal,
inasmuch as it all at once submitted to the examination
of the jurors papers, on which the parties had not been
permitted to explain themselves.*   Some of the accused
complained loudly of this, but, notwithstanding that they
were, *pro tanto*, supported by the opinion of the national
accuser, the Court took no notice of their complaints.

Question as to
the intention.   With no better success, though with
great energy, the accused protested
against the manner in which the question of *intention*
was put, and in which an odious partiality was visible.
The law ordered, on pain of rendering null and void,
that in all cases the jury, after having declared the fact
proven, and the accused party convicted, should add,—
" *I am, or I am not, of opinion that he had committed
such act maliciously, and with design.*"   It was especially on maintaining the adverb *maliciously* that the
accused insisted, because they saw in it, as it were, an
invitation to the Jury to examine the legitimacy of the
motives by which they had hypothetically justified the
conspiracy.   On the question of intention, it was, that
the accused expressed themselves thus in addressing the
jurors :—" Descend into your own hearts; you will there
" find a silent monitor to whisper you—' These men,
·' after all, only meditated on the happiness of their
" fellow-creatures.   The Revolution was not for *them* a
" game of personal interest.'   Let it be deeply impressed
" on you citizens, that there were men who regarded it
" as an event of vast moment to humanity; be well
" assured that that conviction became to them a new
" religion, to which they could, in the spirit of perfect
" self-devotion, sacrifice convenience, riches, repose,
" life itself!   To strike down a friend of liberty, is to
" stretch forth the hand of fellowship to kings.   You sit
" in judgment on liberty; she was fruitful in martyrs,

* A judgment of the Criminal Tribunal of the Seine has since
solemnly decided that the questions relative to the provocations
referred to were put by the High Court *in contravention of the law!*

" and in avengers of their memory. Remember, liberty
" expires when you stifle the generous passions—when
" you present to her inspired worshippers the bleeding
" heads of those who have devoted themselves in her
" defence. The accusers have pretended, that even
" though our arguments were true, the jurors could
" take no account of the motives which might have
" determined the accused, nor see in their intentions
" other than the design to subvert the Constitution of
" the Year III. (1795). If you admit this novel pre-
" tention, then, there is no longer in France either jury
" or country. In the first place, it is not to the over-
" throw of the actual Constitution, but to that of *legiti-*
" *mate authority*, that the jurors ought to turn their
" attention; for could they declare a man guilty who,
" in acting against the Government *de facto*, was im-
" pelled by the conviction that he was acting in favour
" of the Government *de jure*, and of the veritable law
" of the country? What, in that case, would become
" of the internal feeling of good or evil, which renders
" the institution of jurors so invaluable in the estimation
" of pure consciences? To what a nullity you would
" reduce the care which the law has taken of reconciling
" (by questions touching intention and motive) the con-
" tradictions so frequently observable between the pre-
" cepts of natural *law* and those of the actual law ! To
" what a pass you would bring the supreme law of the
" interest of the people, which enjoins its delegates to
" reckon love of country, and devotion to its welfare, as
" a principal circumstance in judging the hearts of
" accused persons."

Some of the jurors joined the accused in demanding
that the questions touching *intention* might be put according to the formula prescribed by the law; they
asked in vain. The High Court persisting in its course,
limited the questions within the following terms :—
" *Has the accused conspired, or provoked with the*
" *intention of conspiring, or of provoking?*" Thus
was interdicted all examination touching the morality of
the act.

There were sixteen jurors ; four were Declaration of
sufficient to acquit. Three only remained the jury.

constantly favourable to the accused. Gauthier Biauzat, whom we name, because we know he has ceased to live, was of the number. He remained throughout faithful to the people; and, had it depended on him, there would have been none condemned. All the questions, however, relative to the conspiracy were resolved negatively. But, unfortunately, thirteen jurors pronounced that there had been provocations, verbal and written, to re-establish the Constitution of 1793, and that Babeuf, Darthé, Buonarroti, Germain, Cazin, Moroy, Blondeau, Meneissier, and Bouin, had participated in it; the two first without palliating circumstances, all the others with these circumstances. From day-break in the morning of the 7th Prairial of the Year V., the rolling of drums, the noise of artillery, and the extraordinary movement of troops, gave the inhabitants of Vendôme a presage of the dénouement of the drama, of which they had been spectators.

Condemnation. Every thing announced to the seven aforementioned prisoners, who were present, their approaching end. They appeared for the last time before the tribunal, which was wrapt in a gloomy silence. A numerous and uneasy multitude filled the Court, of which all the avenues were guarded by a strong military force. The chief of the jury having pronounced the fatal verdict, which he did with a tremulous voice, the accusers followed, demanding sentence of death against Babeuf and Darthé, and of deportation against the rest.

A last attempt was made to arrest judgment. One of the latter, aided by an advocate, demanded of the tribunal to pronounce a general acquittal, on the ground that the law of the 27th Germinal, the application of which had been just required by the national accusers, being prohibitive of the liberty of the press, had ceased to be in force, by virtue of an article of the Constitution, purporting that every law of this description should have effect during only one year at most. The tribunal paid no attention to it, but said to Babeuf and Darthé— " Die !" and to the seven others—" Go and drag along a miserable life, far from your country, in burning and murderous climes !"

At that moment a great tumult is heard; Babeuf and Darthé stab themselves; they cry on all sides—*They are assassinated.* Buonarroti protests and appeals to the people; a general movement is made by the spectators, which is instantly suppressed by a hundred bayonets directed against them. The gendarmes seize those sentenced to transportation, menace them with their sabres, and drag them, along with their dying companions, away from the public view. But the weakness of their poignards, which broke in the attempt, prevented Babeuf and Darthé from accomplishing their self-destruction. They passed a cruel night in consequence of the wounds they inflicted on themselves; the blade of the weapon remained buried in Babeuf's wound, close to his heart.

Babeuf and Darthé stab themselves.

Their courage never belied itself; and strong in conscience they marched resolutely to the scaffold, as to a triumph. Immediately before receiving the stroke of death, Babeuf spoke of his love for the people, to whom he recommended his family. A general mourning prevailed in Vendôme when those generous defenders of equality lost their lives. Their mutilated bodies, which the barbarians had caused to be flung into a ditch, were piously interred by the neighbouring country people.

Bloody execution.

Fifty-six accused were acquitted. Of this number was Vadier, formerly member of the Convention, to whom the High Court adopted a measure that ought not to be forgotten for its palpable injustice. This unfortunate old man, who, by the integrity with which, before the fatal 9th Thermidor, he had discharged the difficult functions of President of the Committee of General Surety, had drawn upon himself the indiscriminating hatred of the enemies of the Revolution and of justice, had hardly escaped a bloody proscription, when a fresh pretext was seized to involve him in another. Though he had no knowledge whatever of the conspiracy, and though not even suspected, he was arrested, dragged, through a thousand dangers, from Toulouse to Paris, put in accusation, and transferred to Vendôme. In the course of the debates, he tried in vain to justify his conduct; he was silenced. Being, how-

Vadier

ever, obliged to acquit him, he was ordered to be detained in prison, on the alleged ground that there was a decree of the Convention authorizing his deportation. Will it be believed? This decree had been revoked, and no longer existed! It was thus, by an error of fact so easy to rectify, that the members of the first tribunal of the Republic—a tribunal to which a law had attributed infallibility—arbitrarily, and without interrogating their victim, inflicted a most severe punishment, which lasted a long time, and might have been perpetual, had not the great crime of the 18th Brumaire (Buonaparte's usurpation) put a period to it.

Generosity of the Municipality of Saint-Lô.   Shortly afterwards the five convicts present were thrown, with Vadier, into the fort constructed on the barren island at the entrance of the Bay of Cherbourg. They traversed this long route in chains, and shut up in barred cages, sometimes exposed to insults and menaces, at other times receiving the most affecting marks of affection and respect. At Falaise, at Caen, and at Valogne, they encountered imminent dangers; but they were received with friendship and honour at Mellereau, at Argentan, and at Saint-Lô. In this latter city the mayor, at the head of the municipal body, complimented and embraced them, calling them, *our unfortunate brethren.* " *You " have defended,"* said the mayor, " *the rights of the " people; every good citizen owes you love and gra- " titude.*" By a resolution of the Council General, they were lodged in its assembly room, where all manner of succours and consolation were administered to them.

Goodness of the people of Vendôme.   For many a long day the good inhabitants of Vendôme used to point out, with tender emotion, to travellers the last abode of the martyrs of equality.*

* [Here ends the history of the conspiracy, after which follow the justificative pieces alluded to in the course of the work. As indicative of the state of opinion, and of the nature of the efforts made by the Democrats in 1795 and 1796, they are documents of great interest. The conspiracy of Babeuf was the last expiring struggle for equality. With the condemnation of its chiefs ended all hope of reviving the Constitution of 1793; and, as a natural consequence, the working masses, losing all interest in public

affairs, abandoned the Revolution to the monied classes. In reference to this portion of French history, Mignet observes :—
" Some time afterwards, Babeuf and his accomplices, amongst whom were Amar, Vadier, and Darthé, the old Secretary of Joseph Lebon, were brought to trial before the High Court of Vendôme. They none of them belied their character ; they spoke like men who were neither afraid to avow their designs nor to die for their cause. At the beginning and ending of each examination, they hummed the air of the *Marseillaise.* This ancient song of victory, joined with their confident demeanour, struck the spectators with astonishment, and seemed to render them still formidable. Their wives having followed them before the tribunal, Babeuf, in finishing his defence, turned towards them, and said, ' They might follow them to the very place of execution, for their punishment could not make them blush.' Babeuf and Darthé were condemned to death, and they both, on hearing their sentence, stabbed themselves with their daggers. Babeuf was the last chief of the old commune, and of the Committee of Public Safety, which had been divided before July (Thermidor), but had afterwards united. The final dispersion of this party, which had been diminishing more and more every day, may be dated from this period. Under the re-action it remained united, and under Babeuf presented a formidable association. From that time Democrats still existed, but the party was disorganized."—BRONTERRE.]

JUSTIFICATIVE PIECES.

PIECE No. I.

THE FRENCH CONSTITUTION,

ADOPTED BY

THE NATIONAL CONVENTION.

Declaration of the Rights of Man and of the Citizen.

THE French people, convinced that the forgetfulness and contempt of the natural rights of man, are the sole causes of the calamities of the world, has resolved to lay open, in a solemn declaration, those sacred and inalienable rights, to the end that all the citizens being always able to compare the acts of the Government with the design of all social institutions, may never suffer themselves to be oppressed and abused by tyranny; and that the people may have perpetually before its eyes the bases of its liberty and its happiness, the magistrate the rule of his duties, and the legislator the object of his mission.

In consequence it proclaims, in presence of the Supreme Being, the following declaration of the rights of man and of the citizen :—

ART. 1. The end of society is general happiness.

Government is instituted for the purpose of guaranteeing to man the enjoyment of his natural and imprescriptible rights.

2. Those rights are equality, liberty, safety, and property.

3. All men are equal by nature and in the eye of the law.

4. The law is the free and solemn expression of the general will; it is the same for all, either in protecting

or in punishing : it can ordain only that which is just and useful to society.

5. Every citizen is equally admissible to public employments. Free people, in their elections, know no other motives of preference, than virtue and talents.

6. Liberty is the power which belongs to a man of doing all that which does not injure the rights of another : it has nature for its origin, justice for its rule, and the law for its protection : its moral bounds are defined in this maxim,—

Do not to another that which thou dost not wish he he should do unto thee.

7. The right of manifesting thoughts and opinions, either by the press or by any other manner, the right of assembling peaceably, and the free exercise of modes of worship, cannot be forbidden.

The necessity of declaring these rights supposes either the presence or the remembrance of recent despotism.

8. Safety consists in the protection granted by society to each of its members for the preservation of his person, of his rights, and of his property.

9. The law ought to protect public and individual liberty from the oppression of those who govern.

10. No one ought to be accused, arrested, or detained otherwise than in the cases determined by the law, and according to the forms which it prescribes : every citizen summoned or seized by the authority of the law ought instantly to obey; by resistance he renders himself culpable.

11. Every act exercised against a man who has not offended against the law, and exercised without the forms prescribed by the law, is arbitrary and tyrannical : the person against whom it is wished to be exercised by violence has the right of resisting it by force.

12. Those who solicit, expedite, sign, execute, or cause to be executed arbitrary acts, are culpable, and ought to be punished.

13. Every man being presumed innocent till the moment that he shall be declared guilty, if it is judged indispensably necessary to arrest him, all severity which is not necessary to secure his person, ought to be severely repressed by the law.

14. No one ought to be judged and punished, till after having been heard or legally summoned, and but in virtue of a law promulgated before the commission of the crime: the law which punishes crimes committed before its existence is a tyranny; a retroactive effect given to the law is a crime.

15. The law ought to decree only punishments strictly and evidently necessary: punishments ought to be proportioned to crimes, and useful to society.

16. The right of property is that which belongs to every citizen of disposing, at his pleasure, of his goods, of his revenues, and of the produce of his labour and industry.

17. No kind of labour, of culture, or commerce, can be forbidden to the industry of citizens.

18. Every man may engage his services and his time, but he can neither sell himself nor be sold. His person is not an alienable property. The law does not acknowledge the state of servitude; there can exist only an engagement of attentions and recompenses between the man who labours and the man who employs him.

19. No one can be deprived of the least part of his property without his consent, except when the public necessity, legally verified, requires it, and under the condition of a just and previous indemnity.

20. No contribution can be established but for general utility. All the citizens have a right of concurring in the establishment of contributions, in watching over their employ, and in causing an account of them to be rendered.

21. Public succours are a sacred debt. Society owes subsistence to unfortunate citizens, either by procuring them labour, or by assuring the means of existence to those who are not in a state to labour.

22. Instruction is what all have need of. Society ought to favour with all its power the progress of public reason, and put instruction within the reach of all the citizens.

23. The social guarantee consists in the action of all for the purpose of assuring to each the enjoyment and preservation of his rights: this guarantee rests on the national sovereignty.

24. It cannot exist, if the limits of the public functions are not clearly determined by law, and if the responsibility of all the functionaries is not assured.

25. The sovereignty resides in the people. It is one
and indivisible, imprescriptible, and inalienable.

26. No portion of the people can exercise the power
of the entire people; but every section of the sovereign
assembled ought to enjoy, with an entire liberty, the
right of expressing its will.

27. All individuals usurping the sovereignty should be
immediately put to death by free men.

28. A people has always the right of revising, of reforming, and of changing its constitution. One generation cannot subject future generations to its laws.

29. Every citizen has an equal right to concur to the
formation of the law, and to the nomination of his delegates, or of his agents.

30. The public functions are in an essential manner
temporary: they cannot be considered either as distinctions or as recompenses, but as duties.

31. The crimes of the delegates of the people ought
never to be unpunished. No one has the right of pretending that he is more inviolable than other citizens.

32. The right of presenting petitions to the depositaries
of the public authority cannot in any case be forbidden,
suspended, or limited.

33. Resistance to oppression is the consequence of
the other rights of man.

34. There is oppression against the social body when
one alone of its members is oppressed. There is oppression against every member when the social body is
oppressed.

35. When government violates the rights of the
people, insurrection is for the people, and for every portion of the people, the most sacred of rights, and the
most indispensable of duties.

CONSTITUTIONAL ACT.

The Republic.

Art 1. The French Republic is one and indivisible.

Division of the People.

2. The French people is divided, for the exercise of its sovereignty, into primary assemblies of cantons.

3. It is divided, for the administration and for justice, into departments, districts, and municipalities.

State of the Citizens.

4. Every man born and domiciliated in France, of the full age of twenty-one years; every foreigner of the same age, who domiciliated in France for one year, lives there on his labour, or acquires a property, or marries a French person, or adopts an infant, or supports an old person: and likewise every foreigner who shall be judged by the legislative body to have merited well of humanity, is admitted to the exercise of the rights of a French citizen.

5. The exercise of the rights of a citizen is lost by naturalization in a foreign country, by the acceptance of functions or favours from a government not originating from the people, and by condemnation to corporal and disgraceful punishments, till again re-established.

6. The exercise of the rights of a French citizen is suspended by being in a state of accusation, or by a sentence of contumacy, so long as the sentence remains unrevoked.

Sovereignty of the People.

7. The sovereign people is the universality of the French citizens.

8. It names its deputies itself.

9. It delegates to the electors the choice of administrators, of public arbitrators, of the criminal judges, and the judges of cashiering.

10. It deliberates on the laws.

Primary Assemblies.

11. The primary assemblies are composed of citizens domiciliated during six months in each canton.

12. They are composed of two hundred citizens at least, of six hundred at most, called to vote.

13. They are constituted by the nomination of a president, of secretaries, and of scrutators.

14. Their police belongs to them.

15. No person can appear there in arms.

16. The elections are made either by scrutiny ro by vote, according to the choice of each voter.

17. A primary assembly cannot in any case prescribe an uniform method of voting.

18. The scrutators shall verify the votes of those citizens who, not being able to write, prefer voting by scrutiny.

19. The suffrages on the laws are given by *yes* or by *no*.

20. The wish of the primary assembly is thus proclaimed:—*The citizens united in the primary assembly of ...... to the number of ...... voters, vote for or against ...... to the majority of ....*

National Representation.

21. Population is the sole basis of the national representation.

22. There is a deputy to every forty thousand individuals.

23. Every union of primary assemblies, resulting from a population of from thirty-nine to forty-one thousand souls, names immediately a deputy.

24. The nomination is made by the absolute majority of suffrages.

25. Each assembly examines the suffrages, and sends a commissioner for the general reverification to the place pointed out as the most central.

26. If the first reverification does not give the absolute majority, a second appeal is proceeded to, and the choice lays between the two citizens who had the greatest number of votes.

27. In case of an equality of votes, the most aged has the preference, either to be balloted or elected. In case of an equality of age, it is decided by lot.

28. Every Frenchmen exercising the rights of a citizen is eligible in the extent of the Republic.

29. Every deputy belongs to the whole nation.

30. In case of the non-acceptance, resignation, exclusion, or death of a deputy, his replacement is provided for by the primary assemblies who named him.

31. A deputy who has given in his resignation cannot quit his post till after the admission of his successor.

32. The French people assembles every year, on the 1st of May, for the elections.

33. It proceeds to elect whatever may be the number of citizens having a right to vote.

34. The primary assemblies meet extraordinarily on the demand of fifty citizens having a right to vote.

35. The convocation is made in this case by the municipality of the ordinary place of assembling.

36. These extraordinary assemblies do not deliberate, unless the half of the citizens who have a right to vote, and one more, be present.

Electoral Assemblies.

37. The citizens met in the primary assemblies name one elector to the proportion of two hundred citizens, present or not, two from two hundred and one to four hundred, and three from four hundred and one to six hundred.

38. The sittings of the electoral assemblies and the mode of elections are the same as in the primary assemblies.

Legislative Body.

39. The legislative body is one, indivisible, and permanent.

40. Its session is of one year.

41. It meets on the 1st of July.

42. The national assembly cannot constitute itself, if it is not composed at least of one half the deputies and one more.

43. The deputies cannot at any time be called to account, accused, or judged, for opinions which they have given in the bosom of the legislative body.

44. They may, for criminal offences, be seized in the fact, but the warrant of arrest, or warrant to bring them before the tribunals, cannot be issued without the authority of the legislative body.

Sittings of the Legislative Body.

45. The sittings of the national assembly are public.

46. The proces verbal of its sitting are printed.

47. It cannot deliberate unless two hundred members at least are present.

48. It cannot refuse the right of speaking to its members in the right of which they have claimed it.

49. Its deliberations are determined by the majority of those present.

50. Fifty members have a right to demand the nominal appeal.

51. It has the right of censure on the conduct of members in its bosom.

52. The police of the place of its sittings, and in the exterior circle which it has determined, belong to it.

Functions of the Legislative Body.

53. The legislative body proposes laws and makes decrees.

54. Under the general name of laws are comprised all acts of the legislative body, concerning—

The civil and criminal legislation;

The general administration of the revenues, and ordinary expenses of the Republic;

The national domains;

The standard, the weight, the impress, and the denomination of coins;

The declaration of war;

All new general distribution of the French territory;

The public instruction, and public honours paid to the memory of great men,

55. Under the particular name of decrees are comprehended all the acts of the legislative body, concerning—

The yearly establishment of the land and sea forces ;·

The permission or denial of the passage of foreign troops over the French territory ;

The introduction of foreign naval forces into the ports of the Republic ;

Measures of safety and general tranquillity ;

The annual and accidental distribution of succours and public works ;

Orders for the fabrication of money of all species ;

Unforeseen and extraordinary expenses ;

Local and particular measures of an administration, a commune, or a public work ;

Defence of the territory ;

The ratification of treaties ;

The prosecution of the responsibility of the members of the council, and the public functionaries ;

The accusation of those charged with conspiracies against the general safety of the Republic ;

All changes in the partial distribution of the French territory ;

National recompenses.

Formation of the Laws.

56. The plans of the laws are preceded by a report.

57. The discussion cannot be opened, and the law provisionally ordained, till fifteen days after the report.

58. The plan is printed and sent to all the communes of the Republic, under this title, *Proposed Law.*

59. In forty days after the sending of the proposed law, if, in the half of the departments, and one over, the tenth of the primary assemblies of each of them, regularly formed, shall not have objected, the plan shall be accepted, and become law.

60. If objections are made to it, the legislative body convokes the primary assemblies.

Titles of Laws and Decrees.

61. The laws, the decrees, the judgments, and all the public acts are titled, *In the name of the French people, the .... year of the French Republic.*

Executive Council.

62. There is an executive council, composed of twenty-four members.

63. The electoral assembly of each department names a candidate. The legislative body chooses from the general list the members of the council.

64. It is changed one-half by each legislature, during the latter months of the session.

65. The council is charged with the direction and inspection of the general administration. It can only act in execution of the laws and decrees of the legislative body.

66. It names out of its own body the agents in chief of the general administration of the Republic.

67. The legislative body determines the number and the functions of these agents.

68. These agents form no council. They are separate, without any immediate connection between them; they exercise no personal authority.

69. The council names out of its own body the exterior agents of the Republic.

70. It negociates treaties.

71. The members of the council, in case of prevarication, are accused by the legislative body.

72. The council is responsible for the non-execution of the laws and decrees, and for the abuses which it does not denounce.

73. It recalls and replaces the agents of its nomination.

74. It is bound to denounce them, if there is cause, before the judicial authorities.

Connection of the Executive Council with the Legislative Body.

75. The executive council is situated near the legislative body. It has an entrance, and a separate place in the hall of the legislative body.

76. It is heard at all times when it has an account to give.

77. The legislative body calls it into its presence, either in whole or in part, whenever it judges necessary.

Administrative and Municipal Bodies.

78. There is in every commune of the Republic a municipal administration. In every district an intermediary one.

79. The municipal officers are elected by the assemblies of the commune.

80. The administrators and municipal officers have not any character of representation.

81. The municipalities and the administrations are half renewed every year.

82. The administrators and municipal officers have not any charter of representation.

They cannot in any case modify the acts of the legislative body, or suspend their execution.

83. The legislative body determines the functions of the municipal officers and administrators, the rules of their subordination, and the penalties which they may incur.

84. The sittings of the municipalities and of the administrations are public.

Civil Justice.

85. The code of the civil and criminal laws is the same for the whole of the Republic.

86. There can be no hindrance given to the right which the citizens have of causing their differences to be decided by arbitrators of their own choosing.

87. If the citizens do not reserve to themselves the right of protesting against it, the decision of these arbitrators is final.

88. Justices of the peace are elected by the citizens of the circles marked out by the law.

89. They conciliate and judge without any charge.

90. Their number and their competence are determined by the legislative body.

91. Public arbitrators are elected by the electoral assemblies.

92. Their numbers and their circles are fixed by the legislative body.

93. They take cognizance of those disputes which have not been definitely settled by private arbitrators, or by justices of the peace.

o

94. They deliberate in public. They give their opinions openly. They decide without appeal on verbal defence, or simple memorial, without process, and without expense. They state the reasons of their decisions.

95. The justices of the peace, and the public arbitrators, are elected every year.

Criminal Justice.

96. In criminal matters no citizen can be judged but on an accusation received by the juries, or decreed by the legislative body.

The accused have counsel chosen by them, or officially named.

The conducting of the process is public.

The fact and the intention are decided upon by a jury of judgment.

The punishment is applied by a criminal tribunal.

97. The criminal judges are elected every year by the electoral assemblies.

Tribunal of Cashiering.

98. There is for all the Republic a tribunal of cashiering.

99. This tribunal takes no cognizance of the more essential parts of affairs.

It pronounces on the violations of forms, and on express contraventions of the law.

100. The members of this tribunal are named every year by the electoral assemblies.

Public Contributions.

101. No citizen is exempted from the honourable obligation of contributing to the public charges.

National Treasury.

102. The national treasury is the central point of the receipts and disbursements of the Republic.

103. It is administered by accountable agents, named by the executive council.

104. These agents are watched over by commis-

sioners named by the legislative body, taken out of its own number, and responsible for those abuses which they do not denounce.

Responsibility.

105. The accounts of the agents of the national treasury, and of the administrators of the public money, are given in annually to responsible commissioners, named by the executive council.

106. These verifiers are watched over by commissioners of the nomination of the legislative body, taken out of its own number, and responsible for those errors and abuses which they do not denounce.

The legislative body passes the accounts.

Forces of the Republic.

107. The general force of the Republic is composed of the whole French people.

108. The Republic keeps in pay, even during the time of peace, a sea and land force.

109. All the French are soldiers, they are all exercised in the use of arms.

110. There is no generalissimo.

111. The difference of ranks, their distinctive marks, and subordination, only subsist relatively to the service, and during its duration.

112. The public force employed to maintain order and peace in the interior, acts only on the requisition in writing of the constituted authorities.

113. The public force employed against the enemies without, acts under the orders of the executive council.

114. No armed body can deliberate.

National Conventions.

115. If in the half and one over of the departments, a tenth of the primary assemblies, regularly formed, demand the revision of the constitutional act, or the change of some one of its articles, the legislative body is bound to convoke all the primary assemblies of the Republic, for the purpose of knowing if there is reason for a national convention.

116. The national convention is formed in the same

manner as the legislatures, and unites the powers of them.

117. It occupies itself, relatively to the constitution only on those objects which have occasioned its convocation.

Connections between the French Republic and Foreign Nations.

118. The French people is the natural friend and ally of all free people.

119. It does not intermeddle with the government of other nations. It does not suffer other nations to intermeddle in its own.

120. It gives an asylum to all foreigners banished from their country for the cause of liberty. It refuses one to tyrants.

121. It does not make peace with an enemy who occupies its territory.

Guarantee of Rights.

122. The constitution guarantees to all the French, equality, liberty, safety, property, the public debt, the free exercise of modes of worship, general instruction, public succours, the indefinite liberty of the press, the right of petition, the right of meeting in popular societies, the enjoyment of all the rights of man.

123. The French Republic honours fidelity, courage, old age, filial piety, and misfortune. It places the deposit of its constitution under the protection of all the virtues.

124. The declaration of rights, and the constitutional act, are engraved on tables in the hall of the legislative body, and in the public places.

(Signed)   COLLOT D'HERBOIS, *President.*
        DURAND MAILLAINE, DUCOS, MEAULE,
        CH. DE LA CROIX, GOSSUIN.
        P. A. LALOY, *Secretary.*

DOCUMENT No. II.

THE TRUTH TO THE PEOPLE,
BY THE PATRIOTS OF 89

Of the 14th July, 10th August, and 13th Vendémiaire.

PEOPLE !—you whom they caress or threaten—whom they exalt or vilify, as may suit the ambitious views of those men who speak of your rights only to trample them under foot—of your sovereignty only to usurp it—listen to great truths ! learn the cause of all the calamities which you have been made to endure, from the 9th Thermidor of the Year II., up to Vendémiaire of the Year IV.

Certain abuses—a few arbitrary acts inseparable from a great revolution—had impressed some blemishes on the great and glorious events of the four first years of the Revolution. To correct those abuses—to put an end to all provisional government—to give the people a constitution which would guarantee its rights and sovereignty —to snatch power from hands that abused it—to strip tyranny of all hopes of raising its hideous head—behold what the Revolution of the 9th Thermidor would have operated for you, if the interest of the people—if general happiness—had been the object of that event. But its results have been most disastrous, because it was the work of vice, of division, of ambition, and of vengeance ; it turned every thing to the advantage of royalism ; it has ended by dragging into one common precipice the pure and courageous Republicans, and the false ones employed to bring it about. From that moment calumny has never ceased to distil its poison. Every *friend of the people*— every *founder of liberty*—was qualified and treated as *knave, miscreant, terrorist,* and *blood-drinker* These denominations were rendered synonymous with *Republican* ; hired journals re-echoed them ; corrupt orators polluted the tribune of the senate with them. Thence were organised famine, massacre, the discrediting of the assignats, the monopoly and forestalling of merchandize. In the people who made the Revolution was no longer to be seen but a mass of slaves ready to crouch in subjection to the *golden million*, which exclusively called itself *sovereign;* pity had all her tears for counter-revolutionists, who represented themselves as being all victims of terror; the prison doors were unlocked to them, and their places speedily supplied by Republicans, under the name Terrorists; and the latter were expelled from all military and civil posts, to be succeeded by returned emigrants, by nobles, by non-juring priests, who had all become patriots *par excellence*. Forthwith our armies were disorganised, treasons burst forth, our arsenals, which a short time before abounded in every thing, were emptied, our fleets beaten were abandoned to the enemy, and our marine annihilated. It then became necessary to our tyrants to proscribe the popular surveillance, to stifle public remonstrances (imprescriptible rights of a free people); accordingly did our new masters hasten to destroy our popular societies, which had been the advanced sentinels of the Revolution, and the terror of Pitt and Cobourg, because they were focuses of public instruction, whence issued sparks that electrified all hearts, and fed the sacred enthusiasm of liberty; because they opposed a formidable rampart to ambition and intrigue; because, in short, they were so many Pharoses or beacon-lights, warning our state-pilots of the rocks which endangered the vessel of liberty.

And, heavens! what means resorted to, to operate and consolidate this counter-revolution!—what liberticidal decrees wrested from the Convention by the faction of the foreigner!—what hordes of emigrants struck out from the proscription lists, and restored to honour, under the qualification of cultivators and workmen!—what bands of refractory priests tolerated, and licensed to fanaticize the multitude! The property of condemned Royalists, which offered a solid mortgage to the assignats, was restored to their kinsfolk, as guilty as themselves; thence the ruin of public credit. An amnesty is offered to the Chouans and Vendean rebels; they spurn it, and insolently demand to be treated on the footing of Power to Power. Miscreant audacity! Oh, shame of our country! Stipulate for peace with Charette, Stofflet, Comartin, Sapino, and the rest of the crew of brigand insurgents!—allow them to arm!—pay them for tearing their country's bosom!—for having murdered thousands of Republicans!—and (by a secret condition) promise them the re-establishment of the altar and the throne! The people's delegates conclude so ignominious a treaty!—one that will dishonour the pages of history—and the French Senate ratify the shame of the first nation on earth! Ah, you will not believe it, future generations; you would not believe it yourselves, men of France, had you not been living witnesses of it. And it is after two years of complete triumph that your delegates stipulate your disgrace, and cover your trophies with crape—it is at the moment when your phalanxes, covered with laurels, had just hoisted the standard of liberty beyond the Rhine, upon the summits of the Alps and Pyrenees, and at the extremities of the Batavian swamps—that treaties of dishonour are ratified in your name with the despots of Berlin and Madrid, whom you had vanquished, and who, had it not been for the Thermidorean reaction, would have come, together with their confederates, to sue for peace upon any conditions that you might have thought proper to impose!

But why should we wonder if the Committees of Government had become a Pandora's box; they were recruited from the factions of Rovère, Boissy, Saladin, Laumont, Auguis, Larivière, Lanjuinais, Dumont, &c., all notorious Royalists, who could no otherwise pay court to the tyrants they served, than by stifling liberty, by replacing the people under the yoke of servitude, and by massacreeing, *en masse*, all the most intrepid Republicans. Blood, however, did not flow in sufficient abundance on the scaffold; accordingly, did they organize in all points of the Republic, hordes of assassins, under the name of *Companies of Jesus and of the Sun*. Boisset was dispatched to Lyons and Bourg; Cadroy, Chambon, Mariette, Isnard, to Aix and Marseilles; and at *their* guilty bidding the assassination of the patriots was made the order of the day throughout the whole south of France. Under their banners the assassins now march, burst in the doors of the prisons, slaughter all the patriots they find within, issue forth like furies, reeking with gore; they violate private dwellings, traverse the streets, sabre every man they meet of known patriotism; the infant is massacred in the bosom of its mother, the old man in presence of his child, and the waters of the Rhone are choked with human carcasses, which are drifted along to the waves of the Mediterranean, already dyed with Republican blood! And these horrid scenes are prolonged in the sight of human tigers, who call themselves delegates of the people! and the Convention crouching under the sway of wretches who have sold themselves to the foreigner, or abandoning itself to prostitute women, has suffered France to be covered with mourning and carnage for ten long months! Nay, the Convention has not punished even one assassin, and Rovère had the effrontery to qualify these assassinations with the name of *popular justice.**

Not content with suffering the murderers to go unpunished—with corrupting the public mind—with subduing the energy and stifling the enthusiasm of liberty—with substituting for the hymns which led our warriors to victory, homicidal songs,† which provoked the immolation of patriots by hecatombs; not content with these, they must needs reduce the people to despair, by giving them but two ounces of bad bread, whilst Boissy d'Anglas came insultingly to the tribune of the Convention to announce that the subsistence of the people was provided for!

* [See page 48 (note), for what Mignet says of the massacres of the people alluded to here.—BRONTERRE.]

† [After the death of Robespierre, Fréron, one of the Thermidorian assassins, in his journal called "*The Orator of the People,*" summoned the counter-revolutionists to arms, and forming the young men of the middling and wealthy classes into a sort of irregular militia called the *jeunesse dorée* of Fréron, placed himself at their head. These young ruffians, armed with short staves *leaded* at the end like bludgeons, used to parade the streets of Paris—to knock down every jacobin or patriot they met—disperse by force all the popular meetings—till, at length, emboldened by impunity and the tacit approval of the Convention, they broke open the doors of the Jacobin Club, and provoked a desperate battle, which gave the Convention an excuse for suppressing popular societies altogether. These young privileged assassins used to march to a tune called the *Reveil du Peuple*, in hatred of the Marselleise and other Republican airs, which so often led the French Democrats to victory.—BRONTERRE.]

Yes!—no doubt, subsistence was provided for the *golden million*, who gorged themselves with the wealth of France, while the mass of the people, destitute of every thing, were dying in thousands of inanition!

And, people of France! in whose hands are your destinies placed? In the hands of men who, after famishing, betraying, ruining, and massacreeing you, still hold seats in your senate; whilst you have seen driven from it, proscribed, and led to the scaffold, the Deputies who opposed its murderous and liberticidal decrees!—for never did perfidious royalism so domineer over the Convention as during the Thermidorian reaction. Yes, you have seen those days of mourning and crime—those fatal days of *Germinal* and *Prairial* —on which you were treated as *seditionists* for having come to the bar of your delegates to demand *bread*, and the execution of that Constitution, which the nation had freely, solemnly, and unanimously accepted.

You remember, courageous inhabitants of the faubourgs, how you were hunted, pursued by Fréron's *golden* band, at the order of the Government—blocked up in your houses, disarmed, dungeoned, and the most energetic of your brethren condemned by military law, and dragged to the same scaffold on which had just flowed the blood of the only delegates who had had the courage to raise their voice in the Senate to support your just remonstrances! You had sworn, virtuous Goujon, Romme, Duroy, Soubrany, Bourbotte, Duquesnoy, to defend the interests of the people, to die for them and for liberty; you have kept your oath! Your generous devotion has turned your executioners pale; it has served the commonwealth; it is engraven in the hearts of the Republicans; it will go down to posterity, and run parallel with that of the Gracchi, of Curtius, and of Regulus. Yes, people of France, you will remember those days of horror, if it were only to consign the abominable authors of them to the execrations of all generations, present and future. You will never forget that during the fifteen months succeeding the 9th Thermidor, your rulers have heaped upon you such vexations, such calamities, as never did the slaves of Rome endure at the hands of their patrician masters, the serfs of

Poland under their palatines, nor even those sons of misery who are sold to bondage by inhuman traffic on Africa's coasts.

Base villains!—they called it a "reign of terror," which had existed only against crime, while they exercised a most bloody and desolating terror against virtue and republicanism.....Miscreants! they boasted of having overthrown a decemviral tyranny, yet never did a direr tyranny grind you down than that which they have exercised during the last fifteen months. Impostors! they had the baseness to saddle men no longer in existence, and whom it is for posterity to judge, with all the evils which they themselves heap upon you. Incapable of continuing the grand operations so nobly conceived and executed by the men they sacrificed, they have only confused and disorganized everything. They pretended to arouse your indignation against the monarchic regime; but the trick was too gross; you were too capable of distinguishing between them and events to be deceived. Too well you knew that the misery which consumed you was not the work of your friends, but of the usurpers— their successors; you were convinced that during the two first years of the Republic, your rights were respected, your enemies crushed, industry and the arts encouraged; your arsenals provided, your fleets well equipped, your flags floating on every sea, your fourteen armies everywhere victorious, la Vendée subjugated, your external enemies routed, the despots of Europe panic-stricken, their thrones rocking beneath them and themselves ready to fall at your feet, the credit of the assignats maintained, the cupidity of proprietors and stockjobbers curbed, your markets well supplied, and abundance guaranteed to you, in return for the countless sacrifices you had made to achieve liberty.

And what are the substitutes given you for such advantages? Alas! what a harrowing picture does the Thermidorian reaction present. Your rights disowned, sneered at, trampled under foot; your friends, your defenders, your brothers, calumniated, proscribed, incarcerated, assassinated; the most unbridled stockjobbing—that destroyer of Republics—substituted for commerce, which vivifies and enlightens them; your fleets beaten, sold, and delivered to the English; your magazines, your arsenals empty, La Vendée and Chouan-nerie * reuniting their forces, the ardor of the Republicans paralysed; the brave fellows who led them to victory banished, and replaced by nobles, emigrants, and Roy-alists; you have seen thirty thousand millions of assignats absorbed in ten months; the rich land-owner—the big merchant—the stock-jobber—the monopolist—divide the spoils amongst them, and suck your blood drop by drop; you have seen famine in the midst of abundance, extreme misery by the side of the most abandoned luxury, public morals destroyed, murder unpunished—even re-commended—crime rendered triumphant over virtue, the democracy annihilated, the steps of the throne raised up again, and a new Tarquin ready to mount it. In a word, liberty would have utterly perished, had it not been for the courage of those brave Republicans—those patriots, so much calumniated and persecuted, who prevented the massacre of the National Convention, and saved the Republic on the memorable days of the 12th, 13th, and 14th Vendémiaire.

Those days, however, have produced no decided tri-umph for democracy. And why? Because the conspi-rators have not been punished, because they still pursue their system of assassination, stock-jobbing, monopoly, and debasing the national money; and find protectors even in the senate! Nevertheless, those memorable days are not altogether lost to us, since they have divested of power the impure hands which had consummated so many crimes; since they have restored to their families such of the Republicans as had escaped the scaffold, and the poignards of the Royalist bands; since they are des-tined to give us a government whose direction will be confided to men of purity—to Republicans who have accomplished much for the general happiness, and will accomplish still more, if *they will clothe themselves with the confidence of the patriots*, who can make no compromise with principles; *if they will strike without*

---

* [The Royalist rebellion in the west of France was sometimes called *Chouannerie*, from three brothers named Chouan, who took a distinguished part in it.—BRONTERRE.]

pity the Royalists, emigrants, and refractory priests,
who incessantly conspire against the Republican Government; *if they will take vigorous means to supply the
markets abundantly, so as to lower the price of provisions;* and if they will retain in office only pure,
enlightened, energetic Republicans: men who would
perish by their side rather than suffer the counter-
Revolution to triumph.

Magnanimous people! your safety consists in resisting
your oppressors with sublime perseverance; disdain not
to use vigilance against them. The calamities they have
incessantly heaped on your defenders have sufficiently
awaked your suspicions to prevent their crafty civism
from any longer imposing on you. Assume your majestic
attitude; arm yourselves with your avenging thunder;
crush those modern Titans who dare to invade your
sovereignty; remember your triumphs; and, if you have
still perils to avoid, you have also trophies to obtain

PIECE No. III.

SOLDIER,
STOP AND READ!

An insidious, perverse Government, and whose luxury
insults the public misery, has just lifted the mask, and
openly attacking liberty, has dared audaciously to close,
and impudently to calumniate, the patriotic unions. In
these assemblies, it is, that the energetic men of the 14th
July, of the 10th August, and of the 13th Vendémiaire,
watched over the rights of the people; and, though
hourly exposed to the bastiles and daggers of the
Royalists, persevered in devoting themselves for the Revolution. They exposed the restoration of the emigrants,
carried to such excess that the list of erasures exceeds
that in which they had been marked out for the contempt of men, and for the vengeance of the laws! They
resolutely claimed for your families the succours so justly
guaranteed to them by the law; and for yourselves, too,

the possessions which the country owes you for having shed your blood in defending her against kings, and which so many solemn decrees justly assure you. The Executive Directory itself had at first favoured those unions, as if an unjust and arbitrary power could love publicity, evidence, and truth. The patriots, confiding in its good faith, repaired in crowds to join them; the snare was craftily laid; they fell into it; patriotic devotion and honesty have little calculation. But the patriots are not sorry; they have acted as became free men. To treat them as anarchists is vain. Europe, more just, even already distinguishes the friends of equality in that name; incorruptible posterity will confirm its judgment.

But whence proceeds this presumption of a few men, clothed with a brief authority? Citizen soldiers! they found their hopes of criminal success upon your courage. They impudently declare, "Our soldiers will defend us." You! their soldiers!!—the vanquishers of tyrants support tyranny!!!....Profligate tyrants!—disabuse yourselves. In vain do you seek to fish out partizans, and to seduce our brethren by brilliant uniforms, by iniquitous bribes, by treats of brandy and cordials: their hearts are not traitors to their country, nor rebels to her voice. Will the same means which unmasked the crime of Capet, and destroyed that tyrant, prove successful for you? No! citizen soldiers! You will not fire on your brethren, as in Germinal and Prairial. Your arms shall no longer be seduced against your friends! It is against tyranny you will direct them; this glorious triumph still remains for you. Like the Greeks of Asia, drawn into the army of Xerxes, you will hearken to the cry of your common country! You will read the lines which your brothers trace in your passage! And should ever the day of a just retribution arrive, you will know what it is that now opposes your return to your homes, where, with us, you desire to establish equality and general happiness!

PIECE No. IV.

EQUALITY.   LIBERTY.

GENERAL HAPPINESS.

Creation of an Insurrectional Directory.

THE Democrats of France, grievously affected, profoundly indignant, justly revolted at the unheard-of state
of misery and oppression of which their unhappy country
presents the spectacle;

Ardently remembering that when a Democratic Constitution was given to the people, and by it accepted,
the preservation of that Constitution was placed *under
the safeguard of all the virtues;*

Considering, therefore, that to the purest, most
courageous virtues, belongs the initiative of undertaking
to avenge the people, whenever, as now, its rights are
usurped, its liberty ravished, and even its existence
compromised;

Believing that the reproach is an unjust one which
accuses the people of cowardice, and that if the people
has hitherto postponed its justice, it was only for want
of proper guides to lead them on;

Recognizing that the overflowing measure of the
crimes of an usurped authority has ripened the inclinations of every virtuous soul, in favour of a revolutionary
explosion, to that degree of maturity, that in order to
render it beneficial—that to put its conductors in a train
to ensure success, it will probably be necessary to moderate rather than accelerate the impetuous burst of freedom,—have resolved as follows :—

Art. 1. They constitute themselves, from this moment,
an Insurrectional Directory, under the name of the
" Secret Directory of Public Safety." In this capacity
they assume the initiative of all movements intended to
lead the people to the recovery of its sovereignty.

2. This Directory consists of four members.

3. This Directory shall be secret; the names of its
members shall be unknown to even its chief agents.
Between these and the members of the Directory there

shall be intermediary agents to carry communications from one to the other.

4. The Secret Directory of Public Safety pledges itself to discharge the immense range of duties which that great title imposes on it.

5. A distinctive mark shall be affixed to such written instructions, as it may be indispensable to give to the principal agents, and this mark shall serve as a precaution against all surprise arising from false instructions; it shall be a guarantee to them, notwithstanding the default of signatures, for the authenticity of the Acts to be communicated by the Secret Directory.

PIECE No. V.

Organization of Principal Agents to the Number of Twelve, and of Intermediary Agents.—Principal Functions of each Class.

The Secret Directory of Public Safety has resolved as follows :—

Art. 1. There shall be twelve principal revolutionary agents—one for each arrondissement of the commune of Paris.

2. Each of these is charged to organize, in his arrondissement, one or more unions of patriots; to foster and direct the public mind in those unions by the reading of popular journals, and by discussions on the rights of the people, and respecting its present situation.

3. These agents shall take note of the daily thermometer of public opinion. They shall render account in those notes of the dispositions, more or less favourable, of the patriots; they shall signify the individuals they may observe most capable of seconding the progress of the movement designed to be brought about; they shall indicate the description of employment, or revolutionary enterprise, to which they may suppose each of these individuals suited. They shall, in like manner, take note of the intriguers—of such impostors who may try to in-

sinuate themselves into the meetings; and they shall, moreover, render account of the impediments and opposition which the latter may offer to the development of energy, or to the inspiration of sound principles and regenerating ideas.

4. There shall be intermediary agents to maintain communications between the principal agents and the Secret Directory.

5. To those agents only shall the twelve principal agents commit the notes of their daily observations.

6. The intermediary agents shall apply successively for these notes every day, or every second day, to each of the principal agents, at their residences, if necessary.

7. The present organization, together with that of the Secret Directory, and the following instruction, shall be transmitted to each of the principal agents.

PIECE, No. VI.

Primary Instruction of the Secret Directory, addressed to each of the Principal Revolutionary Agents.

CITIZENS!—It is not in times of crisis as in ordinary times. When the people enjoys its rights, when the principles of liberty triumph, no one has a right to assume authority over others, without their concurrence; nobody can enterprise measures relating to the general interest without consulting the whole people, and without obtaining its assent. The reason is, that then the best social order reigns, and the best social order is perpetuated only by the rigid maintenance of principles. The man who, in such a state of things, should assume any title whatever for erecting himself (without any concession made to him) into a public magistrate, under pretence of wishing to ameliorate the condition of his fellow-citizens, would be a usurper, even on the supposition that his ultimate intentions were perfectly upright. The reason of this too is plain—it is, that where the people is free, and may be consulted, it is not to be presumed that others can judge better of its interests than the people itself can.

The case is different when a people is in chains—when tyranny has placed it in a state of impotence to emit its will on all that concerns it; when *a fortiori*, it has become impracticable for the people to direct measures of repression against its tyrants; when it has been rendered incapable of wresting from them the usurped power, of which they take advantage, to make it suffer and languish in despair, and to subjugate it more and more every day, till it reaches a limit beyond all calculation.

It becomes, then, just—it becomes necessary that the most intrepid—men most capable of devoting themselves —men endowed with the greatest amount of energy, fire, and force—with those generous virtues, under the safeguard of which has been deposited the preservation of a popular Constitution, which all Frenchmen, having the true spirit of freemen, have never lost sight of—it is then just and necessary that such men, being moreover convinced that the inspiration of their own hearts, or that of liberty itself (which makes them more forcibly—more particulary hear its voice), is a sufficient authority to them to enterprize every thing—it is just and necessary that such men should invest themselves with the dictatorship of insurrection—that they should assume the initiative—that they should arrogate the glorious title of " conspirators for liberty"—in a word, that they should erect themselves into magistrates to save their fellow-citizens.

Such are the motives which have appeared to us to justify our resolution, and to give it a character of grandeur and magnanimity. Having thus satisfied ourselves that our self-conferred mission is eminently legitimate, since the circumstances which render it indispensable for the salvation of liberty, do not admit of its transmission by the sovereign nation, we have furthermore distinguished this very encouraging truth—that the accusation of cowardly apathy, urged against the people, is sheer blasphemy, and that from the general impatience it manifests to burst a yoke really abhorrent to it, we may readily see, that if, up to this time, it has done nothing to break that yoke, we must attribute the circumstance to the fact, that it has hitherto seen itself without guides; and we have remarked, that it is with the deepest regret it postpones the repression of the crimes accumulated on its head. Every thing has announced to us what it would be capable of doing, if it perceived at its head leaders worthy of its confidence.

Animated by such dispositions, we have been immediately led to turn our regards to the men most capable of seconding us in our glorious enterprize. It is you, citizens, who, by a long career of republican conduct, by multiplied acts of pure civism manifested in every stage of the Revolution, by the terrible proofs you have given of your patriotism in times when everything virtuous and patriotic was an object of persecution—it is on you that the first self-constituted avengers of our betrayed country have fixed their regards, to make you the depositaries of their confidence, and to delegate to you the primary and principle divisions of their intended operations.

The portion of trust which the Secret Directory of Public Safety communicates to you is precious and important; its guardianship requires much discretion, prudence, activity, and love of general good; it requires all the virtues of men such as the Secret Directory believes you to be. The Secret Directory has weighed its fundamental organization, and that of its relations with you, in the balance of wisdom and circumspection.

It has deemed it expedient to create twelve municipal agents in the twelve arrondissements of the commune of Paris; and it has so arranged their means of communication with itself, that the correspondence will be almost direct without, however, suffering the twelve principal agents to know the members of the Directory. The reason of this precaution is easily comprehended. It has been felt that the most important part of the secret of the projected insurrection—that upon which depends the success of the whole series of operations—was not so much the existence of an insurrectional committee as the knowledge of the persons who compose it. In fact, should tyranny even learn that such a committee exists, no harm can result to its members, so long as they are personally unknown; neither can any result to the country, unless it be harm to warn despotism to be on its guard, but that

has happened long ago, because despotism has long since
been aware that its crimes must have inspired every
virtuous mind with a disposition to conspire against it.
There would be, therefore, no great danger in divulging
the existence of a committee of general revolution, and
hereafter we may examine whether it would not be even
wise to take advantage of some juncture to let the secret
half-transpire, in order to add fuel to the courage of the
unhappy majority, who only sigh for the opportunity and
moment for emerging from oppression ; whereas everything would be lost by discovering the leading conspirators themselves: in losing them, the combined
ensemble of ramifications emanating, as they will, from
a single centre, would be destroyed, and another certain
and disastrous effect would be, the disconcerting and
terrifying of the most courageous citizens.

Such, Republicans, are the motives which have determined the Directory of Public Safety, notwithstanding
its immense confidence in you—a fact attested by its
choosing you to be its principal and primary agents—to
conceal from even yourselves the names of its members.
The danger of an indiscretion, or that of a counter-
determination—nay, the danger prophetically suggested
to us by a knowledge of human weakness, which too
often supports as a burden the weight of a great confidence, and seems to find comfort in depositing it in the
bosom of friendship, or what appears to be friendship—
all these and the like have been considered by the Secret
Directory, and it could not think of abandoning, perhaps,
the salvation of the country to the hazard of such accidents ; besides, even on the score of fidelity, it is difficult
to persuade oneself of the possibility of that quality
existing with equal strength in the breasts of twelve men,
when made the depositaries of matters of the last importance. The Secret Directory supposes also that it
will not be the less successful in inspiring you with that
entire confidence which the exigency of the case requires.
And why ? Because it has persuaded itself that you will
see in the hardihood, in the devotion, in the fund of
virtue required for such an enterprize, sufficient motives
to accord to it such confidence.

There is another guarantee which the Directory thinks

it may also hold out to you—it is that tone of truth and good faith which malevolence can never simulate. Such tone you will discern in all its acts.

At the same time that we have armed ourselves with every precaution calculated to render ourselves intangible, and our measures impossible to be disconcerted, we desire that you should be secure against any surprise, and that by means of particular marks, stamped upon our acts, you may be always able to recognize their authenticity, notwithstanding the absence of our real signatures.

The Secret Directory has pushed its prudence so far as to isolate its twelve principal agents—each from the rest. They will all receive the same instructions; they will be all charged to do the same things, to concur towards the same end; and, nevertheless, they shall have no mutual knowledge of one another. We have considered such knowledge to be in nowise necessary; *no good could result from it;* it manifestly sufficing that the directing impulse be immediately received from the Secret Directory, by each of its agents, and it being incontestible that success is attainable only through punctuality of execution, and that any concert amongst the twelve agents themselves could only lead to impediments, delays, or modifications, which might possibly diverge from the views and combinations of the regulating Directory. Again, *the greatest harm might result from it,* if in a case—which far be it from us to suspect, after our scrupulous care in selecting the agents (but, in matters of such serious importance, we ought to fear everything, to suppose the worst in everything, and to anticipate every precaution)—there might, then, we repeat, result very great mischiefs from the reciprocal acquaintance and mutual intercommunication of the agents; in case, for instance, that one of them should unfortunately commit an indiscretion, or an act of perfidy, he would then perhaps immolate all his co-agents, whereas, if he did not know them, only himself would suffer from his mal-address or treachery; he could neither involve any one in his defection, nor disorganize the enterprize so as to compromise the fate of liberty.

The same precautions in the way of isolation are taken in regard to the intermediary agents—the same scrutinizing care exercised in selecting them; but independently of this attention, everything is besides arranged in respect of them, in such manner, that no one of them can compromise more than himself, or weaken the strength of our party by more than his individual loss. Furthermore, he will not know what precise part he will have to play, nor that of the principal agent, between whom and the Secret Directory he is to form the connecting link of communication. He will be led to believe himself employed for quite another object; he will not directly deliver his packets of correspondence to the Secret Directory, but everything will reach the hands of the latter without any intermediary being in its confidence : thus, the principal agents will have no cause to fear being betrayed by their co-agents, nor by their intermediary agents, as neither will know them for what they will really be. The principal agents will be known only by the four members of the Secret Directory; and these, whatever may turn up, they can have no cause to distrust.

In general, the Secret Directory having adopted the grand system of isolating everything—of preventing all intercommunication, it will render its entire organization subservient to this plan, in such manner, that no individual it employs, mediately or immediately, will be able to betray any one; and that his ruin will entail no other loss on the Revolutionists. Undoubtedly, such a plan, in which each party concerned will have only himself to distrust, is calculated to embolden all who co-operate towards its success.

As to the precautions which extreme prudence always commands us to take ourselves, in respect of you, in order not to be deceived by the reports and information of any of you, that is our affair. We neither exact nor establish particular marks, to assure ourselves of the authenticity of those reports; but we are sure to distinguish that authenticity by unequivocal signs and proofs.

After having spoken, citizens, of what has appeared to us to legitimatize our enterprize, and of what must render you individually at ease with yourself in participating in it, it is meet to trace out what the Secret Directory considers you will have in the first place to do.

Articles II. and III. of the organization we have designed for you, and which precede this instruction, direct you—

" To organize in your arrondissement one or more
" patriotic reunions; in those unions to feed and direct
" public spirit by the reading of popular journals, and
" by discussions on the rights of the people, and its
" actual situation. To take notes of the daily ther-
" mometer of opinion; to render account in these notes,
" of the disposition, more or less good, more or less
" energetic, of the patriots; to make known to us what-
" ever individuals you will remark most capable of
" seconding the progress of the movement in contem-
" plation; to indicate the sort of employment or revo-
" lutionary task for which you will believe each of those
" individuals best suited; to set a mark on the intriguers
" and traitorous knaves who will try to insinuate them-
" selves into the meeting; moreover, to render account
" of the impediments and opposition they may offer to
" the development of energy, to the inspiration of sound
" principles and regenerating ideas."

Articles IV. and V. of the same organization determine the means by which you will be able to transmit to the Secret Directory the notes, information, or reports, it expects at your hands. You will consign them to the intermediary agents, who will go to receive them directly from your hands, in the same manner as they will consign to you such ulterior instructions as the Secret Directory will find itself obliged to transmit to you.

Such, citizen, is the scope of the mission entrusted to you for the present. Henceforward, we shall have to present to you only those ideas of detail, which you will modify or not, agreeably to your own discretion.

When we invite you to organise in your arrondissement one or more patriotic reunions, we need not suggest the expediency of doing the thing quietly and unostentatiously; and it is possible for you to form such reunions, and even to identify their spirit with your's, without appearing to be either their founder or leader. Let us sacrifice the vanity of appearing to advantage, to the glory of being really useful. There is no stronger guarantee of grand and substantial success, nothing which confers more real self-satisfaction, than the internal consciousness that one is the invisible instrument by which great springs of action are moved. We then render to our genius a merited homage, infinitely supe-rior to that which eager vanity would arrogate, by putting one's self forward as the principal actor in a political scene. It will be time enough to receive the applauses of our brethren, when we shall have saved them.

Thus, then, it appears to us perfectly practicable for the principal agents to institute, organise, and direct the clubs we look for, without appearing to institute, organise, or direct anything. By the way, speaking of organisa-tion, we think, for the like prudential reasons, that we should aim less at making new creations, than to base our edifice on old elements—the old bases already existing. In several arrondissements you have coffee-houses where the patriots are in the habit of assembling; do you quietly endeavour to draw them there in greater numbers, and more frequently. Rather seek, however, to multiply those places of meeting, than to crowd them with an indiscriminate multitude, unknown to one ano-ther, and likely to give umbrage to the Government, as well as to provoke its vigilance. Visit each of those places in turn; even prefer private residences to coffee-houses for holding your meetings, if practicable. In private houses, the patriots will be more completely free —less exposed to police spies—in a better condition to admit none but *brothers* in whom they can confide. In general, avoid giving a public or external importance to those assemblings; do not call them clubs, societies, or unions; avoid all pompous denominations; say, simply, *such* a coffee-house, *such* a dwelling; and the action of going there, call *taking a stroll—visiting*, &c. Let the *things* be, but not the *words*.

We have spoken of another duty after establishing the places of reunion; it is that of using them to foster and direct public spirit. We have laid down that, for that purpose, discussions on the rights of the people, and its actual position, joined to the reading of popular journals, would suffice. Mind! *above all, the reading of popular journals!* The Secret Directory recommends to you this means, as being the most powerful lever. The choice of such journals will not be difficult; you will easily know them. Besides writings, every other means of acting, and of making others act, will be supplied to you at the proper time. The journals we allude to will, in a great measure, serve you as a mariner's compass; they will guide your movements, and serve instead of general instructions. Hitherto they have preached our principles, and those of all true Democrats. They will, doubtless, continue to do so, and in such manner that you will always recognize our doctrine in theirs'. To support and applaud that doctrine—behold! almost the whole ostensible part of you have to act, and in that you have not to quit the circle of demonstrations, which will cause you to be regarded only as simple actors, simpleauditors, and assistants like the rest. As your function of note —taking and reporting can only take place with closed doors; your mission still remains, so far as that is concerned, unknown. This latter part of your mission will not engage you in any observation of detail; its manner of execution is sufficiently chalked out by Article III. of the rules of organization, and by what we have more effectively stated in this instruction.

In stating that the popular journals to be furnished to you will serve as your compass, and as principal supplements to the ulterior instructions we shall give (save where you receive contrary ones from us), it suffices to apprise you that must not make the thermometer of energy rise above the degree fixed by those same journals; and this observation is comprised in that made by the Directory, in its act of creation, where it says,—" That " the overflowing measure of crimes on the part of an " usurped authority, has ripened the dispositions of all " minds in favour of a revolutionary explosion to such a " degree, that to *render it beneficial, to put its directors* " *in a train to ensure complete success, it will be neces-* " *sary, perhaps, rather to moderate, than accelerate* " *the impetuous burst of freedom.*"

Accordingly, however essential it is to warm public spirit up to a certain heat, it would be in the same degree unsalutary, and even dangerous, to inflame it too rapidly until the supreme measure is prepared. We must consider that if the people's opinion is formed, that of the soldier is not; the latter is seduced by the perfidious caresses of a government which desires to *use* him to subjugate the citizens and the soldier himself. Time is necessary to disabuse our armed brethren. It will be wise, then, not to heat the citizens' heads beyond the just progression of the thermometer of opinion, whose varying point will always be indicated by the Secret Directory.

Behold, citizens, nearly all that we have to communicate in this first instruction. Your own zeal, your intelligence, your civism, will supply whatever we may have omitted to trace out in the plan of so momentous a mission. The perfect knowledge we had beforehand of your civic virtues has dispensed us with the necessity of using art to inflame your energy. A simple exposition of things, the acknowledged justice of which is felt in your hearts, as in ours, has appeared sufficient in our eyes to convince you of the essential necessity of the enterprise to which we engage your concurrence. Frenchmen! it concerns your salvation and ours; it concerns the salvation of the existing generation and of posterity—the salvation of our Republic and of the world. Let our courage be the signal to the veritable people to awake! Let them, by us electrified, rise from a fatal sleep which paralyzes them, and establish for ever the reign of happiness, equality, and liberty! All is ready!....The Edifice of Law, which will guarantee abundance for all—equality and liberty for all—to make a grand and majestic appearance, only awaits the overthrow of the existing monument of slavery, oppression, and death, whose place it is to occupy. Let us prepare this happy catastrophe! It will be durable and eternal— the code we are about to establish—because it will ensure the happiness of all. It will not be made to elevate any particular man, but to advantage at once, and for ever, all men whom it is destined to affect. It is time that all the ambitious should disappear—that human pride be confounded. The time has at length arrived for resolving in practice this beautiful problem—*that each of us depend henceforward only on laws and institutions, and that no individual of us shall hold another in his dependance.*

P

PIECE No. VII.

MANIFESTO OF THE EQUALS.

" REAL EQUALITY—THE LAST END OF THE SOCIAL
ART."—Condorcet, *Picture of the Human Mind, page 329.*

PEOPLE OF FRANCE!—During fifteen ages you have
lived slaves, and consequently unhappy. During six
years you breathe with difficulty in the expectation of
independance, of prosperity, and of equality.

EQUALITY!—first vow of nature, first want of man,
and chief bond of all legitimate association! People of
France! you have not been more favoured than the
other nations which vegetate on this ill-fated globe!
Always and everywhere does the unfortunate human
species, delivered over to cannibals more or less artful,
serve for a plaything to all ambitions—for pasture to all
tyrannies. Always and everywhere have men been fooled
by fine words; never and nowhere have they obtained
the *thing* with the word. From time immemorial we
have been hypocritically told—*men are equal;* and
from time immemorial does the most degrading and
monstrous inequality insolently oppress the human race.
Ever since the first existence of civil societies has the
finest apanage of man been uncontradictedly *acknowledged;* but never, up to this moment, has it been once
realized. Equality has never been other than a beautiful and barren fiction of law. Even now, when it is
claimed with a stronger voice, we are answered, " Be
silent, miserables!—absolute equali y is but a chimæra;
be content with conditional equality; you are all equal
before the law. Rabble! what more do you want?"
What more do we want? Legislators, governors, rich
proprietors—listen in your turn.

We are all equal, are we not? This principle remains
uncontested, because, without being self-convicted of
folly, one cannot seriously say that it is night when it is
day.

Well! we pretend henceforward to live and die equal,
as we are born so. We desire real equality or death;

behold what we want. And we shall have this real equality, no matter at what price. Woe to them who will interpose themselves between it and us! Woe to him who will offer resistance to so determined a resolve!

The French Revolution is but the forerunner of another revolution far more grand, far more solemn, and which will be the last. The people has marched over dead bodies against the kings and priests coalesced against it; it will do the same against the new tyrants—against the new political Tartuffes* who have usurped the places of the old.

" What do we want," you ask, " more than equality of rights ?" We want that equality not merely written in the " Declaration of the Rights of Man and of the Citizen;" we want it in the midst of us—under the roofs of our houses. We consent to everything for it—to become as *pliable wax, in order to have its characters engraven upon us.* Perish, if needs be, all the arts, provided real equality abides with us!

Legislators and governors, who are as destitute of genius as of honesty—you rich proprietors, without bowels of pity—in vain do you essay to neutralize our holy enterprize, by saying, " They are only re-producing the old Agrarian law, so often demanded already before them."

Calumniators! be silent in your turn; and in the silence of confusion hearken to our pretensions, dictated by nature herself, and based upon eternal justice. The Agrarian law, or partition of lands, was only the instantaneous wish of certain soldiers without principles—of certain small tribes, moved by instinct rather than by reason. We aim at something more sublime, and more equitable; we look to *common property*, or the *community of goods!* No more individual property in lands. *The earth belongs to no one.* We claim—we demand—we *will* the communal enjoyment of the fruits of the earth; *the fruits belong to all.*

We declare that we can no longer suffer that the great majority of men shall labour and sweat to serve

---

* [Tartuffe is a famous hypocritical character in one of Molière's plays.—BRONTERRE.]

and pamper the extreme minority. Long enough, and too long, have less than a million of individuals disposed of what belongs to more than twenty millions of men like themselves—of men in every respect their equals. Let there be at length an end to this enormous scandal, which posterity will scarcely credit. Away for ever with the revolting distinctions of rich and poor, of great and little, of masters and servants, of *governors* and *governed.*

Let there be no longer any other differences in mankind than those of age and sex. Since all have the same wants, and the same faculties, let all have accordingly the same education—the same nourishment. They are content with one sun, and the same air for all; why should not the like portion, and the same quality of food, suffice for each according to his wants?

But already do the enemies of an order of things, the most natural that can be imagined, declaim against us, —" Disorganizers, and seditionists," they exclaim, " you want but massacres and plunder."

PEOPLE OF FRANCE! We will not waste our time to answer them; but we will tell you,—" the holy enterprise we are organizing has no other object in view than to put an end to civil dissensions and to public disorder. Never was a more vast design conceived and put in execution. At distant intervals in the history of the world it has been talked of by some men of genius—by a few philosophers —but they spoke it with a low and trembling voice. Not one of them has had the courage to speak the entire truth.

The moment for great measures has arrived. Evil is at its height; it has reached its *maximum,* and covers the face of the earth. Chaos, under the name of politics, has too long reigned over it. Let everything revert to order, and resume its proper place. At the voice of equality, let the elements of justice and felicity be organized. The moment is come to found the REPUBLIC OF EQUALS—that grand asylum open to all human kind. The days of general restitution are come. Weeping families, come and seat yourselves at the common table provided by nature for all her children.

PEOPLE OF FRANCE! The purest of all earthly glories has been reserved for you—yes, 'tis you who are first destined to present the world with this touching spectacle.

Old habits, old prejudices, will again seek to oppose obstacles to the establishment of the REPUBLIC OF EQUALS. The organization of real equality—the only one which satisfies all wants, without making victims, without costing sacrifices,—will not, perhaps, at first please everybody. The egotist, the ambitious, will yell with rage. Those who possess unjustly, will raise the cry of injustice. Exclusive enjoyments, solitary pleasures, personal ease and privileges, will cause poignant regrets to some few individuals who are dead or callous to the pangs of others. The lovers of absolute power, the vile instruments of arbitrary authority, will feel it hard that their haughty chiefs should bend to the level of equality. Their short-sightedness will, with difficulty, penetrate into the future of public happiness, however near; but what can avail a few thousand malcontents against such a mass of human beings, all happy, and astonished at having been so long in quest of a felicity which they had within hands' reach. On the day that follows this real revolution, they will say to one another in amazement—" What—universal happiness depended on so little! We had but to will it. Ah, why had we not willed it sooner? Was it then necessary to have it told to us so often? Yes, no doubt, a single man on the earth, more rich, more powerful, than his fellow men, than his equals, destroys the equilibrium, and crime and misfortune come on the world.

PEOPLE OF FRANCE! By what sign then ought you henceforward to recognise the excellence of a constitution? .... That which altogether reposes on actual, absolute equality, is the only one that can be suitable to you, and satisfy all your desires.

The aristocratic charters of 1791 and 1795 riveted your chains, instead of breaking them. That of 1793 was a great practical step towards real equality; never before was equality so nearly approached; but that Constitution did not yet touch the end, nor was it fully competent to attain general happiness, of which, however, it has solemnly consecrated the great principle.

PEOPLE OF FRANCE! Open your eyes and hearts to the fulness of felicity; recognize and proclaim with us the
REPUBLIC OF EQUALS!

PIECE No. VIII.

ANALYSIS OF THE DOCTRINE OF BABEUF.

PROSCRIBED BY THE EXECUTIVE DIRECTORY FOR
HAVING TOLD THE TRUTH!

ARTICLE 1.

Nature has given to each individual an equal right to the enjoyment of all the goods of life.

PROOFS,
DRAWN FROM THE DISCUSSION TO WHICH THIS PIECE GAVE RISE.

1. Previously to their first coming together, or forming societies, all men were equally masters of the productions which nature spread with profusion around them.

2. Finding themselves together upon an uncultivated land, what could have established amongst them the inequality of this right? Is it their natural difference? But they have all the same organs and the same wants. Is it the dependence of some upon others? But no one was sufficiently strong to make servants of the rest, who might disperse on the slightest occasion for discontent; and the advantage of mutual succours, and of co-operative benevolence, rendered it necessary for all to respect in others, the rights with which they felt themselves invested by nature. Is it the ferocity of their hearts? But compassion is the immediate consequence of their organization, and ferocity springs only from the exasperation of the passions. Is it an inborn penchant for humiliation and servitude? But the sight of distinctions is even for the most savage beings a painful sensation—a source of jealousy and hatred.

3. If families have been the first models of societies, they are also the most striking proofs of the right we speak of. Equality in families is the pledge of tenderness on the part of parents—of union and happiness on that of the children. Is that equality broken? Forthwith anger and jealousy introduce disorder and violence. Everything—even the fondness of parents—inspires the

children with a hatred of partialities, which the parents, themselves cannot apply without risking the introduction of dangerous passions into the family.

4. The most strict equality must have been consecrated by the first conventions; for what could have induced persons, hitherto the enemies of all distinction, to consent to privations and inferiority?

5. The forgetfulness of this equality has introduced amongst mankind—

False ideas of happiness;

Perversion of the passions;

Deterioration and decay of the species;

Violences, troubles, wars;

The tyranny of some, and the oppression of others;

Institutions, civil, political, and religious, which, by consecrating injustice, end with dissolving societies, after having for a long time distracted and torn them to pieces.

The sight of distinctions, of pomp, and of pleasures enjoyed only by a few, was, and ever will be, an inexhaustible source of torments and uneasiness to the mass. It is given to only a few philosophers to preserve themselves from corruption, and moderation is a blessing which the vulgar can no longer appreciate, when once their thoughts have been weaned from it. Do certain citizens create to themselves new factitious wants, and introduce into their enjoyments refinements unknown to the multitude? Simplicity is no longer loved, happiness ceases to consist in an active life and tranquil soul, distinctions and pleasures become the supreme of goods, nobody is content with his station, and all seek in vain for that happiness, the entrance of which into society is debarred by inequality.

The more distinctions we obtain, the more we desire, the more we excite jealousy and covetousness; thence that insatiable and criminal thirst for gold and power; thence those sanguinary wars caused by the spirit of conquest, and by the jealousy of commerce, which leave miserable humanity scarcely a moment of repose.

In the midst of this subversion of ideas, sloth and vexations destroy a part of the species, enervate another part, and prepare for society generations incapable of defending it. From the love of distinctions arise the pre-. cautions taken to preserve them, in despite of the envy and discontent they engender; these precautions are, barbarous laws, exclusive forms of government, religious fables, servile morality; in a word, tyranny on the one hand, oppression on the other. However, the voice of nature cannot be entirely stifled; at times she makes her ungrateful children turn pale, she avenges by occasional outbreaks the tears of humanity, and if she rarely succeeds in re-establishing its rights, she ends always by over-throwing the societies which have neglected her laws.

If equality of goods be a consequence of that of our organs and wants—if public and private calamities—if the ruin of societies—are inevitable effects of all criminal attempts against it, this equality is, therefore, a *natural right.*

ARTICLE II.

The end of society is to defend this equality, often assailed by the strong and wicked in the state of nature; and to augment, by the co-operation of all, the common enjoyments of all.

PROOFS.

1. By *Society* is here understood, association regulated by conventions; and by *State of Nature*, that of casual and imperfect society in which men necessarily lived before they submitted to laws.

Without examining here, whether criminal attempts against equality, of the nature mentioned in this article, could have had place in the state of nature, it is evident that if the inconveniences of that state determined men to establish laws, they must have been only such as arose from the violation of equality. At all events, the preservation of equality is the end of association, because, by equality alone can men living together be rendered happy.

2. By uniting their strength, men assuredly desired to procure to themselves the greatest number of enjoyments of which they had the idea, and by the least possible trouble.

Now, the abundance of necessary things ensures these enjoyments, and is itself ensured by the labour of those associated together, which is the least possible for each, only when it is fairly distributed amongst all.

ARTICLE III.

Nature has imposed on each person the obligation to work; nobody could, without crime, evade his share of the common labour.

PROOFS.

Labour is for each a precept of nature.

1. Because man, isolated in the deserts, could not, without some kind of labour, procure himself subsistence.

2. Because the activity which moderate labour occasions, is for man a source of health and amusement.

This obligation could not be weakened by society, either for all or for each of its members.

1. Because the preservation of society depends upon it.

2. Because the labour of each is the least possible only when all participate of it.

ARTICLE IV.

Labour and enjoyments ought to be common.

EXPLANATION.

That is to say, all ought to bear an equal portion of labour, and derive from it an equal quantity of enjoyments.

The justice of this principle follows from the proofs of the preceding Articles I. and III. But what do we understand by community of labour? Is it meant that all the citizens should be engaged in the same occupations? No; but it is meant that the different branches of labour should be distributed in such manner as to leave no able-bodied person idle or unemployed; it is meant that the increased number of workers should, at the same time that it diminished individual toil, guarantee abundance for the whole; it is meant, that in return for his labour each person shall receive from society the means of providing for his natural wants, and for the small number of factitious wants which all may satisfy.

But it may be objected—What will become of those productions of industry, which are the fruits of time and genius? Is it not to be feared that, being no longer better recompensed than other descriptions of work, they will be altogether extinguished to the injury of society?

P 5

Sophism! It is to the love of glory, not to the thirst for riches, that we have been at all times indebted for the efforts of genius. Every day do millions of poor soldiers devote themselves to death for the honour of serving the caprices of a cruel master; and shall we doubt of the prodigies that might be operated on the human heart by the sentiment of happiness, the love of equality and country, and by the noble incentives of a wise policy? Besides, should we have the same longings for the display of the arts, and for the tinsel of luxury, if we had the happiness to live under the laws of equality?

ARTICLE V

There is oppression wherever one part of society is exhausted by labour, and in want of everything, whilst the other part wallows in abundance, without doing any work at all.

PROOFS.

1. *Inequality and oppression are synonymous;* if to oppress an individual consist in violating a general law to his detriment, those whom inequality *overcharges with toil* are oppressed, because inequality violates the natural law, to which it is absurd to oppose human laws.

2. To oppress signifies either to restrain the faculties of a person, or to unjustly augment his burdens; that is precisely what inequality does, by diminishing the enjoyments of him whose duties it aggravates.

ARTICLE VI.

Nobody could, without crime, exclusively appropriate to himself the goods of the earth or of industry.

EXPLANATION AND PROOFS.

If we demonstrate that inequality has no other cause than this exclusive appropriation, we shall have demonstrated the crime of those who introduced the distinction of *mine* and *thine* (*meum* and *tuum*).

From the moment lands were divided arose the exclusive right of property. Then each person became absolute master of all he could derive from the fields which had devolved to him, and from whatever industry he could exercise. It is probable that men, devoted to the arts of first necessity, were at the same time excluded from all territorial possession, which they had not time to cultivate. Thus one portion of the people remained masters of the things necessary to existence, whilst the rest had only a right to such salaries, or wages, as the former chose to pay them. Nevertheless, this change did not involve a very sensible one in the distribution of enjoyments, so long as the number of those receiving wages did not exceed that of the possessors of the soil. But as soon as natural accidents, acting conjointly with the economy or address of some, with the prodigality or incapacity of others, had concentrated the territorial properties in a small number of families, the men of wages became vastly more numerous than the proprietors, and, as a natural consequence, were utterly at their mercy. The possessors, proud of their opulence, soon reduced the labourers to a life of privations.

From this revolution date the sinister effects of inequality, developed in the first Article. Thenceforward we have seen the idle man fatten, by a revolting system of injustice, on the sweat of the laborious man, who sinks under the weight of fatigues and privations. We have seen the rich man take possession of the State, and, like a master, dictate tyrannical laws to the poor man, exasperated by want, degraded by ignorance, and deceived by religion.

Miseries and slavery are consequences of inequality, which is itself the result of property. Property is, therefore, the greatest scourge of society; it is a veritable public crime.

We shall be told, I know, that property is a right anterior to society, which has been instituted to protect it. But how could the idea of such a right have been formed, before conventions had guaranteed to the proprietor the fruits of his labour? How could society have owed its origin to an institution the most subversive of all social sentiment?

Lastly, let it not be said that it is just that the laborious and economical man should be recompensed by opulence, and that the idle man should be punished by misery. No doubt, it is equitable that the active man, having discharged what he owes his country, should receive in return what she can afford to give him, without destroying herself; it is equitable that his conduct be rewarded by public gratitude; but he cannot thereby acquire the right to poison his country, more than a soldier can acquire, by his valour, that of reducing her to slavery.

There are, doubtless, many sad fellows, who ought to impute to their own vices the poverty they are reduced to; but it would be to outrage experience and reason to range all the unhappy poor in this class, which comprises so small a portion of them. What multitudes of labourers and artisans live unpitied and uncared for, upon bread and water, in order that an infamous libertine may squander in peace the accumulations of an inhuman father, and that a *millionaire* master-manufacturer may export fabrics and trinkets at low prices to countries, which, in return, supply our lazy and voluptuous Sybarites with the perfumes of Arabia, and the birds of *Phase.* Would even the bad members of the working classes be what they are, were it not for the vices and follies in which they are involved by our social institutions, which punish in them the effects of passions, whose developments they provoke?

ARTICLE VII.

In a veritable society there ought to be neither rich nor poor.

ARTICLE VIII.

The rich, who are not willing to renounce their superfluities in favour of the indigent, are the enemies of the people.

ARTICLE IX.

No one can, by accumulating to himself all the means, deprive another of the instruction necessary for his happiness. Instruction ought to be common to all.

PROOFS.

1. This accumulation deprives the men of labour, of even the possibility of acquiring the knowledge necessary to every good citizen.

2. Although the people have no need of very great instruction, they require a certain portion to save them

from being the prey of professional craft, and of pretenders to learning and science. The people, above all, require to know their rights and duties.

ARTICLE X.

The end of the French Revolution is to destroy inequality, and to re-establish general prosperity.

PROOFS.

Where is the honest man who could wish to deliver his fellow-citizens to the convulsions and evils of a political revolution, which had no other object than to render them more miserable, or to place them in a condition which should necessarily entail their total ruin? To skilfully lay hold of the proper moment for reform is not the least task of an able and virtuous politician.

ARTICLE XI.

The Revolution is not terminated, because the rich absorb all valuable productions, and command exclusively; whilst the poor toil like real slaves, pine in misery, and count for nothing in the State.

ARTICLE XII.

The Constitution of 1793 is the veritable law of Frenchmen, because the people has solemnly accepted it; because the Convention had not the right to change it; because to succeed in superseding it, the Convention has caused the people to be shot for demanding its execution;* because it has hunted and massacred the deputies, who performed their duty in defending it; because a system of terrorism against the people, and the influence of emigrants,† have presided over the

---

* On the 1st Prairial of the Year III., and the days following, Bourbotte, Duroy, Duquesnoy, Goujon, Romme, and Soubrany, were put to death. Peyssard was deported, and Forestier condemned to detention.

† The men of the popular party were publicly massacred, or thrust in heaps into dungeons. A great number of emigrants, and more especially all who had deserted after the Revolution of the 31st of May, had been recalled since the 9th Thermidor of the Year II.

fabrication and pretended acceptation of the Constitution of 1795, which, nevertheless, had not a quarter of the number of suffrages in its favour that the Constitution of 1793 has obtained; because the Constitution of 1793 has consecrated the inalienable right of every citizen to consent to the laws, to exercise political rights, to meet in assembly, to propose what he deems useful, to receive instruction, and not to die of hunger; rights which the counter-revolutionary Act of 1795 has openly and completely violated.

ARTICLE XIII.

Every citizen is bound to re-establish and defend, in the Constitution of 1793, the will and happiness of the people.

ARTICLE XIV.

All the powers emanating from the pretended Constitution of 1795 are illegal and counter-revolutionary.

ARTICLE XV.

Those who have used violence against the Constitution of 1793 are guilty of high treason against the nation.

PIECE No. IX.

LETTER OF FRANC-LIBRE
(Soldier of the Circo-Parisian Army)
TO HIS FRIEND LA TERREUR
(Soldier of the Army of the Rhine.)

WE are p— upon, my poor friend, La Terreur; yes, we are p—* upon, and without resource, if we swallow

---

* [I do not pretend to do more than render the general sense of this piece. The slang phrases and indelicate allusions in which it abounds, oblige me to occasionally sacrifice fidelity for decency, and to merge in paraphrase what it would be offensive to render literally.—BRONTERRE.]

down the pill that has been crammed into our mouth. In vain have we fleshed our swords in the vile carcases of the miscreant slaves who fight for the crowned wolves of Europe; in vain have we bivouaced, fasted, combatted, sweated blood and water, and killed lice and slaves during four years; we have wasted our shot on sparrows! —we have lost our labour: for liberty, that noble object of our aspirations, and sweet equality, its inseparable companion, are no longer but vain images caricatured on the dishclouts of the kitchen of the heirs of C—, but an empty cloud like the smoke of my pipe. In the names of order and discipline, *we, and all our brother sans-culottes, are chained like dogs in a poultry yard,* with the difference that when the mastiffs bark they fling them some grub for their inside, whereas they treat you and me as if our mouths were sewed up. Damna-- tion!—my brave La Terreur, should we ever have abandoned our fire-hearths, our wives, our children, our fathers and mothers, to thrash the knaves who menaced our country, had we dreamt that whilst we were kicking emigrants and snaffling kings, *a crew of smooth-skinned tigers would have strangled, mangled, and devoured our parents, friends, and Liberty herself?* Yes, my friend, yes; however strange what I announce to you, it is no less true than the fact, that one sturdy cove like you is worth a cart-load of the ricketty abortions who govern us; and the sketch I am going to present of the picture that has been before my eyes for the last ten months, will convince you of it; I will not add any oath to extort credence from you, for since the oath of fidelity to the Constitution of 1793, I have seen none take oaths but beggarly scamps, without souls or honour.

1. The insolent pride of the Court, and of the *ci-devant* great, forced us to overthrow the throne. We had established a popular Government, in which, as Father Latulipe said, every one had the right to think himself a citizen; but whilst we were helter-skeltering before us the ruffian serfs who presumed to take us to account for what we chose to do with our own concerns, the rascals of commissaries to whom we confided the care of our affairs, after slaughtering those of our friends who preserved their fidelity to us, have

established, under the name of an Executive Directory, *five lions, whom they have caparisoned, harnessed, and plumed like mules of Provence, and surrounded with Scapins, Scaramouches, and Cartouches;* who, all together, have quintupled the arrogance, insolence, tyranny, and despotism of that son of a b——h, C——,* their worthy predecessor.

2. The Government we had left in 93 put egoism under contribution to establish magazines of goods and provender necessary to the safety of the country; that which our perfidious commissaries have substituted for it, establishes no other public magazine than that of the charnel-house of Clamar, composed of thousands of carcases of Republicans, dead of hunger, who during eighteen long months have been coming in cart-loads every hour to choke up that horrible depôt.

3. The nobles had always betrayed us, and we had truly conquered only when we had chased them from our armies; to-day, the brave cudgelling officers who led us to victory—who, like ourselves, have their skins all scarified and sewn up again—are basely cashiered, and replaced by Chouans of the aristocratic and perfumed castes.

4. Paris—the beautiful Paris of 93—in which liberty, equality, and abundance had formed the whole of the people into one happy family, no longer presents other than a frightful forest, filled with devouring wolves and expiring sheep; these wolves are the governors and the rich, and the sheep are the patriots, our kinsmen, brothers, and friends.

5. Our companions in arms, mutilated in battle, are here crushed and spit upon, covered with dirt and contempt by our governors and their base lacqueys; and the greater part of them are sunk into beggars, imploring alms, and cursing the ingratitude of a country for which they have shed their blood like ditch-water. They are wrong, you will say, dear comrade. No, my friend, they are not. Their piteous accents of despair will cease only when we shall have avenged them, and that will not be long, I hope, by G——.

* C——, the initial of Capet, I presume. Capet is the surname of the Bourbons, and Buonarroti's work was published during the reign of the last of that imbecile dynasty.—BRONTERRE.

6. The generals who command us here—vile syco-phants of the five plumed mules, who flatter them in return—keep us, under pretence of discipline, in the most abject slavery. Folded up here, at the military school, like a flock of sheep, we are prevented from communicating with our friends and kinsmen. Ah!—no doubt they fear lest their tears should move our hearts, and inspire our courage with a just vengeance; but in vain do the rotten voluptuaries hope to ——! Though they count us only for machines of oppression, essentially obedient, they shall soon know—the tyrants! —that we are also the avengers of the rights of man and of humanity.

7. The Government of 93, my dear comrade, has assured us the spoils of the enemies of the country to reward our victories. The Government *that is*, gives, in the name of restitution, to our enemies, what we had conquered from them, and what served as a national security for our Republican currency; whence it follows, that the miscreants who govern us, after having trampled under foot the red cap of liberty they were unworthy to wear, have shamelessly put a green one on their head; and, to complete their infamy, while they continue to promise us a thousand millions' worth of national pro-perty, they in reality reserve for us no other recompence than the tents taken from us three campaigns back—to make begging wallets of for our families.

I should never end, my dear La Terreur, were I to undertake to trace to you all the horrors which encom-pass us here; but, better used to fight than to whine, as patient in sorrow as terrible in vengeance, I only wait, my dear comrade, with ten millions of oppressed Demo-crats, the moment when peace with the foreign foe shall permit you and your companions in arms to return to your firesides. Then, united once more, we shall prove to France, and to the world, that we know as well how to chastise the traitors, and to keep our oaths of 93, as we did to vanquish the unkennelled packs of b——!

Safety and fraternity.

Your brother,
Franc-Libre.

Paris, 24th Germinal, Year IV. of the
Democratic Republic to come.

PIECE No. X.

*Primary Instruction of the Secret Directory addressed
to each of its principal Military Agents.*

CITIZENS!—It is not in times of crisis as in ordinary
times, &c. [Read Piece VI., from the beginning as far
as the words, " as it would be capable of doing, if it saw
" at its head leaders worthy of its entire confidence."

Animated with such dispositions, we have been led at
once to turn our regards to the men most capable of
seconding us in this most glorious career. It is you,
citizens, who, whether we regard your continuity of noble
conduct, together with the multiplied acts of pure civism
you have evinced throughout the Revolution, or the terrible proofs you have given of courage and incorruptibility,
in times when everything patriotic and virtuous was persecuted ; it is to you, citizens, that those who have constituted themselves the first avengers of a betrayed country
have turned their regards to make you the depositaries
of their confidence, and to delegate to you the first and
principal division of their intended operations.

The portion of trust which the Secret Directory communicates to you is precious and important. Its safe
fulfilment demands much discretion, prudence, activity,
and love of the general good ; it requires all the virtues
of men such as the Directory believes you to be.

The Secret Directory has weighed its fundamental
organization, and that of its relations with you, in the
balance of wisdom and circumspection. It has deemed
it expedient to appoint principal agents near to the different armed bodies placed within and around the commune of Paris, and it has so arranged their means of
communication with itself, that the correspondence will
be almost direct, without, however, any of those agents
being able to know the members of the Directory.

The reason of this precaution, &c. [Read Piece VI.
from the preceding words, as far as the words, " *the
discouragement and consternation of the most courageous citizens.*"

Such are Republicans, &c. [Read Piece VI. again, as far as the words, " *equally unflinching of twelve men,*" instead of which substitute, " *equally unflinching of several men.*" Read on afterwards as far as the words, " *you will perceive it in all their acts.*"]

" At the same time that we have armed ourselves with all the necessary precautions," &c. [Again see paragraph in Piece VI., beginning with these words, and read to the end without any change.]

" The Secret Directory has carried its prudence so far as to," &c. [The same as in the paragraph in Piece VI., beginning with the same words, except to substitute the word *agents* for *twelve agents*, in two places.]

Articles III., IV., V., of the organization we have prescribed to you, and which precede this instruction, indicate to you—

" To form and direct the public spirit of the soldiery " in general, and of the corps and battalions which are " assigned to you, in particular.

" To stimulate and foment this military public spirit ; " first, by facilitating the propagation of journals and " other popular writings ; afterwards, by affording occa- " sion for habitual conversations and frequent discussions " on the rights of the people, on its present situation, " and on the state of the army.

" To take notes of the daily thermometer of opinion ; " to render account in these notes of the dispositions, " more or less good, more or less energetic, of the mass " of the soldiers ; to distinguish the individuals you will " remark most capable of forwarding the movement to " be produced ; to indicate the species of employment " or revolutionary enterprise to which you may believe " each of those individuals best suited ; to fix a mark on " the intriguers, the serviles, the tyrannical subalterns ; " and to render account of the obstacles they may oppose " to the development of energy, to the inspiration of " good principles, and regenerating ideas."

Articles VI., VII., and VIII. of the same organization determines the means by which you will be able to transmit to the Secret Directory the notes, informations, or reports it will expect at your hands.

" You will give them to the intermediary agents, who

" will go to receive them directly from your hands, in the'
" same manner as they will consign to you personally
" such ulterior instructions as the Secret Directory shall
" find itself obliged to transmit to you."

Such, citizens,- is the scope of the task assigned
you in this elementary stage.   Hereafter we shall have
only to offer to you some ideas of detail, which you may
modify as prudence dictates.

When we invite you to stimulate, feed, and direct the
public spirit of the soldiery, by reading, and by discussions
on the rights of the people, on its actual situation, and
on the situation of the army, you will feel how expedient
it is for the interest of the cause, as well as for your own,
that the thing should be done quietly, and without osten-
tatiously aiming at too much.   It is possible for you to
become the leader of a great number of brave fellows,
and to infuse into them your own spirit, without their
being conscious of the source whence they imbibed it :
it would be far more dangerous were their chiefs, and all
who have an interest contrary to the principles we wish
to inculcate, to discern the part you were playing about
them.   You ought, therefore, to look vigilantly to yourselves, and use extreme precaution, lest you betray your
object by inconsiderate avowals, or by reposing confidence
in any person, no matter whom.   It is not on occasions
like this that one can indulge his self-love.   Let us sacrifice the vanity of *appearing* to the advantage of really
being and *doing*.   There is no stronger guarantee of
great and signal success, there is nothing which confers
a prouder internal satisfaction, than the consciousness
that one is the invisible instrument by which great springs
of action are moved ; we then render to our genius and
discretion a merited homage, infinitely superior to that
which eager vanity would grasp, by wishing to pass for
principal actor in a political scene.   It will be time
enough to receive the applause of our brethren after we
shall have saved them ; wherefore, then, it appears to us
very practicable for the principal agents to stimulate,
foster, and guide the soldier's energy without hardly appearing to do so ; for since the only thing required is, to
fix his attention on the violation of all the rights of the
people, and on the cruel and deplorable state to which

the citizen and soldier are now reduced, such habitual conversations and discussions as we have proposed to you to get up, may be effected by the sole means of journals, and other popular writings; and it will not be difficult for you to transmit these writings, whether directly or indirectly, in a safe and quiet way, that will involve no consequences, be scarcely noticed, and leave you to appear throughout only as a simple observer.

The dissemination of writings, then, being the principal means on which we count for promoting those serious discussions in which we desire to engage the soldier, we recommend to you this means. The choice of the writings will not be difficult; you will easily distinguish those of the right stamp. For the rest, it will be the business of the Directory to transmit *such* writings to you, so that you may have them in sufficient quantity for distribution. Besides writings, *all other means of acting, and of making others act, will be furnished to you when occasion demands.* The journals we have alluded to will serve you, in a great measure, as a compass to steer your course, and for general instructions conformable to this. They have, up to the present, preached our principles, and those of all true Democrats. We believe they will always continue to do so, and that you will always recognize our doctrine in their's. To support and applaud that doctrine,—behold nearly the whole of the part assigned you in the new drama, and to play it well you need not travel out of the circle of those demonstrations, which make you appear only as simple actors, simple auditors, and by-standers like all the others present. As your function of note-taking and reporting will take place only with closed doors, it leaves your mission still a secret. This latter department will not engage us in any observation of detail; its mode of execution is sufficiently determined by Article V. of the rules of organization, and by what we have prescribed in the foregoing part of this instruction. In telling you that the popular journals to be supplied to you, &c. [Here the same instruction occurs as in Piece VI., in the paragraph beginning with the same words as this.]

Now, however necessary it be to warm the soldiers' minds up to a certain heat, it would be in the same

degree useless, and even dangerous, to inflame them too
rapidly before the final measure. We are certain that
the people's opinion is formed; we are no less certain
that the same may be said of several battalions; but we
know also that there are many armed bodies whom the
influence of craft and perfidy has hitherto kept in error.
It is essential, then, in order to ensure complete success,
that all, citizens and soldiers, be disciplined to move
simultaneously with us. We must not, therefore, excite
a part to that degree of energy required for the grand
explosion, while the others remain considerably behind
in spirit and disposition. We must allow ourselves time
to undeceive at least the majority of our comrades, and
fortify them against the insidious caresses of a Government which desires to use them as instruments, first to
oppress themselves, and afterwards the people. Accordingly, it will be the part of wisdom not to inflame the
passions of the more ardent Democrats above the
exact progression of the thermometer, whose varying
point will be always indicated by the Secret Directory.

We have not yet proposed the lever, which we deem
the most powerful of all for exciting the soldier's mind
and courage. We proceed to tell it you. It is a long-
acknowledged truth, that to impel men to vigorous
action, you must appeal to their interests. The general
interest is made up of all the particular interests. We
must, therefore, conciliate those particular interests, if
we would operate the real good of the whole; and, since
these same interests are for all men the most powerful
springs of action, it follows that, in employing this grand
instrument, we at the same time perform a thing the
most just and capable of guaranteeing certain success.
Let us appeal, then, to the interest of the greatest
number—that is to say, let us be virtuous and equitable,
for virtue and justice present us with the surest means
of success.

It is for the interest of the greatest number that the
Revolution was undertaken; it is because, previously to
the Revolution, the majority found themselves socially
aggrieved and oppressed, that they desired a change to
improve their condition. The interest of the majority
caused the Revolution to be adored so long as a hope

was entertained that it would operate a change for the better. The same interest has caused the Revolution to be detested, since its more recent events taught the majority to see in it only a change from bad to worse. It is the interest of the majority that now induces us to commence another Revolution, which we wish to be the last, and whose object is to change the *worse* into a perfect good. Let us prove to the majority the possibility of this latter change. Let us do more—let us show them the certainty of it, and we shall see that their interest will determine them to ensure it, by the energetic and irresistible ascendancy of their volition and force.

There are two principal points of view in which we can and ought to address ourselves to the interest and feelings of the men who have defended the country— their interest as applicable to their present lot—their interest as applicable to their future lot.

May you not with perfect truth exhibit to the soldier a picture, in which he will recognize himself miserable, like the people, equally destitute as the people, equally starved and famished, equally cheapened and degraded? I behold a poor fellow returning from the frontier. In what state is he? His bare aspect is enough to let me see that our governors are the best friends of the despots he has combatted! I see him the victim of neglect and suffering, for having made their satellites bite the dust. His person lank—his face pale and haggard—he sinks from inanition. I interrogate him; he tells me that the deplorable state I find him in, is not surprising when the cause is explained. I learn that his pay is more beggarly than that of the vilest German military slave. With thirty sous in assignats, and only two sous per day in cash, it is a miracle that he is not starved to death. In a word, he is worse treated than the wretched German serf, or the vile Italian thief-catcher, who, brutalized, degraded, and with scarcely any pretentions to the name of man, forms part of the legions whom Francis of Austria pays at about the same rate, and whose hungry aspect inspired me with so much pity at the commencement of the Revolution. The soldier of our country not only suffers hunger now-a-days, but he is without

shoes, without clothes; to have his shirt washed is out
of the question, for that would cost thirty francs,* and
where, poor wretch, could he find such a sum? But
he suffers more than the want of clothing and nourishment. He must in addition, be harassed, vexed, crushed
under a multiplicity of tortures decorated with the pompous name of *military discipline ;* and which is, at bottom, a far more galling system of refined tyranny than
existed under the lordly ministers of Louis XVI. It
renders the soldier far more of an automaton, far more
servilely subject to the caprices of subalterns. He is
degenerated, in fact, into a mere moving man-machine,
who must know nothing but the word of command. To
reason, to speak, nay, even to think, are interdicted
from him. Moreover, the tyrants in authority over him
are not the men who accompanied him in the perils of
war. It is not the bravest that are promoted; it is not
the men who most distinguished themselves against the
enemies of liberty that are rewarded by honours. On
the contrary, those now in command are, for the most
part, base, dastardly intriguers, and even counter-revolutionists. Real military merit is devoted to neglect
and opprobrium. Thus is the defender of the country
overwhelmed at once by every calamity incidental to his
state. He is not clothed, he is not fed; he bends
under the cruel rod of contemptible chiefs, who never
fought for the Republic, who detest it, and, with it, all
who have poured their blood for its triumph. If any
exceptions are made to the destitution and privations of
the mass of soldiers, it is only in a sense which caps the
climax of perfidy and national humiliation. Baits and
lures are offered to some, the better to consolidate the
slavery of the rest. Those distributions of wine, of
brandy, &c., made to the battalions, whose service is
more immediately to guard the *extra*-revolutionary city
(Paris), whose energetic bursts for liberty are always
feared; those entertainments more substantial, even
splendid, with which the select companies employed as
the immediate guard of the Government, are regaled;

* [Owing to the depreciation of the assignats, or revolutionary
paper-money.—Bronterre.]

—all that is only the honey, presented at the end of the staff destined to cudgel the people into servitude. If the miserables who receive these largesses vow to the authors of them that blind obedience for which they are offered as a bribe, we can only say that such persons must be regarded as sordid traitors, who sell their country and liberty for a mess of potage.

Such, or the like, is the picture—alas! too true a one —of the present condition of the soldier, which you should continually present to his view, and alongside of it you may place that of his future condition, which you may easily sketch in perspective. The latter, God knows, will not be a much brighter one. Represent to them the scenes which await their return to their firesides. What will they find there? misery profound—a thousand times more profound than that which weighed down their unhappy fathers. The Revolution had promised them a just, a legitimate compensation (too well was it merited!) for their glorious exploits achieved to assure its success; the Revolution had promised them national property, quite enough to secure subsistence for each and all. . With this recompense, worthy of their toils, they might pass, in an honourable retreat, the remainder of their lives tranquil and happy; form new families without number; bring up a new generation in the love of a country whose happiness they might have justly prided themselves in having established, and narrate a thousand times over, and always with a new joy, and new sympathetic affections, to their astonished children, by what combined and consecutive acts of courage they had succeeded in shaking off the yoke of the oppressors and of the rich, and finally in founding their independence. Instead of that, what will they be? Those possessions which had been solemnly promised and guaranteed to them by a multiplicity of decrees—what has become of them? They had been carried to the then valued amount of an effective *milliard*, that is to say, to three hundred *milliards** in value, of the present

* [*Milliard* means a thousand millions' worth (*francs*, of course); and we may infer from this passage that, within little more than twelve months after the death of Robespierre (during whose ascendancy the decrees alluded to were passed), the assignats

assignats. Where are the domains of the Republic
equivalent to this sum? They have been restored to
traitors from whom they had been justly confiscated.
The defender of his country was not on returning to
his cottage to find it domineered over by the turretted
castle of the insolent squire, who, with all the soil in his
possession, made the soldier's father work as a slave,
treated him in all respects as such, allowed him not half
food enough, and never permitted him to be decently
clothed. The defender of his country was to find in the
vast possessions monopolized by this insatiable ogre his
allotted portion, which would suffice with industry to
yield him a comfortable living. Nothing of the kind!
Instead of what was promised, he will find this devouring
monster more furious, more unpitying than ever. The
latter will behold in the poor old broken-down soldier,
the man who fought against him when he was an emigrant, who eagerly desired his utter destruction, and who
still regrets that it was not consummated. The feudal
despot will exact a long and dire repentance for such
crimes. The ancient defender of liberty will pass his old
age in bitter bondage and frightful misery. More
trampled on, more degraded than his forefathers, outraged by the infamous expressions, *beggars, rabble,
populace,* he must, (as the author of a real people's
journal has too truly foreseen and said) " crouch under
" the insolent domination of rich robbers, become their
" galley-slaves, toil for vile wages from sun-rise to sun-
" set, have only his sweat to moisten his morsel of brown
" bread, dried up by the heat of the sun. Still happy
" they who will be able to prolong existence even on
" those terms, the rest will be turned adrift on the world
" to beg or perish. We shall see the lamed, the unfor-
" tunates with wooden legs, with broken jaws, fractured
" arms, &c., cover the streets and highways, painfully
" drag their bodies towards the doors of the bloated sons
" of luxury, present their humiliating prayer to a hundred
" of them, experience ninety-nine rebuffs, accompanied

had so depreciated in value that three hundred francs in assignats
were then only equal in value to one franc of the same currency,
before the 9th Thermidor.—BRONTERRE.]

" with insults, and receive at the hundredth door an
" obolus, the thousandth part of what will suffice to buy
" a breakfast's bread for them."

Such is a too true and sensible sketch of the future
situation of our defenders—a sketch which you are to
use all your endeavours to make them understand and
appreciate. Tell them afterwards that it depends on
themselves alone to avert this horrific perspective—that
to save themselves, they have only to aid the people and
the people's friends to re-conquer the rights of all. Those
to whom you may speak with confidence, and whom you
will deem at the outset calculated to propagate what we
are about to say—*those you may assure, that from the
very day on which they shall have aided the people to
recover its power,* THEY SHALL BE NO LONGER IN
WANT OF ANY THING ; THEY SHALL BE PROVIDED WITH
EVERYTHING NECESSARY FOR MEN. TELL THEM, FUR-
THERMORE, THAT ON THE DAY AFTER THE STRUGGLE
ABUNDANCE AND THE MOST PROSPEROUS CONDITION
OF LIFE SHALL BE GUARANTEED TO EVERY SOLDIER.
It will be no longer in distant promises, and such as are
easy to elude, that we will deal ; *it will be the simulta-
neous and immediate reality.*

In order the better to kindle in them the feelings most
suitable to the people and to themselves ; make them
reflect on what they *are*, and what they are *intended for*
by their rulers ; on the motives for which they have been
drawn around the walls of Paris ; on the ignominious
use which it is in contemplation to make of their bayonets
and arms ; and on the very opposite and glorious part
they may play for their own happiness and that of their
fellow-citizens : present these reflections to them somewhat in the way they have been put forth by the popular
journalist already cited, and from whom we will here
copy some additional reflections.

" What is the business of the numerous phalanxes
" concentrated around the city of Paris—the city of the
" Revolution—the cradle of liberty?....Why are they
" called hither? Are they going to be subjugated? Ah!
" it is not difficult to elucidate these questions.

" It is not for the real people that the soldiers of liberty
" form a formidable fence about the walls of Paris. This

" real people—the industrious, the labouring people—
" are maltreated, muzzled, starved, ruined!....by the
" tribe of stockjobbers, monopolists and robbers, This
" latter description of gentry is indeed in avowed and
" criminal rebellion against the good people; but is it to
" subjugate the oppressive party, and to defend the op-
" pressed party, that our warriors present a triple array
" of bayonets in all the circumference of Paris? No !
" it is quite the reverse!.....The intention is to use their
" arms and force to effect the total subjugation of the
" oppressed under the yoke of oppression—to maintain
" the latter in his odious domination, and the people in
" their pitiful impotence! Ah ! were it the people it
" was the object to defend, there would be no necessity
" for diverting the people's brethren the soldiers from
" their legitimate destination, which is to combat the
" external enemy ; for the rest, the people would suffice
" to defend itself; but, when the object is to sacrifice
" the mass to a fraction, then it is, that there is need of
" hired bayonets—then it is that, Government expects
" to find auxiliaries in men to whom *obedience is*
" preached as the only *essential duty*.....It is when
" the Government and the corrupt caste whom it exclu-
" sively protects have lost all shame; it is when, un-
" blushingly, and without even the decency of disguise,
" and through a most infamous conspiracy, they have by
" atrocious ordinances, audaciously called *laws*, conse-
" crated iniquities of every sort, misery the most frightful,
" slavery the most revolting ; it is when the measure of
" their abominations is filled to such palpable overflowing,
" that the people's patience is exhausted, and its cre-
" dulity will bear no more !.....it is *then* that the tyrants
" turn their eyes to the army ! Yes, it is the same hands
" which chastised ruffian kings, that our new tyrants
" would arm to preserve, to perpetuate, such oppression !
" Yes ! it is a *military government* established to force
" the people to submit to a régime of wretchedness, in
" which it is pretended they can live....without nou-
" rishment, without raiment, without liberty....And they
" are fathers—sons—brothers—who are expected to im-
" pose such a system on—aye, to stab, if needs be, their
" children — wives—fathers—brothers—friends—and

" kinsmen ! ! ! and it is the soldiers of the people, who
" are themselves the people, that are to be marshalled
" out against another portion of the people ! By these
" it is that the robbers would consolidate their system of
" servitude, degradation, and famine....a thousand
" times worse than the old slavery against which French-
" men so justly rose up six years ago.

" No ! the soldiers of France will never be the vile
" satellites, the blind and cruel instruments of the people's
" enemies, and, consequently, of their own.....It is only
" where governments have rendered themselves culpable,
" or would wish to do so, that they encompass themselves
" with bayonets. When power is just, it is always strong
" enough in the voluntary support of the people. Capet
" had fortified himself with an army before the 14th of
" July. We all know what his designs were, and what
" crimes he would have perpetrated with impunity if he
" had succeeded. Would it be culpable to examine
" whether those who imitate him are not equally guilty ?
" for is there not an exact parity of motives between
" Capet's act and theirs ?

" Our soldiers will remember how magnanimously well
" the army of Capet behaved ; though trained in the school
" of monarchic discipline, it did not, with all its training,
" forget that it belonged to the people. The French
" Guards lowering their fasces before the sans-culottes !—
" behold an example that will go down to the admiration
" of all ages !

" No, no!—it shall not be said that the defenders of
" the Republic were less grand, less magnanimous. It
" shall not be said that they held such language as this :
" ' Governors—usurpers of the people's rights—be tran-
" ' quil ; fear nought ; despise the unanimous cry raised
" ' against you by the indignant people, and its bold
" ' tribunes ; shut your ears to all complaints ; trample
" ' under foot its importunate remonstrances against
" ' your oppression, which after all it is born to endure.
" ' Tyrants ! we are your soldiers ; we will prop up your
" ' despotism, and all your acts of brigandism ; we will
" ' crush ; if needs be, we will thunder down upon our
" ' fathers and brothers ! we will embowel our sisters and
" ' mothers ! we will exterminate our children ! to main-

" ' tain your insupportable and unexampled domma-
" ' tion!!! It is our duty to aid you in consolidating the
" ' slavery of our country; our own chains ought to be
" ' rivetted by our own hands.'

" No, no, again! It shall not be said that the de-
" fenders of the Republic consented to be only moving
" machines, only living puppets, only senseless automata,
" to blindly obey every impulse of their leaders. It
" shall not be said that they will no longer use their
" own judgment, or that, captivated by false and vain
" caresses, by debasing distributions of *drink*, they
" helped a Government of usurpation and oppression to
" rivet for ever the chains of twenty-five millions of
' their fellow-countrymen."

And as to you, citizen, to whom we address these first
instructions, after suggesting this sketch of the way in
which you ought to catechise our armed brothers, we
will not add a word more to inspire you with the spirit of
our principles, and the extreme importance of the mission
we have imposed on ourselves. Neither will we further
enlarge on what we have pointed out as the most effective
means of seconding our operations. " Your zeal, your
intelligence, your civism, will supply the rest." [See
Piece VI., beginning with those words, and read on to
the end.]

PIECE No. XI.

DO WE OWE OBEDIENCE TO THE CON-
STITUTION OF 1795.

In swearing to defend Liberty and Equality, we have
reciprocally bound ourselves in solemn engagement to
one another, never to recognise any other authority than
that of the people, and to punish all who, by force or
fraud, should presume to violate its sovereign will. This
solemn engagement renders it a duty imperative on all
of us to examine coolly and scrupulously whether the
Government which now rules France is veritably the
Republican Government desired by the people.

Those whom we have seen uniformly combat in the ranks of the defenders of liberty, reject as counter-revolutionary the Act of 1795. Those, on the contrary, who never appeared decided for anything, except their own selfish interests, extol this Act as the fundamental law, *par excellence.* They deny the former party even the right of examining it, and wish to command for it the same religious respect that was exacted five years ago for the Royalist Constitution of 1791.

In a struggle, the issue of which ought for ever to set at rest the conscience of all upright men, it is of sovereign importance to light our way by the flambeau o. principles, developed and applied by arguments matured and independent of persons and parties; for if, in short, the Constitution of 1795 *do* possess all the characteristics of legitimate law, we ought to submit to and defend it; but if it be devoid of such characters, then is it the duty of freemen to overthrow it, and to punish the men who would have enslaved the people.

I am aware that the bare wish to examine impartially what we are all so interested in knowing, will be called *anarchy, rebellion*—favourite terms of the Court before and after 1789, of La Fayette, of Dumouriez, of the Venetian Senate, of the Pope, of the Grand Seignor, which signify neither more nor less than that the present possessors of power wish to retain it, no matter at what price; but we, who deem it an honour to be rebels and seditious against all anti-popular powers, whatever jargon they talk, whatever masks they wear, will always counsel our fellow-citizens to make use of their reason, and to incessantly rise up against every authority opposed to the principles of popular sovereignty.

Previously to the famous report of the Commission of Eleven, we had the Constitution of 1793, which was generally recognised as being the veritable fundamental law of the French people, because it had received their formal sanction by the suffrages of 4,800,000 voters in the primary assemblies, whose envoys, to the number of 8,000, confirmed the thus-declared will of France, upon the ever-memorable day of the 10th of August, 1793; and what rendered that law, and the people who accepted it, so laudable in the sight of humanity, was the equality of rights it guaranteed to all Frenchmen, without regard to the state of domestic servitude, which it proscribed, and without distinguishing between rich and poor—the necessary concurrence of the people in forming the law, and the latitude secured for giving effect to the people's wishes in the way of having them heard and respected*—circumstances which, whatever our statesmen may pretend, struck at the root of civil convulsion, by extirpating all contrast between the will of the sovereign and that of its delegates. How fine a sight!—to behold perhaps a twentieth of the people arrest the crimes or faults of its agents, and provoke against them the effective judgment of all their fellow-citizens, without a single shock to the public tranquillity?

When we speak of the beauties of the Constitution of 1793 to the partisans of the existing order, they pretend to oppose to us a posterior will of the people, who, say they, had a right to change that Constitution, and have effectually done so in accepting the Constitution of 1795.

Undoubtedly, if the French have freely accepted this latter Constitution, we owe it obedience until it adopts another; but it is precisely on this fact, which is the matter in dispute, that we are to bring the discussion strictly to bear. Is it the people, or even a large section of the people, which demanded the change? Certainly not. The people has loudly and unanimously reclaimed its Constitution of 1793. Witness the numerous addresses of the communes, of the popular societies, and the armies; witness the scenes of Prairial at Paris, and the almost simultaneous ones in the north and south of the Republic; witness the acts of the Convention, which, to render homage to the will of the people, and to calm apprehensions, decreed, on the 1st Germinal, of the same year, the penalty of deportation against whosoever should write or speak against the Constitution of 1793.

The people had ordered, by Article 115 of this Constitution, that all demands for changing it, should essentially originate with the people themselves, and could

* This Constitution, which no feeling man can ponder on without a lively emotion of admiration, offered the first example on record of comfort and instruction being guaranteed to all citizens alike by the fundamental law of the State.

on no account emanate from the legislative body; never-theless, the too celebrated Commission of Eleven, whose powers were limited to merely proposing the organic laws of the Constitution of 1793, came to the body of the Convention to declaim against what it qualified with the term of *popular tyranny;* and that Convention itself, in disregard of its duties and oaths, instead of hurling the Commission into annihilation, had the au-dacity to propose to the people its anti-popular fabrication of 1795. No fact can be more evident than that the Commission of Eleven, and the Members of the Con-vention who voted for the change, have overstepped their powers, and betrayed the people by this open violation of its clear and solemn will.

There took place, however, certain events which the guilty usurpers qualify with the name of *popular accep-tation*—events with which they wrap themselves up to legitimatize their crimes, and to escape the penalties of treason, which they manifestly incurred. The Con-stitutional Act of 1795 has been sent, it is true, to the primary assemblies and to the armies,* the extracts of whose registers, made by those *personally interested in the matter,* have " verified " that 900,000 citizens have voted for its acceptation. If this acceptation be the free expression of the people's will, the Constitution of 1795 carries the day; but if it is but an act of violence. . . . let us see!

4,800,000 citizens have voted for the Constitution of 1793; only 900,000 have assented to the Act of 1795. What has become of the remaining 3,900,000 ? Either their vote has not been verified, or they have not presented themselves at the primary assemblies. If the first sup-position be true, the crime of the Constitutionalists of 1795 is manifest; if the second is to be admitted, then will it be necessary to examine whether the silence of the 3,900,000, who had voted on the former occasion, is suffi-cient to warrant the presumption of a change of will and

* The Constitution of 1793 was not sent to the armies; never-theless, it had 4,800,000 votes. What apology is to be made for the legislator who, having recourse to the votes of soldiers, trained in habits of blind obedience to their chiefs, afterwards commands, in the name of their bayonets, the consent of the rest of the citizens ?

tacit consent on their part, or whether it is only the effect of violence exercised by the counter-revolutionists.

But in order to prove that their silence ought to be taken for consent, it is necessary, according to all rules of law, that it be proved.

1. That the 3,900,000 citizens had it in their power to attend the assemblies, and would have incurred no danger in pronouncing against the Act of 1795.

2. That this Act does not violate the natural and inalienable rights of the citizens; for otherwise, the most formal consent could be considered only as an act of madness and blindness, involving no obligation; and in this case, the acceptation of some would be a palpable act of oppression against the rest.

Let us call to mind what was the fate at Paris, Toulon, Valenciennes, &c.—of those who, in Prairial of the Year III., demanded the execution of the Constitution of 1793; let us call to mind how the Convention caused the people who reclaimed it to be shot and guillotined; how it massacred and hunted down, without regard to the laws and forms it had itself prescribed, and by the most monstrous violation of justice and decency, those of its members who refused to participate in the disgrace of its treasonable proceedings; let us call to mind the protracted and atrocious persecution which indiscriminately menaced the defenders of the Constitution of 1793, in the interior and in the armies; and let us afterwards judge of the state of liberty, when there were citizens found to kill themselves in the primary assemblies, in order to escape the bloody proscription which her new tyrants were then exercising all over France.*

Ah! if this silence, so imperiously commanded by the exercise of terror over the good—a terror operated by the execution and incarceration of all the warmest friends of the people—if such a silence can justify in France the Order of 1795, let us cease—yes, let us cease to declaim against the despotism of the East, which reposes exactly upon a similar basis.

And the 200,000 citizens dying in dungeons, and the

---

* It is right to remind the victims of terror, that the 8,000 envoys of the people had not as yet invoked it (terror), at the epoch when the Constitution of 1793 was accepted.

100,000 others in exile to avoid the poignards of the counter-revolutionists, and all those to whom they caused the right of suffrage to be refused in the primary assemblies—will you say that these also have tacitly consented? Is it not true that the Act of 1795 despoils the people of the inalienable right of changing its Constitution, and of sanctioning the laws? Is it not true that it strips of the right of citizenship such Frenchmen as cannot pay a contribution equal to the value of three day's labour, or who are in a state of domestic service?* Is it not true that in five years, no one will be able to exercise the right of citizenship, if unable to read or write, unless the Constitution assures the means of instruction to the indigent class? Is it not true that nobody can be either an elector or juror unless he pay, at the least, a rent equivalent to 150 days' work in towns, and unless he be a farmer or proprietor in the country?† Is it not true that the representatives, who are appointed or accounted to declare the people's will, are not elected by the people, but hold their power only from the most opulent, most cruel, and most vicious part of the nation? Frenchmen! if you doubt it, open the Act of 1795, and you will find all these iniquities sealed by the blood of our friends, immolated last Prairial to the furious ambition of the patricians.

You desire, tyrants, that this silence should be reputed a tacit consent? But will you also say that 25 millions of people, thus despoiled of all rights, have consented to their own servitude? Will you say that the French, whose blood has flowed in torrents for liberty, have renounced all participation in the national sovereignty—to crouch, like the negroes of America, under the inexorable scourge of the planter? Rather say that such was the will of a minority which holds the keys of power and of enjoyments, and we shall reply that whenever equality of rights towards each member of the association is violated, *then* society no longer exists—there only remains oppression on the one side, and the obligation to resist on the other.

---

* This exception comprehends at least a sixth part of all the citizens.

† A condition which excludes all the journeymen and labouring classes.

RECAPITULATION.

The Constitution of 1793 has had 4,800,000 suffrages.
That of 1795 has had posteriorly.. 900,000 ditto.
With respect to the latter, no votes
 were given by .... 3,900,000 citizens.
Silence is not a tacit consent.

. 1. Because it has been commanded by a long system of terror—by the assassination and bastilizaticn of the patriots.

2. Because the Constitutional Act of. 1795 violates the natural rights of man, which no one can renounce.

This silence is therefore a formal disavowal. It follows from this reasoning, which we defy all the partisans of inequality to answer :—

1. That the Constitution of 1793 is the sole and veritable law of the French people.

2. That the Act of 1795 is the result of violence and tyranny, which cannot be defended without crime.

3. That no one can exercise, without treason towards the people, the powers which emanate from the Counter-revolutionary Act.

At Paris, this 24th Germinal of the Year IV.

PIECE, No. XII.

ADDRESS OF THE TRIBUNE OF THE PEOPLE

To the Army of the Interior. *

SOLDIERS !—In a Republic which was once superior to what our Republic is now, the army and the people had what we have not. Rome had her Tribunes of the People and her Military Tribunes. They were magistrates whom the law appointed to be perpetual defenders of the people and of the army. The Tribunes of the People were elected by the people, and their duty consisted in keeping incessant watch lest any criminal attempt should be made on the people's rights; they were to be

* Extract from No. 41 of the *Tribune of the People.*

incessantly attentive to curb the ambition and injustice of the senate and patricians, or of the rich; and they had the privilege of opposing every law which might seem to them contrary to the people's interest or to general happiness. The Military Tribunes, chosen in the same way by the soldier, were similarly employed in keeping watch for him, in defending his rights, and in always opposing whatever might tend to harass, betray, or deceive him.

In France this august tribunitian magistracy has not been established. The person now addressing you has felt the utility of its existing, at least morally. I have constituted myself, by means of a periodical paper, Tribune of the People. My office is but a faint miniature of the tribuneship of the Romans. I enjoy only the right (and even for this I have a hard struggle) to follow and watch the march of the Government, and to warn my fellow-citizens when I discern acts which I deem inimical to justice and to their common interest. The right of *opposing* such acts is wanting to me. I exercise only a portion of influence on public opinion, and this portion is measured by the degree of confidence I inspire.

If I judge rightly, the striking evidence which I have succeeded in placing along side all the truths I have presented to the people, has attached to me the sound and honest part of this people—the major, the interesting, the useful part—the part from which you, soldiers, are drawn—the part, in short, which is insolently called *plebeian*. So strongly attached, indeed, that, without any Constitutional institution, this title of Tribune, by the assent and sanction of the people, is not illusory. The people has, therefore, in France, as in ancient Rome, the tribuneship in reality. I dare say they possess it as veritably as did the Romans under their best tribunes, under Lucius Junius, under Viscellinus, under Arsa, under Dentatus, under Canuleius, under Stolon, under the Gracchi. Like them, it is my pride to have earned the hatred of traitors—the confidence and esteem of the major part of my fellow-citizens.

With this confidence, the right of *opposing*, which I have not, for want of the legal institution, is, nevertheless, in great measure realized to the advantage of the

people, by means of the sanction it gives me in repro-
bating such acts of the Government as I demonstrate to
be contrary to its just interests and rights.   The people,
when enlightened respecting the injustice it experiences,
renders feeble the decisions of its guilty delegates ; and
the vast and universal expression of discontent it sends
abroad is equivalent to a *formal opposition*, because it
is impossible for tyranny, however expert and crafty, to
give durability to what a whole nation rejects.

Why, then, with such advantages, almost equal to
those of the Tribunes of Rome, have I not yet obtained
the same success which they were accustomed to obtain ?
Ah ! my brothers, you must have foreseen the reason.
You will perceive, according to what I have stated, that
something is still wanting to place us on a level of
advantage with the Romans.   I am but a tribune of the
people; you have no military tribunes.   Thus referring
to what certain parties say, you may easily perceive this
deficiency on our side.   To believe these persons, your
public spirit, your revolutionary intelligence, are not, in
general, equal to the intelligence and public spirit of the
other citizens. . . . Nay, they go so far as to assert that
you are prepared to justify, by your conduct, the expression which escaped from some of your rulers—" *Our
soldiers will defend us !*"   I know, however, that it is
far from true. . . . that the aggregate of your body
is locked up within such a narrow and servile circle of
ideas and opinions.   Nevertheless, it cannot be dissembled that a large portion of your body might be
easily led into disastrous errors from the want of good
instruction.   Such instruction I now offer you, and I
also propose myself to be your military tribune.   Most
naturally does this title amalgamate with that of tribune
of the people. . . . Are not you the people also ?   Do
your interests differ from those of your brothers who
compose the class of citizens ?   And may not the man
who enjoys their confidence likewise inspire yours ?   Give
ear to him, then, and hear him frankly plead your cause!
courageously support your noblest rights ! and tell you
what you have to do. . . . for yourselves, and for the
people of whom you form part, and to whom you
belong.

For what purpose are you congregated in such large numbers around this metropolis?—the city of the Revolution?—the cradle of liberty? Why are you called here? Are its inhabitants rebels? Is it required to subjugate them? These are questions which it is not unimportant to throw some light upon.

Soldiers! it is not for the real people that you form around our walls a formidable pale! This real people—the industrious, working people—is maltreated here, muzzled, outraged, despised, starved, ruined, by the people of stock-jobbers and public robbers!....It is this latter description of people which is in a most criminal state of rebellion against the good people! But is it to subjugate the oppressive party, and to defend the oppressed party, that you present a triple array of bayonets around the circumference of Paris? No! but quite the contrary....The tyrants mean to use your arms and force to utterly crush the oppressed under the oppressors' yoke!—to maintain the latter in their odious domination, and the people in its sufferings and despairing impotence! Ah! if the object was to defend the people, there would be no necessity to draw off from the frontiers their brethren, whose destination is to combat the external foe! For the rest, the people would suffice to defend itself. But when it is sought to sacrifice the mass to a fraction, then are distant succours required. It is then the tyrants expect to find such succours in the men whose duty they pretend to be *unqualified obedience*. ....It is when the Government, and the corrupt caste it exclusively protects, have lost all shame—it is when, without even the decency of disguise, the infamous accomplices of despotism have, by atrocious ordinances (audaciously called *laws*), consecrated iniquities of every sort, misery the most frightful, slavery the most revolting —it is when the measure of their misdeeds is carried to such an overflowing fullness, and with such glaring effrontery—that the long patience of the people is exhausted, and its credulity can bear no more—it is then they turn their eyes to you! It is your hands they would arm to maintain—to perpetuate such oppression! It is the *Government of arms* that is sought to be established, in order to force the people to bend to a

regime in which it is pretended they can live without
nourishment, without clothes, without liberty! And
they are the fathers, husbands, sons, brothers, kinsmen,
&c., that our rulers would have impose on—nay, strike
(should circumstances require it) their children, wives,
fathers, brothers, sisters, friends, kinsfolk! &c. And it is
through you, who are of the people!—you, soldiers of the
Republic!—who are thus placed in opposition to another
portion of the people!—it is through you it is sought
to consolidate this state of bondage, degradation, and
famine, a thousand times worse than the old servitude
against which we rose in arms six years ago!

No!—you will not be the vile satellites, the cruel and
blind instruments of the enemies of the people, and, consequently, of your own enemies! I repeat, that it is only
when authority has rendered itself culpable, or wishes to
aggravate its guilt, that it encompasseth itself with bayonets. When power is just, it is always strong enough
in the people's strength. Capet had fortified himself
with an army before the 14th of July....We know what
his designs were, and for what a complication of crimes
he wanted to secure impunity for himself. Would it be
wrong to examine whether those who imitate him are not
influenced by an exact parity of motives?

Remember, soldiers, that the army of Capet, though
trained in the school of monarchic discipline, exhibited a
noble conduct. It remembered that it was part of the
people! The French guards lowering their fasces before
the sans-culottes was an example which will be handed
down to the admiration of all ages. Alas! why must
we remind you of an epoch more recent and less glorious?
On the 12th Germinal and on the 1st Prairial batallions
born amid the Republic, and which had made themselves
illustrious in battle against the satellites of kings, have tar-
nished their laurels by obeying two slaves named Pichegru
and Menou!—by slaughtering (under their orders) a
people covered with rags and dying of hunger! Ah! had
it not been for this fatal and dishonouring conduct, our
degradation and misery would be now past. That battle
against the people has done it more harm than all the
victories gained in its name have done it good. The
French armies have a deal to do to repair that calamity.

It is true we owe them gratitude for the 13th Vendemiaire, for if, as a general rule, the arm of the soldier should always wither in presence of the real people, he should make exceptions with respect to the gilded sons of luxury, who are not the people. But how many Vendèmiaires would be necessary to expiate the infamous days of Prairial? In Vèndèmiaire you vanquished these gilded Do-nothings, you made aristocracy and royalism bite the dust. So far well... Every blow dealt to these two monster-species is useful and worthy of the French armies. But in dealing the blow, it is right to have a wise object in view. Is it enough to conquer? No, it is further necessary to turn the victory to account. This is what you neglected to do in Vendèmiaire. We read these words in the address of *Solignac*, which has just appeared under the name of the first division of the army of the interior. *The men of the 13th Vendèmiare combatted for the Government.* It is a sad truth that, and perhaps the only truth contained in that contemptible document. The vile Adjutant Solignac was equally worthy of drawing it up, as he was of committing the forgery of attaching the name of the army of the interior to his servile effusion. Yes! unfortunately you combatted and conquered in Vendèmiaire only for the Government! You might have rendered the victory fruitful and decisive for the people and for yourselves; instead of which, the Government for whom you triumphed has shown you its gratitude by making both the people and you worse slaves than you were before. Will you not be wiser when the like occasion offers again? Will it not be for the people that you will then combat? I cannot believe that this degrading language—that these grovelling phrases which the dishonoured Solignac has put into your mouths can express your real sentiments! What! you could have said, *it is our chiefs who direct our bayonets! our hands are armed in favour of the depositaries of the national authority! ....we are the protectors....of the Government!* Gods! this language of slaves to be spoken by republican soldiers!— *their lips to be soiled by these liberticidal blasphemies!* It is you who could have said—" Governors! usurpers of " the people's rights! be tranquil, fear nothing.... " despise the almost unanimous cry raised against you

" both by tnis indignant people and its resolute Tribunes;
" close your ears to all its complaints, trample under
" foot its importunate remonstrances against your op-
" pression, which, after all, it is born to support. Tyrants!
" we are your soldiers—we will maintain your despotism
" and all your brigand acts—we will crush—if necessary
" we will fulminate upon our fathers and brothers!—we
" will rip up the bellies of our sisters and mothers!..we
" will exterminate our children....................
" ....
" to maintain your insupportable and unparalleled domi-
" nation. Our duty is to aid you to consolidate the
" slavery of the country; our own chains ought to be
" rivetted by our own hands! For what else are we but
" moving machines, living puppets, senseless automatons,
" who are blindly to obey every impulse of our leaders?
" *It is our chiefs who direct our bayonets.... We are*
" *the protectors of the Government!* Besides, are we
" not well enough paid for it? What have we to com-
" plain of? Have we not for some time a double and
" triple pittance of brandy? What is there to put in
" the balance against that? What signifies it that for
" this inestimable douceur we are required to chain down
" our contemporaries and posterity? What signifies it
" that soon—in a month, in a week, perhaps, or it may
" be to-morrow—our families and ourselves shall have
" nothing? We have brandy to-day—that is everything.
" Formerly, indeed, we had been promised (and even
" assured by solemn decrees) possessions—lands—pen-
" sions—but are we born for such advantages? Is it
" not folly to believe that the Revolution was made for
" us? By the way, of our chiefs—ought we not to be
" sufficiently flattered at seeing the Directory give our
" General Buonaparte 800,000 francs to furnish his
" house? To Duvigneau, chief of our staff, a most
" gorgeous carriage and equipage.*

---

* It is said that the same corrupting means were tried with
Jourdan. It is added, that to render them effectual, or propor-
tionate to the degree of resistance anticipated on the part of this
General, the means employed to win him were somewhat more
seductive than those employed for the rest. Report speaks of six
beautiful steeds, and of a complete suit of armour—of magnificent
galas at the house of Baron de Bénezech—of brilliant fêtes given

" All that is charming. All that ought to glad the sight
" of the soldier, and no doubt it is enough for him to
" have his eyes feasted with such a spectacle. What
" more do we want?—we, the greater part of us miserable
" peasants, sons of workmen, and the scum of society?
" Our fathers were a herd of *canaille,* who thought them-
" selves too happy to be allowed to admire the gen-
" tilities of their lords and masters. It was even a favour
" to suffer them to look the 'respectable' folk in the
" face. Their happiness consisted in doing each the
" work of four, in never more than half-satisfying their
" hunger, and in having the satisfaction of knowing that
" the fruits of their sweat gave superfluities of pleasure
" and enjoyment to a small number of debauchees,
" abandoned to every vice. What more do we demand?
" Are we not the descendants of this *populace?* And
" is it not this populace which caused us to be born
" with naked breech? Wherefore we ought to pretend
" to no other rights than they had. Why talk to us of
" lands and pensions to reward our exploits against the
" enemies of the Revolution? No, no, those rewards
" were not made for us. They were very good to
" promise at the time it was necessary to tempt us to
" enlist in order to repel the invaders who wished to set
" fire to the four corners of France, but we have no
" right to suppose that such promises could have been
" made in seriousness. On returning home to our beg-
" gars of fathers, we ought to expect to be beggars like
" them, to crouch like them under the insolent domi-
" nation of the rich; to be their galley slaves; to labour
" for vile wages from sunrise to sunset; to have only
" our sweat to cool and moisten the half-mouthful of
" brown bread dried in the sun's heat! Yet happy
" those of us who will be able even thus to prolong their
" existence! The rest—will go alms-gathering. We shall
" see the lamed, the wooden-legged, those with broken

by this *beloved* Minister of the Directory to the wife of the hero of
the Army of the North—of the additional and quite peculiar
honour of giving to *Citizen-ess* Jourdan the arrangement of the car-
.iages of the Luxembourg Court. But it is confidently stated that
Jourdan, little affected by these cajoleries, remains no less the
General of liberty notwithstanding, and that he continues to
merit the confidence of the people and of the soldiers.

" jaws and fractured arms, cover the streets and high-
" ways, drag themselves painfully up to the doors of the
" wallowers in luxury, present their humiliating suppli-
" cations to a hundred of them, experience ninety-nine
" refusals, accompanied with outrages, and receive at
" the hundredth door an obolus, the thousandth part of
" what would buy a breakfast-meal of bread. But,
" soldiers of the Republic, let us make a joke of all
" that. The Government gives us brandy now. Let us
" stultify ourselves, and not look to the future. Let us
" not examine even why it gives us this brandy. Let us
" keep aloof from those sad sermonizers who come to
" tell us that the brandy is meant to captivate our blind
" obedience, in order to give to the Revolution a result
" quite opposite to the one for which it was undertaken.
" They say it is to induce us to keep down the people
" who would re-conquer its rights and ours against the
" Government which has usurped all. They say that it
" is in order to afterwards work specially against us ;
" that it is to consolidate and guarantee to the emigrants
" and counter-revolutionists, the restitution of their pos-
" sessions, legitimately confiscated, which had been set
" aside for our recompense, and the resumption and
" restitution of which have caused the destruction of the
" assignats and the ruin of the people. They say that
" by supporting the Government in such operations,
" after having concurred in the Revolution, we are now
" consummating the counter-revolution, since we make
" the Revolution turn to the profit of its enemies; since
" we help them to resume the wealth which had become
" ours, and which, consequently, we more than re-
" nounce for ourselves, by protecting the men who are
" wresting them from our hands. Behold all that these
" folks say who pretend to be more clear-sighted than
" others. But let us not hearken to them. The Govern-
" ment gives us brandy—that is all we want. Let us
" oppress the people, our families, and ourselves—*let us
" see only our chiefs, let us hear only their voices,
" they alone ought to direct our bayonets.* We are
" but automatons, beasts, barbarians, incapable of re-
" flecting, of feeling, and of judging. *To the right
" face—to the left*—behold all that we ought to know.

" *Take aim—fire*—we ought to ask no questions about
" what is passing before us !"

Such, soldiers of the Republic, is the atrocious and
mad reasoning held out to you. But it is fortunate that
this reasoning is not yours. No, you will not be the
assassins of your country, and your own executioners.
You love the people as it loves you ; you will constantly
protect it as it protects you. If it were possible that you
could forget yourselves, that you would not support, that
you would not reclaim your incontestible rights, the
people would reclaim them, would sustain them for you.
You must have already remarked how far from indifferent
it is to your condition, how its fraternal solicitude is incessantly occupied with it. Its cares on your behalf, its
alarms respecting your future destiny, reflects the image
of the parent's tenderness for his children. Nay, are
they not also the reality ? And that affectionate mother,
your country, which never loses sight of you ; which,
with restless eye and soul of love follows you everywhere
in the hazards and perils of glory ; which, when tyrannic
villany, stronger than her benevolence, condemned you
to privations and bad treatment of every sort, payed you
the last tribute of her heart by melting in tears over your
condition—this tender mother, I repeat, takes always the
same interest in your welfare. Doubtless, she will not
find you ungrateful children. Hear what she implores
of you by the voice of her popular writers. Hear it again
in the last dying accents of those patriotic reunions dissolved and proscribed principally for the reason that they
demanded for you what was solemnly promised you in
the fine days of the Republic—in 1793 ! The Society
of the Pantheon rendered itself very culpable in the eyes
of despotism when, in an address to the Council of Five
Hundred, it dared to express these words :—

" The public fortune has been impaired by the indis-
" criminate restitution to the families of traitors, of the
" domains which had been justly confiscated. The
" nation has been, in great measure, abandoned to the
" mercy and brigandism of commerce, and the rich man
" alone has had a patent of privilege for existence. All
" the decrees now emanating from the legislative body
" are tainted with the spirit of last year's system.

" They augment prejudices and distrusts, instead of
" calming or diminishing them.   In establishing dif-
" ferences between the metallic money and the assignat,
" by fixing the proportion at 150 capitals for *one*, you
" have yourselves given the assignat its death-blow."

The Pantheon!—soldiers of the country....At this
sound—at that of Jacobins—those of you led astray by
the prejudices artfully implanted in you by the aristocracy, start back as though smitten by some indescribable repugnance.   Those who appreciate things
better, and who are not susceptible of delusion, know
that those two terms are synonymous with that of *best
friends of the people*.   Again, the same parties ask,
Where are those Jacobins and men of the Pantheon?
Take courage, my friends; they are not dead.   A troop
in retreat is not routed.   Each member of those societies
is still secretly at work for the citizen at home, and for the
soldier under arms.   The Pantheon is not at Paris only;
it is also at every point of the Republic.   We, the
Tribune of this entire Republic — an honorary and
affiliated member of all those academies of pure republicanism, who collect together the results of their best
labours—to us it belongs to make them known to our
brothers, to show them where are their most solid
bulwarks.   Warriors! go to the north; seek the real
supporters of your rights in those climates where the
temperature forms geniuses more profound than brilliant,
more perseveringly firm than carried away by momentary
enthusiasm—more frankly zealous to achieve good, than
blessed with the wit of giving us the superfices for the
substance of it.   Go to that city which has given birth
to the hero of democracy,* and where your tribune consummated a term of exile. At Arras is also a Pantheon,
no less plebeian than that which absolute power judged
it expedient to reduce to ruins, in the Central Commune
(Paris).   It is there republican soldiers, where you—
where the people—have still courageous and energetic
friends.   Read, in consecutive order, what they have
done for you, and tell us whether they do not serve you,
in intention, at least, as well as you could serve yourselves.

* [Robespierre was born at Arras.—BRONTERRE.]

Address of the Undersigned Patriots of Arras to the Council of Five Hundred.

" LEGISLATORS!—The intention of the National Con-
" vention in passing the decrees of the 4th and 16th of
" June, 1793, 16th Vendémiaire, 5th Nevôse, 21st
" Pluviose, 24th Floréal, and 13th Prairial of the Year
" II., undoubtedly was to assure to the families of the
" generous defenders of the country the succours re-
" quired for the relief of the pressing wants they expe-
" rience. The excessive dearness of provisions, the
" total discredit of the assignats, in which they are paid
" for, the want of employment for the labourers, and
" the miserable wages they receive—all these circum-
" stances must thoroughly convince you that the sums
" hitherto granted to them are not only insufficient, but
" immeasurably far from fulfilling the original intention
" of the Conventionalists. . . . Legislators ! to *you* it be-
" longs to remedy these abuses as disastrous to humanity
" as they are dishonouring to the Republic. . . . For you
" is reserved the glory of executing the laws recently
" passed in favour of the brave and courageous de-
" fenders of liberty ! . . . . One decree states that there
" shall be reserved to the amount of 300 millions of
" national domains, to be distributed in shares to each
" of the soldiers, upon their definitive return from the
" army ! The resolution you have latterly taken ex-
" pressly purports that there be excepted from the sale
" of these same possessions, and placed in reserve the
" equivalent in value of an effective milliard.* These
" provisions are, doubtless, good ; but they do not
" suffice to guarantee our soldiers, and the friends of
" equality, against the oscillations of legislative bodies.
" Why may you not ordain the immediate execution of
" these measures?—measures equally calculated to in-
" fuse new courage into our brothers in arms, as they
" are necessary to make them cheerfully support the

---

* An effective milliard—that is to say, a milliard paid in specie
(as originally projected when the assignats were at par), would
be equivalent to 300 milliards in assignats of the present depreciated currency—a sum well worth the trouble of claiming. But
where were the national domains reserved to meet this demand ?—
BRONTERRE.

" fatigues and dangers of the war? Why, in waiting
" for their return, should not their families—almost all
" of them plunged into the most frightful misery—enjoy
" the recompense, awarded to the valour of their hus-
" bands, brothers, and protectors?" Why should they
" not occupy and cultivate those lands for the posses-
" sion of which so many heroes have shed and are still
" shedding their blood every day on the frontiers?....
" Legislators! we will not dissemble—we fear there is
" still a design to frustrate and render null an advan-
" tage so dearly earned by the people's blood! If you
" be sincere, begin by putting a stop to the calumnies of
" the enemies of the Republic! Hasten to prove to the
" *Democrats* that the promises made to our warriors
" are not illusory! Ordain on the spot the distribution
" of the part of the national property which you have
" allotted to their intrepidity! Procure for their unhappy
" families the satisfaction of enjoying, beforehand, the
" fruits of their courage! Give to all of them the means
" of immediately raising, on the apportioned lands,
" habitations suitable to receive them, upon the ter-
" mination of their glorious campaigns. Let them
" henceforward only have to offer up vows for the
" prosperity of a state whose glory they will have so
" powerfully contributed to render eternal!"—[*Here
follow the signatures.*]

Soldiers! it is the real people which thus speaks for
you! But it is not for this real people that the present
Government would interest your arms! It is not to
induce you to serve this people that you are loaded with
false caresses, and that you are primed and plied with
liquors and brandy. On the contrary, it is to determine
you to sell yourselves against the people, that the filthy
bribes are offered you. How little they know you,
soldiers!—the wretches who would thus corrupt you.
They judge you by their own standard. They fancy,
because they have themselves signed an odious compact
against the people, that you, too, could be seduced to
participate in their guilt and ignominy. No, no. Be
always the soldiers of the people. Swear by your sabres
to die only for the people. You have seen it; you will
see it again; it is equally ready to die for you and with

you. I leave you to day, or otherwise I should offer you many other testimonials of its friendly wishes, similar to what the Democrats of Arras have expressed towards you. In deferring this exposition till another time, I would meanwhile warn despotism, that on all sides the voice of liberty and equality soars above all their humanicidal complots. Let them try again to day to stifle that voice, together with the energy of those who are its organs! Schooled by adversity, exasperated by the recollection of the deep-laid, refined, multiplied perfidies of which they have been victims; forewarned of what would be their fate if they suffered another defeat, the Democrats have all fully prepared themselves to resist any new projects of tyranny. They are perfectly aware of what art and force they will require against the villains who have made this encampment around Paris. Do you also be enlightened, magnanimous warriors, and you will be neither accomplices nor dupes of the partisans of oppression. In vain have the usurpers brought all their trickeries into play; in vain have they put all their wiles in requisition. Not one of them shall succeed. One of their stratagems is to frequently renovate the army of the interior. When they fancy that disabused by us, you begin to regard us as friends instead of enemies, they send you off to a distance! The columns which hold us here, as it were, in a state of siege, are continually and almost every hour relieved by other columns. To what will all this *finessing* lead? Why, to this—that all the French armies will come in succession to receive instruction at our school, to read our inflaming papers, and to rend (each in turn) the veil which prevented them from knowing the truth, and from forming a right estimate of the villains who deceived them and us.

GRACCHUS BABEUF,
Tribune of the People.

Paris, 10th Germinal, Year IV. of the Republic.

R

PIECE No. XIII.

TO GRACCHUS BABEUF,

Tribune of the People.

Paris, 30th Pluviose, Year IV.

And I too would desire real equality. I am almost
sixty years old—I have nothing, or almost nothing, in
the shape of property—I am burdened with six children,
as yet too young to work—I have the misfortune not to
know any profession or trade—I am neither merchant,
nor courtier, nor stockjobber, nor broker, nor even
clerk in an office. How many pressing motives for desiring real equality. But, alas—is it possible? Of what
use to show me this blissful state in so remote and obscure a distance, that I despair of ever arriving there?
How are we to give it existence? Always the *word*,
and never the *thing*.

I have read of agrarian divisions of land, but that has
not endured. The cause of this is what needs to be
fathomed. It is not a question of new distribution
merely, but of the durability of such distribution. The
lands are not all that would require to be newly distributed; and I have nowhere read of even the attempt
being made to distribute the productions of mind and
invention, except in religious communities, or some such
establishments. Shall we divide ourselves into small
communities? Suppose we do that, and that I bring,
for example, my charming picture, my perfect machine,
my excellent invention, my discoveries in physics, in
chemistry, in hydraulics, in natural history; my music,
my poetry, my volubility on the violin, the harp, and
the harpsichord; the harmonious sounds of my voice. &c.
to the general magazine of real equality, along with my
neighbour the cobbler, to receive our equal portions of
good things, such as meat, bread, liquor, &c.; still this
is not all that is required—it is necessary that such a
state should be durable, that, moreover, it should not
extinguish taste, genius, and the passion for the beau-

tiful, and for perfection in the arts and callings. But suppose me gifted with the self-abnegation of a monk—capable of renouncing my most pleasurable tastes and *penchants*, for the sake of a real equality with my neighbour the cobbler—still shall we not need superiors, priors, abbots, executive directors, &c., for names make no difference in the matter? Shall we not want laws, that is to say, mutual conventions? Will it not be necessary to confide to perfectly disinterested chiefs, a force equal in action to the re-action we must always calculate on, and calculate too with a precision as nice as the weight of a turnspit or the spring of a watch. What a crowd of reflections come to offer themselves here!

I hear Jean Jacques Rousseau and Mably quoted on your side. The first has positively said, that to live under a pure democracy we should be demi-gods. The second is very far from believing in the possibility of real equality in a country so extensive, so considerable, and so well peopled as our's. When I think on it, and I often think on it, my head loses itself in bewilderment.

Tribune!—lay us down a plan; prove to us, in a clear manner, the possibility of equality; that such equality can be durable; and show us the positive steps or means of arriving at it, that is to say, that we may not continue for years in anarchy; and that, after so many great movements, after so many painful and fruit-less sacrifices, we may not behold ourselves in a worse condition than we are at present.*

(Signed)   M.... V.

* [My readers of the Owenite or co-operative school will be f,rcibly reminded, by the above letter, of the many doubts and queries addressed to Robert Owen, touching the possibility of reducing his system to practice. To all such readers and doubtful inquirers, the following reply of Babeuf to M. V. will prove a gratifying treat.—BRONTERRE.]

Babeuf's Reply to a Letter signed "M. V," published and addressed the 30th Pluviôse, to Gracchus Babeuf, Tribune of the People.

" In a veritable society there ought to be neither rich nor poor."
" The rich who will not renounce their superfluities in favour of the indigent are enemies of the people."
" The end of the Revolution is to destroy inequality, and to re-establish the happiness of all."
" *Articles 7, 8, and 10 of the Analysis of the Doctrine of the Tribune, posted up and proclaimed the 20th of this month of Germinal.*"

The following truths, addressed in reply to the author of the letter of the 30th Pluviôse, ought to have been published sooner. I am not sorry, however, that particular reasons obliged me to wait till now. The doctrine discussed in this paper is more than ever the order of the day, and I flatter myself that I shall at present attract a reasonable attention to the greatest of all subjects which interest man.

Every true Republican ought to rejoice at the doubts advanced by the Citizen M. V., as to the possibility of executing the system of real equality. If the contest engaged in, touching this supreme point of human regeneration, be supported by the friends of liberty with the same warmth of zeal which they recently evinced in demolishing the scaffolding of feudality and monarchy, it is beyond doubt certain that we shall soon witness the fall of the barbarous system of private properties, and, as a consequence, the re-establishment on earth of the happiness of the Golden Age, and of practical fraternity, which ambition and avarice have hitherto entirely banished from our monstrous societies.

Generous souls!—you who launched into the revolutionary career, impelled by the sole love of humanity, the time is come for attacking with the thunderbolts of reason, that ever-existing cause of all calamities, of all tyrannies—individual riches. The doctrine we preach has in support of it the cool calculations of philosophy, and the authority of some of the greatest men of antiquity and of our own age. It alone offers a reasonable boundary to the revolution which would be a crime, if in changing the mere form of oppression it left the multitude in misfortunes and servitude, aggravated by the false hope of mitigation, and consolidated by the increased number and perversity of its oppressors.

Before touching on the proofs of the possibility, of the justice, and of the charms of the system of real equality, in answer to the doubts of M. V., we must set him right on a question which he seems to misunderstand, when, after speaking of the division of lands, he adds, " the difficulty of the question regards not merely the division of lands, but to provide that such division be durable."

Nothing of the kind. The system of equality excludes all division. Nay, it is to this very division, that our societies—the offspring of the wants, passions, and ignorance of our ancestors—owe all the tyrannies and all the afflictions of which we are at present the victims. Before any of our forefathers could have said that a field belonged to him, it was necessary that a convention—express or tacit—should have guaranteed him the enjoyment or possession of it. Happy for mankind had that fatal convention never taken place ! That convention it was which first introduced into the *social* state the disastrous consequences of force and cunning, of which there was so much reason to complain in the *natural* state.* That it is which has isolated and divided human kind, which has excited their cupidity, and founded upon this destructive vice the conservation of societies. That it is which has furnished force, cunning, and perversity, with the means of evading the natural conditions of the social compact, and delivering over simplicity and virtue to exhausting labour and penury and sorrow. That it is which has condemned the producers of all wealth to every privation, and heaped all manner of luxurious enjoyment upon the idle. That it is which has subjected the multitude (constrained to be ignorant) to the snares of ambition and fanaticism. It is it, in fine, which is the source of all tyrannies—1st, Because, were it not for the hope of wallowing in pleasure without doing any-

---

* The right of nature differs essentially from what is called the *state* of nature. The former is the result of experience and reflection ; the latter is the offspring of first impressions and of ignorance.

thing to earn his living, nobody would desire to be either
a monarch, or a noble, or a governor; 2d, Because it
is the perfection of perfidy to call men free who, condemned to labour to exhaustion, without hoping ever to
enjoy, are incapacited to make known their feelings and
sufferings by the want of leisure, and by the constrained
ignorance in which our social state retains them. Behold
why nothing is more contrary to equality and to happiness than private property, or the division of lands
which is its fountain-head.

Nay, more—this division of lands to which, according
to some, the *maximum of our social happiness* is re-
ducible, would aggravate the general evil, inasmuch as
it would alarm the egoism of our proprietors, which forms
the only basis of what at present is called public prosperity,
and open the way to the immediate return of disorders
of which it is pretended that it would be the remedy.

Now, let us see what is understood by real equality.
It has for its basis two essential conditions:—*work in
common ; enjoyment in common.*

In the first place, labour being a necessary condition,
without which society would perish, nobody can evade
his share of it without injustice; the man who has done
so, has either diminished the public stock of wealth, or
else thrown his own burden upon his neighbour.

Two powerful considerations occur in support of this
system. 1. This common labour would augment the
riches of society, which in the actual state can count
upon the useful labour of only a small portion of its
members. 2. If the general labour were fairly distributed
amongst all the valid members of society, it would deliver
from an insupportable burden those whom we have condemned exclusively to drudgery, and would transfer to
the rest only a very moderate portion of labour, which
would soon become for all a source of pleasure and
amusement. I do not comprehend how one can *honestly*
regard our present state as the best possible, whilst the
great mass of the people lead a more miserable life than
they would in a state of simple nature. Look at the
savage—if he hunts, if he fishes, if he cultivates the earth,
the fruits of his sweat is entirely his own, and he enjoys
all the happiness he knows. Our journeymen operatives

—our peasants—on the contrary, far from keeping the enjoyment of their productions, and of tasting the happiness of which our civilization gives them the idea, are obliged to surrender nearly all to greedy and worthless proprietors, and to a certainty, suffer hunger, thirst, and the inclemency of the seasons.

Let each work for the great social family, and let each receive in return the means of living and his fair share of the general pleasure and happiness. Behold what nature wills—behold the state in which equality is not a chimera, and in which the liberty of each individual is substantially assured.

You speak, citizen M. V., of the abnegation of all tastes, of all penchants, of the equality that would take place between the living of an artist and that of a cobbler, and of the decay of the fine arts, as so many disastrous consequences of the system of real equality, whose absurdity you would thereby prove. The objection only proves that you are still enthralled by our old prejudices. To suppose that to return to equality would be to become savage and brutal, is only to misconceive its constitution. To fling in our teeth the scarecrow of abnegations, when we wish to put an end to the incalculable and perpetual privations of the majority of the people—when we wish that the labour of each person should secure him a commodious and agreeable existence—is either not to comprehend us, or to show oneself the accomplice of those whom idleness and hatred of work render the enemies of equality.

It would, to be sure, be an indescribable horror, my dear M. V., that your bread, your meat, your wine, and your clothes, should come out of the same magazine and have the same taste as those of a cobbler! But then, why did Nature choose to give to this inferior animal a stomach and senses like yours? Miserable! when you swim in abundance, do you want in addition the picture of another's griefs to complete your happiness?

The pretended decay of the professions and the fine arts is another of the "unanswerable" objections of those *clever* persons who would have you believe that the world is at end the moment you snatch from them their distinctions, their privileges, and their usurped consideration. Assuredly, even if this decay were to take place, the mass of the people, who are utter strangers to the advantages of the fine arts, would not experience any great inconvenience in consequence. But in truth, no such event is to be feared, for it is manifest that the arts would receive, in our system of equality, advancements of general utility, and a sublime impress conformable to the grand sentiments which an immense association of happy beings should necessarily give birth to. The citizens would be well-fed, well-clothed, well-amused, without inequality, without luxury; the Republic alone would be rich, magnificent, all-powerful.

Some crafts, it is true, whose productions only serve to relieve the *ennui* of a very small portion of parasites, and to pump enormous masses of money into their hands, should give place to others which would augment the well-being of the great mass of society. But where is the man who could regret this happy change? The sciences and the fine arts once relieved from the goad of ever-pressing, ever-crippling want, the man of genius would no longer have any other stimulus than the love of glory: and, soon shaking off the yoke of flattery, and of selfish Mecænas-like patrons, his only object would be the prosperity of the social body.

To frivolous poems, to architecture of bad taste, to pictures without interest, we should see succeed circuses, temples, and sublime porticos, whither the sovereign people (at present worse lodged than our brute animals are) would repair to imbibe, in the monuments and works of philosophy, the doctrine, the example, and the love of wisdom.

In this enchanting system, of whose charms I only pretend to sketch the outlines, we should witness the solution of the problem—*to find a state in which each individual might, with the least trouble, enjoy the most commodious life*. Thus the very-diversified productions of all would belong to the mass, who would afterwards distribute them for the greatest happiness of each. You see, then, citizen M. V., that it is not proposed to condemn men to abnegations, but, on the contrary, to diminish the privations of the mass. You ought also to see that in such a state the uprooting of avarice, having put an end to jealousies, cunning, and distrusts, men would be really brothers, strictly interested in the conservation of an order of things which would make the happiness of all.

It was due to the French Revolution to put in practical execution the conceptions of philosophy, hitherto regarded as chimerical. We have commenced the great work; let us finish it. Were we to stop at the point where we now are, humanity and posterity would have little to thank us for.

In order to pass from our present vicious state to the one I advocate, it is necessary,—

1. To place all the existing wealth of the country in the hands of the Republic.

2. To make all the valid citizens work, each according to his capacity and actual habits.

3. To utilize the objects of labour, by bringing together those which mutually aid one another, and by giving a new direction to such as are only the effect of the existing stagnant masses of riches.

4. To bring together (so as to have a continued supply) into the public depôts all the productions of the land and of industry.

5. To effect an equal distribution of productions and enjoyments.

6. To dry up the source of all property, of all individual or private commerce, and to substitute for them a wise distribution confided to the public authority.

7. To establish common halls of education, in which each individual should be trained to the employment or work most suitable to his strength and inclinations.

Thus egoism would be no longer the spring of action or the stimulus to labour for individuals, who, whatever the variety and use of their productions, would receive the same retribution in food, clothing, &c. &c.

From this consequence our rich folk elicit the two following objections:—

1. The necessity of procuring subsistence, and the hope of ameliorating our condition in life are the great sources of labour and reproduction; this necessity and this hope once destroyed, labour ceases, the spring of reproduction is dried up, and society perishes.

2. If every species of labour were to receive the same recompence, there would no longer exist any motive for pursuing those scientific researches, which produce discoveries useful to society.

I answer, 1st, It is easy to make every one understand that a few hours' occupation per day would secure to every individual the means of living agreeably, and permanently relieve him from those anxieties by which we are now continually undermined; and surely the man who now slaves himself to exhaustion in order to have a little, would work a little in order to have much.   Moreover, the objection rests entirely upon the disagreeable idea we are accustomed to form of labour, which, if wisely and universally distributed, would become in our system a mild and delightful occupation, of which no person would have either the inclination or interest to elude his share.

2d. It is, I think, a well ascertained fact that the progress of science depends more on the love of glory than on the avidity for riches; and in this case, our society, truly philosophic, embodying every possible means of effectually and impartially honouring its benefactors, would have therefore a right to expect more from science than our present corrupted associations, in which genius and virtue, despised and devoted to indigence, have the mortification to behold folly and crime almost invariably loaded with riches and honour.

I have said enough to satisfy my readers in good earnest, that the principle of avidity and selfishness, which forms the basis of all our present institutions, is detestable; and that to terminate for ever the agitations, misfortunes, and tyrannies which divide and oppress us, we must replace ourselves in a veritable state of society, where each individual, having equal stake and interest, may derive an equal profit; for all the reasonings of the political economists will never convince men of sense and honesty that it is supremely just that those who do nothing should possess every thing, and chain down, brutalize, and maltreat those who doing everything, possess almost nothing.

Citizen M. V. presents as another objection to our

system of equality—the necessity of a Government, and the too large extent of the Republic. The answer is obvious.

1st. The persons commissioned to preserve this system, the machinery of which is extremely simple, would be regarded as workers necessary to the general prosperity; and never being able to obtain more enjoyments than the other citizens (too deeply interested in watching them) there would be no occasion to fear any attempts on their part to retain their authority in contempt of the people's will.

2d. If all the difficulties which prejudices oppose to the community of labour and enjoyment in a small state or tribe can be easily vanquished, there is nothing to prevent the like result in a great association like the Republic of France. In the first place, it is readily conceived how all the citizens might be employed, each in his respective locality, and agreeably to the nature of the soil. As to the equal distribution of objects of consumption to all the communes of the Republic, or to all that might participate in it according to their relations with the differerent climates, I cannot see why a wise authority, unembarrassed by the obstacles with which these sorts of operations are now-a-days thwarted by the greedy selfishness of governors and governed, could not execute it with far more satisfaction to all the citizens than they experience in the actual state of things, abandoned, as they frequently are, to scarcity and famine, by the crafty calculations of speculators.

I behold, in the new order of things—

1. The arts placed, by providential institutions, in the localities where they would be most useful; and, by commingling with the agriculturists, working the extinction of those receptacles of every vice, large cities; and covering France with villages, adorned with immense and happy populations, whose propagation and multiplication there would be nothing to retard.

2d. Men, enlightened and trained to labour by *education in common*—loving their country more than they at present love their families—and deliberating, with a knowledge of causes on public affairs—I behold them giving to the world the first example of democracy.

and virtue, defended with the courage of a lion by an immense population.

3d. Frenchmen without money, without privations, without ennui, without blue-devils, without the desire of amassing against the future—I behold them paying cheerfully to their country the common tribute of all—*labour;* I behold them luxuriating in the pleasures of nature, and passing their unoccupied time in the gaieties of public festivals, in the discussion of laws, and in the instruction of youth.

4th. Society disenthralled from the litigations, the hatreds, the jealousies, and all the disastrous consequences of private property.

5th. Legislation reduced to a few simple elementary principles; reduced, in fact, to the art of augmenting the knowledge and pleasures of society.

6th. The country, when threatened with danger, able to find, in the increase of a half-hour's work per day, more soldiers and resources than can, in the present order of things, be furnished by all the financiers of Europe.

Oh, my fellow-countrymen! contemplate this picture of liberty, of peace, of happiness! Behold the only possible remedy for so many distractions, convulsions, and factions—evils which must terminate either in universal slavery or universal happiness. What, then, are the powerful obstacles to prevent us (upon returning to the ways of reason) from putting an end to our mutual jealousies, our fierce contests, and our propensities to destroy one another? The stupidity of some, the sloth of others, and the vicious habits which have puffed with false pride the hearts of those who look cold-bloodedly on the misery of their fellow-creatures—the fruit of their baneful opulence —such are the obstacles that mar our progress.

Friends of the country! patriot philosophers! to you it belongs to finish the Revolution. To your reasonings —to your writings, it belongs to extirpate selfishness— the source of all misery and woe. To truth, in short, it belongs to destroy royalism, which, at once the cause and effect of monstrous inequality, will ever subsist under any and every form of government, until *actual equality* and democracy shall have amalgamated all interests, destroyed all partialities, and divested one portion of society of the anti-social faculty of constraining, harassing, wounding, and oppressing the remainder.

If power had no interest in opposing the progress of human sociability, I would regard the success of this enterprise as certain; for if we speak clearly and honestly to the people, I feel satisfied they will immediately declare themselves for equality. But whereas such state is not relished by the vitiated hearts and perturbed imaginations of the powerful, those who will have the courage to fulfil their duties towards the mass, must expect, not only to be tortured and persecuted in a thousand ways, but also to be represented (which already happens) as *brigands, incendiaries,* and *royalists.* True, it will with difficulty be believed that those who have destroyed the throne, and who cannot endure any inequality, not even that of idleness and riches, can love royalty the *maximum* of inequalities! But still there will be fools to believe it, and therefore the patriots must be prepared to bear with fortitude this new indignity; indeed, unless they shall make up their minds to risk life itself in defending the general good, the Revolution will only appear in the eyes of posterity as a blot on history and a crime on themselves.

It still remains for me to dissipate the last doubt of citizen M. V, who fears anarchy in the transition from the existing system to that of equality.

Patriots! join your voices to mine when I exclaim—Oh! fellow citizens, let us cast our gold into the sea—let us all work—let us all enjoy—let us banish idleness and luxury—and this seductive language, supported by the reasons of wisdom, will set reform beyond the reach of all the incertitudes, all the alarms which seemingly are feared. But were it even true that this transition should necessarily involve convulsive extravagances (which, however, have never accompanied our great national movements), I would only call them the last effects of expiring anarchy. For, properly speaking, disorder and anarchy do really exist at present in every actual society in Europe, where, under divers pretexts, and by different means, the population is despoiled of all its rights. And surely it would be well worth risking some momentary

irregularities, in order to put an end to the present
grand organized and perpetual anarchy, and to establish
a system of prosperity which, realizing the predictions ot
philosophers on the Revolution, would, according to all
appearances, work the utter demolition of the Governments which still disquiet us, because their subjects have
not hitherto discovered in our innovations the clear and
decisive stamp of the general felicity we have so long
heralded and proclaimed.

Paris, 28th Germinal, Year IV. of the Republic.

SUPPLEMENT TO PIECE XIII.

A NEW SONG, FOR THE USE OF THE FAUBOURGS. *

Air : *C'est ce qui me désole.*

Mourant de faim, mourant de froid,
Peuple dépouillé de tout droit,
    Tout bas tu te désoles :   *bis.*
Cependant le riche effronté,
Qu'épargna jadis ta bonté,
    Tout haut, il se console.   *bis.*

Gorgés d'or, des hommes nouveaux,
Sans peines, ni soins, ni travaux,
    S'emparent de la ruche :   *bis.*
Et toi, peuple laborieux,
Mange, et digère, si tu peux,
    Du fer, comme l'autruche.   *bis.*

Evoque l'ombre des Gracchus,
Des Publicola, des Brutus ;
    Qu'ils te servent d'enceinte !   *bis.*
Tribun courageux, hâte-toi,
Nous t'attendons : trace la loi
    De l'*égalité* sainte.   *bis.*

Qui, tribun, il faut en finir.
Que tes pinceaux fassent pàlir
    Luxembourg et Verône ! †   *bis.*
Le règne de l'*égalité*
Ne veut, dans sa simplicité,
    Ni panaches, ni trône ! ‡   *bis.*

* Par Sylvain Maréchal.
† La royauté et l'aristocratie, dont les chefs résidaient au
Luxembourg.
‡ Les panaches étaient la décoration des membres du directoire.

Certes, un million d'opulens
Retient depuis assez long-temps
   Le peuple à la glandée :   *bis.*
Nous ne voulons, dans le faubourg,
Ni les chouans du Luxembourg,
   Ni ceux de la Vendée.   *bis.*

O vous, machines à décrets,
Jetez dans le feu, sans regrets,
   Tous vos plans de finance :   *bis.*
Pauvres d'esprit, ah ! laissez-nous :
L'*égalité* saura sans vous
   Ramener l'abondance.   *bis.*

Le directoire exécutif,
En vertu du droit plumitif,
   Nous interdit d'écrire :   *bis.*
N'écrivons pas ; mais que chacun,
Tout bas, pour le *bonheur commun,*
   En bon frère conspire.   *bis.*

Un double conseil sans talens,
Cinq directeurs toujours tremblans
   Au nom seul d'une pique :   *bis.*
Le soldat choyé, caressé,
Et le démocrate écrasé :
   Voilà la république.   *bis.*

Hélas ! du bon peuple aux abois
Fiers compagnons, vainqueurs des rois,
   Soldats couverts de gloire !   *bis.*
Las ! on ne vous reconnaît plus.
Eh ! quoi ! seriez-vous devenus
   Les gardes du Prétoire ?   *bis.*

Le peuple et le soldat unis
Ont bien su réduire en débris
   Le trône et la Bastille :   *bis.*
Tyrans nouveaux, hommes d'état,
Craignez le peuple et le soldat
   Réunis en famille.   *bis.*

Je m'attends bien que la prison
Sera le prix de ma chanson ;
   C'est ce qui me désole ;   *bis.*
Le peuple la saura par cœur ;
Peut-être, il bénira l'auteur.
   C'est ce qui me console.   *bis.*

ANOTHER SUPPLEMENT TO PIECE XIII.

Un code infame a trop long-temps
Asservi les hommes aux hommes :
Tombe le règne des brigands !
Sachons enfin où nous en sommes.

Réveillez-vous à notre voix
Et sortez de la nuit profonde,
Peuples! ressaisissez vos droits,
Le soleil luit pour tout le monde.   } *Refrain général.*

Tu nous créas pour être égaux,
Nature, ô bienfaisante mère!
Pourquoi des biens et des travaux
L'inégalité meurtrière?—Réveillez, etc.

Pourquoi mille esclaves rampans
Autour de quatre à cinq despotes?
Pourquoi des petits et des grands?
Levez-vous, braves sans-culottes.—Réveillez, etc.

Dans l'enfrance du genre humain
On ne vit point d'or, point de guerre,
Point de rang, point de souverain,
Point de luxe, point de misère!
La sainte et douce égalité
Remplit la terre et la féconde:
Dans ces jours de félicité,
Le soleil luit pour tout le monde.

Tous s'aimaient, tous vivaient heureux,
Goûtant une commune aisance;
Les regrets, les débats honteux,
N'y troublaient point l'indépendance.—Réveillez, etc.

Hélas! bientôt l'ambition,
En s'appuyant sur l'imposture,
Osa de l'usurpation,
Méditer le plan et l'injure.—Réveillez, etc.

On vit des princes, des sujets,
Des opulens, des misérables,
On vit des maîtres, des valets,
La veille tous étaient semblables.—Réveillez, etc.

Du nom de lois et d'instituts
On revêt l'affreux brigandage;
On nomme crimes les vertus,
Et la nécessité pillage.—Réveillez, etc.

Hélas! vos généreux desseins,
Fils immortels de Cornélie,
Contre le fer des assassins
Ne peuvent sauver votre vie.—Réveillez, etc.

Et vous, Lycurgues des Français,
O Marat! Saint-Just! Robespierre!
Déjà de vos sages projets
Nous sentions l'effet salutaire;
Déjà le riche et ses autels,
Replongés dans la nuit profonde,
Faisaient répéter aux mortels:
Le soleil luit pour tout le monde.

Déjà vos sublimes travaux
Nous ramenaient à la nature :
Quel est leur prix ? les échafauds,
Les assassinats, la torture.—Réveillez, etc.

L'or de Pitt et la voix de d'Anglas
Ont ouvert un nouvel abîme :
Rampez ou soyez scélérats,
Choisissez la mort ou le crime.—Réveillez, etc.

D'un trop léthargique sommeil,
Peuples, rompez l'antique charme :
Par le plus terrible réveil,
Au crime heureux portez l'alarme.
Prêtez l'oreille à notre voix,
Et sortez, etc.

NOTA.—Ces chansons furent distribuées à la même époque, par
les soins du directoire secret.

[These songs were distributed at the same epoch by the care of
the Secret Directory.].

———

The following English lines comprise the substance,
and are, as near as may be, a literal version of the second
song :—

By tyrant codes enthralled, by knaves borne down,
Man stoops to man, and villains wear the crown :—
Where is the freeman's voice? the warrior's steel ?—
Shall we not stoutly fight as well as keenly feel ?
Awake! arise, at Liberty's command !—
Th'Aurora of our freedom is at hand,
And slavery's night is o'er, if we'll but bravely stand!

Oh Nature, or whatever power it be,
Which said to man, " *Be happy and be free !*"—
Say by what strange mischance thy laws o'erthrown,
Have yielded place to slavery and a throne?
Is there not *one* will dare assert the cause
Of outraged manhood, and thy broken laws?
How long shall man quail 'neath the despot rule
Of a usurper or a king-born fool?
Nations! arise, at Liberty's command,
Th'Aurora of your freedom is at hand,
And slavery's night is o'er if you'll but bravely stand!

In ancient times, when yet our race was young
Nor gold nor war the soul to madness stung,

Each in the land possessed an equal share,
No kingly luxury known, no gaunt despair;
Then peace and competence went hand in hand,
Unfear'd the assassin's knife, the foeman's brand—
These days are our's again if we'll but bravely stand!

In those bless'd days when man, of man the friend,
Nor yet had learn'd to borrow or to lend,
Nature on all alike her bounty poured,
No starving wretch was seen, no pampered lord—
Till fraud and priestcraft, by ambition led,
Taught man his kind to hate, his blood to shed;
Then princes, subjects, masters, serfs were known,
And shuddering Freedom fled before—a THRONE!
Then started into life the warrior's trade—
Then groan'd th' assassined sire, the ravished maid!
Pillage and murder still the steps pursued
Of *heroes*, glorying in the path of blood.
Then first were heard the ravings of despair,
And dying wretches rent with shrieks the air.
Nations! arise, at Liberty's command,
Th' Aurora of your freedom is at hand—
And slavery's night is o'er, if you'll but bravely stand!

Where is the difference 'tween the serf and peer?
Why meanly quail ye then with idiot fear?
Bring front to front the oppressor and oppressed—
Wealth cannot strength import, nor title steel the breast.
Lay on! lay on! the death sigh of the brave
Be our's and not the death-bed of the slave!
Nations! arise, at Liberty's command,
Th' Aurora of your freedom is at hand—
And slavery's night is o'er if you'll but bravely stand.

PIECE No. XIV.

A PRESSING WORD TO THE PATRIOTS

FRIENDS! —I did not intend addressing you to-day.
I interrupt a work that requires much time, in order to
address you a few urgent words in haste. Give ear to
them; they interest you exceedingly.

Truth triumphs. All the oppressors are pale. The
eyes of the people are opened by its friends. The army

sees also. The torrent of popular energy can be no
longer restrained by any dyke or bulwark. Our rulers
have perceived all this, and they have just got upon a
new tack, in order to escape the fall, the expectation of
which is our consolation and their despair.

Within the last ten or twelve days they have discovered that persecution and outrages against citizens of
the best character, were no longer efficacious arms in
their hands. They have substituted for them craft and
disgusting cajoleries. The ferocious wolves have transformed themselves into supple and cautious foxes. Be
not deceived by it; they are still and always the same
carnivorous animals; they have not changed their nature
nor their evil will. They caress you to-day, as it were,
with velvet paws; to-morrow they will devour you if they
can. Hear me as to the points upon which I wish to put
you on your guard.

The emissaries of the Talliens, the Legendres, the
Barrases, and those *honest* personages themselves, are
in a great flutter, and have all their irons at work to
make you fall into the most abominable of snares; they
take advantage of the dispositions you have shown
against all the culpable authors of your calamities,
amongst whom they have themselves figured in the first
rank; they have the impudence to pretend that *they* were
not amongst your oppressors, or, at least, they affect to
separate themselves from the crew of persecutors who
marched only as *they* ordered, and agreeably to *their*
instigations. They dare to insinuate that they are now
ready to constitute themselves avengers of the crimes
which they themselves committed, or caused to be committed! It is of importance to unmask their designs, to
show you the tendency of their views, and to point out
the new deep abyss they are digging beneath your feet;
but, antecedently, it is necessary to give you a clue to
their intrigues.

Aux-Fer, and the rest of that crew, have been
hugging a new set of knaves, of whose names we could
here give you the complete list; but for the present we
content ourselves with signalizing two of them, whose
acts have been most prominent. *Rich*.... and *Soul*....
(the latter calls himself a man of letters) have been for

the last few days employed in tampering with the groups
assembled near the Tuilleries. Admirably do they acquit
themselves of their mission, which is to excite popular
effervescence to an extreme point.   They there give out,
to whoever will hear them, that the two councils are,
without exception, composed of villains—that Barras
and Carnot are excellent Republicans, most anxious to
terminate the sufferings of the people, and to save the
country—that there has been, therefore, formed an infamous plot to assassinate them—that consequently, it is
the duty of the people to rally around them and their
friends, to arm without delay, and to sound the tocsin
(alarum bell).

A true Democrat, whom the emissary Rich.... had
set upon within the last few days, on the terrace of the
Tuilleries, in order to inoculate him with his collusory
ideas, was in the act of hearing Rich....'s objections
touching "the strange precipitation with which it was
sought to hurry on so important an affair;" when meanwhile they were interrupted by *Legendre*, of whom
Rich.... inquired the news of the day.   The butcher
of Prairial replied, that he did not understand how the
patriots could follow the instigations of the *Tribune of
the People*, who seemed to single out the best patriots,
such as Barras and Carnot, for his most furious invectives; that it was necessary to fall vigorously only upon
the acknowledged workers of mischief, such as *Isnard*
and his *clique;* that the patriots should unite to annihilate these men; but that the little errors and differences they had mutually to reproach one another
with, ought, for the sake of the common cause, to be
reciprocally forgotten, &c.

Close to where this affair took place, another syco-
phant asked a certain other Democrat if he had seen
such a man who possesses influence over a certain
quarter of Paris, hinting that something good was to be
communicated to him on the part of *Tallien;* and the
intriguer added—" You are a patriot; you are not an
" intruder amongst us; the mine must spring in a few
" days, the tocsin must be sounded; I am in quest of
" the man alluded to, to apprise him of what is pass-
' ing—"

The plot is well got up, the bait is not worse laid than so many others of which you have been the dupes and victims ; but could you possibly be duped on this occasion as on the former ones ? The intentions of the men who have never ceased to assassinate, starve, and load you with chains, are manifestly these.

In the first place, *to save their guilty heads*, upon which they see that the grand jury of the people, convinced of their unparalleled and countless crimes, is ready to execute the terrible sentence long since pronounced against them. They see no other means of accomplishing this than by feigning to throw themselves into the arms of the Democrats, whom they flatter themselves they will be able the more easily to captivate, by persuading them that the people is incompetent to work out its own salvation, without the aid of some of the parties in authority.

But through what means are we to suppose them desirous to effect the object of saving their heads ? What subsequent *intentions* are we to credit them for ? Have the patriots the simple good nature to suppose it will be by frankly serving the democracy, in order to expiate the infamy of having destroyed it by proceedings the most criminal, and to obtain from them a generous pardon on account of this reparation ? Are the patriots simple enough to believe that these hypocrites would divest themselves of power, of supremacy, and of the initiative, during, and after the revolutionary movement, with the view of living peaceably under simple democratic laws, and under the protection of a sacred amnesty, awarded them by an indulgent nation ? No, no ; that is not *their* plan ; they have no such intentions. The truth is, these oppressors have perceived that the principles of democracy predominate—that their throne is tottering—that they have lost all confidence—that the true defenders of the people possess that confidence entire—that, in short, the question now uppermost in the public mind is not whether this or that party is to succeed to power, but how the evils are to be remedied which the hypocrites have brought upon us. Nor must we be foolish enough to believe them, shou'd they even confess (which they do not) that they are willing to expiate their past wickedness by being themselves instrumental in terminating its horrid results. No; we must not suffer these odious beings even to take a musket and enter our lines as private soldiers. Were the people of France capable of acting otherwise towards them, it would be the basest people on earth; it would be ever after unworthy that a single individual of courage and wisdom should devote his faculties to the achievement of liberty.

Citizens! attend well to this truth. Fear not so much the Royalists in the senate; they are rather serviceable to us than otherwise. Whatever evil they may intend against us—we are on our guard against it; and as to their contest with the opposite party, *that* is useful to us. Whenever the rulers of a country form but a single party, they are always strongest, as against the people. The party of the people must put itself in train to vanquish, single-handed, both the Royalist party, whose idol is at Verona, and the Royalist party, whose idols are at the Luxembourg, without needing the assistance of one or the other. It would be folly to pretend to conceal from either our hostile intentions under pretence of disarming their vigilance. These intentions are long since known to them, and they have tried every means to neutralize and render them abortive. No longer able to defeat us by force or opinion, behold why they now resort to stratagem. But this last resource we will also triumph over. I oppose to them not masked but open batteries. The geese, the cacklers, the fools of the faction of *prudents* will say, perhaps, that it would be better policy to cover ourselves with some disguise. I say, it is absolutely necessary, and the time is come, that the mass of the sans-culotte army should see the camp, and that its existence can be no longer concealed from the enemy. It is no longer by surprise that we either can or wish to vanquish it—it is in a manner more worthy of the people—it is by open force. Far from us the vile pusillanimity which would persuade us that we can do nothing by ourselves, and that we shall always need a part of the government to be on our side. Governments make revolutions only for themselves—only that the governors may always govern. We, on the contrary, want a real revolution, that will

establish the perpetual happiness of the people on the
basis of true democracy.   Sans culottes! let us fling
from us all paltry ideas of mere animadversion against
certain men; it is for bread, for ease, for liberty, that we
have kindled the revolutionary flame.   Let us not suffer
ourselves to be imposed upon—let not our attention be
diverted from the real object which interests us.   I tell
you, I repeat it to you, it is an error to suppose that you
can effect nothing single-handed and by yourselves.
Never will there be anything great and worthy of the
people done, except by the people, and where there will
be only the people.   Make no movement, then, until
you see the men of the people move and appear.   Do
not fall into any trap; look not elsewhere for liberators;
recognise no other standard.   Do not allow yourselves
to be abused by that other sophism of the government
spies, who interpret the deceitful inductions of our enemies; they say, *they have their soldiers.*   They lie, the
rascals! they are our soldiers, not theirs.   They are ours
by their very institution, but they are still more so by
their actual dispositions.   Yes, the soldier will march
only *with* us, and *for* us.   So much the better that the
villains, who harass us, have collected a great army here.
Better still should they augment it; we shall be only the
stronger in consequence.   The seed has been sown; the
good doctrine has taken root amongst our enlisted
brethren, who, like us, are of the people, and who have
but the same cause that we have; tyranny deceives itself
again in changing them every hour from place to place.
The troops arriving to-day, receive lessons from those
who have been before them, and the troops that are
marched away only carry elsewhere the doctrines we
have inculcated, so that our popular " *poison* " takes
everywhere.   No, no! it is no longer in the power of
any inquisition, civil or military, to prevent our soldiers
and workpeople from reading writings which they devour
with avidity, and from which they imbibe the leaven of a
democratic contagion the most active and intoxicating.
People! behold the reason why your own party suffices
for your triumph; it is because we have *you* altogether
with us, and already a considerable portion of the *sans
culottes,* whom the usurpers vainly hoped to seduce

against you. Thus shall we all march united on the *people's day*, to a certain victory in the train, and under the sole direction of the *men of the people*, the moment they shall give us the signal that such happy day is arrived.

GRACCHUS BABEUF,
Tribune of the People.

PIECE No. XV.

THE INSURRECTIONAL COMMITTEE OF PUBLIC SAFETY TO THE PEOPLE.

Act of Insurrection.

EQUALITY.　　　　　　　　LIBERTY.
GENERAL HAPPINESS.

THE Democrats of France, considering that the oppression and misery of the people are at their height—that this state of tyranny and woe results from the acts of the existing Government;—

Considering that the numerous crimes of the governors have excited against them the daily-repeated and ever-unavailing complaints of the governed;—

Considering that the Constitution of the people, sworn to in 1793, was placed by the people under the safeguard of all the virtues; that, consequently, when the entire people has lost all its constitutional guarantees against despotism, it belongs to whatever virtues are most courageous, most intrepid, to take the initiative of insurrection, and to direct the emancipation of the mass;—

Considering that the Rights of Man, acknowledged at the same epoch (1793), prescribe to the entire people, and to each portion of it, as the most sacred of rights and the most indispensible of duties, *that* of rising against the Government which violates its rights, and that they direct every freeman to instantly put to death those who usurp the sovereignty;—

Considering that a faction of conspirators has usurped

the sovereignty by substituting its own particular will for
the general will, freely and legally expressed in the
primary assemblies of 1793, by imposing on the French
people (under the auspices of persecution and assassination directed against all the friends of liberty) an execrable code, called the Constitution of 95, in place of
the Constitution of 1793, which had been accepted with
so much enthusiasm ;—

Considering that the tyrannic code of 95 violates the
most precious of rights, in that it establishes distinctions
among the citizens, interdicts them the faculty of sanctioning the laws, of changing the Constitution, and of
assembling together ; limits their liberty in the choice of
public agents, and leaves them no guarantee against the
usurpation of governors ;—

Considering that the authors of this frightful code
have maintained themselves in a state of permanent
rebellion against the people, since they arrogated to
themselves, in contempt of the sovereign will, an authority which the nation alone could confide ; that they
have appointed themselves, either by their own act, or
by that of a handful of factious enemies of the people,
some, kings, under the disguised name of *directors*—
others, legislators, independent of, and irresponsible to
the people ;—

Considering that these oppressors, after having done
everything to demoralise the people; after having outraged, degraded, and proscribed the attributes and institutions of liberty and democracy; after having caused
the massacre of the best friends of the Republic, restored
and protected its most atrocious enemies, robbed and
exhausted the public treasury, sucked the national resources dry, totally discredited the republican currency,
effectuated the most infamous bankruptcy, delivered over
to the cupidity of the rich even the last ragged garments
of the poor, who, for nearly two years, have been slowly
perishing of hunger ; that, not content with so many
crimes, they have at length, by an unheard-of refinement
of tyranny, robbed the people of even the right of com-
plaining ;—

Considering that they have originated and favoured
plots to foster civil war in the western departments, in

s

deceiving the nation by a patched-up pacification, whose
secret articles stipulated conditions contrary to the will,
to the dignity, to the safety, and to the interests of the
French people;—

Considering, that more recently still, they have surrounded themselves with a band of foreigners, and that
the principal conspirators of Europe are at this moment
in Paris to consummate the last act of the counter-revolution;—

Considering that they have just disbanded and treated
with indignity such of the battalions which have had the
virtue to refuse being parties to their atrocious designs
against the people; that they have had the audacity to
send to trial those of our brave soldiers who had displayed
most energy against oppression; and that to this infamy
they have added the more execrable one of representing
their (the soldiers) generous resistance to the will of tyrants,
as being itself the work of Royalist inspiration!—

Considering that it would be difficult and unnecessarily
tedious to follow up and trace completely the populicidal
march of this criminal government, whose every thought,
whose every act is a felony against the nation; that the
proofs of all these treasons are traced in characters of
blood all over the Republic; that all the departments are
unanimous in invoking its repression; that it belongs to
that portion of the citizens in nearest contact to the
oppressors to attack oppression; that this portion is
accountable to the entire state for the safe protection of
liberty; and that too long a silence would render it an
accomplice of tyranny;—

Considering, in fine, that all the defenders of liberty are
prepared;—

After constituting themselves an insurrectional committee, they take upon their heads the responsibility, and
the initiative of the insurrection, and decree as follows:—

Art. 1. The people is in insurrection against tyranny.

2. The end of the insurrection is the re-establishment
of the Constitution of 1793, of liberty, of equality, and of
the happiness of all.

3. To day, and this very instant, the citizens, male
and female, shall proceed from all points in disorder, as
it may be, and without awaiting the rising of the neigh-

bouring quarters, whose populations they will carry along with them. They shall rally at the sound of the tocsin and trumpets, under the guidance of patriots to whom the Insurrectional Committee shall have confided banners bearing the following inscription :—

CONSTITUTION OF 1793.
EQUALITY.   LIBERTY.
GENERAL HAPPINESS.

Other banners shall bear these words :—

" When the Government violates the rights of the " people, insurrection is for the people, and for each " portion of the people, the most sacred of rights and " the most indispensable of duties !"

" Those who usurp the sovereignty ought to be put to " death by freemen."

The generals of the people will be distinguished by tri-cololoured ribands floating in striking profusion around their hats.

4. All the citizens shall repair with their arms, or wanting their arms, with any other offensive weapon, under the sole direction of the aforesaid patriots, to the *rendezvous*, or chief place of their respective arrondissements.

5. Arms of every sort shall be seized and carried off by the insurgents, wherever they find them.

6. The barriers and the course of the river shall be sedulously guarded; no person can quit Paris without a formal and special order of the Insurrectional Committee; there shall be free to enter Paris, only the carriers and conductors of eatables, to whom protection and surety will be given.

7. The people shall take possession of the national treasury, of the post-office, of the ministers' houses, and of every magazine, public or private, containing provisions, ammunition of war, or military stores.

8. The Insurrectional Committee of Public Safety orders the sacred legions encamped around Paris, who have sworn to die for equality, to support everywhere the efforts of the people.

9. The patriots of the departments, who are refugees

s 2

at Paris, and the brave destituted * officers, are invited to distinguish themselves in this holy contest.

10. The two Councils, and the Directory, usurpers of the popular authority, shall be dissolved. All the members composing them shall be immediately judged by the people.

11. All existing authority, ceasing in presence of that of the people, no pretended deputy, member of the usurping government, director, administrator, judge, officer, sub-officer of the national guard, or any public functionary whatever, shall exercise any act of authority, or give any order. Those found contravening this injunction shall be put to death on the spot. Every member of the pretended legislative body, or director found in the streets, shall be arrested and conducted forthwith to his ordinary post.

12. All opposition shall be instantly put down by force. The parties resisting shall be exterminated. Also shall be put to death those who will beat, or cause to be beat, the *generale ;* all foreigners, no matter of what nation, who shall be found in the streets; all the presidents, secretaries, and commandants of the Royalist conspiracy of Vendémiaire, who may dare to show their faces in public.

13. All envoys of foreign powers are ordered to remain in their domiciles during the insurrection; they are under the safeguard of the people.

14. Provisions of all sorts shall be brought to the people on the public places.

15. All the bakers will be in requisition to continue the baking of bread, which will be distributed *gratis* to the people : they shall be paid according to their invoices.

16. The people shall take no repose till after the destruction of the tyrannic government.

17. All the property of emigrants, of conspirators, and of all the enemies of the people, shall be distributed without delay amongst the defenders of the country and the unhappy poor. The poor of all the Republic shall be immediately accommodated with lodging and furniture in the houses of the conspirators. The effects belonging

---

* *Destitué* (in French) means deposed, or removed from office.

to the people in pledge at the pawn-offices shall be gratuitously restored on the spot. The French people adopts the wives and children of the brave fellows who shall have fallen in this holy enterprise ; the French people will feed and maintain them ; it will do the same towards their fathers and mothers, brothers and sisters, and all to whom the existence of the deceased was necessary. The proscribed patriots in exile throughout the Republic shall receive all suitable succours and means to enable them to return to the bosom of their families. They shall be indemnified for the losses they may have suffered. The war against domestic tyranny being that, which most opposes general peace, such of our gallant defenders as will prove their services in aiding to terminate it shall be free to return with arms and baggage to their firesides. They shall, moreover, be put in immediate enjoyment of the rational recompenses so long promised them. Those who may prefer continuing to serve the Republic shall also be immediately rewarded in a manner worthy of a great and free people.

18. All property, public and private, shall be placed under the safeguard of the people.

19. The care of terminating the Revolution, and of giving to the Republic liberty, equality, and the Constitution of 1793, shall be confided to a national assembly, composed of one democrat for each department, named by the insurgent people on the presentation of the Insurrectional Committee.

20. The Insurrectional Committee of Public Safety shall remain *en permanence* until the complete accomplishment of the insurrection.

PIECE No. XVI.

The Sans-Culotte People of Paris to the Legion of Police.

GENEROUS BROTHERS !—Your signal is heard, your conduct is approved, your firm resolve gives us joy. The moment is arrived for shivering the sceptres of the new

upstart tyranny? Has liberty ordained that the times in
which we live shall see the last of universal oppression?
The people is prepared.

No!—you will not desert us. No—you will not depart for the frontiers to have yourselves immolated beneath the steel of foreign slaves, the accomplices of our
slaves. Such is the fate intended for you. Our tyrants
have made a frightful compact with the miscreants we
have been six years combatting against. They have
stipulated to give them a holocaust offering of all the
faithful defenders of the people. Judging by your acts,
you, brothers, deserve to be amongst the first sacrificed.
You have espoused the interests of the people; you have
protested, with the people, against all the crimes of its
oppressors; you have shown that you would not become
part of its executioners, in presence of the bloody pre-
paratives marshalled around us by the assassins. Paris
blocked up—Paris threatened to be deluged in blood
and fire, because it complained of being, in common
with the rest of the Republic, starved, despoiled, famished, degraded; Paris, in short, under the yoke of
a handful of barbarian usurpers, is become for all men an
object of compassion and public interest. Dearest comrades!—it depends on you to save us, and to cover yourselves with glory. You can take the initiative against
the enemies of the people. You *will* take it. Your
friends, your brethren, your wives, your kinsmen and
parents, invoke you, that while you refuse to expose
yourselves to the massacre intended for you on the frontiers, you will not abandon them to another massacre
within those walls. Already have you made the accents
of truth to penetrate the ears and hearts of your encamped brethren. Your example will perfect their conviction. They will learn, *in despite* of all the watch-
words and instructions—in spite of all the interdictions
of their officers to prevent their inter-communication
with the citizens—that in the struggle of the people
against its governors, *it is the people that are in the
right.* They will feel that it is not the people they
ought to immolate. Let us make an appeal to these
brave fellows, and they too will come over to our side.
As to the people, it tells you, itself, that it is prepared.

Its leaders are about to give it the signal. It hears them; it is by the side of you. Its tyrants are dispersing—liberty reappears—abundance and prosperity lift their heads again—the Republic triumphs on all hands, and effectual measures are taken to render its re-establishment perpetual.

9th Floréal.

PIECE No. XVII.

Note to be added.

CONVINCED how important it is to completely baffle the Royalists, and to deceive them respecting our real intentions in the movement which is preparing, in order to prevent both them and the Government from employing against us, during the movement, their old proscriptive epithets of *terrorists, jacobins, seditionists, men of Prairial*, &c. I think we should all, from the outset, have chalked upon our hats—*Army of the people; down with the tyrants.*

Also, there shall be borne three sorts of banners, upon which will be the following inscriptions—*Army of the people; down with the tyrants; vengeance of the people.* This appears to me a capital expedient to make our very enemies subserve our designs. You may judge of it by the applauses given at the theatres to the words, *Tremble tyrants,* &c. When success shall have declared itself for the popular party, it will be then necessary to make a theatrical display of banners, as if descending from the clouds, and bearing the inscriptions, *Constitution of* 1793; *general happiness; victory of the people*, &c. In the midst of applauses, and of bravos (a hundred thousand times repeated), you will see the insurrection march instinctively to its natural destination.

Thus only can we flatter ourselves with being able to give to the efforts of all a simultaneous direction against the common enemy, to turn public indignation to proper

account, and to evade the opposition of the **Royalist**
faction, which might prove very injurious to us at the
commencement of the action.

PIECE No. XVIII.

Address to the Delegate from the Mountainist Committee.

You are aware, citizens, of the efforts of certain Democrats to recover the rights of the people; you are
aware that, in the midst of proscriptions and scaffolds,
we had courage and firmness enough to plead the
sacred cause of humanity, and that we have persevered
up to this moment in confronting all dangers, in order to
form an opposition party against tyranny.

At the epoch of Vendémiaire, we emerged from our
dungeons (where we deserved enough from tyranny to
be buried alive for ever) only to attack it anew; the
sacred fire was then extinct; the mass of the people was
royalized; a portion of the patriots subdued, worn out,
degenerated in the prisons, found themselves too happy
in their enlargement to think of aught else; nay, previously to their discouragement, they were disposed to
make terms with an atrocious and usurped Government
—to serve it even, and to accept its plans and conditions. If some few men, still worthy of liberty, represented to them the dishonour and disgrace of such a
compromise, the greater number excused themselves by
something still more disgraceful; they said, they had a
mental reservation, and that if they fraternized with
their enemies, it was only the better to surprise their confidence, so that, when strong enough, they might be
able to overwhelm and extinguish them.

Such conduct was unpalatable to us. We desired to
infuse a sort of chivalrous honour into the war of virtue
against crime. Front to front we attacked the latter;
we gained over the waverers; we induced the Republicans to play a part more worthy of them, we restored

them to their primitive dignity; we unroyalized the
people also; we disabused them of the false opinion by
which the villains had induced them to believe that their
then deplorable condition was the result of the Republican system; we succeeded in demonstrating to them,
that, on the contrary, it was the result of the atrocious
reminiscences of royalism, and of the decay of the Republican edifice, which, if it had been completed, would
procure them the *maximum* of happiness. Well, we
had the advantage of bringing about the end sought by
this tuition—that of disposing the patriots and the mass
of the people to overthrow the existing tyrannic Government, in order to substitute for it one more worthy of
the great Revolution which the French have had the
courage to undertake.

We have felt that revolutionary journals are not sufficient to conduct us to our end. It is now several months
since we found it to be our duty to form ourselves into a
committee of several courageous Democrats; to organize
ourselves insurrectionally, and to organize around us all
the elements necessary to consummate a successful insurrection.

We have done much to effect that purpose. We
think we have brought together the greater part of the
requisite materials, and made nearly all the arrangements
essential to such object.

We have information as to the places where ammunition and arms are to be found, and as to the means of
getting possession of them.

We have lists of the patriots; of all the men of character in Paris; we have the means of effecting a simultaneous rising of the people at the first signal.

We have more—we have an organization of civil and
military agents fully prepared to act. We have printed
at length the manifesto of our insurection.

In short, the insurrection was ready to burst forth,
when certain information we received, and observations
we caused to be made, led us to some serious reflections.

It is our duty to address you in perfect frankness.
We had resolved, in making this insurrection, to dis-
pense with everything which had belonged to the different
National Assemblies. Strangers to all factions, working

s 5

only for the people, we had considered it to be of prime importance to keep aloof from our new Government everything which might, by reviving former passions or prejudices, prove prejudicial to the people's complete regeneration.

You will excuse us, citizens, for expressing to you certain truths somewhat strongly—you will ascribe them to our extreme frankness. We upbraided the Mountainists with not having fully discharged their duty in the mission entrusted to them by the people. We reproached them for not having died in support of the people's rights rather than submit to see them trampled on. We were further apprehensive that in calling them once more to the helm of affairs, we should witness the revival of quarrels and distracting recriminations—the natural fruits of the old points of dispute—the leaven of which still exists in the heads of the majority of them. In a word, we persuaded ourselves that we could do *all* and *better* without them than with them.

We fancy, however, that within the last few days, we have acquired, if not a positive proof, at least a very strong presumption of the contrary, and besides, we are tender how we risk the ruin of the country. Several overtures have been made to us, in which we have been told that, labouring on your side in the same views and objects as ourselves, you are most anxious to form a coalition with us for the common object.

We are determined to accept this proposition, and the more readily, inasmuch as we have been fearful lest your measures and ours might reciprocally clash with and mar one another; and lest (since we must speak it) you might obstruct our projects at the decisive moment, and lest, on the arrival of different companies of the people's defenders on the ground, they might feel no disposition to harmonize together, but, on the contrary, add a civil war, amongst themselves, to all the others which the Republic has to sustain against all its different species of enemies. A calamity such as that, and all the consequences likely to result from it, have filled us with alarm. We have resolved to prevent them, by accepting your proffered coalition. We have invited you, for the purpose of transmitting to you this decision. Most desirous are we that it may prove agreeable to you, and that we may come to a good mutual understanding; that we may effectively concentrate and combine our means to save the people, and rescue it from tyranny; let us forget everything in order to attain this happy end.

PIECE, No. XIX.

The Directory of Public Safety to the Agents of the Twelve Arrondissements.

CITIZENS!—Never was conspiracy holier than ours, whether we regard its motives or its end. Neither was there ever a conspiracy whose agents showed themselves so worthy of the confidence of which they were made the sacred depositaries. Never did conspirators labour in secret against a perfidious Government so long and so successfully as we have done. In vain has its restless vigilance racked itself, and exhausted every resource of inquisition the most atrocious; not one material proof has it yet been able to obtain against us.

This result does honour to our choice of you, and gives us the strongest guarantee for a confidence still greater, if possible, than that already reposed in you. With men of your stamp, we need to practice no reserve. What is engraven in our hearts ought to be equally familiar to you as to ourselves, and we owe you the truth complete and entire.

For some days past our correspondence with you is less active on our part. The tone of it is less firm, less decided, more vacillating, than it has hitherto been. A sort of negligence, of languor, of incertitude, must have been visible to you in our movements. At what a time, however!—at a time when, apparently, our vigour ought to have been redoubled, whilst the patriots and the mass of the people called aloud for battle, and that circumstances appeared to offer them many chances of gaining it. This communication will put you in a condition to pronounce whether our conduct is not justifiable not-

withstanding.   If we cannot justify it, it is the duty of
you, and of the patriots you direct, to throw all the
blame on us, and even to punish us for the non-fulfil-
ment of our mission.

We might content ourselves with telling you, that in
considering our means of attack, we had well-grounded
reasons for believing them inadequate, and that we,
therefore, felt it our duty to suspend a patriotic outbreak, which might only prove the signal of extermination to the Democrats ; and the more strongly, because
the terrible lessons of Germinal and Prairial ought to be
constantly before the eyes of Republicans, and that only
one more similar lesson was required to ruin them for
ever.

But this is not the only consideration that stopped us.
We know that in an insurrection we must be daring—
we must be (to so speak) more than rash.   Behold
the principal cause of the apparent slowness on our
side.

You know we are all desirous that this insurrection
should be the last—that it should, in fact, constitute the
happiness of the people.   It was accordingly our duty
to take every precaution capable of assuring this result.
We have wished that the manifesto proclaiming it
should guarantee as the first benefit—as a simple preliminary step to the state of felicity we propose for the
people ; we have willed, we say, that this manifesto
should guarantee, in the first place, *the distribution
amongst the unhappy poor of the property of all the
conspirators ;* that in the next, it should declare that
the unhappy poor would be lodged, and *provided with
furniture, in the houses of the conspirators,* &c. &c.
In order that these, and other equally advantageous
changes, may be executed, we must assure ourselves
that the power, in passing from the hands of the villains
who now hold it, shall fall into those of true, pure, and
absolute Democrats—of men of the people—of the
people's friends, *par excellence.*   How are they to get
hold of this power ?   Behold the difficulty which has
stopped, and still stops, us.   It is the discussion of this
ticklish point which has forced us to let several opportunities be lost, which might otherwise have been pre-

cious to us, and probably determined in our favour the success of the battle we have to fight.

. To gain the battle. is nothing, unless we can make sure of profitting by the victory. Behold why we had printed a first manifesto to the number of thirty thousand copies, in which we had laid it down that the Directory of Public Safety would substitute for the existing tyrannical authority a national assembly, composed of one member for each department, chosen from amongst the most energetic and tried Democrats, of whom the Directory would itself furnish the list to be approved by the people. This assembly, acting in concert with the Insurrectional Directory, would have been charged to finish the Revolution, and to assure the well-being of all.

Numerous considerations subsequently led us to believe that we should augment our strength and chances of success by recalling the proscribed deputies of the old Mountain, who had no share in violating the Constitution of 1793, and who owed to violence alone the loss of their seats in the Assembly. We considered that, in the eyes of the democratic party, these Mountainists constituted the legal authority, which the people had not superseded, and which, consequently, did then exist. We did not, however, dissemble that this section of the Conventionalists was almost as culpable and ruinous to our cause as the rest; in the first place, for having, after the 9th Thermidor, permitted and taken part in the counter-revolutionary reaction; for having allowed the democratic edifice to be demolished piecemeal, and without opposition; for not having sounded the alarm on the 5th Messidor, when the infamous Boissy D'Anglas appeared in the Tribune, and obtained the adoption of his populicidal code; for having afterwards had the cowardice not to protest aloud against this execrable treason;* in fine, for having had the egregious baseness to accept (the greater part of them) missions from this government of usurpation and oppression. But *powerful reasons, which we will hereafter explain to you and to the people, had obliged us to close our eyes for a moment to these circumstances,* and to make great sacrifices of feeling, in

---

* These three latter imputations, thus generalised, appear to me exaggerated.

order to secure the aid of men, without whom we felt it would be perhaps impossible to rescue the country from the unbearable slavery it endures. We had come, then, to the resolution to make use of them, but we had, at the same time, taken measures to secure the people against refalling under a new tyranny in their hands. We had agreed to re-establish the less corrupt remnant of the Convention—that is to say, the proscribed party (to the number of about 68 members); and to raise a counterpoise to their ambition by uniting to them a new body, composed of one Democrat from each department, and whose election, made by us and the people in insurrection, would present an opposition-front of more than one hundred Democrats of the most energetic and decided stamp; moreover, to retain, *up to the moment when the entire people should be placed in secure possession of tranquility and prosperity,* the title and authority of Insurrectional Committee of Public Safety.

To this effect had we stipulated with the ex-Mountainists; they had accepted all our conditions, and promised to aid us with all their means. We had, in consequence, printed 50,000 copies of a fresh manifesto, and were taking measures to put it in immediate execution. Would you believe it, citizens? These Conventionalists have altered their mind, and have come to tell us that they will give the patriots no guarantee against their foreseen tyranny; they have come to tell us that they would no longer consent to the adjunction to their body of one Democrat from each department—that is to say, they demand the destruction of one despotism only to put another in its place—to overthrow the existing oppression in order to set up their own !

In support of their pretensions they urge the most wretched sophisms, and they count as nothing a single reason which we consider supreme—it is, that we desire to subvert the dominion of robbers, *only that we may the better establish that of the people on a durable foundation.*

Behold, my friends, a frank explanation of the causes of our delay. We are still at the same point. These honest Mountainists hold us in check, and, whether from ambition or pride, they seem to care little if, whilst they.

are disputing about terms, the country is exposed to eternal perdition. It is unfortunate, we repeat, that circumstances, which we cannot just now explain to you, place us in the condition of not being able to dispense with them. The conclusion of this letter is to inform you that if we can, we shall, nevertheless, dispense with them, and that if we cannot, we must only direct the people in such manner as to prevent the evil which they (the Mountainists) might still cause us; in a manner, to oppose to their ambition, in despite of them, the counterpoise they reject.

The people accuses us of inactivity. How lamentable that we cannot apprise them, as we do you, of what obstructs us ! Our popular writers could not do it without compromising matters of the last importance. In this position—a most painful one for us—do you at least undeceive the patriots, not by transmitting to them all the particularities which we have just now communicated in exclusive confidence to you, but by assuring them that their leaders merit their continued trust, and by exhorting them to be patient, and to sustain their energy, which, in one way or another, will be released in a very few days from further restraint.

Die or vanquish is the word. Better, far better, to perish in a glorious struggle than to await assassination in one of the thousand ways which our tyrants employ, and will employ against us.

Wait, then, in steady expectation of the decisive moment. Be not alarmed one way or the other—whether you will see the remnant of the Mountain ranged on our side, or otherwise; but bear in mind that one of the most important instructions is to surround the Insurrectional Committee with a great mass of popular force at the moment when it may present itself at the sitting of the resuscitated Convention to make known the people's pleasure, to the end of assuring the happy effects of the insurrection; as also to assure what the then assembled people will insist on, and expect, at the hands of the new representation (to be added to the skeleton of the Convention), in order to effectually accomplish the regeneration we have in view.

P.S.—Inform us immediately whether you have prepared the standards; it is a point of detail, but a very essential one.

N.B.—On the 18th, at nine in the evening.—We learn this moment that the Mountainists give way to the pressing arguments we have so repeatedly plied them with. They consent definitively to all we ask; accordingly, we proceed not to lose a moment. The conclusion of our letter relative to the marching of the people *en masse,* in the train of the Insurrectional Committee—this conclusion, we repeat, *holds always,* and the measure it demands is most particularly recommended to you.

Paris, 18th Floréal, Year IV. of the Republic.

PIECE No. XX.

LIBERTY.   EQUALITY.

GENERAL HAPPINESS, OR DEATH.

The Author of the Letter of Franc-Libre to his Republican Brothers of the Executive Directory.

BROTHER REPUBLICANS!—I have received, with inexpressible pleasure, the instructions and commission of secondary agent, which your confidence has entrusted to me, through the medium of our brother, D. T. H. I hope soon to justify the opinion you have conceived of me; if not by my talents, at least by my zeal, my constancy, my courage, and, above all, my discretion.

To the particular knowledge I have of Paris, where I have resided eight years, I unite that, more valuable still, of the military spirit, which I have studied in all its bearings, as a Government agent, during seven years, and essentially during the campaigns of the present war. It is in consequence of this practical experience that I have felt it my duty to draw up the following reflections, which I submit to your wisdom.

It is a real delusion to suppose that the same stimulants which operated the insurrection of the military corps in 89, can be still used with effect to work a new insurrection now. The machine has acquired a new form; we shall, therefore, require a new combination of springs to put it in motion. I will explain myself.

Under the monarchic regime, the soldier was less a slave than he is now-a-days, it is true; but he knew that he was a slave, because the contrary was never pretended to him, and because his officers neglected no means to remind him of it; the immense distance there was between them and him made the latter too acutely feel his degradation. The consequence was, that in 1789 the soldier embraced the popular cause, far less from love of liberty and equality, of which he could then have only a confused idea, than from the inveterate hatred he bore towards his officers—a hatred whose explosion was terrible, in proportion as it had been long pent up. This hatred, this leaven, was then, if not the only one, at least the most powerful spring which moved our armies to insurrection; and this truth is too evident to be contested.

To-day the case is altogether different; except in the superior grades alone, the great mass of officers is composed of men formerly privates, who have only their pay to live upon, which is reduced, for a chief of battalion, to about eight effective sous per day, which obliges the major part of them, captains and others, to eat at the same mess with the privates, and consequently to contract the most intimate familiarity with them.

This equality of misery between the soldier and his officer produces a friendship, an attachment, and a mutual confidence the reverse of what existed before 89. The result is, that the soldier, accustomed, like all men, to judge of his condition by comparing it with that of others, finds, in respect of his officers, too small a difference between them and him to be envious or jealous; and the officer, who is fooled by the hope of an approaching better lot, makes the private participate in this chimerical expectation, which mutually consoles and sets both to sleep in a sort of lethargic stupor. Besides, the existing civil state offers to the majority of military men a still worse condition than their present one, as foot soldiers—a circumstance which, in no small degree, contributes to keep them servilely under the yoke.

But, it will be said, how is it that amongst the officers,

who are not all automatons, there are not some few to
open the eyes of their comrades? How! the reason is
simple; all whom real love of liberty, and that alone,
had induced to take arms, have, as far as they were
able, withdrawn from the service since the 9th Thermidor
—that is to say, since the overthrow of the cause they
had undertaken to defend. The impossibility of retiring
had made some still remain; but the Executive Directory, which will have no soldiers not essentially slaves,
has made these latter retire, by its decree of the 6th
instant, on the new organization of the army. The result
must, therefore, be that we shall have henceforward for
officers, only those vile beings destitute of fortune, of
talents and resources, who, moreover, grown old in
slavery, will be incapable of disobeying, through fear of
losing their epaulettes, which they regard as the *ne plus
ultra* of their possible good fortune; only those creatures, in short, who, under the reign of kings, thought
themselves honoured in carrying worsted lace on their
sleeves, and in the privilege of striking the privates with
the flat of their swords. Behold a just description of
the officers who alone are relished by the existing
Government.

As to the soldiers in general, they are no longer those
ardent defenders of liberty we had in 1792 and 1793.
The major part of those brave fellows have fallen on the
bed of honour; the mass of what remain is composed
of country recruits, who serve liberty as convicts serve at
the galleys. In a battalion of four hundred men you can
seldom find forty privates who know anything of reading
and writing. The youth of our towns, who are somewhat better informed, have almost all contrived to escape
from the service. The only aspiration of most of the
soldiers (who, ridiculously enough, are called *volunteers*)
is to return in all speed to their firesides; and I can
vouch for it, there are thousands of them who care so
little about the Revolution, that they would willingly
barter the Republic for one of their village-cakes. But
to make amends, we have, on the other hand, about a
third, who, being soldiers by trade, and destined to be so,
no matter under what regime, are fit instruments for any
and every purpose, when one knows how to employ

them ; of these the greater part are fool-hardy *hot-brains*
who always carry along the timid and apathetic by their
ascendant audacity. To put these men in motion, it is
not fine or long speeches that are wanted; wine, and
the hope of pillage, are sufficient. These are what they
best understand, and without them you must expect nothing. The Convention knew right well the virtues of
this recipe, and right well it used it on the 13th Vendémiaire.

The cavalry, in general, is of the class I have just
described to you, more especially the dragoons, hussars,
and chasseurs.

After these observations, I proceed to trace the means
which, in my opinion, it would be expedient to employ
to operate the general resurrection desired.

1st, To vigorously undermine the generals and their
staffs, but to spare the subaltern officers. 2dly, To provoke, if not the disorganization of the forces, at least the
utmost possible relaxation of their discipline, in order the
better to operate their dissolution afterwards, if necessary.
3dly, To speak at once of pillaging the rich, and of
absolute disbanding (you will easily know how to evade
your promises afterwards, as circumstances turn out);
not, however, to speak too much of absolute equality,
for their chiefs (Chouans as they are) have long since
fortified the minds of the soldiery against that system, to
the degree that they not only deem it impossible, but in
general think it a certain mark whereby to recognise the
Royalists. This will appear strange, but it is not the less
true notwithstanding. And 4th, and lastly, when the
grand day of operation arrives, it would, in my opinion,
be of most essential use to establish balls or dancing
parties in the tea-gardens in the vicinity of the barracks,
whither the soldiers might be attracted, and then, by
plying them with *lush*, we might artfully work up their
spirits to the proper pitch of exaltation.

These reflections, brother Republicans, I offer you in
the way of consultation. If you find my opinions worthy
of adoption, I pray you to let me know it. I mean to
occupy myself for the next few days with a work which
I shall entitle, *A Dialogue between Jambe-de-bois*
(wooden-leg) *and Franc-Libre*. This dialogue will

turn upon the details of the misery and actual degradation of the soldier, compared with the lot he enjoyed in 1792. This work (to be written in the true soldier slang) will be immediately followed (so far as leisure will permit me) by another, entitled, *Reply of La Terreur to Franc-Libre*.

I have read and re-read your instruction, and I shall read it again, in order to imbibe its spirit, and to follow it *punctually*.*

I salute you fraternally.

26th Germinal, Year IV.

PIECE No. XXI.

Franc-Libre to the Secret Directory, &c. &c.

FOR three decades (thirty days) I had laboured in vain to find a brother amongst my comrades of the camp of Grenelle. I already began to despair of success, when a lucky chance procured me one who is of the sort to soon procure me other and more substantial ones.

Here is the fact.

I passed some hours yesterday after dinner drinking over a bottle with Montion (that is his name) lieutenant of my battalion (a man of oratorical and military abilities, and an old Flemish soldier.) I had long before surmised that his principles were good, and it was to sound him that I took him aside. After a long talk on politics in general, and after making him drink enough to make him speak (for he is naturally very discreet), he owned to me, in that sort of heartfelt effusion which is a certain sign of frankness, that he had never ceased to be a Democrat; but that he had lost the hope of seeing the Republicans so soon lift their heads again, and that, in consequence, he, and several of his old Flemish friends, making a virtue of necessity, affected to appear Government-men.

---

* This letter is by the traitor Grisel.—[What an accomplished miscreant!—BRONTERRE.]

I seized this opportunity to arouse his courage; and avowing to him that I professed the same political creed as himself, I gave him to understand that I knew, for a positive fact, that more than forty thousand sans-culottes were ready to rise, and that they would have already overthrown the tyrants, had they not apprehended the finding themselves in the necessity of combatting us— us, soldiers of the Government. I added, that everything presaged an immediate insurrection notwithstanding, and that to a dead certainty we should be victimized, like the Swiss on the 10th of August. I said no more, but that sufficed to produce an understanding between us. 1st, That he would see, to-day, three of his old friends, whom he knew at bottom, and would engage them to join him in preparing the troops to second the people at the decisive moment; he will enable me to know his friends, without letting them know me; he will tell them (an enssential point) and assure them that there are already three hundred gained over, but that it is agreed that they shall be known to one another only in parties of four and four, in order to avoid the effects of treason; At a rough guess, the number may mount up to fifteen or twenty, of whom three only are officers (for it is the least accessible grade.) When this little nucleus is formed, I shall get transmitted to each of them about a thousand francs in assignats to gain the soldiers, and to spread insubordination. The way I shall get this money (for money, I take it, is the grand lever) is this—1st, I have in the hands of one of my brothers, at Abbeville, thirty-five thousand livres in assignats; these will soon be here, for a letter is already despatched for them. 2d, I have a cousin-german, named Ponticourt, a notary in the street *Sainte-Croix de. la Bretonnerie*, whom I rarely see, because he is very rich, and consequently a great royalist; he has often offered to advance me money to equip me better than I am now equipped, for, as he says, I have more the air of a sans-culotte than of a captain; I have always despised his offers, as I do his person, without however breaking or quarrelling with him, out of a certain regard to his father, &c. &c. I will go find this cousin—I will tell him that I have just got a place in the War-office—and will ask him to lend me ten

thousand francs to equip myself, a thing he will jump to
do for me.*

17th Floréal.

PIECE, No. XXII.

THIS piece is the same as Piece XV., except the following modifications. Between the fourth and fifth
Considering, read as follows :—

" Considering that the National Convention has never
" been dissolved; that it was only dispersed by violence
" and by the tyrannic will of a counter-revolutionary fac-
" tion; that it still exists of right; that it could not be re-
" placed, unless by a legislative body, freely elected by
" the people, and, consequently, according to its demo-
" cratic Constitution."

Between Articles 10 and 11, read the following Article,
which becomes the 10th :—

" The Convention will immediately re-assemble, and
" resume its functions."

The numbers of all the following Articles augment by
an unit. At the end of Article 11, which becomes the
12th, add these words :—

" The members of the Convention will be recognised
" by a particular sign; it will be that of a red envelope
" around the form of the hat."

In place of Article 19th, which becomes the 20th,
read what follows :—

" On account of the void which will take place in the
" national representation, in consequence of the expulsion
" of the usurpers of the national authority; and by reason
" of the actual impossibility of resorting with effect to
" the primary assemblies, for a choice of representatives
" worthy of the people's confidence, the National Con-
" vention shall forthwith unite to itself one member for
" each department, taken from amongst the most decided
" Democrats, and especially amongst those who shall have

---

* This letter is also by the traitor Grisel, who wrote it after
having given information of the projects of the Democrats.

" most actively concurred in the overthrow of tyranny.
" The list of them will be presented by the delegates of
" that portion of the people which shall have taken the
" initiative of the insurrection."

PIECE No. XXIII.

PROJET.

EQUALITY.   LIBERTY.
GENERAL HAPPINESS.

THE Insurrectional Committee of Public Safety, considering that the people has long been wheedled by vain
promises, and that it is time at length to provide effectively for its own well-being—sole end of the Revolution :

Considering that the majestic insurrection of this day
ought for ever to destroy poverty—perpetual source of
all sorts of oppression—decrees as follows :—

Art. 1. When the insurrection is over, the needy citizens, who are actually ill-lodged shall not return to their
ordinary dwellings, but shall be forthwith installed in the
houses of the conspirators.

2. The furniture of the aforesaid rich shall be immediately used to furnish comfortable accommodation to
the sans-culottes.

3. The Revolutionary Committees of Paris are charged
to take all the necessary measures for the prompt and
punctual execution of the present decree.

PIECE, No. XXIV.

FRAGMENT.

Draught of a Decree concerning the Popular Judgment.

THE Insurrectional Committee of Public Safety—
Considering that the punishment of faithless delegates,
and of the usurpers of the national sovereignty, is the first

duty which the insurgent section owes to the entire people ;—

Considering that this punishment ought to be inflicted in such manner as to strike terror into traitors only, and to remove from the enemies of equality all pretext for calumniating the Parisian people ;—

Decrees as follows :—

Art. 1. The usurpation and tyranny of the members of the two councils, and of the Executive Directory, are evident. The law* punishes with death the usurpers of the popular sovereignty.

2. A commission, appointed by the insurgent people, sits in judgment on the aforesaid individuals.

3. This commission conducts its proceedings in presence of the people ; after having heard the Insurrectional Committee, or the accuser named by it, it pronounces *whether there are grounds for recommending the delinquent to the mercy of the people.*

4. The insurgent people convened by sections, and in the form to be pointed out, accords or refuses the mercy demanded.

5. Such and such citizens....actual members of the two councils, are worthy of the people's confidence; they are placed under its special protection.

6. For the purpose of accelerating the punishment of traitors, each agent of arrondissment names and presents to the acceptation of the assembled people four citizens per section.

7. The commission is divided into six sections ; each section pronounces to the number of twenty-two members. Others replace the absent ; the oldest presides ; the composition of each section is decided by lot.

8. ....(Left blank.)

* Article 27 of the Declaration of Rights of 1793.

PIECE, No. XXV.

The Secret Directory to the Agents.

ALL the steps are taken, the measure of our tyrants' crimes is full to overflowing ; *we must rise !*

Here are the orders and instructions to which we desire you to conform strictly :—

1. To-morrow morning, at....o'clock, you will cause the tocsin to be rung in all the sections of your arrondissements, and as many trumpets as you can possibly procure, to be sounded in the streets. The general-in-chief will send you some, after the insurrection commences, if he can take possession of the place where they are deposited. It were desirable that the platoons, or, at least, the arrondissements, should be preceded, as they march, by sound of trumpet.

2. At the same instant you will cause the manifestoes we send you, to be placarded and spread profusely; and you will make the mass of the people rise by means of your agents whom you should have previously apprised.

3. The Directory has nominated the following citizens to be the people's generals during the insurrection—to wit, &c. &c. You will cause them to be recognised— first, by the subalterns whom we have chosen, and afterwards by the entire people, and you will see that their orders be punctually followed.

4. You will find herein annexed the list of citizens of your respective arrondissements, whom, agreeably to the information transmitted by you, we have deemed most competent to lead the people to the conquest of its rights. Each of them shall command one of the platoons into which the people is to be divided ; the citizen appointed as chief, shall command the arrondissement ; the sub-chiefs will command the sections.

5. You will immediately apprise the chiefs of arrondissements to whom you will make known the names of the generals they are to obey, and you will enjoin them at the same time to apprise the sub-chiefs to hold themselves in readiness, without telling them anything more :

T

the same intimation shall be given to the commanders of platoons in whom you can fully rely; the rest shall be apprised only at the moment of rising. You are at liberty not to employ such commanders of platoons as you may have reason to suspect or doubt.

6. You will consign to the chiefs, sub-chiefs, and commanders of platoons, the standards referred to in the Manifesto.

7. You will order them to take immediate possession (and at any cost or price) of the arms and ammunition which may be found at the adjutants' houses and at the chief stations of the sections.

8. You will make all the cannoneers that may offer themselves, to muster in a body, that they may be ready to execute the orders of the generals.

9. You will make choice of energetic patriots, to whom you will confide the business of haranguing and electrifying the people. You will, at the same time, turn to account the pathetic and persuasive eloquence of the women, whom you will direct; as we have already told you in our preceding instructions, towards the soldiers, to whom they will present civic crowns, while they exhort them (by all the powerful considerations they know so well how to employ) to mingle and amalgamate with the ranks of the people.

10. From the instant the effervescence begins, you will encourage it by causing the report to be spread, that the camps of Grenelle and of Vincennes have already ranged themselves on the people's side. It is necessary, that in fraternising with the people, the soldiers should mingle in the ranks of the sans-culottes, and that they should neither march in bodies, nor under the directions of their officers.

11. You will order the chiefs and commanders to seize, or disperse all persons attempting to rally to the orders of the Government; and under the command of the officers of the National Guard. All warrants, ordonnances, or messengers bearing orders from any existing authority whatever, shall be stopped and arrested.

12. You will be careful to follow and rally the mass of your arrondissements; you will set the example of devotion and courage; and you will render us an account

every quarter of an hour, by expresses, of the state of the insurrection.

13. Should the generals order the mass of your arrondissement to divide itself, you will follow the larger division, and you will confide the surveillance of the remainder to some zealous citizen, whose name you will forthwith transmit to us, and whom you will order likewise to send us expresses every quarter of an hour.

14. You will communicate all your instructions to whatever sans-culotte most deserves your confidence, that he may replace you in case any accident should happen to you personally.

15. You will order (on our part) three members of the revolutionary committees of each section of your arrondissement, who were in activity on the 9th Thermidor, and who have preserved themselves most incorrupt, to resume their functions at the first sound of the tocsin. Failing these, you will choose other patriots, whom you will charge to take, in concert with us, all the requisite measures for executing the Insurrectional Act; above all, they must occupy themselves with the articles concerning the bakers, and the refreshments to be furnished to the people.

16. You will also order them to forthwith put in requisition the horses, mules, and vehicles necessary for the transport of provisions, ammunition, and the wounded. In taking possession of the magazines of flour, you will be careful to establish guards to watch them, and to secure to the bakers, in the vicinity, a continued supply.

17. The instant the insurrection begins you will send us (to remain near us) ten armed and resolute sans-culottes of your arrondissment; they will serve to carry orders, and in the last extremity we will bury ourselves beside them under the ruins of liberty.

18. The Insurrectional Directory will hold its sittings at ....

19. It will instal the National Convention immediately after the insurrection at .... You will make known its existence to the people.

20. You will see that the orders of the generals, for guarding the barriers, be punctually executed; and you will be particularly vigilant that the bridges be guarded,

and that all inter-communication be cut off between the existing authorities.

21. You will take advantage of the first moment of victory, to make the people of each arrondissement repair to us *en masse*, that they may concur in the presentation of the list of Democrats to be added to the National Convention, and to support the popular and regenerating laws which will be proposed by us on the spot, and drawn up in such a manner as not to leave a single poverty-stricken citizen in the state.

PIECE No. XXVI.

FRAGMENT

(Of the Draught of an Address to the Victorious People).

TRIUMPHANT PEOPLE!

CITIZENS!—If to command the interest of his audience, the subject of an orator's address should contain matters of the highest importance, never did orator deserve to be listened to with more attention than I am about to experience. I implore this attention at your hands. I beg it, and desire to prepare you for it beforehand, happy people! in the name of this blessed day, which now shines upon us. I would seek to augment it by intimating that the things I have to address you on, are more important still than the sublime conquest you have just achieved. In short, if confidence in him who speaks, and in those in whose name he speaks, can augment the degree of application in one's auditors, I fancy that I do not prejudice my claims on your attention when I announce that at this moment you hear speak the organ of the Insurrectional Committee of Public Safety. · · ·

People once more free! people unfettered and victorious! abandon yourselves to unconstrained transports; *your masters are no more!* The time is passed when in your presence, and while they treated of your liberty, your lives, your dearest interests, they wished to make a vile automaton of you. We do not ask you—*we* do not—to give any signs of approbation or of disapprobation. Sovereign people! if we betray you—if henceforward our words were also (like the rest of your deceivers) to be only the forerunners of our perfidy and crimes—in the name of our country, and of liberty, do not suffer us to finish them; instantly, on the spot, rebuke us; punish us!

Again I deem it suitable to my exordium, people of France, to declare to you here who the members are of this Insurrectional Committee of Public Safety, in whose name I address you. Here are their names . . . .

France! it is thy universal self that hearest me! And you, my auditors, who, with us, compose her first liberators, I have promised you, as well as her, to speak of matters worthy of this great day—of matters more interesting than even the distinguished triumph it has shone upon. I will state and propose things which will guarantee the people against ever losing the fruits of this triumph.

It is ever to the people I address myself; I still see only the people here. The Insurrectional Act makes mention of a representation; such representation does not yet exist, since it is not yet recognized. It does not as yet exist, since the people, still in insurrection, continues to exercise its rights and power undelegated—since all other power disappears in its (the people's) presence. A representation does not as yet exist, because the fruits of the insurrection are not yet gathered in, nor even assured to the people. Citizens, take effective advantage of this circumstance. Let no old juggling trick illude you. It is you who are here. I see no senate here; it is, consequently, to you, to you alone, I am going to address myself; and I repeat, it is important—of sovereign importance—that you give me all your attention. The moment is precious—it is unique—it will never again arrive. On the use we are about to make of it may depend our lot for ever.

[*The remainder of this address was either lost, or probably not completed.*—BRONTERRE.]

PIECE No. XXVII.

PROCLAMATION TO THE SOLDIERS.

SOLDIERS!—The moment approaches to save or ruin the country for ever! Our people, wearied under the weight of afflictions, is about to rise in its wrath against oppression. It is resolved to destroy tyranny, or expire with liberty. No; they cannot be patriots who would longer endure the existence of a government raised up (against the people's will) on the tombs of its warmest friends, on the violation of its rights, and on the destruction of all popular laws. The misery of the people has reached its *maximum*, and all means of making its voice be heard are taken away. It no longer has either society or public assembly to echo its complaints or support its remonstrances. The councils and the Directory which show themselves so humane and gracious towards the *great*, and the *respectables*, have neither heart, nor bowels, nor ears, nor voice for the people.* If any one speaks or writes for the latter, he is imprisoned, he is destroyed. No, never was tyranny more atrocious, more insupportable; the people, for whom the Revolution was made, are treated by our rulers as a vile rabble that must be chained down for their (the rulers') safety; and the men, whom such excessive barbarity revolts—the very men who overthrew the Bastile and the throne—are called Royalists by these same villains, in order to deceive and arm the weak and ignorant against them. By such perfidious Machiavelism do they hope first to delude, and afterwards bayonet you as they did in Germinal and Prairial of the Year III. You are sans-culottes, and you will not fight against those who, like you, have uprooted royalty! Listen, and do not abandon yourselves to illusion.

The people desires the Constitution of 1793, which it unanimously accepted, but of which it has been perfidiously despoiled, through the massacre and incarceration of the patriots under the name of terrorists. It desires

---

* Might not one suppose that this description was intended for our own House of Commons?—BRONTERRE.

this Constitution, because in abrogating all distinctions of riches, this Constitution renders all men equal before the law; because it assures property and relief to the defenders of the country and to the poor; and because it authorises the people to put a veto on all laws which they may deem prejudicial to their interests.

If you are not the friends of kings, of nobles, and of monied vampires, you will be on our side; you will not heed the deceitful language of your staff-officers, who, in contempt of their oft-repeated oaths, have flung themselves, body and soul, into the arms of the present government, because it pays a good price for their baseness, and above all, because it permits them to exercise over you the intolerable despotism which you had overthrown in 1789.

Ah! little dreamt ye, when you were shedding your blood on the frontiers to defend the country, what horrors were meanwhile committed in the interior! You fancied you were fighting for liberty, for the people; while your victories, your blood, only served to raise up a new tyranny—new distinctions—a new insolence on the ruins of the old despotism.

Look at this Directory! Do you not recognise the court of the Capets in its insolent pomp, its magnificent palaces, its numerous body-guard, its arrogance, the parasitical baseness of its courtiers? And our generals, so elegantly costumed, do they not exhibit, by their luxury and disdainful pride, the exact counterpart of the haughty nobles whose palaces they have usurped? Ah! too well you now perceive, brave soldiers! that the Revolution, which was destined to re-establish equality, has hitherto done no more than replace a band of old robbers by a multitudinous crew of new ones.

Patriotic administrators were guiding the Revolution towards the relief and comfort of the oppressed poor, Chiefs, friendly to equality, were leading you to victory; they have been destituted under the name of Terrorists. Terror, which had saved the country, became a crime, and the courageous men who, in the noblest spirit of devotion, had braved all dangers, were pointed out for the poignards of counter-revolutionists as the most abandoned of villains.

Well! after two years of counter-revolutions, you ought to be disabused. The Terrorists are those who, throughout the whole of the Revolution, have been combatting for the rights of the people; who incessantly invoke and demand the promised recompenses for *you*, and relief for the distressed poor—who gave death to the enemies of the people; they are the men, in short, by whose sides you have so often made the satellites of tyrants turn pale. See then, whether we or our enemies are best entitled to your esteem.

Soldiers! open your eyes; you are of the people. Could you arm against the people? Why this animosity against your brothers of the Legion of Police? They are banished to a distance, because they see clearly; because they will not cut our throats; in a day or two you also will be undeceived, and made the subjects of the like treatment.

Soldiers! whether with red collars or white collars, are you not all children and defenders of the country? Have you not all fought together for the triumph of liberty? Friends, embrace one another, and turn your combined arms against the usurpers, who, fearing the just vengeance of the people, hope to find a support in your divisions. But should you dare it, the country, your common mother, exasperated by the blood of your slain brethren, will overwhelm and crush you under the weight of her maledictions.

The tocsin sounds.

You are not the Government's soldiers, but the people's soldiers. It is not the Government, but the people, that pays you by its sweat and privations; and should you arm against the people, as your tyrants pretend you will, whatever the danger, we will combat you. The die is cast; to be silent is the greatest of crimes; to endure it now is to sanction the slavery of future generations. We will rise up, and we shall see if you are the defenders of liberty or the slaves of tyranny. Ah! soldiers, you, too, are the people, oppressed, miserable like ourselves; you will, therefore, join our ranks, and help us to avenge the country of your and her oppressors.

PIECE No. XXVII.

*Fragment of a Projet, or Draught of a Decree of
Police (left by the Conspirators).*

Art. 1. Individuals who do nothing for the country
can exercise no political rights in it. They are strangers
to whom the Republic accords hospitality.

2. They do nothing for the country who do not serve
it by some useful occupation or labour.

3. The law considers as useful occupations :—
Those of agriculture, pastoral life, fishing, and navigation ;
Those of the mechanical and manual arts ;
Those of retail dealing ;
Those appertaining to the transport of men and things ;
Those appertaining to war ;
Those of instruction, education, and the sciences ;

4. Nevertheless, the occupations of teaching and the
sciences shall not be reputed useful, if those who exercise
them do not produce, within a given time, a certificate
of civism, delivered after forms to be hereafter regulated.

5. The exercise of political rights is preserved to citizens whose useful occupations have been suspended by
the infirmities or circumstances of the Revolution.

6. Foreigners are interdicted from entering the public
assemblies.

7. Foreigners are under the direct surveillance of the
administration in chief, which may temporarily remove
them from their ordinary domicile, and send them to
places of correction.

8. Every foreigner admitted to the rights of hospitality,
becomes an aspirant to the rights of citizenship, if he
enters into the national community. He exercises these
rights as soon as he can present a certificate of civism.

9. The law determines the period after which no one
shall be competent to exercise the rights of citizenship
who is not a member of the national community.

10. All the citizens shall be armed.

11. Foreigners shall deliver, under pain of death,

whatever arms they are possessed of, in the hands of the revolutionary committees.

12. On the first decadi next following the promulgation of the present decree, the citizens shall meet in general assembly to re-organise the National Guard.

13. There shall be formed, within the shortest possible time, in the environs of Toulon, Valence, Grenoble, Mâcon, Metz, Clermont, Angoulême, and Toulouse camps destined to maintain tranquillity, to protect the Republicans, and to favour reform.

14. For this purpose, the revolutionary committees shall select, and make depart immediately for the places designed, four Republicans from each company of the National Guard, completely armed, equipped, and provided with whatever is necessary for encampment.

15. The provisions or contents of the military decree are applicable to the above camps.

16. These camps will be broken up as soon as the new laws may be peaceably executed.

17. The Isles Marguerite and Honoré, d'Hières, d'Oleron, and de Rhé, shall be converted into bridewells, or places of correction, whither shall be sent (to be bound to hard labour in common with other convicts) suspected foreigners, and all persons arrested in consequence of the proclamation to the French people.

18. These isles shall be rendered inaccessible; they shall have administrations directly subject to the Government.

19. Those of the prisoners who will furnish proofs of amendment, of activity in the works, and of good conduct, shall be privileged to re-enter the Republic, and acquire therein the rights of citizenship.

PIECE No. XXIX.

Fragment of a Draught of an Economical Decree

Art. 1. There shall be established in the Republic a grand national community.

2. The national community holds proprietorship of the possessions hereinafter mentioned—to wit:—

The possessions which, being declared national, were not sold up to the 9th Thermidor of the Year II.

The possessions of the enemies of the Revolution, which the decrees of the 8th and 13th Ventôse of the Year II. had vested in the unhappy poor.

The possessions forfeited, or to be forfeited, to the Republic, in consequence of judiciary condemnations.

The buildings now in occupation for the public service.

The possessions which the communes enjoyed previously to the law of the 10th June, 1793.

The possessions appropriated to hospitals, charitable institutions, and establishments for public instruction.

The lodgings occupied by the needy citizens, in execution of the proclamation to the French on the . . . .

The possessions which may be voluntarily abandoned to the Republic by their present owners.

The usurped possessions of such as have enriched themselves in the exercise of public functions.

The possessions of which no use is made by their present holders.

3. The right of succession, whether by inheritance or will, is abolished. All the wealth actually possessed by individuals shall lapse, at their decease, to the national community.

4. Will be considered as actual possessors the children of a father now living, who are not called by the law to form part of the armies.

5. Every French person, of either sex, who makes a voluntary surrender to his country of all his effects, and devotes to it his body, and whatever service he is capable of, is a member of the great national community.

6. Old men who have attained their sixtieth year, and the infirm, if they are poor, are, of right, members of the national community.

7. As also, all young persons brought up in the national houses of education.

8. The possessions of the national community are employed in common by all its valid members.

9. The grand national community maintains all its

members in an equal and honourable mediocrity; it provides them with everything they want.

10. The Republic invites all good citizens to contribute to the success of reform, by a voluntary surrender of their possessions to the community.

11. After the date of ...., no one can be a civil or military functionary, who is not a member of the said community.

12. The grand national community is administered by local magistrates, freely chosen by its members, agreeably to the laws, and under the direction of the supreme administration.   *   *   *   *

13. [*The remainder of this* projet, *like several other papers of the conspirators, appears to have been lost, or left imperfect.*—BRONTERRE.]

Of Occupations in Common.

Art. 1. Every member of the national community owes to it such labour as he is capable of, in agriculture and the useful arts.

2. Are excepted, old persons of sixty years, and the infirm.

3. Citizens who, by the voluntary abandonment of their possessions, will become members of the national community, shall not be subjected to any painful labour, if they have attained their fortieth year, and if they did not exercise a mechanical art before the publication of the present decree.

4. In each commune the citizens are distributed by classes. There are as many classes as there are useful arts; each class is composed of all those who profess the same art.

5. There are, amongst each class, magistrates named by those composing it; these magistrates direct the works—see to their equal repartition—execute the orders of the municipal administration, and set an example of zeal and activity.

6. The law determines, for each season, the daily duration of the labour of the members of the national community.

7. There is with each municipal administration, a council composed of old men, delegated by each class of

workers; this council enlightens the administration upon everything which concerns the distribution, the mitigation, and the improvement of works.

8. The supreme administration will apply to the works of the national community the use of such machines and processes as are suited to diminish the labour of men.

9. The municipal administration attends to and regulates the condition of the workers of each class, and that of the task to which they are appointed. It regularly informs the supreme administration of what passes.

10. The displacement of workers from one commune to another is ordered by the supreme administration, according to its knowledge of the powers and wants of the community.

11. The supreme administration condemns to forced labour, under the surveillance of communes nominated for the purpose, individuals of both sexes, whose incivism, idleness, luxury, and dissoluteness, set pernicious examples to society—their possessions are appropriated by the national community.

12. The magistrates of each class cause to be deposited in the magazines of the national community, the fruits of the land, and the productions of art susceptible of conservation.

13. The new verification of these objects is regularly communicated to the supreme administration.

14. The magistrates attached to the class of agriculture superintend the propagation and improving the breed of animals proper for food; they also see that the people be well clothed, that they have the means of transport and conveyance, and that they be supplied with proper refreshments, and every other means of mitigating their burdens.

Of the distribution and use of the possessions of the National Government.

Art. 1. No member of the national community can enjoy or use anything but what the law assigns him, by the actual delivery of the magistrates.

2. The national community guarantees, from this instant, to each of its members—

A healthy, commodious, and well-furnished habitation;

Clothing for work-hours, and clothing for the hours of respite, linen and woollen, conformably to the national costume;

Washing, lighting, and firing;

A sufficient supply of food in bread, meat, fowl, fish, eggs, butter or oil, wine, and other drinks, used in the different climes or regions; vegetables, fruits, seasoning, and other articles, the due combination of which constitutes a competent and frugal state of comfort. Also, medical aid and attendance.

3. There will take place in each commune, at stated periods, repasts in common, at which all the members of the community will be bound to assist.

4. The keep of public and military functionaries is the same as that of the members of the national community.

5. Every member of the national community who receives pay, or hoards money is punished.

6. Members of the national community can receive the common ration only in the arrondissement where they are domiciled, except in cases of removal authorised by the administration.

7. The domicile or settlement of actual citizens is *that* which they enjoy at the publication of the present decree; that of young people, brought up in the national houses of education, is in the commune where they were born.

8. There are, in each commune, magistrates charged to distribute, at the respective domiciles, to the members of the national community, the productions of agriculture and of the arts.

9. The law determines the rules of such distribution.

10. [Left unfinished.]   *   *   *   *

Of the administration of the National Community

1. The national community is under the legal direction of the supreme administration of the state.

2. Relatively to the administration of the community, the Republic is divided into regions.

3. A region comprises all the contiguous departments whose productions are pretty nearly the same.

4. There is in each region an intermediary adminis-

tration, to which the departmental administrations are subordinate.

5. Lines of telegraph accelerate the correspondence between the departmental administrations, and the intermediary ones between the latter and the supreme administration.

6. The supreme administration determines (according to law) the kind and quotation of distributions to be made to the members of the community of each region.

7. Agreeably to this determination, the departmental administrations make known to the intermediary ones the *deficit* or the superfluities of their respective arrondissements.

8. The intermediary administrations compensate, as nearly as may be, the *deficit* of one department by the superfluity of another, direct the necessary payments and transports, and render account to the supreme administration of their wants and superfluities.

9. The supreme administration provides for the wants of the deficient regions, by the superfluity of those which have too much, or by exchange with foreigners.

10. Above all, the supreme administration causes to be previously levied and deposited every year in the military magazines, the tenth of all the harvests of the community.

11. It provides that the superfluities of the Republic be carefully preserved, as provision against years of scarcity.

*   *   *   *   *   *

Of Commerce.

Art. 1. All private commerce with foreigners is forbid; any merchandize so acquired will be confiscated to the profit of the national community; contraveners will be punished.

2. The Republic procures for the national community whatever commodities it wants, by exchanging its superfluous productions of agriculture and art for those of foreign states.

3. For this purpose commodious entrepôts are established on the frontiers, by land and water.

4. The supreme administration negociates with foreigners through its agents; it makes the latter deposit the superfluities to be exchanged, in the entrepôts, where it receives from foreigners the commodities agreed for.

5. The agents of the supreme administration in the entrepôts of commerce are frequently changed; prevarications are severely punished.

*   *   *   *   *   *

Of Transport and Conveyance.

Art. 1. There are magistrates in each commune charged to direct the transport of communal possessions or goods from one commune to another.

2. Each commune is provided with sufficient means of transport, whether by land or water.

3. The members of the national community are called in rotation to conduct and superintend the commodities transported from one commune to another.

4. Every year the intermediary administrations charge a certain number of young people (chosen in all the departments subordinate to them) with the more distant transports.

5. Citizens charged with any transport whatever, are maintained and provided for in the commune where they happen to be.

6. The supreme administration causes to be transported from commune to commune, by the shortest rout, under the surveillance of inferior administrations, such commodities as are required to make up the *deficit* of regions which experience a scarcity.

*   *   *   *   *   *

Of Contributions.

Art. 1. Individuals not belonging to the national community are alone subject to contribution.

2. They are liable to the contributions already stated.

3. These contributions will be gathered in *kind*, and paid into the magazines of the national community.

4. The total of the quotas of those liable to contribution, for the current year, is double of that of last year.

5. This total will be divided and levied amongst the

departments *progressively*,* on all rendered subject
to it.

6. The non-communionists may be required, in case
of need, to pay into the magazines of the national community, *on account* of future contributions, their superfluous provisions or manufactured articles.

     *   *   , *   *   *   *

Of Debts.

Art. 1. The national debt is extinguished for all
Frenchmen.

2. The Republic will pay over to foreigners the capital
of the funded debts it owes them. Meanwhile, it appro-
priates to its use both the perpetual dividends and the
life-interest annuities payable to foreigners.

3. The debts of every Frenchman, who becomes a
member of the national community, are extinguished as
regards all French claims upon him.

4. The Republic charges itself with the debts due
from the members of the national community to
foreigners.

5. All fraud in this respect is punished with perpetual
slavery.

     *   *   *   *   *

Of Money.

Art. 1. The Republic coins no more money.

2. The monied metals, or materials which may lapse
to the national community, will be employed to purchase
the commodities it will require.

3. Every individual not participating in the community, who will be convicted of having offered any
species of money to one of its members, will be severely
punished.

4. There shall be no more gold or silver introduced
into the Republic.

     *   *   *   *   *   *

---

* The word *progressively* has been explained in treating of the
progressive impost.—BRONTERRE.

PIECE No. XXX.

THE LAST LETTER OF GRACCHUS BABEUF.

(To my Wife and to my Children.)

FAREWELL, my friends. I am about to enter the night of eternity. The friend to whom I address the two letters you will see—to that friend I describe my situation and feelings towards you, better than I can describe them to yourselves. It seems as if I felt nothing from feeling too much. I place your fate in his hands. Alas! I know not that you will find him in a condition to be able to do what I ask of him; I know not how you will be able to gain access to him. Your love for me has led you here through all the obstacles of our misery. You have supported yourselves in the midst of pains and privations; your constant sensibility has made you follow every moment of this long and cruel procedure, of which, like me, you have drank the bitter chalice. But I know not what steps you mean to take to return to the place whence you came; I know not how my memory will be appreciated, though I am conscious of having conducted myself in the most irreproachable manner. I know not, in short, what is to become of all the Republicans, their families, and even their little ones at the breast, in the midst of the royal furies which the counter-revolution is going to excite. Oh, my friends! how harrowing are these reflections for my last moments! ......To die for my country—to leave a family, children, a beloved wife, would, after all, be more supportable, if I did not behold liberty destroyed, and every thing that appertains to sincere Reupblicans involved in the most horrible proscription. Ah! my dear children! what will become of you? I cannot at this moment help feeling the most intense emotions....Think not that I feel regret for having sacrificed myself for the noblest of causes; even should all my efforts prove unavailing for it, I have fulfilled my mission ....

If, contrary to my expectation, you can survive the

terrible tempest which now rages over the Republic, and
over all that was attached to it; if you can restore yourselves to a tranquil situation, and find some friends to
aid you to triumph over your bad fortune, I would recommend you to live well-united together. I would recommend my wife to endeavour to bring up and guide
her children with mildness, and I would recommend my
children to deserve their mother's goodness, by respecting
and always obeying her. It belongs to the family of a
martyr of liberty to give the example of every virtue, in
order to attract the esteem and attachment of all good
people. I would desire my wife to do all in her power
to give education to her children, by engaging her
friends to yield her all the assistance possible towards
such object. I invite Emilius to comply with this wish
of a father, whom I believe he much loves, and by whom
he was so tenderly beloved; I invite him to comply
with it without loss of time, and as soon as he possibly
can.

My friends, I hope you will remember me, and often
speak of me. I hope you will believe that you were
always most dear to me. I knew no other way to render
you happy, than by promoting the happiness of all. I
have failed. I have sacrificed myself; it is for you, as
well as for liberty, I die.

Speak often of me to Camille; tell him a thousand
and a thousand times that I bore him tenderly in my
heart... Tell Caius as much, when he will be capable of
understanding it.

Lebois has announced the printing of our defence in
separate parts; let mine receive the greatest possible
publicity. I recommend my wife—my sweet friend—not
to give Baudouin, Lebois, or others, any copy of my
defence, without having another perfectly correct one in
her possession, as a security that that defence may never
be lost. You will feel, my love, that this defence is precious; that it will be always dear to virtuous hearts, and
to the friends of their country. The only possession that
will remain to you, from me, will be my reputation; and
I am sure that both you and your children will derive
much consolation from the enjoyment of it. You will

love to hear it said by all feeling and upright hearts, in speaking of your husband—of your father—

He was perfectly virtuous.

Adieu! No more. I hold to the earth but by a single thread, which to-morrow's light will sever. That is certain; too clearly I see it. The sacrifice must take place. The wicked are in the ascendant; I yield to them. At all events, it is sweet to die with a conscience so pure as mine; the only thing harrowing or cruel in it, is to be torn from your arms, oh, my tenderest friends! Oh, all that I hold dearest!!!....I tear myself away ....the violence is done....Adieu, adieu, adieu, ten millions of times, adieu!

One word more. Write to my mother and sisters. Send them by diligence, or otherwise, my defence as soon as it is printed. Tell them how I died, and endeavour to make these *good, kind creatures* understand that, far from being dishonourable, such a death is most glorious.

Adieu, then, once more, my dearest, tenderest friends. Farewell for ever. I wrap myself in the bosom of virtue's sleep.

GRACCHUS BABEUF.

THE END.

TO MY FRIENDS AND READERS

Babeuf's letter to his wife and children is the last of the justificative pieces. I have now concluded a work which, were I to die to-morrow (leaving unexecuted the larger and more important ones I am preparing), would console me for the misspent part of my life. The history of Babeuf's conspiracy ought to be preserved, if it were only to undeceive mankind respecting the true character of the French Revolution, and of the causes which occasioned its failure.

My readers are aware that, at the commencement of the work, I was ignorant whether Buonarroti was living or dead. Judge my surprise and delight when, some five weeks ago, a letter, dated Paris, and from Buonarroti himself, came to apprise me that he was still living, and to furnish me with a list of the real names of the conspirators, of which I was previously only able to give the anagrams. The handwriting of the letter is exceedingly small—so small as almost to require a microscope to read it. The following is a *verbatim* copy, as well as I could make it out :—

(*From Buonarroti to Bronterre.*)

Paris, May 3, 1836.

Mon Frère—N'ayant pas encore quitté la vie je suis heureux de pouvoir vous témoigner la satisfaction que j'ai éprouvée en apprenant par le prospectus que vous venez de répandre le zèle avec lequel vous vous-êtes déterminé à publier en Anglais, mon histoire de la conspiration de Babeuf. Agréez en mes remercimens les plus empressés. Je les dois à l'homme à qui l'amour de ses semblables fait braver les injures et les persécutions partage toujours réservé a quiconque ose élever la voix contre les institutions oppressives, et frayer le chemin aux progrès de la vérité et de la justice. Je vois avec une joie véritable, que l'Angleterre a aussi dans son sein des amis sincères de cette pure égalité, pour laquelle j'eus le bonheur de joindre mes faibles efforts à ceux bien plus glorieux de mes amis qui les scellerent de leur sang.

Quoique un océan de mœurs invétérées et de passions viles offusquent encore la raison et enchaînent les volontés il ne faut pas désespérer—du salut de l'humanité. Elle avancera; j'en ai la conviction, dans la route, de la sociabilité et du bonheur; et nous jouirons dans une vie plus heureuse du bien que nous avons entrevu, et dont nos successeurs plus sages que leur pères sauront se mettre en possession. Ci jointe une note des noms véritables que je vous prie de substituer aux anagrams que des motifs de prudence, me firent employer lors de la publication de mon ouvrage. Ces motifs sont aujourd'hui sans valeur, et il est juste de faire connoître ceux qui partagerent les travaux et les dangers de Babeuf.

Mon intention n'est certainement pas de vous parler de moi. Qu'est ce que l'humanité gagnerait à être exactement instruite des details, bons au mauvais, de ma vie? je me borne à vous prévenir que les receuils d'où vous avez tiré ma biographie fourmillent d'anachronismes et des fautes: on m'attribue des choses que je n'ai pas faites; celles que je pouvais revendiquer sont ou tronquées ou mal rendues; les événements sont quelquefois deplacés, et la bonne opinion que vous voulez bien avoir de moi vous a dicté en ma faveur des éloges que je suis honteux de ne pas mériter.

Une occasion particulière que je saisis avec empressement me fournit la facilité de vous envoyer un essai biographique sur Robespierre dont la publication me paroît utile; peut être jugerez vous àpropos d'en faire usage.

C'est pour moi une fort bonne aubaine que l'événement qui m'a procuré votre connoissance; les hommes de la trempé que vous paroissez posseder sont assez rares par le temps qui court, et je me félicité d'avoir appris la science certaine qu'en Angleterre tout n'est pas avidité de richesses et esprit de Boutique et qu'à côté de vos seigneuries et de vos prêtres de Plutus il y a des penseurs profonds, des amis dévoués du peuple et, d'admirables contempteurs des folies humaines.

Croyez, mon frere, que si vous prenez la peine de m'écrire je m'estime raihenreux de cultiver votre connoissance.

Votré devoué Frére,

PHILIPPE BUONARROTI,

Agé de 75 ans.

TRANSLATION.

MY BROTHER,—Not having yet taken leave of life, I am happy in being able to testify to you the satisfaction I have felt in learning, through the prospectuses you have distributed, the zeal with which you have determined on publishing, in English, my history of the conspiracy of Babeuf. Please to accept my most earnest thanks. I owe them to the man whose love of his fellow-creatures induces him to brave insult and persecution—the lot always reserved for whosoever dares to raise his voice against oppressive institutions, and to pave the way for the progress of truth and justice. It is with real joy I see that England also contains sincere friends of that pure equality, for which I had the happiness of joining my feeble efforts to those far more glorious ones of my friends, who sealed them with their blood.

Although an ocean of inveterate habits and vile passions still obscure reason, and chain down men's wills, we must not despair of the salvation of humanity. It will advance, I am convinced, in the road of sociality and happiness; and we shall enjoy, in a happier life, the good which we have dimly foreseen, and of which our successors, wiser than their fathers, will be able to possess themselves. Annexed to this is a note, containing the real names (of the conspirators), which I beg you will substitute for the anagrams that prudential motives made me employ at the time of publishing my work. These motives have no longer any weight, and it is just to make known the persons who shared the labours and dangers of Babeuf.

It is certainly not my intention to speak of myself. What would humanity gain by becoming acquainted with the exact details, good or bad, of my life? I content myself with apprising you, that the compilations whence you have gleaned my biography abound in anachronisms and errors. Things are attributed to me which I have not done; those which I might justly claim are either mutilated or badly expressed; events are sometimes out of place; and the good opinion you are disposed to entertain of me has dictated to you eulogies in my favour, which, I am ashamed to say, I do not merit.

A particular opportunity, of which I gladly avail myself, affords me the facility of sending you a biographical essay on Robespierre, of which the publication appears to me desirable; mayhap you will deem it suitable to your purpose to make use of it.

I consider myself very fortunate in the event which has procured me your acquaintance. Men of the stamp you appear to be are rare enough as times go; and it is a source of satisfaction to me to learn, for certain, that in England there is something besides greediness of riches and the spirit of the shop; and that, by the side of your lordships, and your priests of Plutus, there are to be found deep thinkers, and admirable despisers of human folly.

Believe me, my brother, that if you take the trouble to write to me, I will esteem myself happy in cultivating your acquaintance.

Your devoted brother,

PHILIPPE BUONARROTI,

Aged 75 years.

Bedon	lisez	Debon.
Laujen de Dorimel		Jullien de la Drome.
Hannac	..	Chanan.
Sombod	..	Bodsom.
Glartou	..	Goulard, imprimeur (printer).
La Tilme	..	Maillet, homme de loi (lawyer).
Chintrard	..	Trinchard, menuissier (carpenter).
Vélor	..	Révol, imprimeur (printer).
Golacain	..	Solignac, tanneur (tanner).
Rivagre	..	Gravier, marchand de vin (wine-merchant).
Lihppi	..	Philp, marin (seaman).
Tismiot	..	Mittois, homme de lettres (man of letters).
Lussorillon	..	Roussillon, chirurgien (surgeon).
Reuf	..	Feru, de Toulon.
Eriddi	..	Didier, ferrurier (locksmith).
Filipe le Rexelet	..	Felix le Pelletier.
Be Naumbet	..	Baudement.
Adery	..	Beray.
'Eris	..	Reys, sellier (saddler).
Crexel	..	Clerex, tailleur (tailor).
Le Himug	..	Guilhem, courrier (courier.)
Perrino	..	Pierron.
Allinoget	..	Laignelot, ex conventionnel. ⎰ Ex-members
Euduchoi	..	Choudieu, idem. ⎱ of the Convention.
Sasemy	..	Massey.

I have felt it my duty to publish this letter, not only because it supplies the real names of the conspirators (which, *pro tanto*, gives the translation an advantage over the original), but also because it impeaches the accuracy of the compilations from which I gleaned the few facts recorded in my short sketch of the author's life. As I write only for utility's sake, whatever may be my own predilections, I owe it to truth not to indulge them to the extent of misleading my readers. I therefore avail myself of Buonarroti's own testimony to correct

any erroneous impressions I may have been betrayed
into respecting him, leaving it to the reader to judge
how much of the error (if any) is imputable to the modesty of the author himself. I will merely observe that
the only sources I have had access to for my biographical
sketch are " *Phillips' Biographical Anecdotes of the
Founders of the French Revolution,*" and some few
English periodicals, including the *Quarterly Review* in
particular. I have distorted nothing, discoloured nothing,
added nothing to what is contained in these sources. If
I am wrong, they are wrong—and if I have been too
laudatory of the author, it is because I found the friends
and enemies of his principles equally zealous to do
homage to his virtues. I expect very soon to have the
pleasure of a personal interview with Buonarroti, in which
case I shall avail myself of the opportunity to learn those
details of his life which his modesty prevented him from
transmitting by letter. Such details, as also any other
information I may collect in Paris, shall be laid in some
shape before my friends and readers.

BRONTERRE.

P. S. The similarity of Mr. Owen's doctrines to those
for which Babeuf died, induces me to annex the following
documents to this work. My Parisian and other foreign
readers I know will be much gratified by their insertion.

THE LEGACY OF ROBERT OWEN,
TO THE POPULATION OF THE WORLD.

" Sacred to Truth, without Mystery, Mixture of Error, or Fear of Man."

MORE than half a century ago I discovered that there was some grievous error deep in the foundations of society, which created evil, and prevented the good which man by his nature was evidently destined, in some stage of his progress, to attain and permanently to enjoy.

From that period to the present, I have never ceased honestly and fearlessly to search for that truth which should enable me to detect the error, remove the evil, and for ever establish the good.

Having found this truth, and proved it to be such by the only criterion of truth known to man; that is, by its undeviating consistency with ascertained facts, I now give it to you, that through its influence you may be regenerated, your minds born again, and your posterity be made partakers of the endless blessings which this truth, and this truth alone, can insure permanently for the human race.

This great truth which I have now to declare to you is, that *the system on which all the nations of the world are acting is founded in gross deception, in the deepest ignorance, or in a mixture of both. That, under no possible modification of the principles on which it is based, can it ever produce good to man; but that, on the contrary, its practical results must ever be to produce evil continually.*

And, consequently, that no really intelligent and truly honest individual can any longer support it: for, by the constitution of this system, it unavoidably encourages and upholds, as it ever has encouraged and upheld, hypocrisy and deception of every description, and discouraged and opposed truth and sincerity whenever truth and sincerity were applied permanently to improve the condition of the human race. It encourages and upholds national vice and corruption to an unlimited extent; whilst, to an equal degree, it discourages national virtue and honesty.

The whole system has not one redeeming quality: its very virtues, as they are termed, are vices of great magnitude. Its charities, so called, are gross acts of injustice and deception. Its instructions are to rivet ignorance in the mind, and, if possible, to render it perpetual. It supports, in all manner of extravagance, idleness, presumption, and uselessness; and oppresses, in almost every mode which ingenuity can devise, industry, integrity, and usefulness. It encourages superstition, bigotry, and fanaticism; and discourages truth, common sense, and rationality. It generates and cultivates every inferior quality and base passion that human nature can be made to receive; and has so disordered all the human intellects, that they have become universally perplexed and confused, so that man has no just title to be called a reasonable or rational being. It generates, under the title of glorious war, violence, robbery, and murder, and extols and rewards these vices as the highest of all virtues.

Its laws are founded in gross ignorance of individual man and of human society; they are cruel and unjust in the extreme, and, united with all the superstitions of the world, are calculated only to teach men to call that which is pre-eminently true and good, false and bad; and that which is glaringly false and bad, true and good. In short, to cultivate now with great care all that leads to permanent vice and misery in the mass, and to exclude from them, with equal care, all that would direct them to true knowledge and real happiness; which alone, combined, deserve the name of virtue.

In consequence of the dire effects of this wretched system upon the whole of the human race, the population of Great Britain (the most advanced of modern nations in the acquirement of the means to create riches, power, and happiness) has created and supports a theory and practice of government, which is directly opposed to the real well-being and true interest of every individual member of the empire, whatever may be his station, rank, or condition— whether sovereign or subject. And so enormous are the increasing errors of this system now become, that, to uphold it, the government is compelled, day by day, to commit acts of the grossest cruelty and injustice, and call such proceedings laws of justice and Christian mercy.

Under this system, the idle, the useless, and the vicious govern the population of the world; whilst the useful and truly virtuous, as far as such a system will permit men to be virtuous, are by them degraded and oppressed.

Under this system, those who daily and hourly practise the art of poisoning the body, deranging the intellects, and reducing individuals to the lowest stage of human existence, are openly fostered and encouraged, until they build palaces of temptations, to excite to every conceivable vice and crime, and at the same time to teach almost a continued language of the vilest and most demoralizing oaths: whilst those who, to protect themselves and their helpless families, by their industry and good conduct, from these dire effects, meet together to aid and encourage each other in their wise and virtuous proceedings, and engage to do so by righteous oath, taken solely to unite these, the producers of all good to society, in a virtuous bond of brotherhood and sisterhood, are hunted like beasts of prey, incarcerated in demoralising prisons, subjected to a worse than farcical trial, found guilty by ignorant and prejudiced individuals, and sentenced to a cruel, ignominious, and grossly unjust punishment.

Men of industry, and of good and virtuous habits! this is the last state to which you ought to submit; nor would I advise you to allow the ignorant, the idle, the presumptuous, and the vicious, any longer to lord it over the well-being, the lives and happiness, of yourselves and families, when, by *three days* of such idleness as constitutes the whole of their lives, you would for ever convince each of these mistaken individuals that you now possess the power to compel *them* at once to become the abject slaves, and the oppressed portion of society, they have hitherto made you.

But all the individuals now living are the suffering victims of this accursed system, and all are objects of pity: you will, therefore, effect this great and glorious revolution without, if possible, inflicting individual evil. You can easily accomplish this most-to-be-desired object. Proceed with your Union on the principles you have latterly adopted; they are wise and just; and wisdom and justice, combined with your Union, will be sure to render it for ever legal.

Men of industry, producers of wealth and knowledge, and of all that is truly valuable in society! *unite your powers now to create a wise and righteous state of human existence; a state in which the only contest shall be, who shall produce the greatest amount of permanent happiness for the human race.* You have all the requisite materials awaiting your proper application of them to effect this change, and circumstances have arisen within the last week to render delay a dereliction of the highest duty which you have to perform to yourselves, to your families, and to the population of the world.

Men of industrious habits, you who are the most honest, useful, and valuable part of society, by producing for it all its wealth and knowledge, *you have formed and established the Grand National Consolidated Trades' Union of Great Britain and Ireland, and it will prove the palladium of the world.* All the intelligent, well-disposed, and superior minds among all classes of society, male and female, will now rally round the Consolidated Union, and become members of it; and, if the irrationality of the present degraded and degrading system should render it necessary, you will discover the reasons why you should willingly sacrifice all you hold dear in the world, and life itself, rather than submit to its dissolution or slightest depression.

For your sakes, I have become a member of your Consolidated Union; and while it shall be directed with the same wisdom and justice that it has been from its commencement, and its proceedings shall be made known to the public as you intend them to be, my resolve is to stand by our order, and support the Union to the utmost of my power. It is this Consolidated Union that can alone save the British empire from greater confusion, anarchy, and misery than it has ever yet experienced. It is, it will daily become more and more, *the real conservative power of society;* for its example will be speedily followed by all nations, and through its beneficial example the greatest revolution ever effected in the history of the human race will be commenced, rapidly carried on, and completed over the world, without bloodshed, violence, or evil of any kind, merely *by an overwhelming moral influence;* which influence individuals and nations will speedily perceive the folly and uselessness of attempting to resist.

Experience has forced these important truths into my mind, and I give them now to the population of the world as *the most valuable legacy that man can give to man.*

March 30, 1834.

THE CHARTER OF THE RIGHTS OF HUMANITY,

Passed at a great Public Meeting of the Producers of Wealth and Knowledge, held in the Metropolis on Wednesday, February 12, 1834.

The period has arrived when we, the producers of wealth and knowledge, have decided that we will not waste any more of our time or labour on objects of minor importance, which, if obtained, could effect no permanently beneficial change in our condition ; but that, overlooking the local advantages of class, and considering only the general and permanent interest of humanity, we will henceforth devote all our energies to the attainment of those superior objects and advantages developed in this our charter.

1. A graduated property tax, equal in amount to the full exigencies of government, when wisely administered.

2. An abolition of all other customs, duties, and taxes—national, county, and parochial.

3. Free and protected ingress and egress for all persons into and out of all countries; and the free interchange of all improvements and commodities between all nations.

4. Wars to cease; and all differences between nations to be adjusted by an annual congress, to be held in rotation in each of the different states.

5. Liberty of expression of conscientious opinions, upon all subjects, without limitation.

6. No dominant religion to exist, nor any one to be encouraged by any worldly temptations whatever; but all persons to be equally protected in the rights of conscience.

7. National, scientific, physical, intellectual, and moral education for all, who from any cause cannot be otherwise well trained and cultured in all these respects.

8. National employment for all who cannot otherwise find productive or beneficial occupation, that thereby the greatest amount of wealth may be produced for every individual.

9. The children of all classes, without any exception, to be trained and employed, physically or mentally, to produce *for* society as much as they require *from* society.

10. National measures to set the poor and unemployed immediately to beneficial employments, under arrangements which shall reform their feelings and habits, and secure their comfort and happiness.

11. National arrangements to distribute the new wealth, created by the national employment of the poor and unemployed, beneficially for them and the nation.

12. Unlimited freedom for the production and interchange of all commodities and riches, until more wealth shall be produced than is necessary for the happiness of the population of every country.

13. A change of the vicious and degrading circumstances by which the productive classes are now surrounded, for others possessing a virtuous and superior character.

14. The present property of all individuals, acquired and possessed by the usages and practices of old society, to be held sacred until the possessors shall discover that it can no longer be of any use or exchangeable value, from the facility with which a surplus of wealth will be produced for all; thus destroying the *motive* to accumulate individual wealth, as the *motive* to accumulate water, where it is in abundance, has been destroyed, although it is the most intrinsically valuable of all our wealth.

15. The just rights of both sexes to be universally established.

16. The congress of nations to determine on some one language, which shall be taught to all the children of each state, in addition to their mother tongue.

17. Arrangements to be adopted, as soon as practicable, to put an end to individual and national competition and contest, now unnecessary, and producing innumerable grievous evils to all classes.

THE RATIONAL SYSTEM.

Experience has proved that man has always been the creature of the circumstances in which he has been placed, and that it is the character of these circumstances which inevitably makes him ignorant or intelligent, vicious or virtuous, wretched or happy. It is, therefore, necessary to acquire a knowledge of the influence which individual and general circumstances have over human nature; that is, to learn what particular circumstances produce among mankind ignorance, vice, and misery, and what intelligence, virtue, and happiness; and to discover how to remove the former, and to secure the latter; and this will be acquired by the study of the following fundamental laws of human nature :—

WHAT HUMAN NATURE IS,
AND THE FACTS FROM WHICH THE RATIONAL SYSTEM OF SOCIETY IS DERIVED.

1. Man is a *compound being*, whose character is formed of his constitution or organization at birth, and of the effects of external circumstances upon it, from birth to death; such original organization and external influences continually acting and re-acting each upon the other.

2. Man is compelled by his original constitution to receive his *feelings* and his *convictions* independent of his *will.*

3. His *feelings* or his *convictions*, or both of them united, create the motive to action called the *will*, which stimulates him to act, and decides his actions.

4. The organization of no two human beings is ever precisely similar at birth; nor can art subsequently form any two individuals, from infancy to maturity, to be the same.

5. Nevertheless, the constitution of every infant, except in case of organic disease, is capable of being formed or matured either into a *very inferior* or a *very superior* being, according to the qualities of the external circumstances allowed to influence that constitution from birth.

ADDRESS OF ROBERT OWEN,

At the Great Public Meeting, held at the National Equitable Labour Exchange, Charlotte-street, on May 1, 1833, denouncing the Old System of the World, and announcing the Commencement of the New.

The existing condition of mankind makes it evident to those who can reflect, and who have been formed with minds capable of generalizing the ideas acquired from the past and present history of the human race, that the associations of men, from their commencement, have been founded upon a false basis, and that, in consequence, man has been formed to be the creature of error and deception, of sin and of misery.

All associations have been based on the supposition that man possesses the power to believe and to feel according to the bidding of others; and that virtue consists in thus believing and feeling, and vice in refusing so to believe and feel. And by analyzing the complex proceedings of mankind, it has been discovered that the system of forming the human character, and of governing the human race, derived from these notions, is the only system that has ever been known in any part of the world, and consequently is the only one that has yet been practised.

The experience of the past, the only valuable knowledge which man has acquired, proves that this system continually generates, and effectually cultivates, all the inferior animal passions—is opposed to the progress of real knowledge, to natural sincerity; to all the higher moral virtues, and to the finest and best feelings of our nature. Also, that as long as this system shall be supported, ignorance, poverty, and of necessity, sin and misery, must continually pervade all the associations of men ; while pure charity and affection must remain as hitherto, unknown and unpractised.

Clearly perceiving this wretched state of human existence, and knowing that all governments are blind to its errors, inconsistencies, and wickedness, I have decided, after the most calm and deliberate reflection, to *renounce* on this day, thus publicly, in what may be justly called the metropolis of the civilized world, for myself and my disciples, the entire of this old system, and to declare my conviction that to countenance it any longer will be *the grossest act of folly and the greatest of all crimes.*

I also thus announce my determination henceforward to advocate thus openly and fairly *another system*, founded upon *opposite principles*, and leading to a *totally different practice.*

It is also my determination to recommend to all who think with me, to adopt the same course, and now to put these principles into full practice, and to assert the natural right of all men to act conscientiously, according to their convictions, as long as their conduct shall be beneficial to the public and not injurious to others.

If the existing laws of this country cannot protect the people in this moral and only really virtuous line of conduct, it is evident a despotism exists over the public mind which ought now to cease, and that the constitution of this and other countries ought to be changed to meet the improved intelligence of the age.

It is now the time to try the moral courage of men, and to ascertain who possesses virtue and knowledge sufficient to abandon falsehood for truth, folly for wisdom ; yes, the period has arrived when the moral courage of man will be put to the test, and it will be proved who are prepared to overcome the mental bondage in which, hitherto, all have been held from their infancy.

Do you feel desirous to ask me what we of the " New World" now mean to relinquish, and what to adopt ?

That none may misunderstand our proceedings, or falsify our intentions, I now thus openly, before the world, declare that—1. We abandon all the false religions that have been forced upon the human race, founded on the supposition that man, by his will, has the power to believe or feel as he likes, or to believe contrary to his convictions, or feel contrary to his nature, at the bidding of others.

2, We now adopt the only religion which can be *true,* because it is derived immediately from the unchangeable and everlasting laws of nature, which never lie, or deceive the human race. The basis of this RELIGION OF TRUTH, the only one which ever can conduct man to the practice of pure charity and real virtue, and to the enjoyment of unalloyed happiness, is the knowledge that the laws of nature have given the power to *adult* man, so to controul

the mental faculties and physical powers of his infant, as to force
it to receive *error*, however absurd and inconsistent, or to imbibe
truth only, known to be truth by its undeviating consistency with
the ascertained laws of nature; and to acquire the most wretchedly
vicious and injurious, or the most highly virtuous and beneficial
habits through life: and thus, through our new religion, we attain
the invaluable knowledge of the certain mode by which, without
individual reward, or punishment, or responsibility, to make the
whole human race morally, intellectually, and physically, either
inferior or superior, good or bad, miserable or happy; and yet no
two of them is likely ever to be formed to be without various
desirable physical and mental differences.

3. Our future practice will be in conformity with this new religion, as far as the rapidly expiring errors of the old system shall
be removed to admit its adoption, and the evils necessarily emanating from this old system we shall now adopt every means to
make manifest to the human race.

4. We shall be opposed to no men, but solely to the old errors,
which in the period of their mental weakness they have been
compelled to receive.

5. In conformity with the principles of the new religion of de-
monstrable truth, we shall adore in admiring silence, as alone
becomes man, that, to us, at present, INCOMPREHENSIBLE POWER,
which acts in and through all nature, everlastingly composing,
decomposing, and recomposing the materials of the universe, producing the endless variety of life, of mind, and of organised form.

6. We will not degrade, blaspheme, or merely humanise this
power, so far beyond man's present knowledge, as to attribute to it
the human form and passions, or any of the qualities of our limited
senses and vague imaginations.

7. Neither will we attempt to force others to receive or acknowledge *our impressions* upon this subject, seeing that up to this
hour similar attempts have confounded and perplexed the human
mind, making man in every district in the world a degraded mental
slave, irrational and miserable. On the contrary, we shall patiently
wait until an evident accurate knowledge of this power shall be
made manifest to all mankind, who will then, by the law of their
nature, be compelled to admire and to love it, in proportion to the
extent and the goodness of the qualities which it shall be discovered
to possess.

By this course of proceeding, dictated by common sense, or plain
right reasoning from self-evident facts, all *injurious* differences of
opinions respecting religion will cease from among men; charity
unlimited will take the place of presumption and violence; anger,
ill-will, and irritation of all kinds will cease, and in place thereof
pure love and affection, through a superior education, will be
made to pervade and direct all the proceedings of mankind.

8. Directed by this knowledge and these feelings, we will, as
soon as it shall be practicable, form arrangements to create *New
Institutions to new form the general character of the rising generation,
and to regenerate the existing adult population ;* for the period is near
at hand when the *minds* of men must be born again; when they
shall no longer see as through a glass darkly, but face to face, and
know each other even as they know themselves.

To effect this change, other arrangements, very different from
those which now exist, will be formed to insure a superior education from birth, such as will give a new and very superior character
to all children : arrangements that will preclude any child, free

from mental disease, or bodily defect, from acquiring physical, intellectual, or moral injurious habits or qualities; and that will render the succeeding generations a superior order of beings, compared with those who have hitherto lived.

9. As a knowledge of facts has now disclosed to us that, liking or disliking, or loving or hating, depend not upon the *will* of man, but upon the manner in which his organization is affected by the ever-varying qualities of external objects, none will be required to perjure themselves, as they are compelled to do under the old system of the world, before they can legally enjoy the natural rights of the sexes, by solemnly declaring that they will love to the end of life a being who is liable to perpetual change, and whom they may be forced to dislike or hate before the year expires. No! instead of this blasphemy against the laws of nature, other arrangements dictated by common sense, or right reason,* will be formed to insure all the good that can be derived, and to avoid all the vice and evil that has been experienced from the social converse between the sexes. All will then be fully conscious, and will openly acknowledge that pure chastity consists in forming this connexion only when affection exists between the parties, and that it is a vile, abominable, and injurious prostitution to form or continue this connexion when there is no affec-

---

* Many persons grossly mistake our views on the subject of the union of the sexes. Our object is to remove the causes of the immense amount of sexual crime and misery, and consequent physical and mental disease which now exist. It is nature's laws, now disregarded, which we desire to discover and implicitly obey; there being none other which can produce virtue and happiness. In the present absence of real knowledge derived from experience, and with the existing irregular feelings of the population of the world, created by a false education, we propose that the union and disunion of the sexes should take place under the following regulations:—Persons having an affection for each other, and being desirous of forming a union, first announce such intention publicly in our Sunday assemblies. If the intention remain at the end of three months, they make a second public declaration which declarations being registered in the books of the society will constitute their marriage.

In our new world, marriages will be solely formed to promote the happiness of the sexes, and if this end be not obtained, the object of the union is defeated. Should the parties, therefore, after the termination of twelve months at the soonest, discover that their dispositions and habits are unsuited to each other, and that there is little or no prospect of happiness being derived from their union, they are to make a public declaration, as before, to that effect, after which they return, and live together six months longer, at the termination of which, if they still find their qualities discordant, they make a second declaration, both of which being duly registered and witnessed, will constitute their legal separation.

The above cases apply only when both parties unite in the declarations. Should one alone come forward upon the last declaration, and the other object to the separation, they would be required to live together another six months, to try if their feelings and habits could be made to accord, so as to promote happiness. But if at the end of the second six months, the objecting party shall remain of the same mind, the separation is then to be final, and the parties may, without diminution of public opinion, form new unions more suited to their dispositions.

As all the children of the new world will be trained and educated under the superintendence and care of the Society, the separation of the parents will not produce any change in the condition of the rising generation. Under these arrangements, we have no doubt, a much more virtuous and happy state of society will be enjoyed than any which has existed at any time in any part of the world.

tion between the parties, even when they are what is called legally bound to each other. The union between the sexes will be, in consequence, always pure and chaste ; it will be a union of affection only ; it will continue as long as that affection can be maintained, and cease only, under well-devised public forms and regulations, when the affection between the parties can no longer be made to exist. And the experience of the world has proved that affection is much more disinterested, pure, and durable, without than with these legal bonds. In order to prevent confusion or any evil whatever by these changes, *other* arrangements, very different from the existing *family* arrangements, will be made, in conformity with this superior union between the sexes, and the superior national education to be provided for the children.

10. We shall abandon the present degrading and demoralizing mode of distributing wealth by the ordinary method in practice, of buying cheap and selling dear, through the medium of the common money of the old system of the world. Arrangements will be made, as speedily as possible, to effect an equitable exchange of labour for equal value of labour throughout society, by the intervention of the *labour note*, the most perfect money in all respects ever yet introduced into society. But this method of transacting the business of life will be an intermediate and temporary arrangement only, and will be continued no longer than till permanent arrangements can be formed to re-constitute society upon scientific principles, giving to each separate division of society, in practice, the due proportion of the producing, distributing, educating, and governing principles, so combined and organized that more of all kinds of wealth, possessing intrinsic value, may be, with advantage to all parties, so easily created, that those made to be the most penurious or avaricious will cease to desire any individual accumulation of it ; and all contests, private or public, for the possession of wealth, will terminate for ever. And then all the human powers and faculties will be directed, to promote in a straightforward manner, to the exclusion of all private interests, the general happiness of the whole of society.

11. Conscious of the unlimited powers possessed by the British nation when wisely united in its operations, to produce wealth through all future time, far beyond the wants or desires of its population, we renounce the principle of individual competition in the production and distribution of wealth, as being, in its immediate and remote consequences, not only the most demoralizing principle on which man can now act and govern his affairs, but as being, also, the greatest obstacle, in practice, to the beneficial production and distribution of wealth, to the formation of a superior individual and national character, and to the well-ordering and good government of the people.

12. We shall, therefore, as soon as the means can be obtained, exchange the principle of competition, and of mistaken individual interest, for the principle of unlimited union and of undivided national interests. And by this change in conducting the affairs of this empire, we know that more and better wealth can be produced in *one day* than is now produced in *one week* ; that this greater amount and better quality of wealth can be more advantageously distributed for the whole population, by *one day's* occupation of those at present employed to distribute wealth, than is now effected by them under the existing competitive system of

distribution in *one month;* that by this change, with less labour and capital than are now applied to the task, the individual and national character can be formed to be many hundred-fold superior to that which *has been,* *is,* or *can be* found under the competitive system, and that by the abandonment of the principle of division of interests, the empire will be more easily and far better governed than it ever has been under the old system, with *one per cent.* of the capital and labour which are now required.

13. As the false basis upon which the moral part of the old system has been founded, united with the principle of competition, when applied to practice, form together the *sole cause* which renders law, or codes of law, *necessary* in society, we, of the new world, renounce all law proceedings in our transactions with each other, and we will form arrangements to adjust whatever differences may arise between individuals, or associations of individuals, by the decision of three persons selected for their superior knowledge and experience in the new principles, and their known love of justice; these individuals to be annually chosen by the elders of their district.

Courts of law, and all the paraphernalia and folly of law, with its animosities and ruinous expense, cannot be found in a rational state of society, and will, therefore, not be found among the children of the new world.

14. As the principles on which this new system is based will immediately check, and effectually prevent the growth of anger and ill-will, and speedily remove all the *causes* of dislike from among the children trained from infancy in the new world, war will be discountenanced, and ultimately abrogated as a practice, the most grossly ignorant and vicious that a well-ordered or rational mind can conceive; a practice contrary to our new religion, and to be followed only by those who have been made irrational from their birth, or by wholesale murderers and robbers.

Charity, peace, and good-will to the whole family of mankind, without regard to any of the petty artificial or irrational causes of division now existing between them, will be the inevitable, and therefore, uniform practice of all the children of the new world; and one of their chief offices, until the ignorance which causes the evil shall be removed, will be to reconcile man to man, and nation, to nation, throughout the world, and to enable all to understand that they have but one interest, which is, to insure the permanent happiness of each and all, to promote which, by every means that the aggregate of knowledge and power can devise, will be the great business of human life, and then will be seen how easy and straightforward is the true path to real virtue and the most refined enjoyments.

15. But although private and public warfare and contests, with their endless train of unavoidable crime and misery, will be unknown among the children of the new world, effeminacy, with *its* train of evil, will also be discountenanced and discarded. The new mode of forming the character of the children of the new world will cultivate, and bring forth to maturity and perfection, all the physical, intellectual, and moral faculties and powers which have been given to human nature. Arrangements will be formed to admit and encourage the due exercise of each of these faculties and powers up to the point of temperance, for it is *only* by *all* of them being called into action at the period designed by nature, that man can feel satisfied, contented, and happy. Anxiety is the natural feeling which arises when *any one* of these propensities or

qualities is not duly exercised. The physical powers will, therefore, be better cultivated than they were in the best days of Greece
and Rome, and a far superior form of body and expression of mind,
and a duly regulated activity of both will be obtained for all the
future generations.

\.In consequence, *celibacy, in either sex, beyond the period designed
by nature,* will be no longer considered a virtue, but, on the contrary, it will be known to be, as it is, a great crime against nature,
causing other unatural crimes, all of which produce disease of
body and mind, giving a false direction to both thoughts and feelings, and thereby making the human race the most artificial, unnatural, and criminal beings in existence. The earth is yet a
wilderness for want of people to drain its marshes and cultivate its
soil, nor does it yet produce one-thousandth part of the excellence
and enjoyment which it is capable of bringing forth and permanently sustaining. Upon this, and almost all other important
subjects, the world is in gross darkness, because it has hitherto
been instructed and governed, or rather uninstructed and mis-
governed, by men trained to possess only the most feeble and
puny knowledge of themselves, of nature, and of wise and good
gavernment.

16. We now also renounce the separate interests which have
been created by the errors of the old world ; and we will adopt
another mode of carrying on the general business of society. Originally many and various occupations were performed by one
individual ; but as population increased in particular places, the
variety of employments practised by one person gradually diminished, until they are now become so much divided, that many
individuals have their time and attention taken up and occupied in
making a small part of a common pin, a needle, or of thread, to the
destruction of their health, their mental faculties, and all the
higher enjoyments of a rational existence. Experience has now
developed the means by which the *union* and *division* of labour may
be *combined* to secure the peculiar *advantages* of both, without the
evils of either. The science of society, so totally unknown in the
old world, has disclosed the necessity for, and the benefits of,
uniting a due proportion of agriculture, manufactures, commerce,
education, and government, in every separate association, for
carrying on the business of life : and in the new world all these
individualised and opposing interests will become one, and each
part thus united, will essentially aid and promote all the others.
The communities of the new world, when the public shall acquire
any rational notions respecting them, will be found to be nothing
less than a combination of all these interests, so united as to ensure
to every individual living within them, the greatest amount of
advantages, and the highest degree of individual freedom and
happiness that human nature, in its present state of knowledge, is
capable of enjoying. Thus will man, as a member of an association
formed purposely for his benefit, experience the utmost share of
individual freedom that is compatible with the still higher privileges of a social state of existence.

17. We consequently abandon all the arrangements to which
these separate interests have given birth ; such as large cities,
towns, villages, and universities, as well as the existing arrangements for carrying on the business of agriculture, detached from manufactures, education, and commerce. These accidental individual
circumstances, formed without knowledge or foresight, are not
such as can ever form men into a rational being, or insure to him

more than a very small portion of the wealth, health, and happiness, which his nature may be made to enjoy.

18. We also abandon, to the irrationality of the old system of the world, all places for ceremonial worship of an unknown Power, and with them all mysteries in every department of life, as being much worse than useless. In like manner, we abandon to the same system, all places of punishment and confinement, such as prisons, penitentiaries, houses of correction, and workhouses ; and all charitable institutions, as they are called, as being prominent and magnificent monuments of the utter incapacity of the rulers of human affairs, to form arrangements to insure a superior character, wealth, and health of body and mind, to the respective populations which they have governed, or do now attempt to govern.

19. We abandon also all individual ambition and desire for personal distinction, knowing we possess nothing but what we have received, and that these personal distinctions cannot benefit mankind, but are, in themselves, the *cause* of endless errors, crimes, and miseries, and tend to keep men in perpetual ignorance of themselves, and to make them highly irrational.

20. We also dismiss, for similar reasons, all envy and jealousy from the new world, in which all will partake of the advantages derived from the excellencies of each ; all will, therefore, feel their happiness to be increased in proportion as each excels in all superior qualifications, and in consequence all will aid to enable each individual to acquire and enjoy them. Thus will unity of design, of duty, of interest, and of sympathy, among the human race, supersede the division, competition, and opposition of man to man, and nation to nation, and remove the causes of all the envy and jealousy which instigate to crime, make man a demon, and the earth a pandemonium.

I therefore now proclaim to the world the commencement, on this day, of the promised millennium, founded on rational principles and consistent practice.

MANIFESTO

OF THE PRODUCTIVE CLASSES OF GREAT BRITAIN AND IRELAND, TO THE GOVERNMENTS AND PEOPLE OF THE CONTINENTS OF EUROPE, AND OF NORTH AND SOUTH AMERICA.

(*Passed unanimously at the Great Public Meeting, held at the National Equitable Labour Exchange, Charlotte-street, Fitzroy-square, London, on the 13th May, 1833.*)

MEN OF THE GREAT FAMILY OF MANKIND,—

We, your relatives and friends, have been enabled, through past experience, aided especially by modern improvements and discoveries, and late political events, to acquire the knowledge of a *new life*, and, in consequence, to perceive all things through a new light. We have thus arisen from a mental lethargy, which had overwhelmed our reasoning faculties, and benumbed all our finest and best feelings. But we are now wide awake, and have become fully conscious of all the evils which we and you have so long suffered. Our eyes have been opened to our real position in society; we have at length discovered the true source of our power, and the most effectual mode of applying it for the benefit of all future generations.

To accomplish the great work which we are about to undertake, many and most important changes in conducting the affairs of life must of necessity be made; and we now put forth this statement to obtain your approval and ardent co-operation, because we desire that these changes should be effected by reason, and not by force.

We, therefore, intend now to make manifest the necessity which has arisen at this period for the adoption of these changes, and also to convince the population of the world of their truth and justice, and thus to carry the minds of all with us; and, in the spirit of charity and kindness, to prevent all future revolutions of violence, by removing the causes which germinate and bring them to maturity.

We perceive that the evils which have afflicted the human race have arisen from ignorance; our remedy is to remove this ignorance.

The materials for the production of happiness superabound—they are now unused, or misused. We mean to bring them into action, and give them a right direction.

The materials for the production of happiness are the *earth* and *human beings*. The former requires but to be well cultivated, and properly arranged to produce abundance, and to form a terrestrial paradise. The latter, but to be trained from birth according to the laws of their nature, and all their faculties and qualities to be made available, and properly directed, to insure the perpetual happiness of each individual.

To effect these important results, another and a very different arrangement of society from that which has hitherto existed must now be made.

The whole powers of the *soil* and of *man* must be brought into action; no portion of either can remain dormant when population can be advanced to require the wastes and wildernesses of the earth, which are now, for want of cultivation, fruitful sources of disease and discomfort to man.

But all our powers are now misapplied. The arrangements of society are random or chance proceedings, arising chiefly from the supposed private interests of one family, in opposition to all others.

We, the *producers of real wealth*, have been, and now are, held in disesteem; while the *unproductive*, useless, and injurious members of society, riot to their own hurt in riches, and are trained to consider us their servants and slaves. By these ignorant and unnatural proceedings, the Earth and his own nature have been made the perpetual source of evil instead of good to man.

We *will*, that this irrational state of society shall now cease, and that, henceforward, *all*, except those of the present generation too far advanced in life for the change, shall be trained to become producers of physical wealth or of intellectual gratification, and that none shall be maintained who are not occupied in producing or acquiring that which will benefit society, or be deemed equivalent to their consumption of its productions.

We now know that all will become far better and happier, by

being made to be producers, physically or intellectually, or both, of the means of gratification to society, that they can be by living a life of idleness or uselessness, and that the individual who is not trained, and afterwards employed to effect something beneficial to society, must be, of necessity, not merely a useless but a positively injurious member of the great family of mankind.

That it is, therefore, the first duty of all governments to adopt national measures to train and place all the population of their respective dominions within such arrangements as shall make them physically, intellectually, and morally, useful members of society.

But, to effect this change, an entire new organization of society is necessary. None of the professions, as they are now exercised, will be required; nor can any of the present modes of transacting the business of life be retained. Instead of these errors of the old world, arrangements will be adopted to re-organize the whole of society, and to re-model the proceedings of mankind. We know that, whatever shall be discovered and proved to be for the permanent interest of the human race, will of necessity be carried into execution; and we know it to be for the permanent interest of the human race that the natural powers and faculties of each individual should be fully developed and brought into action for the direct benefit of all, that he himself may thereby be the most permanently benefitted.

That each individual should be trained to become, as his natural faculties may direct, a producer of wealth, or of something of real value to society; that is, of something that shall contribute to the well-being or happiness of some portion of the population; or, in other words, as all may be trained to be useful or useless, no one shall be formed to become a worthless or useless member of our new social state.

We also know that, by arrangements founded on these simple principles, the human race may be emancipated from ignorance and poverty, and, consequently, from sin and all its frightful train of miseries and evils innumerable.

The union of these few principles, properly combined in practice, will constitute the foundation for a very superior local and general government of the human race; and the general business of society, which has been hitherto so complicated and perplexed, will become, as it ought to be, so plain that any individual may be trained easily to comprehend the principles, and to apply them advantageously to practice.

We, therefore, now proclaim to you that a new *era* has commenced—one in which wealth of the most intrinsic value can be created to an unlimited extent, and in which the individuals of the human race may be trained and educated to become beings possessing all the good and superior qualities only which belong to their nature.

And this era we do not hesitate to pronounce the commencement of that period, which, under the term Millennium, the human race has been so long taught to expect.

It is a period when all deception and artifice must cease—when man will know and acknowledge the laws of his nature, and act in perfect accordance with them, and when, in consequence, he will become a natural and superior being.

We invite you now to co-operate cordially with us to effect this great and glorious change—we invite you as relatives and friends, without desire to create hostile feeling of any description—we invite you purely from the affection which our newly acquired knowledge of our common nature has created within us. We dismiss all fear and suspicion, and all the inferior feelings which a system of error had generated and matured within us; for we have now full confidence that we ourselves can attain these grand and noble results without the aid of any, and, notwithstanding' the opposition of any, or all parties, whoever or whatever they may be. The old power of the old system of error is vanishing away as a mist disappears before the refulgent influence of the sun. It had no strength but that which it derived from *public opinion*, and from public opinion it can no longer obtain support.

And why should any of you lament that public opinion is withdrawn from giving power to an old system of error which has produced evil continually? Is there any one, from the occupier of the most powerful throne to the meanest individual of the lowest tribe, who is not most grievously injured by the necessary effects of this system? It makes now, of all mankind, slaves to passions or to persons—a state of human existence which can never produce either virtue or happiness. Not one of you has a real interest in the longer support of this system; but, on the contrary, your future happiness must arise from its now dying a natural death.

Come, then, and for your own happiness, co-operate with us as friends. We are the producers of all the wealth and means of comfort you have hitherto possessed—we can make arrangements by which, in future, you may enjoy these good things in safety, and without fear; but, were we so inclined, we could effectually withhold them from you and your children; and force applied to us, would demonstrate only the weakness and folly of our mistaken opponents. The reign of terror, of carnal arms, or of physical force of any kind or description in opposition to public opinion, has for ever ceased. It is now useless to speak of these old worn-out means to effect any great or permanent object. We discard them as being worse than useless; as means of power gone by, never more to be called into action by *beings* claiming a rational nature.

We call upon you to discard them also, and to turn your thoughts from the destruction of your fellow men, and of their wealth, to the acquisition of that knowledge which will enable you to assist materially to improve the former, and greatly to increase the amount of the latter. To act thus is your duty and your interest, for it is the only course that can insure you permanent satisfaction, or that can now give you a chance of happiness.

In conclusion, we again earnestly call upon you to unite cordially with us in measures—

First, To produce a surplus of all kinds of wealth.

Second, To distribute wealth the most beneficially for all parties in all countries.

Third, To form a superior character for the rising generation, and to improve the adults of the present generation.

Fourth, To govern well and wisely for all parties.

Fifth, And to form arrangements to carry these measures into immediate execution, to stop the evident progress daily making toward a revolution of violence.

TABLE OF CONTENTS.

JUSTIFICATIVE PIECES.

ERRATA.

The following errors, which are partly my own, partly the author's, and partly the printer's, have inadvertently crept into the translation, owing to unavoidable haste in sending the numbers to be stereotyped as they appeared.

Page	Line	Instead of	Read
xv	42	1st of May	31st of May.
xviii	11	Desodoard	Desodoards.
17	38	supineness	suppleness.
27	38	prints	provisions.
45	19	our new lords	our lords.
71	18	danger	advantage.
354	35	equipage	equipage of the late D'Orleans.

I am not aware of any other errors except one or two literals in the anagrams of the names, and for the correction of these the reader will please to see Buonarroti's letter to me, in which he furnishes the real names of the conspirators.—BRONTERRE.

H. HETHERINGTON, PRINTER, 126, STRAND.